THE NEW AMERICAN LITERATURE

THE NEW
AMERICAN LITERATURE
1890–1930

BY

FRED LEWIS PATTEE

Author of "A History of American Literature since 1870,"
"The Development of the American Short Story,"
and other studies in American Literature

THE CENTURY CO.
NEW YORK   LONDON

First Printing

To

MY DEAR WIFE GRACE

without whom this book
never could have been

PREFACE

My "History of American Literature since 1870" covered the years from the Civil War decade to the beginning of the 1890's. It concerned itself for the most part with one single generation—the later Victorians, to speak in British terms—the immediate successors of the Emerson-Longfellow-Holmes-Lowell-Whittier group of writers. The present study, taking up the story where the earlier volume ended, carries the history on to the present day, though, with a few exceptions, it deals with no writer whose first book appeared after 1920. The volume is built upon the general thesis that the thirty or forty years since the 1890 decade constitute a distinct and well-rounded period in American literary history, that literature during this single generation of marvelous change departed so widely from all that had gone before that it stands alone and unique, that the soul of it and the driving power of it were born in the new areas beyond the Alleghenies, and that during its thirty or forty years was produced the greater bulk of those writings that we may call distinctively our own, work peculiarly to be called *American* literature.

In the opening chapters I have trespassed a little upon the areas of the earlier volume by reconsidering with more perspective and richer materials certain works and workers on the border line between the two periods, notably Garland, Norris, Crane, Davis, Wilkins. I have minimized too one feature prominent in the earlier volume, the bibliographical summaries at the ending of chapters. With such a work as Manly and Rickert's "Contemporary American Literature: Bibliographies and Study Outlines," 1929, exhaustive and accurate, within easy reach of everybody, why du-

vii

plicate materials? Only in special cases not covered by this work or in the case of materials in addition to those furnished by its bibliographies have I departed from this practice.

My study of a period so near us, with, in most cases, practically no perspective, cannot hope to arrive at final values, but that such a preliminary survey is needed I am fully convinced. Someone must do the pioneer work with a new period, mapping—crudely it may be, yet the best he can with materials at hand—the new trails. Some one must do it. Let others in later years with more perspective and fuller materials correct my outlines.

My thanks are due to all who have helped me in the collection of my materials. Especially would I thank Professor William L. Werner of the Pennsylvania State College for his careful work upon the proof sheets.

F. L. P.

Bread Loaf, Vermont,
July 9, 1930.

CONTENTS

THE NEW AMERICAN LITERATURE

THE NEW
AMERICAN LITERATURE

CHAPTER I

THE FIN DE SIÈCLE

IT is a convention of late to describe the closing decade of the nineteenth century with colorful adjectives. We have had "the mauve decade," "the yellow nineties," "the romantic nineties," and lately, from the pen of Irving Bacheller, "the highbrow decade." The ten years were indeed picturesque, deserving, perhaps, even the rococo treatment of Beer's mauve-tinted volume; but they were more: the decade was a culmination; it was the end of an era; it was an equinox between two creative periods, a moment of pause, of sterility, an Indian summer, silent, hectic with colors, dreamy with the past, yet alive with mighty gathering forces. The vital twentieth century was opening; in reality it began in the nineties.

I

First of all, it was a decade of swift change. The world that had been, the period of the post-Civil War, the age of Bret Harte and Cable and Thomas Bailey Aldrich, vanished in a night. There had come the emergence of the new West, the disappearance of the frontier, the rise of modern journalism, the war with Spain and the new imperialism, the amazing new applications of electricity,

3

the automobile. America all in a moment was forced out of the localized provincialisms that had been so dominating a characteristic of the mid-century, out of the narrow nationalism that had come as a result of the Civil War, and was now entering a totally new era of internationalism that was filling it with uneasiness and apprehension.

The first hintings of revolution came from the West. The census of 1890 had revealed startling facts: the center of population had crossed the Alleghenies, and was now in the Midwest. Moreover, it was discovered that the Government had disposed of the last of its free lands. For the first time in the history of America there was no frontier. The old Border, which had lured to adventure and new hope—"the golden West," had reached the Pacific. For a century and more it had stood for freedom, for youth seeking adventure, for escape, for rebellion against the conventional, for rampant individualism. If one failed in the East there was still hope in the free lands of the boundless West. Congress in the sixties and the seventies had given vast areas to the northern veterans of the Civil War, and as a result there had been no slump in the morale of the nation following the disbandment of the great army at the close of the conflict. As long as America still had free lands and a frontier there was optimism.

But the Border was gone. Jack London and others sought to create for romance a new Border in Alaska and even in the Solomon Islands of the Pacific, but they could create only a literary thing. The old Border had disappeared, and with it the chief elements that rendered it picturesque: the Plains Indian, the bison, "the great American desert," the Sante Fé trail, the cowboy. The year 1890 begins the era of the new West, the new America, indeed. The great desert of the school geographies in the early seventies was now a vast garden-spot rich beyond dreamings in wheat and corn, with great cities of the plain now dominating railroad centers. The West was becoming stabilized; sharply was it beginning to impinge upon the East. It was individual, self-contained, aggressive, uncolored by anything save its own soil. "Europe ends with the Alleghenies": Emerson had realized it in the forties.

The first voicings of revolution from the new lands had been a burst of pessimistic criticism like the first murmurings of a storm. Partly it was dissatisfaction at the manipulation of the early free lands. The sections and quarter-sections taken up in the first flush days of the settlement had passed often into the hands of speculators and capitalists. Then had come a tide of "renters," many of them European immigrants, and to understand their problems and their tragedies one needs but to read such stories as Garland's "Under the Lion's Paw," Howe's "The Story of a Country Town," Cather's "My Ántonia," or the editorials of William Allen White of Kansas. The result was the agrarian revolution of the seventies and eighties, a conflict which first expressed itself in the organizing of the Grange and of the Populist Party.[1]

The second impingement of the West upon the East became dramatic in 1892. The four hundredth anniversary of the discovery of America was to be celebrated with an exposition which was to be made one of the wonders of the modern world. All America was to exhibit its greatest achievements, the heights of its civilization; and after a hot battle Chicago was chosen as the locale of the exhibit. The consternation of the East was extreme, but Chicago proved worthy of her assumed responsibility. The Exposition became a colossal success. W. D. Howells, voice of the cultured East, in a letter to A. S. Hardy wrote, "I have just had my first glimpse of the World's

---

[1] For a full bibliography of the land problems of the period see "The Frontier in American Literature," Lucy L. Hazard, 1929, p. 274. The best treatment of the subject is "The Agrarian Crusade," Solon J. Buck, Yale Press, 1921.

Fair and am speechless." The West had awakened like a sleeping giant and was beginning to threaten the dominion of the East. Even Boston voiced itself in superlatives. From Chicago Charles Eliot Norton, quintessence of the Harvard culture, sent home in a letter:

I have never seen Americans from whom one could draw happier auguries for the future of America than some of the men I saw at Chicago. The "Fair," in spite of its amazing incongruities, its immense "border" of vulgarities, was on the whole a great promise, even a great pledge. It, at least, forbids despair.

A certain condescension in Easterners, perhaps; one bitterly resented by the West and returned by them in hatred of all Eastern things; but it was founded in truth. The West, so long the area of lawlessness and high adventure, was becoming the dominating "America." Norton, type of the exclusive East, felt this as he walked the streets of the great White City of the Exposition. It meant a new hope for the world.

Here are sixty or seventy millions of people of whom all but a comparatively small fraction have come up, within two or three generations, from the lower orders of society. They belong by descent to the oppressed from the beginning of history, to the ignorant, to the servile class, or to the peasantry. They have no traditions of intellectual life, no power of sustained thought, no developed reasoning faculty. But they constitute on the whole as good a community on a large scale as the world has even seen. Low as their standards may be, yet taken in the mass they are higher than so many millions of men ever previously attained.[2]

At the Exposition one saw the beginnings of world-revolutionizing things: applications of electricity, the phonograph, the germ of the cinema, the perfected telephone, the "horseless carriage" which soon was to dis-

2 "Letters of Charles Eliot Norton," 1913, vol. II, p. 220.

place completely the "safety" bicycle then so enormously in vogue. The gas-engine had come, and it was to turn civilization upside down in two decades: Ford had demonstrated that his machine would work; the Wright brothers already were experimenting with aëronautics— Orville Wright was to make his first flight in December, 1903. The world of the Centennial of 1876 was as far removed from the Columbian Exposition of 1893 as the England of Dr. Johnson was removed from the England of the Victorian Jubilee. The old provincial, static world was vanishing like a dream of the night. *Things* had vaulted into the saddle; machinery had become king. The virile West had arrived: it was as if the lid had been removed from the magic jar containing materialistic power.

II

In literature, however, especially in the American area, the old forces that had sprung into control during the Victorian mid-century were still in control. No "newness" permitted here. A venerated group of the leaders of that period was still alive and still writing. In every season's output, the swan-song volumes and December offerings of these "masters" were most widely advertised products. There was Holmes's "Ultima Thule" and "The Iron Gate," Whitman's "November Boughs" and "Good-Bye My Fancy," Whittier's "Hazel Blossoms," Higginson's "Cheerful Yesterdays," Mrs. Fields's "Authors and Friends." Then one by one, the quavering old voices ceased. Lowell, Bancroft, and Melville passed in 1891, Whittier and Whitman and Curtis in 1892, Parkman in 1893, Holmes (not quite "the last leaf") in 1894, Mrs. Stowe in 1896, D. G. Mitchell in 1898, and Higginson, Nestor of the group, in 1911. Their passing left behind the sense that something irrevocable had departed from American life.

The generation, however, that had made possible a new period in the years following the Civil War was a partial compensation; it was at the height of its powers, and it was more and more dominating the literary output. H. C. Vedder for his volume "American Writers of To-day" made studies of what he considered the nineteen living leaders in 1894: E. C. Stedman, Francis Parkman, W. D. Howells, Henry James, Charles Dudley Warner, T. B. Aldrich, Mark Twain, F. Marion Crawford, Mrs. Burnett, E. E. Hale, Edward Eggleston, George W. Cable, R. H. Stoddard, Frank Stockton, and Joaquin Miller. Add to this list eight others: Bret Harte, Sarah Orne Jewett, Joel Chandler Harris, Sidney Lanier, John Muir, John Burroughs, Thomas Nelson Page, and R. W. Gilder, and the group that produced what I have termed elsewhere the "National Period" is fairly complete. In 1894 all save Lanier were alive; their average age was sixty, and each was adding at least one volume every year to the mass of published books.

At sixty, one adds nothing new and one sympathizes not at all with revolution. Aldrich was busying himself with the editorship of the conservative "Atlantic" and writing "Ponkapog Papers." Howells had left Boston, and though more than half of his voluminous product was yet to be written, the list of books that now are regarded as his contribution to the American "classics" was then complete. In 1895 he was already lapsing into Nestoriana and self-explanation. "My Literary Passions" begins the long list of his volumes reminiscent. Henry James had been taken over by the English as one of their own. Mark Twain, his best work done, was running to pessimism and dollar-making; John Burroughs had turned philosopher; Cable was immersed in work philanthropic; Harte, long an exile in England, was turning out, with painful industry, replicas of his early tales, alleging that only in England could he receive prices that would satisfy the demands of his extravagant family at home.[3] Most of the others were writing marketable books and tales. In quantity American literature was flourishing, but in quality it was at lowest ebb. The new generation of critics already was damning it with superlatives. Take a single sample from the pen of young Francis Otto Matthiessen:

The emptiness of the literature of the late nineties cannot be exaggerated. A symbol of it is the number of the "Atlantic" that marked the completion of its fortieth year in October, 1897. There is a paper by the distinguished French critic Brunetière, but the American names are hardly loud enough to be even an echo of the names that are gone. Stedman and Aldrich are now the principal poets. And except for Sarah Jewett's "Martha's Lady," the fiction consists of nothing more permanent than Kate Douglas Wiggin, and F. Hopkinson Smith. It is perfectly quiet and harmless, for it's thoroughly dead.[4]

The creative period that followed the Civil War was over. The nineteenth century, gibbous in its last quarter, was fading out seemingly into nothingness.

III

The first symptom that the old period was nearing its end was the appearance at the very opening of the decade of a new and vigorous group of young writers, born, most of them, in the sixties and the seventies. In the single year 1891 appeared the first significant offerings of James Lane Allen, Kate Chopin, Richard Harding Davis, H. B. Fuller, Hamlin Garland, and Mary E. Wilkins. Before the decade ended there had been added to the list Stephen Crane, Booth Tarkington, John Kendrick Bangs, Alice Brown, Richard Burton, Theodore Dreiser,

[3] See "The Letters of Bret Harte," edited by Geoffey Bret Harte, 1926. An enlightening volume.
[4] "Sarah Orne Jewett," Francis Otto Matthiessen, 1929, p. 110.

Ellen Glasgow, James Huneker, Jack London, Bliss Perry, George Santayana, Ernest Seton, O. Henry, and Edith Wharton.

A group it was that had been nurtured on the regional fiction of the eighties, and it had learned the art of poetic twittering from the French villanelles and rondeaux and triolets according to the Dobson echoings. It was debauched too by the historical romance, which was at the height of its vogue in the years of their apprenticeship. All of the group sooner or later were aware of European conditions, and were reading French and Russian and Scandinavian literature. The conservative old "Harper's Magazine" was issuing as serials Thomas Hardy's latest work and even George Du Maurier's *risqué* novels.

Original work was hard to do: all the strong influences were against it. Irving Bacheller, who as presiding genius of the new Bacheller syndicate was constantly in contact with editors, presents this indictment of the times:

The editors of the great magazines were regarded with awe in those days. They knew their power. Their bearing was king-like. Their retainers had the Olympian look and tone. They dwelt in the rarefied and chilly atmosphere of high levels. "The Satraps of the Century" was a current phrase on Park Row. It was a sober recognition of rank and authority. There was no touch of derision in the words. From 1884 to 1895 was the highbrow decade. Never since the time of Samuel Johnson was the brow of literature so exalted and so serenely self-satisfied. The brow of statesmanship was on a like level of altitude—the Conkling level.[5]

England, however, always a decade or more behind France, was in the throes of a literary revolution: the strange new art of Aubrey Beardsley, the audacity of Oscar Wilde, the amazing cockiness of the "Yellow Book," the Irish impertinence of Bernard Shaw who

[5] "Coming up the Road: Memories of a North Country Boyhood," Irving Bacheller, 1928.

could in all seriousness put himself on an equality even with Shakespeare, the wild new atmosphere of the Kiplings and Wellses and Doyles, were filling the Victorians with alarm. Everywhere talk of yellowness, decadence, degeneration. The "Yellow Book" soon became the symbol of the *fin de siècle*. A most mild and ladylike affair as we view it to-day against the background of modern "realism," it was everywhere looked upon as a kind of red flag of revolution, a literary bombshell with spluttering fuse. "It was considered," according to S. S. McClure, "a very bold publication in those days, a rather daring book to have on one's table."

In May, 1894, the staid old "Critic," edited by the Gilders, lost its poise completely at the sight of the yellow thing, which it dubbed "the Oscar Wilde of periodicals," a literary indecency, "vulgar and impertinent":

The amount of attention that this periodical has attracted is proof, if any were needed, that the mountebank in his motley can call the crowd; but is that all that the editors of this quarterly are aiming at? Have they yet to learn that notoriety is not fame? They claim that the "Yellow Book" is the embodiment of the modern spirit. If this is true, then give us the good old-fashioned spirit of "Harper's," the "Century," and "Scribner's" whose aim is to please intelligent people and not to attract attention by "tripping the cockawhoop" in public.

At the same time Charles Dudley Warner in the "Editor's Study" of "Harper's Magazine" launched out against the just-born little periodical as another symptom of the general disease that was killing the literatures of the world. It was a variety of the "yellows," he believed, something like the scourge so fatal to peach trees. To him as writer of this critique has generally been attributed the first use of the term "yellow literature," but in this same article he quotes Thoreau as having said the same thing about the literature of his own day.

Spurned by the East, the "Yellow Book" was hailed by

the West generally as the morning star of a new day. There was in it, they believed, the time-beat of something vigorous and vital and modern. The young Chicago "school" quickly launched out with an imitation, "The Chap Book," a publication as we read it to-day really remarkable. It was read widely: at one time it boasted a circulation of 15,000. Imitations of it quickly came by the dozens. San Francisco followed with the "Lark," and East Aurora, New York, with the "Philistine," long edited by Elbert Hubbard. None of them all is more deserving of record than Gelett Burgess's "Lark," an exquisitely printed thing and most distinctively edited. It survived for two years, and one fragment of it is still surviving. No other poem of the decade has been more quoted than Burgess's nonsense quatrain, published in the "Lark," May, 1895:

> I never saw a Purple Cow;
> I never Hope to See One;
> But I can Tell you, Anyhow,
> I'd rather See than Be One.

It echoed through a whole decade, like Mark Twain's

> Punch, brothers, punch with care!
> Punch in the presence of the passenjare.

These literary mushrooms, "fourteen of which sprouted, bloomed, and withered during the first half of 1897," [6] were as far as America got in the revolution.

Much talk there was, however. Young Booth Tarkington in Princeton believed that literature surely was in the sere and yellow leaf. Was not Nordau's volume "Degeneration" among the American best sellers?

Never did an epoch more placidly believe itself the last word than did the *fin de siècle*—and every country newspaper glibly used that phrase, so sophisticated was our whole nation

[6] "Some Contemporary Americans," Percy H. Boynton, 1924, p. 17.

in those days. The *fin de siècle* was the last word in scientific achievement, in modern inventions, in literature and the fine arts, in good taste, in luxury, in elegance, in extravagance, in dress, in cleverness and in the art of being *blasé*. Civilization had gone about as far as possible; we had reached the summit of the peak, and after us must come the decadence, which was, indeed, already setting in with Oscar Wilde's writings and the strange drawings of Aubrey Beardsley.[7]

In England the revolution made headway even against the tides of Victorian conservatism. According to Richard Le Gallienne, himself a member of the London "Yellow Book" circle, there was in progress a veritable renaissance:

The amount of creative revolutionary energy packed into that amazing decade is almost bewildering in its variety. So much was going on at once, in so many directions, with so passionate a fervor. Those last ten years of the nineteenth century properly belong to the twentieth century, and, far from being "decadent" except in certain limited manifestations, they were years of immense and multifarious renaissance. All our present conditions, socially and artistically, our vaunted new "freedoms" of every kind—including free verse —not only began then, but found a more vital and authoritative expression than they have found since, because of the larger, more significant personalities engaged in bringing them about.[8]

On the Continent too there was revolution, with strong literary leaders everywhere emergent: in Russia, Tolstoi and the "realists"; in the north, Ibsen; in France, Flaubert, Maupassant, Zola; in Germany, Sudermann and Hauptmann; in Italy, d'Annunzio.

In one way America, too, was of the revolution: it imported whole editions of the new authors, it paid unheard-of prices for their magazine articles; America

---

[7] "The World Does Move," Booth Tarkington, 1928.
[8] "The Romantic 90's," Richard Le Gallienne, 1928.

"paid the freight." For years the novels of the so-called
Scotch "Kailyard school"—Barrie, Maclaren, Crockett—
were among the best sellers. Kipling and Doyle and
Stevenson found their best markets in America. Du
Maurier and Hardy ran in the magazines *risqué* serials
that no American could have got published. And the
whole public, led by the newspapers, welcomed the revolutionists when they deigned to visit us, and paid them
lavishly for their readings.

America always from the days of Dickens in the 1840's
had been the land of gold for English writers. Though no
copyright protected foreign authors, "Harper's Magazine" had paid Charles Dickens $6000 for the American
rights of "Great Expectations," Wilkie Collins $3750 for
"The Woman in White," Charles Reade for a single novel
$5000 and George Eliot for "Daniel Deronda" $8500.
Now in the *fin de siècle* the amounts paid ran into vastly
larger figures. America has always welcomed English newness with copious dollars and given substantial comfort to
English literary rebellion.

Thus America in the 90's became a part of the European
revolution, but it furnished no revolutionists. The old line
held: the youngsters might rage, but they were powerless
to break through—powerless at least for a decade. The
old order was strongly entrenched behind a dozen or
more dominating publishing houses, one or two in Philadelphia, two or three in Boston, and the rest in New York
City. Even as Bacheller has said, conservatism sat upon
every one of them like a Connecticut Blue Law. They
were timid, they were afraid of their patronage, even
to jumpiness. There were no wild-cat magazines to publish the writings of the insurgent youngsters, and the
old standard ones like "Harper's," the "Atlantic," and
the "Century," were supported by a clientele of the old
order. To offend this conservative group meant ruin to
the magazine—ruin to established business. Foreign
writers of note could be tolerated in their frankness of

"revelation." The editors, however, expurgated with thoroughness daring manuscripts, even by the more famous of these writers, and even though the latter could be pardoned on the ground of their foreignness. "Jude the Obscure" was so "carved and emasculated" for its run through "Harper's Magazine" that its author declared in wrath that when it was published in its original text as a volume those who had read the magazine version considered it a new creation. Gilder when editor of the "Century Magazine" subjected Mark Twain's manuscripts to drastic expurgation.

There is much of his writing that we would not print for a miscellaneous audience. If you should ever carefully compare the chapters of "Huckleberry Finn," as we printed them, with the same as they appear in his book, you will see the most decided difference. These extracts were carefully edited for a magazine audience with his full consent.[9]

This could not continue. No younger generation can be repressed forever. It was soon discovered that the rascals were demanding books rather than magazines and that they had strange new manuscripts that they wanted made into books. To print them new wild-cat firms began to appear. Hamlin Garland's first work was issued by the Arena Publishing Company. His later "Main-Travelled Roads" and his more daring "Rose of Dutcher's Coolly" were issued in Chicago by the new firm of Stone & Kimball which specialized in daring books. Then had come the Bobbs-Merrill Company of Indianapolis, which soon was issuing best sellers with every publishing season.

In the meantime the standard publishing houses were busy with "safe" ventures, centering attention almost wholly upon the new works of the older authors, whom they kept constantly before the public. The "Critic" at the opening of the decade issued a Lowell Birthday number

---

[9] "Letters of Richard Watson Gilder," 1916, p. 399.

with a letter from every member of the older American literary Valhalla—a most fulsome outpouring. Twenty years later the dominating forces were still selecting the safe and the sane and the unrebellious. Witness the list of the American Immortals chosen for the American Academy organized in 1913:

Woodrow Wilson
William Dean Howells
Henry Adams
Thomas R. Lounsbury
Theodore Roosevelt
John S. Sargent
Alfred Thayer Mahan
Daniel Chester French
John Burroughs
James Ford Rhodes
Horatio W. Parker
William Milligan Sloane
Robert Underwood Johnson
George W. Cable
Andrew D. White
Henry van Dyke
William C. Brownell
Basil L. Gildersleeve
Arthur T. Hadley
Henry Cabot Lodge
Francis Hopkinson Smith
Edwin Howland Blashfield
Owen Wister
Augustus Thomas

William M. Chase
Thomas Hastings
Hamilton Wright Mabie
Brander Matthews
Thomas Nelson Page
Elihu Vedder
George Edward Woodberry
Kenyon Cox
George Whitefield Chadwick
Abbot H. Thayer
John Muir
Charles Francis Adams
Henry Mills Alden
George de Forest Brush
William Rutherford Mead
John W. Alexander
Bliss Perry
Francis D. Millet
Abbott Lawrence Lowell
James Whitcomb Riley
Nicholas Murray Butler
Paul Wayland Bartlett
George Bowne Post

What H. L. Mencken termed the "pianissimo revolt" of the early nineties, the Populist soap-boxings of Hamlin Garland, and the European transplantings attempted by the early Norris, the flourishings of the "Chap Book" and the "Philistine," amounted to little. It was a rebellion of frogs against storks.

But new forces were gathering. Gradually in the book-lists appeared names uncouth and strange—Bodenheim, Dreiser, Huneker, Mencken, Oppenheim, Sandburg, Santayana, Kreymborg, Crapsey, Guiterman, Orrick Johns, Giovannitti; and soon their works and others began to be handled by new publishing houses bearing such un-Puritanic names as Knopf, Boni & Liveright, Covici. Sons and grandsons of immigrants these men were for the most part, men who had borne into America ideals and conceptions totally un-Anglo-Saxon.

The literary revolution made slow headway in America, but it came at last. Started by English and Continental influences it eventually became autochthonic, original, dominating, reacting even upon the European world that had given it its birth.

BIBLIOGRAPHICAL REFERENCES

"The Eighteen Nineties," Holbrook Jackson, 1922. A careful study of the *fin de siècle* decade in England, free from superlatives and soundly critical.

"The Mauve Decade: American Life at the End of the Nineteenth Century," Thomas Beer, 1926. Picturesque, uncritical, often smart. The opening sentence sets the key: "They laid Jesse James in his grave and Dante Gabriel Rossetti died immediately." Literary vaudeville.

"The Romantic 90's," Richard Le Gallienne, 1926. A beautifully written appreciation of the decade in England by one who had been a part of what he wrote about. A book of great value.

"The Modern Current in American Literature," Paul Elmer More, "The Forum," January, 1928.

"The Significance of the Frontier in American History," Frederick Jackson Turner. This study, given as a paper at the meeting of American Historical Association in Chicago in 1913, began a new era in American historical study.

"The National Letters," in "Prejudices," Second Series, H. L. Mencken, 1920.

CHAPTER II

CHICAGO

I

THE history of American literature even to the portals of the new century has been an Anglo-Saxon matter. All of the thirteen original colonies were organized solidly upon Anglo-Saxon ideals, religious and social and political. For the prejudices and values and manners of the non-Anglo-Saxon world these colonial areas had no tolerance, even after independence from England and the shaping century which followed. As time went on, they viewed with uneasiness their own western annex beyond the Alleghenies. A flood of "barbarians" was pouring into the land, the greater number of them absorbed by the cities and by the vast farm areas of what the early school geographies had termed "the great American desert." These barbarians prospered amazingly. Their children went to school, where they learned with facility the English and the American languages, and where they mingled on equal terms with the children of the early settlers, vigorous stock, free and individualistic. Many of them were enabled to go to the new State Universities, those seed-beds of the newest America. Soon there emerged leaders, young intellectuals, born Americans but with ideals still fundamentally European, rebels against the conventional idea of democracy. Everywhere in the new and vast trans-Allegheny world rebellion was fomenting, everywhere was the demand for freedom—freedom from the outworn in religion and manners and art, freedom to tell the truth, freedom to build into new and better

living even if it meant the destruction of the whole elder
civilization.

And the new movement centered first in Chicago. The
Exposition had opened the eyes of the world to the values
of the great inland city. To touch Chicago was like
touching electric power. Here was the new world, the
rising school of young Westerners preached it with emphasis. Fuller in his novel "The Cliff-Dwellers" has given
us a typical figure in young Fairchild:

"Does it seem unreasonable that the State which produced
the two greatest figures of the greatest epoch in our history,
and which has done most within the last ten years to check
alien excesses and un-American ideas, should also be the State
to give the country the final blend of the American character
and its ultimate metropolis? . . . Chicago is Chicago. It is
the belief of all of us. It is inevitable; nothing can stop us
now."

And McDowell in the same volume:

"You've got to have snap. You've got to have a big new
country behind you. How much do you suppose people in Iowa
and Kansas and Minnesota think about Down East? Not a
great deal. It's Chicago they're looking to. This town looms
up before them and shuts out Boston and New York and the
whole seaboard from the sight and the thoughts of the West
and the Northwest and the new Northwest and the Far West
and all the other Wests yet to be invented. They read our
papers, they come here to buy and to enjoy themselves."

The whole Middle West, and even Middle South,
looked upon the East, and especially Boston, as outworn,
lost in contemplation of her own past, effete. Provincialism, declared the vigorous younger voices, brings life:
the Eastern cities kill it. Hear a voicing like this:

Why not insist that the provinciality of the American literature is the essential quality of all literature, the one quality
that gives distinctiveness to literary effort? It seems almost

like sacrilege to hear Mr. James making excuses for Hawthorne to English readers by enumerating the surroundings that the American lacked. He had no sovereign, no court, no personal loyalty, no aristocracy, no church, no clergy, no diplomatic service, no palaces, no castles, no manors, no cathedrals, no abbeys. All these things and many more are catalogued by Mr. James to show the difficulties under which he labored, this man who had before him all the ruins of human passion and who was surrounded by the antiquity of the human soul. How paltry, how shrivelled and shrunken does the swallow-tail culture of the literary snob appear in contrast with the provinciality which invests the works of Hawthorne with the swift passion of New England summers, the wild desolate beauty of her autumns, and the strange penetrating gloom of her winters.[1]

Joel Chandler Harris speaking. "Swallow-tail culture"— the spirit of the new West was in it, as well as of the new South.

New England and the East looked at the phenomenon with mildly uplifted eyebrows. "What temperament, what gusto," said one of the most prominent of Bostonians, commenting on Rabelais. "Everything beginning to hum —like culture in Chicago."

Chicago in the minds of a vigorous young group was the center of American civilization, not only industrially and socially but artistically and intellectually. A literary center must be a publishing center, and accordingly young Herbert Stone, son of the founder of the Associated Press, with another Harvard graduate, Ingalls Kimball, set out to give the city a model publishing house. They would make books more mechanically beautiful, more distinctive in type and binding and decoration than any yet published in America. For a time as Stone & Kimball they succeeded in their object. Their book-list, with such names as Paul Verlaine, Henry James, Stevenson, Santayana, for a time was really distinctive. They

[1] "Life of Joel Chandler Harris," Robert L. Wiggins, 1918, p. 148.

issued too the "Chap Book," which they made their trade organ and which, under the editorship of Bliss Carman, vied even with the English "Yellow Book" in freshness and vigor and mechanical beauty. In the brief period of its flourishing it distinguished itself with contributions from Anatole France, Pierre La Rose, Paul Verlaine, William Sharp, William Vaughn Moody, Thomas Bailey Aldrich, Richard Hovey, Bliss Carman, Alice Brown, Louise Chandler Moulton, Josephine Preston Peabody, Richard Henry Stoddard, and others.

The dreamings of these young Westerners, who saw an Athens in the raw metropolis of their native region, seem ludicrous now. There was young Hamlin Garland, with his "Main-Travelled Roads" volume, which Howells was praising in superlatives, settling down for a literary career and deliberately choosing Chicago: "In the belief that it was to become the second great literary center of America. [To Garland, Boston was forever to be the first.] I was resolved," he continued, "to throw myself into the task of hurrying forward on the road to new and more resplendent achievement." But even Garland did not wholly unpack his trunk in Chicago:

I had burned no bridges between me and the Island of Manhattan, however! Realizing all too well that I must look to the East for most of my income, I carefully retained my connection with "Harper's," the "Century" and other periodicals. Chicago, rich and powerful as it had become, could not establish—or had not established—a paying magazine, and its publishing firms were mostly experimental and not very successful; although the Columbian Exposition, which was just closing, had left upon the city's clubs and societies (and especially on its young men) an esthetic stimulation which bade fair to carry on to other and more enduring enterprises.[3]

Stimulating enterprises seemed indeed everywhere beginning. Contemporaneous with the Exposition had come

[3] "A Daughter of the Middle Border," Hamlin Garland, 1921, p. 2.

the spectacular rise of the University of Chicago, which, under the vigorous leadership of William Rainey Harper, had opened its doors to students in October, 1892. The grants of money in seven-figure instalments from John D. Rockefeller and others, amounts amazingly large in that early period of philanthropic giving; the establishment of the Yerkes Observatory with the "largest telescope in the world"; the unprecedented salaries offered scholars to head departments in the University, a movement that seemed to threaten to draw to Chicago all the best teachers of the world, until according to the wags of the day no professor had reached the summit of his career until he had attained the degree C.T.C.—"Called to Chicago"; all this put the city vividly before the country and the world.[4]

Then, too, Chicago was issuing a literary journal of national, if not international, importance—E. A. Browne's "Dial," which with the New York "Nation" was to lead for years the journalistic critical forces of the country. To be reviewed favorably in these two journals, and in the "Atlantic" in addition, was fame enough for any American volume. The "Dial" held to Chicago even into the second decade of the new century.

As a result of all these forces there began to pour into the newspaper offices of the city a remarkable tide of young men, most of them with journalistic ambitions, with dreamings of literary fame to be achieved in time. The newspapers of the city had long been vigorous and original. Eugene Field with his column "Sharps and Flats" in the "Morning News" had made himself a national figure. It is not too much to claim for him the distinction of being the originator of the newspaper "column" in its modern form—as later we shall see. Soon was to come George Ade, who for ten years was to pour the earliest pressings of his original wit into columns next to Field's. And one may add to the group John T.

---

[4] See Robert Herrick's novel "Chimes."

McCutcheon, pioneer newspaper cartoonist, and passing to later days, Bert Leston Taylor—"B.L.T."—most inspired of all newspaper columnists with the possible exception of Field.

Not all the gathering group were exotics, however: Frank Norris and Henry B. Fuller were natives. But the greater number came in from the newspaper offices of other Western cities. A noteworthy group it was. For a time there were resident in Chicago most of the literary leaders of the new period. H. L. Mencken could speak of the city as at one time "the literary capital of the United States" and add, with characteristic exaggeration: "Go back twenty or thirty years and you will scarcely find an American literary movement that did not originate under the shadow of the stockyards." Harry Hansen has presented the roll of those who at one time or another were members of the "Chicago school":

Edgar Lee Masters, Sherwood Anderson, Carl Sandburg, Henry B. Fuller, George Ade, Finley Peter Dunne, Ernest Poole, William Hard, Edwin Herbert Lewis, Francis Hackett, Will Payne, Henry Kitchell Webster, Samuel Merwin, Joseph Medill Patterson, Emerson Hough, Edith Franklin Wyatt, Robert Morss Lovett, William Vaughn Moody, Robert Herrick, Charles D. Stewart, Earl Reed, I. K. Friedman, Ernest McGaffey, Stanley Waterloo, Opie Read, Edwin Balmer, Rex Beach, William MacHarg, Floyd Dell, Clarence Darrow, Ben Hecht, Maude Radford Warren, Eunice Tietjens, Clara Louise Burnham—these and many more were sharpening their pencils and working honestly and earnestly, making more or less of a dent in the literary sphere, running the gamut of romance, sentiment, realism and naturalism, in this atmosphere of smoke and grime.[5]

II

During the years of the *fin de siècle* the most active member of the group was undoubtedly Hamlin Garland.

[5] "Midwest Portraits," Harry Hansen, 1923, p. 193.

He lectured to the literary clubs on "Impressionism in Art," and he issued through the new press of Stone & Kimball a smart collection of iconoclastic essays called "Crumbling Idols," "a small screed which aroused an astonishing tumult of comment, mostly antagonistic. Walter Page, editor of the 'Forum,' in which one of the keynote chapters appeared, told me that over a thousand editorials were written on my main thesis." In 1898, to concentrate the best elements of the art and literary circles of the city, he founded the Cliff-Dwellers' Club, but he was himself only a transient member. Soon he was off to New York City, where literary income was more certain, and the inevitable sterility followed.

Born on the Wisconsin border in 1861, moved by his pioneer father into the new prairie lands of Iowa where he grew into boyhood and young manhood amid early settlement conditions, then thrust by his own restlessness into the East of his dreams, into Boston where, living in an attic on scantiest fare, he absorbed the "Brahmin culture" and acquired perspective until he was able to return to his native West and see it with new eyes, Garland was peculiarly fitted to be for a time an inter-sectional interpreter and prophet. There seemed to be promise in the man of rebellious leadership in the played-out period which had gone completely over to conventionalities and echoings.

He had been started as a novelist by the pioneer fiction of Joseph Kirkland of Chicago, whose "Zury, The Meanest Man in Spring County," together with E. W. Howe's "The Story of a Country Town," was the beginning of American Western realism in its modern phases. Visiting Kirkland on his way back from Boston, he had been told to go home to Iowa, into the neighborhood of his boyhood, and write down without a thought of the conventions what he actually saw. And he had gone back, and had been tremendously moved by what his new Boston eyes revealed of the conditions in his mother's home and in the homes of his old neighbors on the prairie farms. With angry pen—not too angry, since at heart he was a romanticist dealing with the lands of his boyhood—he wrote his "Main-Travelled Roads" series of tales. Some bite like acid, but others are fundamentally propaganda, and even sentimental twaddle. Garland, beneath his surface culture, was a pioneer, a development-pusher, a soapboxer. From first to last he has been an enthusiast, a man with a program, an exhibitor, first of his native region, then of the wilder West, then of the marvels of spiritualism and psychic phenomena, then of Henry Georgism, and Populism, even at times of Socialism. He is as innately American as George Follansbee Babbitt—"a hundred percent American"—eternally vocal.

His little volume "Crumbling Idols" preached the gospel of western Americanism in art and literature. Bumptious it was, adolescent, cocksure; but it voiced the new "Middle Border" which had wakened to a civilization of its own.

Today, in the year of 1894, the commercial dominance of the East is distinctly on the wane. Henceforth the center of commercial activity in the United States is to be the West. Henceforth, when men of the Old World speak of America, they will not think of Boston and New York and Philadelphia, they will mean Chicago and the Mississippi Valley.

Literary horizons also are changing with almost equal swiftness. Centers of art production are moving westwards; that is to say, the literary supremacy of the East is passing away. There are other and subtler causes than commercial elements at work. Racial influences are at work, and changes in literary and social ideals are hastening a far-reaching subdivision, if not decentralization, of power.

Boston has claimed and held supremacy in American literature for more than half a century. Made illustrious by Emerson, Hawthorne, Whittier, Longfellow, Holmes, Lowell, the New England group, it easily kept its place as the most important literary center in America. New York was second and Philadelphia third. The Cambridge group has been called "the polite group" and the "library group." Its members took things for the most part at second hand. They read many books, and mainly wrote gentle and polite poems on books and events. Whittier and Hawthorne, notwithstanding their larger originality, were after all related. They took things in a bookish way.

The school of book-poets is losing power. The rise of Chicago as a literary and art center is a question only of time and of a very short time; for the Columbian Exposition has taught her her own capabilities in something higher than business. . . . Henceforth St. Louis, New Orleans, Atlanta, Denver, San Francisco, Cincinnati, St. Paul and Minneapolis, and a dozen more interior cities are to be reckoned with.

The literature which is already springing up in those great interior spaces of the South and West is to be a literature, not of books, but of life. It will draw its inspiration from original contact with men and with nature.

And in a burst of rhapsody he ends:

O sayers and doers of this broad, free, inland America of ours, to you is given the privilege of being broad and free in your life and letters. You should not be bound to a false and dying culture. . . . Yours not to worship crumbling idols; your privilege and pleasure should be to face life and the material earth in a new way.

And the "new way" as he outlined it he called "veritism," which was but another name for the "naturalism" of France and of the school in England which was to follow Thomas Hardy. He would have his West free, original, autochthonic, but he would have it study European "expressionism" and "symbolism" and the older rules of art.

After his "Main-Travelled Roads" sketches, he tried to follow his own advice with a novel, and he produced "Rose of Dutcher's Coolly," a promising volume, one so "veritistic" that it was ruled out of public libraries as unsafe reading—mild stuff it was indeed, as viewed against the fiction of three decades later—and then he went off into literature as a business, literature that was safe and salable. As a result the earliest sheaf of his short stories of his native Midwest, and the first two volumes of his November gleanings in autobiography, his "Middle Border" series, are alone of all his work destined long to endure.

III

"With the exception of Eugene Field's clever sketches," wrote Hjalmar Hjorth Boyesen in 1894, "I know nothing that can properly be called Chicago literature. But here we have it for the first time in 'The Cliff-Dwellers' of Henry Blake Fuller, a serious study of the social conditions of the western metropolis. For many years I have been looking for such a book." [6] Fuller, unquestionably, from the time of this volume until his death in 1929 was the dean of the Chicago "school." Field and all the others, save Dunne, had come into the Chicago circle from without; Fuller was native-born. Garland and the others were birds of passage settling in the half-way station to the East only until sure of a position in New York; Fuller remained with his city to the end. He was indigenous to the place. His grandfather, of old Massachusetts stock, had settled in Chicago when it was a mudhole on the prairie. His son had followed him in his business and had prospered. The grandson too had served his apprenticeship in business. But there was artistry in the boy, a bent that expressed itself first in music. Abandoning the ancestral career, he went to Italy, where for two years he lived in an atmosphere artistic and musical. He learned the language, read the new literature that was pouring from the European presses, forgot at length his dreams of music and architecture, and began to write— little things infinitely revised, tiny sketchings, literary cameos cut without haste and without models. Returning

[6] "Cosmopolitan," January, 1894.

to America he tried to market his resulting volume, which he called a novel—in vain. The market did not demand sketches without action. The title he had chosen, too, was hardly a commercial one—"The Chevalier of Pensieri-Vani." Despairing of a publisher, he issued the little volume himself, in Boston, under a pseudonym, but there was no publicity. The book would have died still-born and have been buried had not an amazing bit of good fortune come to its rescue: Charles Eliot Norton, attracted undoubtedly by the Italian title, bought a copy and sent it to Lowell, who read it with huge approval. It had a Knickerbocker atmosphere and style; it was like the work of his own literary adolescence. The result was a second edition issued by the Century Company, and the serialization of a second volume by Fuller: "The Châtelaine of La Trinité," in the "Century Magazine." And now followed a second bit of rarest fortune: Agnes Repplier discovered "The Chevalier" and made it the theme of one of her essays. "A beautiful, cultivated, well-spent inactivity is the keynote of this serene little book," was her summary of the volume; and she added, "he has the faculty for delicate and sympathetic delineation."

Fuller's third venture was "The Cliff-Dwellers," a serial in "Harper's Weekly" during the Exposition year 1893. The dilettante dreamer had been swept into the new current of the excited decade: he would picture Chicago as Zola had pictured Paris, as Hardy had pictured Wessex. His first chapter is an impression of the city after Hardy's own manner in "The Return of the Native" —Chicago pictured impressionistically as if it were an area in "The Bad Lands." The inhabited cliffs are skyscrapers; the loftiest of them, the "Clifton," inhabited by more than four thousand souls, savages preying upon each other with ferocity. And behind them the counter-tribe of women—vain beyond belief, extravagant, dominating, ruinous. The *motif* of the novel is in its last sentence: "He knew that she was Cecilia Ingles, and his heart was constricted by the sight of her. It is for such a woman that one man builds a Clifton and that a hundred others are martyred in it." In the picture of its women the novel grips and bites. Otherwise it is a *tour de force,* a book after the Howells pattern but without the Howells clearness and the Howells fluidity of movement. Tame and colorless it seems to-day after Dreiser and Anderson, but it fell into the nineties like a meteorite. The novel that followed, "With the Procession," was even more caustic in its treatment of Chicago society, more biting in its delineation of feminine ruthlessness. In it, says Miss Dondore, "Fuller has done a unique thing: with firm line he has drawn the feminine parallel of the victorious and irresistible ascent of the self-made rich man, the heiress of the spirit that won the frontier." [7]

"With the Procession" was the last of his popular triumphs. In the full tide of success he dropped his realism and went to Europe to dream in the soft atmospheres of an accomplished past. No more realism: realism had been with him but a moment of excitement. After 1895 his volumes were written without thought of popular acclaim. A dozen of them he produced first and last, but they were fruits of his solitude, serene and wrought out, things that fell gently upon the book stands of three decades to be seen by the few and to vanish. He was a dreamer, a man alone, a stylist, a worshiper of the beautiful. Desultory was his product: his books range from romance to drama, from poetry to essays and sketches and short stories. Always was he enamoured of technique, a cutter of cameos, an unhurried dilettante who worked after his own ideals. As a result his books were completely out of print before he died; most of them are still in their original editions.

The explanation is not hard to find: though Chicago-born he was as alien to the Chicago spirit as Keats to his

[7] "The Prairie and the Making of Middle America," Dorothy A. Dondore, 1926, p. 378.

father's stables. He would escape to dream in some distant Valhalla of the soul. Time and again, in 1892, 1894, 1897, he escaped to Europe where at least there was the atmosphere of art and beauty. Literature to him was a thing of the ethereal world, not a vulgar *exposé* of the social régime of the stockyards. He lived in Chicago because of family bonds—nothing beyond this.

"During these later years," he wrote, "I have had to keep in America and almost altogether in Chicago, where practical concerns have often been unfavorable to literary production." Add this from Garland and you have full explanation: "To him the town was a pestilential slough in which he, at any rate, was inexorably mired." He could dream, however, in Chicago, and dabble at his art, and let the vulgar world roar by.

But a curious thing has happened: everywhere is he praised now as one of the leading formative influences in the period of change. James Huneker in his volume "Unicorns" has hailed him as his literary master; Theodore Dreiser has declared that it was Fuller's work which started him as a novelist; and such younger writers as Carl Van Vechten and Percival Pollard and H. L. Mencken have acknowledged his influence. Despite his seeming failure he must be reckoned with as one of the forces of the period. According to Mr. Van Vechten:

His contribution to American fiction is a certain calm, a repose of manner, a decorative irony, exquisite in its not too completely hidden implications, a humor which is informed with abundant subtlety, a study of human nature abroad and at home as searching as it is careful, and above all, a delicate, abiding charm.[8]

Perhaps even yet his gentle little volumes—strange products to come from the area of the strenuous life— may be rescued from their oblivion and be re-issued for

[8] Quoted by Victor Shultz in "Henry Blake Fuller: Civilized Chicagoan," in the "Bookman," September, 1929.

the few who still are enamoured of beauty as a literary necessity, of the dreamings of a poetic soul rather than the foulness of a manufactured actuality, of style and finish rather than journalistic vigor and compelling force.

IV

Criticism of Chicago civilization came with varying degrees of emphasis from the little group of exile scholars from the East gathered by President Harper for the faculty of his new John Rockefeller university. Chief among these from a literary viewpoint were William Vaughn Moody, whose letters, since published, are illuminating documents, and Robert Herrick, who voiced his protest in satirical novels.

Herrick was an Easterner who stood aloof and unsympathetic. His novel "Chimes," written in later years, 1926, semi-autobiographical, tells with satiric touches his opinion of Western culture as centering in the youthful university. He was the first of his Puritan line to settle outside the New England borders; a Harvard man with his education finished in Europe; and he had taught English in the Massachusetts Institute of Technology under the supervision of George Rice Carpenter. Called at twenty-six to organize the English department of the new University after the Harvard pattern, he remained for twenty-five years.

Immediately began his career as short-story writer and novelist. European literature—he had lived in Europe three years—first molded his style: Zola, Sudermann, Ibsen. Like Frank Norris, whose work he admired, he knew his French thoroughly and was inclined to the Gallic type of realism though never with grossness. Realism to him was only another term for normalcy:

The realist writes a novel with one purpose in view. And that purpose is to render into written words the normal aspect of things. The aim of the romanticist is entirely different. He

is concerned only with things which are exciting, astonishing
—in a word, abnormal. I do not like literary labels, and I think
that the names "realist" and "romanticist" have been so much
misused that they are now almost meaningless. The significance of the term changes from year to year; the realists of
one generation are the romanticists of the next.

His earliest novels—the first, "The Gospel of Freedom," came in 1898—are realistic in the sense of being
areas of normal life normally told. Often militant they
are, in their attack upon social evils and business im-
morality. The novel made for mere entertainment he
scoffed at. To him the novel was a lance, a lancet, a
Damascus blade, a delicately wrought rapier, not the jaw-
bone of an ass such as was wielded by the men of wrath
like Upton Sinclair, and the Sinclair Lewis of "Elmer
Gantry."

Behold a Harvard scholar, a Puritan with lines of New
England ancestry, in the Chicago of the *fin de siècle,* the
Chicago of the first sky-scraper era, of the early university
dream—the "Harvard and Yale of the West," of the
Chicago of the stockyards scandal, and the Columbian
Exposition excitement. The rawness of it shocks the
young esthete even as it did Fuller the native, who returned again and again from Europe to mourn its ugliness. Yet the thrill of bounding life in it all held both of
them. Both of them set out to educate it in morals, to
show it its crudeness.

First, the young Herrick scored the unscrupulous materialism of the city. In an early novel he showed the
moral gangrene that ate the soul out of a young architect
who, fighting between the slow gains of legitimate work
and the mushroom product of get-rich-quick methods,
surrendered and made a cardboard tenement house, advertised as "fire-proof," and later watched it burn and
roast its inmates, the lying sign the last thing consumed. In
his "Memoirs of an American Citizen" he exposed the

stockyards methods and the meat-trust a full year before
Sinclair's "The Jungle."

But the rapier is no weapon for such fights. To attack
the stockyards one needed mauls and manners understood
and appreciated not alone by the esoteric few but by the
all, by the commoners in the lowest ranks.

More effective was he in the second area of his fiction,
his diagnoses and exhibited specimens of all that may be
classed as the social relations between men and women.
Especially did he consider the problems of the new
femininity of the new West: a half a dozen of his novels
might be given, each of them, the title "Misfits." The
culminating volume was, of course, his "Together," 1908,
which to the disgust of its author headed the list of the best
sellers, a novel in which he sided with the woman who
revolted against a misfit marriage and made her own law.

It was in a way a surviving spirit of the old frontier
that Herrick was fighting, not only the frontier spirit of
independence which had affected women as well as men,
but a survival of the frontier sentimentalism concerning
women, an exaggerated chivalry of which the later women
took advantage. A sorry gallery has he created of feminine
selfishness, of despicable "cats," of pathetic specimens of
the unequally yoked.

His satire, however, has accomplished little. He has
refused to be popular, he has refused to be advertised in
superlatives, he has more and more abandoned his fighting
weapons altogether. As he has himself expressed it:

My books fall into two classes—those strictly of realistic
technique, such as *The Memoirs of an American Citizen* and
The Common Lot; and those of a freer, more poetic technique,
such as *The Real World, A Life for a Life,* and *Clark's
Field.* I need scarcely say that these latter are the books
nearer my heart, but they are not the ones which appeal most
widely to the public.

Not great are his novels, not especially original nor compellingly distinctive, but as documents in the history of a unique era they will always have a certain vitality that will hold them on library shelves. Those most frequently starred as important are these seven:

"The Real World," 1901
"The Common Lot," 1904
"The Memoirs of an American Citizen," 1905
"Together," 1908
"A Life for a Life," 1910
"Clark's Field," 1914
"Chimes," 1927

And it is pleasant to be able to note that in the opinion of the present critic the last-named novel has the best claim and the best chance for permanence.

v

The vogue of the Chicago "school" was brief. In the words of Harry Hansen, "they came at an impecunious moment in their career, struggled and suffered in an ill-ventilated hall bedroom, wrote one or two books, and then answered the call of the East." There was nothing to hold them. Hamlin Garland in "A Daughter of the Middle Border" has told the outcome of the Chicago dreams:

Chicago, rushing toward its two-million mark, had not, alas! lived up to its literary promise of 1894. In music, in painting, in sculpture and architecture it was no longer negligible, but each year its authors appeared more and more like a group of esthetic pioneers heroically maintaining themselves in the midst of an increasing tumult of material upbuilding. One by one its hopeful young publishing houses had failed, and one by one its aspiring periodicals had withered in the keen wind of eastern competition.

And the reason for it all, according to Hansen, was the fact that the Chicago "mass" was not ready for culture.

The various institutions which had seemed to promise so much for the city "had not come into being in answer to popular clamor. All are monuments of the patience, the culture, the tolerance, or the wealth of certain individuals who could dream in a stifling atmosphere."

The individuals of the "school," men like Dreiser and Anderson and Masters, we shall treat in due time. Chicago, as it affected the period, fills more than a single chapter.

BIBLIOGRAPHICAL REFERENCES

"Midwest Portraits: a Book of Memories and Friendships," Harry Hansen. A valuable study of half a dozen modern literary leaders, with Chicago as background. Full-length studies of Sandburg, Anderson, Herrick, Masters, Harriet Monroe, Lew Sarett, Ben Hecht, and others.

"George Ade" in "Prejudices," First Series, H. L. Mencken, 1919.

"Chicago: the History of its Reputation," Lloyd Lewis and Henry Justin Smith, 1929.

"A Daughter of the Middle Border," Hamlin Garland. The opening chapters record the author's experiences in Chicago during the early nineties.

HENRY BLAKE FULLER, 1857–1929

"The Chevalier of Pensieri-Vani," 1891; "The Châtelaine of La Trinité, 1892; "The Cliff-Dwellers," 1893; "With the Procession," 1895; "The Puppet-Booth," 1896 (dramatic sketches); three volumes of short stories, viz.: "From the Other Side," 1898; "Under the Skylights," 1901; "Waldo Trench and Others," 1908; "The Last Refuge," 1900; and then "Lines Long and Short," 1917 (experiments in free verse), and three final novels: "On the Stairs," 1918; "Bertram Cope's Year," 1919; "Gardens of this World," 1929; "Not on the Screen," 1930.

CHAPTER III

FRANK NORRIS

I

THE Chicago movement failed for want of an adequate leader. As the decade was closing, however, the leader appeared, but not in Chicago. It was young Frank Norris, Chicago-born, but long since removed to San Francisco. Again, as in the eighteen sixties, it was a voice from California that precipitated a new period, a voice free from provincial narrowness and Puritanical intolerance. Moreover, it was the voice of a leader fitted for leadership. Unlike Garland, he had been reared in a wealthy home with every advantage of education and cultural atmosphere; and he had been Harvard-trained, and he had been broadened by residence in Europe.

His father, a business man, first in New York and then in Chicago, had settled finally in California because of failing health. It was from his mother—at the time of her marriage an actress of national fame—that the boy inherited his artistic bent. He was eleven when he left Chicago, a dreamy lad, stored with romance from his cradle, and the training in the San Francisco schools and the fashionable Belmont seminary did not curb in the least his romantic individualism. At seventeen he would quit school: he would be an artist, and, like Fuller of an earlier day, he would study nowhere but in Paris. His whim was granted, and for two years he roamed the Latin Quarter and learned French. And along with other things he became conscious of the literary revolution in progress in the city

—Zola, Flaubert, Maupassant, Daudet, and the rest. Realism *à la française*—"naturalism"—was in the air. But fundamentally the boy was a romanticist: romanticism was in his blood. The literary ferment, however, laid hold upon him. He began to scribble, incessantly scribble, romance for the most part, airy nothings built from his voluminous reading and his dreaming. His art no longer interested him: he dropped it and only scribbled—until his father stepped in and ordered him home.

In 1890 the boy was entered in the University of California, but it was only to dawdle and dream. Nothing in the great State college awoke the lad. Like Jack London a little later, he found an English department desiccated and useless, and after three unprofitable years he left it to go to Harvard where he was admitted to the senior class. And now for the first time Norris found his real work. In the class-room of Professor Lewis E. Gates there was sympathy even with youthful extravagance. There was guidance, moreover, and there was an atmosphere that awakened all the youth's latent powers. He found himself now a Zolaist. His residence in France had at least given him a knowledge of the French, and he read now with a new conception of literary art. He had awakened. To his surprise he found himself in agreement even with the extremists. He, too, was a realist, even a "naturalist" *à la française*. And now he, too, began to write realism, throwing himself into his work with Western extravagance. Under the professor's eye he produced much of the material which afterwards became "McTeague" and nearly all of "Vandover and the Brute," a novel that found no publisher until twelve years after its author's death.

Again at home, with his Harvard degree now, another wave of restlessness swept over him. He would go into journalism, but it would be as a special correspondent in some wild field of adventure. And just as he was ready the miracle happened: a San Francisco paper sent him to South Africa to report the Boer war then fomenting with England. He arrived just in time to be a part of the Jameson raid, to be captured and threatened with death, and then to fall a victim to African fever, which all but finished him on the spot and did end him completely some years later.

Returned at length to San Francisco, he was given a desk in the office of "The Wave," a free-lance journal afterwards to be made famous through the editorship of Gelett Burgess, of "purple cow" fame, and Will Irwin. Now it was that his literary career really began. It had come to him with emphasis that the time was ripe for a literary leader, an American Zola, and he now set out himself to be that leader. In a series of papers he had announced the principles of the new revolution. This in a single paragraph was to be his creed:

The people have a right to Truth as they have a right to life, liberty and the pursuit of happiness. It is not right that they should be exploited and deceived with false views of life, false characters, false sentiment, false morality, false history, false philosophy, false emotions, false heroism, false notions of self-sacrifice, false views of religion, of duty, of conduct, and manners.

The new literature must be first of all a literature of Truth, free from all artificialities, free from all conventions, including prudishness and sentimentality. It was a condemnation of the local colorists, who had run to extremes, and of the historical romancers who by the mid-nineties were occupying the entire center of the literary stage. It was more than this: it was the rallying cry of a new generation of creators; it was the voice of the new period. All the elements of the new revolution were in it.

Now began the real work of Frank Norris. In seven years seven volumes. First came his journalistic sketchings for the "Wave." The editor, a congenial soul, allowed him to work his will, and the result was scribblings, paragraphs, impressionistic settings, and soon a weekly column, "Little

Stories of the Pavements." During the years that Jack London was living melodrama in the city and laboring with intensity for literary recognition, Norris also in the same city was throwing his soul into literary creation. For materials he drew upon his observations in San Francisco and its environs, heightened always and vivified by a Stephen-Crane-like imagination. The old Chinatown of the days before the earthquake still lives in his gruesome tale "The Third Circle." Everywhere one is reminded of the later Jack London: "Shorty Stack, Pugilist" undoubtedly was the original for London's "The Abysmal Brute," and "Moran of the Lady Letty" suggests at every point "The Sea Wolf," written years later. And surely "A Man's Woman" could be picked up by mistake and read from cover to cover as another tale from the author of "The Mutiny of the Elsinore." From Zola the young Norris learned to represent life in all its dimensions, life as it is. From Kipling he learned that realism to be effective must give the impression that the author has gained his facts from personal presence in the areas involved. Moreover, from Stevenson—"Waverley" romanticist—he had learned again what his mother had taught him: that even "naturalism" to be effective must have a soul as well as a body, must have in it a drop of that magic something that defies the test-tubes of science—that something we often call romance.

The young reporter's weekly trickle of sketch and tale soon broadened into a lake. He began a novel for serialization in the "Wave" entitled "Moran of the Lady Letty," a wild improvisation, feeding the copy into the press from week to week until the story reached its climax. A red-blooded tale it was, a veritable "shocker," as brutal in atmosphere and incident as anything in all Jack London's repertoire. It had vigor, however, and what London would call "punch." And it seemed like actuality—certainly the author of it must have known the sea as only a sailor could know it: the same argument that later was to declare that only a veritable soldier of the Civil War could have written Crane's "Red Badge of Courage." It was instantly successful: it caught the attention of the East, even as "The Luck of Roaring Camp" had done a generation before, and as London's "The Son of the Wolf" in the "Overland Monthly" soon was to do, and the result was an offer from "McClure's" and the departure of the young writer for the East.

The rest is quickly told. A series of novels followed: "Blix," "McTeague," "A Man's Woman," and then "The Octopus," first volume of a trilogy, "the epic of the wheat," then the second in the series, "The Pit." The third, "The Wolf," was to follow, but this he never wrote. Suddenly he died—dead at thirty-two with dreamings in his brain of another trilogy, the colossal epic of the Gettysburg battle, a volume for each day; but it was not to be. Frank Norris must be reckoned with those dead young authors who live most gloriously in the works they dreamed of writing, the volumes of their years that were not to be.

With Norris, however, one is inclined to feel that the end came not too soon if he was to be reckoned among the leaders of his period. From the moment he reached New York City more and more in his work are to be found symptoms of surrender. "New York," Ambrose Bierce once wrote, "is cocaine, opium, hashish."

Norris's own story, "Dying Fires," written in the vigorous days of his apprenticeship on the "Wave," is emblematic of his career. Young Overbeck, its central figure, is Norris himself, living in the actuality of life in the Rooseveltian areas "where men are men," in "Clipper Gap," where the mountain ranches began, and where the mountain cowboy lived up to the traditions of his kind.

This life, tumultuous, headstrong, vivid in color, vigorous in action, was bound together by the railroad, which not only made a single community out of all that part of the east slope of the Sierras' foothills, but contributed its own life as well—

the life of oilers, engineers, switchmen, eating-house waitresses and cashiers, "lady" operators, conductors.

And this life Overbeck put into a novel, crude but alive; it stirred the East, and he was called to New York. And the spirit of New York laid hold of him.

By rapid degrees young Overbeck caught the lingo of the third-raters. He could talk about "tendencies" and the "influence of reactions." Such and such a writer had a "sense of form," another a "feeling for word effects." He knew all about "tones" and "notes" and "philistinisms." He could tell the difference between an allegory and a simile as far as he could see them. An anticlimax was the one unforgivable sin under heaven. A mixed metaphor made him wince, and a split infinitive hurt him like a blow.

Slowly the fires died within Overbeck; he finished his novel and in every way was it in the mode of art; but it was a dead thing. And now he saw his great mistake:

The golden apples, that had been his for the stretching of the hand, he had flung from him. Tricked, trapped, exploited, he had prostituted the great good thing that had been his by right divine, for the privilege of eating husks with swine.

Then Overbeck tried to return, but it was too late: the fires were dead; the ashes were cold.

Norris by no means came to such tragic limits, but the tale is a prophecy. America in 1900 was not ready for revolt: the old conventions still held strongly. Even with such lusty young revolters as the young Hamlin Garland and Norris, Jack London and O. Henry, David Graham Phillips and Theodore Dreiser—all of them publishing vigorously in 1900—America was still satisfied with the Kailyard school of imported fiction and with such sugary compounds as "When Knighthood Was in Flower." The magazines overflowed with imported popularities; Arthur S. Hardy, editor during this period of the "Cosmopolitan," records with pride his conquests for his magazine:

Flammarion writing on "The End of the World"; Francisque Sarcey, the dramatic critic, contributing a monthly note; Madame Adam, editor of the "Nouvelle Revue"; Valdès, Kipling, Charcot, Clark Russell, who furnished a serial seastory, Zangwill, Paul Verlaine, Edouard Rod, François Coppée, Guy de Maupassant, etc.

America was being educated for revolt, but the revolt must come through foreign writers. Norris in New York ceased to fight. His last novel, "The Pit," is conventional work. His rebellion, like Garland's, had seemingly failed. All the rebels had surrendered.

II

By temperament and by training Norris was an innovator. He was free, untouched by the New England inhibitions and wholly outside of the closed circle of the Brahmin literary aristocracy. He was unlocalized, unconcerned with the provincial uniqueness which had so obsessed the novelists of locality during two decades. Moreover, unlike his predecessors Harte, Clemens, Eggleston, Cable, Howells, Jewett, Murfree, and Harris, he had come to his work with college training, with a literary program from the start, one from which he did not swerve until the enervating atmosphere of New York loosened his grip.

From the first he conceived of himself as a leader. As early as 1892 he was condemning in the "Critic" "the estate of American letters" and was suggesting radical changes:

The estate of American letters is experiencing a renaissance. Formality, the old idols, the demigorgons and autocrats no longer hold an absolute authority. . . . To-day is the day of the novel. In no other day and by no other vehicle is contemporaneous life so adequately expressed; and the critics of the twenty-second century, reviewing our times, striving to reconstruct our civilization, will look not to the painters, but to the novelists to find our idiosyncracy.

And to him the novel must deal with common life and be written not for the few but for *all*—for the People.

It is all very well to jeer at the people and at the people's misunderstanding of the arts, but the fact is indisputable that no art that is not in the end understood by the people can live or ever did live a single generation. In the larger view, in the last analysis, the People pronounce the final judgment. The People, despised of the artist, hooted, caricatured and vilified, are, after all, and in the main, the real seekers after Truth.

His mission, as he conceived it, was to tell the Truth to his generation, to *all* of his generation.

The difficult thing is to get at the life immediately around you—the very life in which you move. No romance in it. No romance in *you,* poor fool. As much romance on Michigan Avenue as there is realism in King Arthur's court. . . . To know life around you, you must live—if not *among* people, then *in* people.

And the great novelist looking back over his life when his last novel has been written should be able to feel that it all has been—

sincere work, telling the truth as he saw it, independent of fashion and the gallery gods, holding to these with gripped hands and shut teeth—he will think of all this then, and he will be able to say: "I never truckled; I never took off the hat to fashion and held it out for pennies. By God, I told them the Truth. They liked it or they did not like it. What had that to do with me? I told them the truth; I knew it for the truth then, and I know it for the truth now."

III

Two books in Norris's list stand among the notable creations of the period—two books for the short shelf of American "classics": "McTeague" and "The Octopus." "McTeague" in every way was a pioneer book: it was an illustration to the full of its author's theories. It attempted to record without idealization a bit of actual life as it happened, a sordid bit usually found only in the news columns of sensational papers. Its author weakened a little at the end: the opportunity for melodrama was too tempting; but the book as a whole is a definition of what Norris called "Truth" in fiction.

It was Truth, however, seen through a temperament. The eye of the man was telescopic, not microscopic like the local colorist's. He saw life always in epic proportions. He saw his leading characters, as did Jack London in later days, as supermen, as Nietzschian "blond beasts." Here is McTeague:

McTeague was a young giant, carrying his huge shock of blond hair six feet three inches from the ground; moving his immense limbs, heavy with ropes of muscle, slowly, ponderously. His hands were enormous, red, and covered with a fell of stiff yellow hair; they were hard as wooden mallets, strong as vises, the hands of the old-time car-boy. Often he dispensed with forceps and extracted a refractory tooth with his thumb and finger. His head was square-cut, angular; the jaw salient, like that of the Carnivora.

So in all his novels: Bennett in "A Man's Woman":

He was an enormous man, standing six feet two inches in his reindeer footnips and having the look more of a prize-fighter than of a scientist. Even making allowances for its coating of dirt and its harsh, black stubble of a week's growth, the face was not pleasant. Bennett was an ugly man. His lower jaw was huge almost to deformity, like that of the bull-dog, the chin salient, the mouth close-gripped, with great lips, indomitable, brutal.

His women also are of "blond beast" texture. This is Travis Bessemer in "Blix":

She was young, but tall as most men, and solidly, almost heavily built. Her shoulders were broad, her chest was deep, her neck round and firm. She radiated health; there were exuberance and vitality in the very touch of her foot upon the carpet, and there was that cleanliness about her, that freshness, that suggested a recent plunge in the surf and a "constitutional" along the beach. One felt that here was stamina, good physical force, and fine animal vigor. Her arms were large, her wrists were large, and her fingers did not taper. Her hair was of a brown so light as to be almost yellow.

And this was Miss Moran of the *Lady Letty:*

She drank whiskey after her meals, and when angry, which was often, swore like a buccaneer. As yet she was almost, as one might say, without sex—savage, unconquered, untamed, glorying in her own independence, her sullen isolation. Her neck was thick, strong, and very white, her hands roughened and calloused. In her men's clothes she looked tall, vigorous, and unrestrained.

One thinks of Frona Wilse in Jack London's "A Daughter of the Snows." It was pioneer work for the "red blood" school soon to come in the era of "the strenuous life."

Everywhere was Norris epic in his literary plans. The trilogy that was to tell the story of the wheat exceeds the continent in its bounds. This was the plan as outlined in his preface to "The Octopus":

The Trilogy of the Epic of the Wheat will include the following novels: *The Octopus, a Story of California; The Pit, a Story of Chicago; The Wolf, a Story of Europe.* . . . The first novel, *The Octopus,* deals with the war between the wheat grower and the Railroad Trust; the second, *The Pit,* will be the fictitious narrative of a "deal" in the Chicago wheat pit; while the third, *The Wolf,* will probably have for its pivotal episode the relieving of a famine in an Old World community.

At times the novel seems like a pioneer "muck-rake" production: the railroad is the villain of the book, and mercilessly is it scored. But quickly one forgets this. One is gripped by the tremendous thesis of the trilogy. Out of the vast Northwest a stream of the life-fluid, the flood of wheat moving steadily eastward. It is like the Gulf Stream in the Atlantic: nothing can stop its tremendous onward flow. In "The Octopus," the Railroad Trust with its millions of money and its ruthless supermen tries to regulate the tide; it sweeps over them and rushes on. In Chicago unscrupulous speculators try to corner it: in vain. Nothing can stop the restless tide flowing ever to the East, where stalk hunger and famine and death. All of its episodes are of epic intensity, told with emotion, gripping, compelling: the plunge of the Pacific express through the flock of sheep on the track; the death of the railroad magnate drowned in the wheat of the elevator; the chase of the freebooter Dyke —but through it all the tremendous thesis: seemingly the railroad won, but—

the wheat remained. Untouched, unassailable, undefiled, that mighty world-force, that nourisher of nations, wrapped in Nirvanic calm, indifferent to the human swarm, gigantic, resistless, moved onward in its appointed grooves. Through the welter of blood in the irrigation ditch, through the sham charity and shallow philanthropy of famine relief committees, the great harvest of Los Muertos rolled like a flood from the Sierras to the Himalayas to feed thousands of starving scarecrows on the barren plains of India.

Much was written during the seventies and the eighties of "the great American novel"—the novel that was to do for America what a dozen great novels have done for England. Foolish speculation it was undoubtedly, and yet what novel written in America before 1900 comes nearer being the "great American novel" than "The Octopus" by the young Frank Norris?

BIBLIOGRAPHICAL REFERENCES

There is at present no life of Norris. His brother Charles prepared an advertising pamphlet with biographical data at the time of the Golden Gate Edition in 1903, but it has long been out of print. A new edition of Norris's works coördinate with the *de luxe* edition of Stephen Crane, with a competent editor for each volume, has been promised. Several studies of Norris's life and work are particularly helpful:

"Literature and Insurgency, Ten Studies in Racial Evolution,"
John Curtis Underwood, 1914. Chapter 4 deals with Frank Norris. The author is an extremist with a thesis which he never forgets. His summaries and epitomes of Norris's books are excellent.
"Some American Story Tellers," Frederic Taber Cooper, 1911. An article of book-review texture by a veteran journalist. An excellent approach to Norris, but to be read with caution.
"Frank Norris, or, Up from Culture," Charles Caldwell Dobie, in the "American Mercury," April, 1928. Often "smart" as the title would indicate, written in the "American Mercury" style, but the best study yet of Norris's early life.

Several magazine articles are worth consulting, though the point of view of most of the early criticism dealing with Norris is archaic:

"Norris as a Novelist," W. D. Howells, "North American Review," 175 : 769.
"The Work of Frank Norris," Hamlin Garland, the "Critic," 42 : 216.
Introduction to "The Third Circle," Will Irwin, 1909. Important. Best authority on Norris's "Wave" period.
"The Novels of Norris," H. W. Preston, "Atlantic," 91 : 691.
"Frank Norris," W. S. Rainsford, "World's Work," 5 : 3276.

FRANK NORRIS, 1870–1902

"Yvernelle" (romantic narrative poem), 1892; "Moran of the Lady Letty," 1898; "Blix," 1899; "McTeague, a Story of San Francisco," 1899; "A Man's Woman," 1900; "The Octopus, a Story of California," 1901; "The Pit, a Story of Chicago," 1902; "The Responsibilities of the Novelist and other Literary Essays," 1903; "Complete Works of Frank Norris, Golden Gate Edition," 1903; "A Deal in Wheat and Other Stories," 1903; "The Joyous Miracle," 1906; "The Third Circle," 1909; "Vandover and the Brute," 1914.

CHAPTER IV

THE NEW JOURNALISM

I

THE decade of the nineties witnessed a change in newspaper and magazine publication that in itself was a revolution. The Sunday edition with its "literary" supplement, the invention of photo-engraving, the rise of "yellow journalism," the ten- and fifteen-cent price for magazines, and the enormous growth of advertising in the daily and the weekly and the monthly literary mediums projected literature into a totally new world.

The revolution centered about some half a dozen remarkable men, vigorous personalities, the first of them in point of time Edward Bok, who in October, 1889, took the editorial supervision of the "Ladies' Home Journal." A native of Holland, an immigrant, a youth migrating to America with nothing but bare hands, he had approached the new world of the West with dreams as vivid and romantic as those which two generations before had filled the young Washington Irving when he had made the reverse journey eastward to the land of his fathers. He had no local prejudices, no provincialism, no American "isms" of any kind, and he set out to make a journal for *all* the people and at a price to suit *all* the people. And by a miracle of good judgment, an uncanny ability to concentrate upon topics interesting to the great American mass, and, added to all, a business sense that was able to advertise his wares in ways peculiarly effective, he drove the circulation of his magazine to figures before unheard-of in the magazine world—a million and a half copies a month. "As much as $400,000," he declares, "was spent in one year in advertising only a few features—a gigantic sum in those days, approached by no other magazine." It was his dream to make—

a magazine that would be an authoritative clearing-house of all the problems confronting women in the home, that brought itself closely into contact with those problems and tried to solve them in an entertaining and efficient way; and yet a magazine of uplift and inspiration: a magazine, in other words, that would give light and leading in the woman's world.[1]

His sense of what was wanted was remarkable. At one period he received a million letters a year from his subscribers, and with a force of thirty-five editors he answered them all in full. With no thought of the money involved, he secured articles from Kipling, President Harrison, Mark Twain, Bret Harte, F. Marion Crawford, Conan Doyle, S. O. Jewett, J. K. Bangs, Kate Douglas Wiggin, Hamlin Garland, Mrs. Burton Harrison, Joel Chandler Harris, and a dozen others as prominent. He was able to secure even Theodore Roosevelt, while the latter was President, to take charge of a monthly column. To quote Algernon Tassin:

He . . . placed the two hemispheres on a family basis. He did not go forth to the family-circle as the mid-century *Harper's* had done; he inscribed the circle around himself like Richelieu holding the maiden Julie. Nobody could step outside of it unless he stepped off the planet. Unknown Wives of Well-known Men, Unknown Husbands, Famous Daughters of Famous Men, How I Wrote This or Did That—everybody who was somebody and everybody who was nobody were soon engaged in counting his or her pulse-beats to a breathless world and to the tune of the periodical's increasing circulation. One touch of Mr. E. W. Bok had made the whole world kin. . . . As for the editors of the new cheap magazines,

[1] "The Americanization of Edward Bok," p. 162.

they looked upon Mr. Bok and at once did likewise. Personal publicity became the proof of aggressiveness and enterprise. It was part of the advertising age.[2]

Following Bok came a group of other active individualists who viewed literature solely through business eyes. There was W. R. Hearst with his yellow journals, a distinct growth of the nineties; there was Joseph Pulitzer, a revolutionary force in New York journalism; there was Melville E. Stone, whose Associated Press soon became a world power; and there were the vigorous two who wrought havoc in the world of magazine publication, Frank A. Munsey and S. S. McClure.

First had come Munsey, who started his "Munsey's Weekly" as early as 1889, changing it in 1891 to "Munsey's Magazine." Munsey was first of all a business man, an organizer and financial manipulator with rare powers. Unlike his two rivals Bok and McClure, he was native-born, reared in an isolated village in Maine, uneducated save for what he got at the red schoolhouse of his town, the grocery store, and the county telegraph office where at length he found employment.

McClure was scholarly and bookish. He was a college graduate with Greek and Latin and smatterings of world classics. When he dreamed of a magazine it was one founded on the old literary conceptions with, of course, modern variations. He started his magazine on high literary levels, appealing to the best readers. To quote from his autobiography:

One of the distinctive features begun in the first number was a series of "Real Conversations," carefully prepared interviews with noted men about their life and work. The first of these was an interview with William Dean Howells, by H. H. Boyesen. Later came interviews with Eugene Field, Frank R. Stockton, Jules Verne, Alphonse Daudet, Professor Alexander Graham Bell, and many others. The "Human Docu-

2 "The Magazine in America," Algernon Tassin, p. 355.

ment" series, begun in the first number of "McClure's," was another feature, so successful that we would have kept it up forever if the supply of great men had held out.

Munsey, however, approached literature from unliterary levels. He had been reared on Beadle's novels and the sentimental trash which had been issued in such amazing quantities from a publishing house in Augusta, Maine—fiction for housemaids and mill-hands and shop-girls. Such stuff, he soon realized, found an enormous market. If successful at Augusta, Maine, he reasoned, what would it not be if issued from New York, with all the added facilities for distribution and advertising and the securing of contributors? A purely business proposition it was to him, though when he set out for New York his trunk was full of stories of his own which he was to sell for the money that was to be his business capital. His adventures in these early years of his start read like his own fiction. After unheard-of difficulties he succeeded in borrowing enough money to start his weekly, an Augusta-Maine-like journal edited on the lower literary levels of the American mass. It started without impetus; it sold not at all. Frantically he borrowed more money and poured it into advertising. No results. The American News Company refused to handle him. He was soon on the brink of ruin.

I had no money. I had an indebtedness of nearly a hundred thousand dollars. But it wasn't money that was to win this fight: it was the magazine and the price—the theory of giving the people what they wanted and giving it to them at the right price. Though I had no money I still had credit, and this credit had to serve in the place of cash.

He decided to sell over the heads of the news company— deal directly with the people. By every law of business it meant ruin, but by sheer nerve the man won. No more epic battle was ever fought, and his success was as epical as his fight. Magazine followed magazine, then newspapers were added. He acquired the New York "Press," the New York "Sun," then the "Herald," then the "Evening Sun" and the "Telegram," and two papers in Baltimore. At last he was a veritable power.

His theory that the price of the magazine was the dominating thing had made him a pioneer of enormous influence. Always were his magazines "cheap" in every sense of the word, keyed to the general, but the selling price was low and the advertising prices were high. In 1891 "Munsey's Magazine" was twenty-five cents, while all the standard magazines hovered about thirty-five cents. Then had come the day of S. S. McClure.

Like Bok an immigrant, he had come from his native Ireland at the age of nine, landing in Quebec in 1866. Settled in Valparaiso, Indiana, the little family—a widowed mother and four children—struggled with poverty. Never lad more restless or more irresistibly bent on self-improvement, and never one more self-reliant. By severest labor in every variety he worked his way through Knox College, a seven years' task, since he was forced to begin in the preparatory grades. His degree won, he settled in Boston in the employ of the "Wheelman" magazine, then later in New York, first in the De Vinne printing establishment, then in the office of the "Century Magazine."

And at this moment came a new force into the magazine world, one destined greatly to change the whole complexion of American publishing: the literary syndicate. Irving Bacheller seems to have been originator of it.[3] Manuscripts had been brought to him to market and he had succeeded with them; then it had occurred to him to go abroad and secure still more salable material. He amazed young Conan Doyle by offering him double the prices he was receiving from English magazines, and soon he was back in New York with a goodly cargo from various

[3] "Syndicate Stuff," by Dewey M. Owens, "American Mercury," June, 1927, states that the syndicate was originated in 1884 by S. S. McClure.

sources. The Bacheller syndicate was organized. It discovered Stephen Crane and not only gave him publication but commissioned him to search the Southwest and Cuba for new materials for articles and books. S. S. McClure now awoke to the new idea and himself scoured England for manuscripts. Now there were two syndicates bidding for everything worth while, especially materials for newspaper publication. The golden period for English authors had opened; prices were advancing. Then had come to McClure the idea of a magazine of his own in which to issue his captured riches. He has told the story in detail:

It was about eight years after I had founded my newspaper syndicate business that I first began seriously to consider founding a magazine. The originators of the cheap magazine in the English-speaking world were, I should say, the late Sir George Newnes, editor of the *Strand* and *Country Life,* and William T. Stead, whose great career was ended by the *Titanic* disaster. The success of Newnes' magazines and Stead's *Review of Reviews,* and the success of the *Ladies' Home Journal* at ten cents in this country, made me think that a cheap popular magazine would be possible in the United States.

The development of photo-engraving made such a publication then more possible. The impregnability of the older magazines, such as the *Century* and *Harper's,* was largely due to the costliness of wood-engraving. Only an established publication with a large working capital could afford illustrations made by that process. The *Century Magazine* used, when I was working for it, to spend something like five thousand dollars a month on its engraving alone. [4]

"McClure's Magazine" issued its first number in June, 1893, charging for it the then startling price of fifteen cents. Immediately opened the famous magazine war, which for a time was like a price-cutting battle between rival grocery stores. John Brisben Walker after the first issue

[4] "My Autobiography," S. S. McClure, p. 207.

of "McClure's" cut the price of his "Cosmopolitan" from twenty-five cents to twelve and one-half cents, though soon he went up to fifteen cents. Munsey thereupon cut his price from twenty-five cents to ten cents in October, 1893, making his the first ten-cent magazine of anything like standard size and character. Not long was Walker a force, however, and not long did McClure and Munsey clash, for they were feeding two very different markets. McClure was securing material of really remarkable quality, and was paying for it. He scoured the English markets with tireless energy, offering prices before unheard-of, and securing the earliest work of some of the young authors who soon were to be dominating figures. He was able to make terms with Rudyard Kipling and to turn most of his early work into American first editions; he offered Stevenson $8,000 for "St. Ives" and paid other authors prices as startling. His adventures as we read them to-day are most interesting, often most surprising, as for instance: "I bought the first twelve Sherlock Holmes stories from Mr. Watt, Conan Doyle's agent, and paid £12 ($60) apiece for them. . . . When I began to syndicate the Sherlock Holmes stories they were not at all popular with editors." Unquestionably the American syndicates and the American newspapers, and above all the American magazines, now thrilling with new life, did more to advance the "English" literature of the time than anything that was working in England itself. It gave, however, for a time the impression that America was bare of authors; that only in England could one find real literary merit.

And America was able to market these authors and pay the increasing prices for their wares, sometimes fabulously large as money went in those pre-war days, largely because of the rediscovery of what Bonner had found out in the sixties: the principle that it is advertising that sells goods. Bok and McClure and Munsey—especially Munsey—were not only advertising their wares in a modern way but were combining literature and advertising in their magazines in such a way as to make the advertising pay the bills. Magazines all at once became advertising journals with literary matter of secondary importance. The "Saturday Evening Post," with a full table of literary contents equalling that of the best magazines and produced by the highest-priced writers of the time, could reduce its subscription to five cents a copy. The result was a circulation of millions: literature plus advertising had become a "big business" matter, and writings of all varieties, but predominatingly fiction, were now demanded for it in amazing quantity.

In 1902 came the powerful impetus of George Horace Lorimer, born in Louisville, Kentucky, in 1868. After a college course at Colby and at Yale, he assumed in 1899 the editorship of the "Saturday Evening Post," an editorship the most brilliant in American magazine annals. His "Letters of a Self-Made Merchant to His Son," 1902, and "Old Gorgon Graham," 1904, created a new fictional genre, the hustling American business story. Elbert Hubbard's "A Message to Garcia" was also a keynote. Magazines like the "American," for instance, emphasized with increasing heaviness "go get 'em" business success tales, and "Everybody's" and "Collier's" and the "Saturday Evening Post" centered their short fiction about this compelling motif. Abe and Mawruss in the "Potash and Perlmutter" tales of Montague Glass, and the Scattergood Baines of Clarence Budington Kelland, are lineal descendants of old Gorgon Graham.

The effect of all this upon the new American school of writers just forming for the new century was marked:

For another romantic movement was afoot: the romance of journalism as the school of letters was well established now, and the delusion brought boys scurrying to the offices of the New York papers in droves. Had not Richard Harding Davis, Julian Ralph, Edward Townsend and, more brilliantly still, Rudyard Kipling emerged from that battering apprenticeship? So journalism took hold of the national fiction and for a

decade fiercely attuned it to the key of commonplace perceptions and to the flattery of an inferior city.[5]

There came from it a school of prose writers trained in
the mechanics of composition as no other has been in the
history of literature. The newspapers have demanded of
their armies of contributors and reporters clearness, facility
of expression, picturesqueness, "punch," and a smart atmosphere of seeming reality. Of beauty in its every shade,
of distinction in diction, of uniqueness of expression, of individuality, and of the graces of style that distinguish great
literature, the reporter need take little heed. The work is
for the day: why look beyond it? And the greater number
of all the writers of magazine articles and books during the
period came to literary production through the newspaper
offices.

II

Of the school of journalists evolved by the nineties, the
era of the special-correspondent type of reporter and the
peripatetic war correspondent, Richard Harding Davis
undoubtedly is the leading type. Others there were as active
at times as he: Julian Ralph, undoubtedly, and David Graham Phillips, Frederick Remington, Jack London, Stephen
Crane, and a dozen others; but Davis always will stand as
the typical figure, the leader, and perhaps the last representative of his peculiar type of worker. For the World
War demonstrated the fact that the war correspondent of
the old variety had been rendered obsolete. The propagandist, the news-distorter and concealer had taken his place.

Son of Rebecca Harding, author of the first bit of
mordant realism in the history of American literature—
"Life in the Iron Mills," in the "Atlantic" of 1861—and
of L. Clark Davis, prominent newspaper editor of Philadelphia, Richard Harding Davis was from his earliest years

[5] "Stephen Crane, a Study in American Letters," Thomas Beer,
1923, p. 71.

surrounded by literary influences. When he was five years old his mother was given a place on the editorial staff of the New York "Tribune" and was writing novels that were among the best sellers of their day. His education was the conventional one for boys of his social class: the city schools, the best preparatory schools, and finally Lehigh University, followed by courses in journalism at Johns Hopkins. Then as a matter of course newspaper work, first in Philadelphia and then in 1888 with the New York "Evening Sun."

His rise to literary success was rapid. His early short stories in the "Sun" and elsewhere, notably his "Gallegher," 1891, became exceedingly popular, and his powers as a journalist were quickly recognized. For a period he was editor of "Harper's Weekly." Then came a most extraordinary career as a special reporter sent to every part of the known world. He reported "The West from a Car Window"; he toured the Mediterranean, making a complete circuit of all the ports; he represented his paper at the coronation of the Czar, the millennial celebration in Hungary, and the Jubilee of Queen Victoria; he toured Central Africa and the wilds of South America; and he was present in all the wars for two decades in both hemispheres. He was peculiarly fitted for his work: he was restless, audacious, self-reliant, confident of his own powers, unlimited in energy. Moreover he had mastered the easy fluency of the newspaper reporter, the ability to be entertaining whatever his subject, and all the powers that make for the presentation of "news." He had a style that was very readable but seldom distinguished. It was made for the readers of the newspaper, and the newspaper must perish with the day that brings it forth.

Davis's long list of published books lies in three divisions: six volumes of republished reporter's correspondence, like "The Rulers of the Mediterranean" and "The Congo and Coasts of Africa"; seven volumes of war correspondence; and a small shelf of popular fiction—juveniles, romances, and short stories collected from the magazines. His "literary nose," to use the slang of his profession, was unerring. Always was he a little ahead of the fashions: when historical romance was the vogue he issued his "Soldiers of Fortune," and it became a best seller; when "The Prisoner of Zenda" filled all the book-stands, he produced "The Princess Aline."

For a time his Van Bibber tales were highly praised. They seemed to come from an authority, one who knew to the full the life of the idle rich in the Four Hundred circle of New York. But time has proved the work but tinsel. It was good Sunday newspaper stuff and it fed the lean readers of its day. His literary fame will rest ultimately perhaps on a small group of his short stories headed by "Gallegher." Other stories like "The Exiles," well told, with the aura of strangeness about them because of their unusual settings, are to be classed among the best products of an era peculiarly rich in short-story classics.

III

The fate of Davis has been the fate of most of his journalistic contemporaries. Frederic Taber Cooper summed up the matter in the "Bookman" as early as March, 1905:

One powerful factor in modern fiction, which is in danger of becoming a detriment, is the journalistic training which a majority of our younger writers have received and the exaggerated importance which they attach to the so-called "news interest." The novelist of to-day chooses characters who will attract you from the opening sentence, men of audacious achievement, women of flamboyant picturesqueness, people whose lives would make effective scare-heads in the yellow journal. They will not, they dare not, take time to make the reader understand the quiet beauty of unpretentious lives, outside the rush and turmoil of the world at large.

What H. W. Boynton has termed "the higher journalism" undoubtedly has created essays and even "stories" of permanent value, but the creation of permanence is by no means the work of the daily press. The newspaper prints the news, the story of the preceding day, as a bare record of facts; literature adds to it interpretation: "It must bear upon some universal principle or emotion of human life."

The popularity of journalism in America has . . . reacted upon most of our magazines so strongly that they are distinguished from the better daily journals by exclusion of detail and modification of method rather than by essential contrast in quality. Upon the character of the daily press, that is, depends the character of our entire periodical product; and this means, in large measure, the character of the public taste. To afford a vast miscellaneous population like ours its only chance of contact with literature entails a responsibility which may well appal even the ready and intrepid champions of the daily press.[6]

One may add to all this another fact most significant: more and more during the period the newspaper office has been the door through which young writers have entered the world of literary creation. Most of the successful writers of to-day have learned their art from the city editors of metropolitan journals.

Edward W. Townsend, born in 1855, may be instanced as typical. He began newspaper work at fifteen. After an apprenticeship on the San Francisco "Examiner," he joined in 1892 the staff of the New York "Sun." His Sunday special for his paper—the "Chimmie Fadden" papers—soon attracted wide attention. Published in book form in 1894 and 1895, they headed for a time the lists of the best sellers and brought their author into the ranks of the most promising writers of the decade. Chimmie Fadden was a mixture of local color, vaudeville dialect, and Zola naturalism. He brought a new literary "kick," as he himself would have explained it. Like Davis's Van Bibber, however, he

6 "Journalism and Literature, and Other Essays," H. W. Boynton, 1904, p. 22.

was a manufactured thing; he was no more true to the Bowery of which he was supposed to be a typical specimen than the end-man of a minstrel show is true to negro character. It was good journalism, however: it made the people laugh, and it made the Bowery more than ever a household word. The volumes that followed, "A Daughter of the Tenements," 1896, and "Near a Whole Cityful," 1897, attempted to do what Crane did with his "Maggie, a Girl of the Streets." Ephemeral it all was, like the fiction which it neighbored in the Sunday journals. Its author disappeared from the best-seller lists as suddenly as he had appeared, went into politics, became a Congressman, and later wrote a volume on the United States Constitution.

To be able to rise above the iron régime of the newspaper office and to make one's daily work so individual that it can stand by itself independent of the paper that first made it possible, as Joel Chandler Harris had done with his Uncle Remus stuff and George Ade with his fables, requires genius. A few have done it. Says George Ade:

The laws of the Medes and Persians were rubber-like in their pliability as compared with the traditions and precedents and unwritten rules of every newspaper shop. . . . One of the first slaves to escape from the galleys and begin bailing his own boat was Arthur Brisbane. He had opinions and the artist's trick of edging around until he found an entirely new angle from which to view the landscape. He had a vocabulary and the gift of combining force with what seemed to be the easiest kind of writing. So he became known by his real name and had money and was cordially envied and disliked. . . . The years have vindicated Brisbane and to-day he continues to give sane and helpful and entertaining advice to millions of readers.

Not many have the power to escape. Men like Julian Ralph, to cite a single name, most promising and brilliant newspaper workers in their day, never broke from the machine and to-day are mere names like the journals of yesterday that they helped to build. Journalism demands constantly the best of every generation, and it wastes fearfully that best; it destroys for literature the major part of all who enter it.

BIBLIOGRAPHICAL REFERENCES

"The Magazine in America," Algernon Tassin, 1916. The only reliable work at present covering the history of the later magazines. Frank Luther Mott's "A History of American Magazines," a most valuable work, carries the story only to 1850 in Vol. I. Vol. II is promised.

"History of Coöperative Newsgathering in the United States," Victor Rosewater, 1930.

"The American Magazine," in "Prejudices," First Series, H. L. Mencken, 1919.

"My Autobiography," S. S. McClure, 1914.

'The Americanization of Edward Bok," 1920.

RICHARD HARDING DAVIS, 1864–1916

The best biography of Davis is "Adventures and Letters of Richard Harding Davis," by his brother Charles Belmont Davis, 1917. The best approach to his work is the elaborate volume "Richard Harding Davis, a Bibliography, being a record of his literary life, of his achievements as a correspondent in six wars, and his efforts in behalf of the allies in the great War," by Henry Cole Quinby, 1924.

His leading separately-published books may be listed under three heads:

WAR CORRESPONDENCE AND WAR THEMES

"Dr. Jameson's Raiders," 1897; "A Year from a Reporter's Notebook," 1898; "Cuba in War Time," 1898; "The Cuban and Porto Rican Campaigns," 1898; "Notes of a War Correspondent," 1900; "With Both Armies in South Africa," 1900; "Somewhere in France," 1915; "With the Allies," 1914; "With the French in France and Salonika," 1916.

GENERAL CORRESPONDENCE

"The West from a Car-window," 1892; "Our English Cousins," 1894; "The Rulers of the Mediterranean," 1894; "About Paris," 1895; "Three Gringos in Venezuela and Central America," 1896; "The Congo and Coasts of Africa," 1907.

FICTION

"Gallegher and Other Stories," 1891; "Van Bibber and Others," 1892; "The Exiles and Other Stories," 1894; "The Princess Aline, 1895; "Cinderella and Other Stories," 1896; "Soldiers of Fortune," 1897; "The King's Jackal," 1898; "The Lion and the Unicorn," 1899; "In the Fog," 1901; "Ranson's Folly," 1902; "Captain Macklin: His Memoirs," 1902; "The Bar Sinister," 1903; "Vera the Medium," 1908; "The Consul," 1911; "The Man Who Could not Lose," 1911; "The Red Cross Girl," 1912.

Collected editions of his works are as follows: 1898, eight volumes; 1899, six volumes; 1903, six volumes; 1916, twelve volumes. To each of the volumes there was a preface by a personal friend: Booth Tarkington, C. D. Gibson, E. L. Burlingame, Augustus Thomas, Theodore Roosevelt, Irvin S. Cobb, John Fox, Jr., Finley Peter Dunne, Winston Churchill, Leonard Wood, Gouverneur Morris, John T. McCutcheon. The prefaces were later published with the title " R. H. D. —Appreciations." 1918, twelve volumes. Six of his books were published in the Tauchnitz edition.

Davis's plays and comedies, some twenty-five in all, I have not listed. See Quinby's Bibliography, p. 99.

CHAPTER V

STEPHEN CRANE

THE one genius of the decade was Stephen Crane. Into the pale ending years of the century he came as Walt Whitman had come into the period before. To the prim little boys of the nineties with long curls and "Little Lord Fauntleroy" suits he offered attractive volumes full of *damns* and *Oh, hells!* Nothing could have been more awful. And he told things about life that no decent person ought to know. He had begun with "Maggie, a Girl of the Streets."

As with all geniuses, his life was a series of paradoxes. To begin with, he was the son of a Methodist minister who on the pitiful salary offered by a small-town church was rearing a family of fourteen children. Stephen was the fourteenth. And his mother was a fundamentalist in the days before the word had received its modern connotation: she wanted her boy to be a minister.

No genius ever more restless. The itineracy of his father's profession gave him the variety he craved, but by no means all the variety. On the back lots of his town he became a skilful ball-player and at Lafayette College where briefly he resided he made the team at once, as he did again at Syracuse University where he was active for a year in all save his studies. Before he was twenty-one he was in New York City an adventurer living upon what he could make from the city dailies. He was, however, no reporter. Says his biographer Beer:

Apparently he did not even try to report. Of what use to any newspaper was an impression of impatient horses kicking "grey ice of the gutter into silvery angles that hurtled and clicked on frozen stone" when the boy had been sent to get the facts of a large and important fire? The stamping horses hitched to the engine and the stolid movement of a young fire-man stepping back from a falling wall, these things took his eye and went on paper. The name of the building's owner, its number on the street, and the question of its insurance simply wafted from the brain behind the plunging blue eyes. Nor could a city editor accept an interview with a prominent alder-man when that dignitary, under charges of corruption, "sat like a rural soup tureen in his chair and said, 'Aw!' sadly when-ever ash from his cigar bounced on his vest of blood and black." [1]

The passage is illuminating: it explains Stephen Crane. One need not look for his masters: he was himself. Style was the man. Forever was he caught by the fundamentally characteristic, forever was he seeking to convey scenes and feeling to his reader by similitudes, and always they came with a strong flavor of unexpectedness and originality. His mind worked impressionistically. He thought and saw in images. The conventional aspects he dwelt upon not at all.

His explorations in the Bowery, at that time the sup-posed summit of New York's sinfulness, gave him ma-terials for his first long fiction, a Zola-like picturing of the environment and adventurings of a girl ruined by an un-scrupulous drug clerk. Sordid indeed the atmosphere of the little volume. It is true to the slang and profanity and "feeling" of the low street it reproduces; but of animal uncleanness and pornographic realism, be it recorded, the book contains nothing to offend. Richard W. Gilder of the "Century" was shocked by the manuscript. It was "stark realism," and America, he believed, was not yet Paris. The "Century" had its clientele of readers who trusted him as editor to give them what they could enjoy. To publish

[1] "Stephen Crane, a study in American Letters," Thomas Beer, 1923, p. 82.

"Maggie," he argued, would be to be unfaithful to his trust. All the other magazine editors of the city offered the same excuse. Then Crane borrowed a thousand dollars of his brother and published the thing himself, hiding his own identity, however, with the pseudonym Johnston Smith. In vain, however. No publication ever fell flatter or deader. Even New York lifted its skirts and tiptoed by the thing. "It's because it's too honest," complained the boy, and he wondered what was the matter with the world.

At this point appeared Hamlin Garland who read the book and realized its freshness and originality. It was precisely the type of volume that he had been calling for. He reviewed it in the "Arena" and brought it to the attention of Howells who also felt its promise. As best they could they helped the lad; Howells took him to his home and later found a publisher for his writings, the new Irving Bacheller syndicate who were willing to give publicity to his new book "The Red Badge of Courage" and employ him to furnish other stuff like it. It was serialized widely, and, on the advice of Ripley Hitchcock, was taken over by the Appletons and issued by them in attractive form. The public again was indifferent. Then suddenly it was learned that England had gone into superlatives over the book, that English army officers were declaring that only a seasoned veteran could have written it. Thereupon the American demand for it grew into something like a stampede. It became a best seller, the book of the season. But not without caustic criticism and more caustic rebuttal. There were "damns" in the book— as if anything realistically true to military life could avoid them. Despite the report in the "Critic" of February, 1896, that Crane was now "the author of the hour in London" and that the book was now hailed there as a modern classic even by conservative British critics, the old guard in America ignored the volume. Barrett Wendell recognized it to the extent of calling it "sensational trash." Edgar Saltus, representing a younger and more cynical estheticism, wrote to a friend, "A man sometimes yearns for the power to write vulgar inanity and sell it by the cart-load to fools. I hear that Stephen Crane has made twenty thousand dollars out of his trash."

Crane's little volume of poems, "The Black Riders," published earlier in the same year, had no success, however, despite the success of his novel. Not even Garland could sponsor such poetic heresy as that; to the general, even to the rebel few, it was nonsense. To Crane the beaten path was always an insult. He would make his own path. Un-questionably, hints from other original souls often started him on his strange new trails. There had been an evening when at dinner at the home of W. D. Howells he had heard the novelist read from the newly discovered poems of Emily Dickinson, and had gone home with new ideas whirl-ing in his brain. And this he wrote with his strange new pen:

> Tradition, thou art for suckling children,
> Thou art the enlivening milk for babes;
> But no meat for men is in thee.

Four years later he issued his second volume of poems, "War Is Kind," undoubtedly a book that influenced in some degree the new poetic school already evolving.

Thus with volumes in two distinct fields, both of them written before he was twenty-two, Stephen Crane became a pioneer force in both the fiction and the poetry of a new period.

Over the rest of Crane's brief and headlong biography one need not linger. Special correspondent we may call him, with a commission to wander without rest. At the call of the Bacheller Syndicate he explored the wilder areas of Texas and Mexico, dropping at intervals articles and stories and impressions for the newspapers. For them a little later he undertook a filibustering expedition to Cuba, then fighting for independence from Spain. The old rat-trap of a ship foundered and sank a few hours out of port. What happened is recorded in the vivid tale "The Open Boat." No more graphic, no more compellingly circumstantial, reproduction of an adventure was ever penned. Conrad considered it "one of the supreme modern stories." One is admitted into the very heart of the tragedy and is a part of it.

The fifty hours in the open boat, the constant drenching with sea water, the lack of food save for a few sea biscuits soaked in whiskey, planted the seeds of disease that a few years later ended Crane's life. Despite the grilling experience, however, he scoured the swamps about Jacksonville for weeks after his rescue hoping for another chance at Cuba, and thus added malaria to his shattered nerves and exhausted vitality.

Then came orders that he go to Greece to report the war with Turkey. He was lionized in London and was delayed there by illness, but finally he reached the battlefields in time to see the ending of the struggle. Again he was in London, where he became intimate with the vigorous new group of writers, especially Conrad, who were so changing the currents in literary England. A moment, and he was off to Cuba to report the new war with Spain. The war over, however, he was in London again, his health shattered.

In a grand old house rented at a ruinous rate he kept open house, entertaining literary London like a prince and writing furiously in snatched moments to meet expenses. Here came Conrad and all the younger group. He was at the height of his fame. In March, 1900, he was dead, dead at twenty-nine, and nothing save a few short pieces completed—most of his work being fragments thrown off at excited moments, impressions, short dashes in verse and fiction. Twelve volumes it totals in the definitive edition collected of late from all sources and edited by friends and admirers, but it is largely a collection of improvisations. The set, however, is an impressive one when one considers the youth and the headlong life of its author. A view of its contents is worth reproducing in full:

I. The Red Badge of Courage and The Veteran; II. Tales of Two Wars; III. The Monster and The Third Violet; IV. Active Service; V. Whilomville Stories; VI. The Black Riders, and Other Verses; VII, VIII. The O'Ruddy; IX. Wounds in the Rain; X. Major Conflicts; XI. Midnight Sketches and Other Sketches; XII. The Open Boat and Other Tales.

Prefaced with introductions by Joseph Hergesheimer, Robert H. Davis, Wilson Follett, Carl Van Doren, William Lyon Phelps, Amy Lowell, Thomas Beer, Willa Cather, Sherwood Anderson, William Dean Howells, and H. L. Mencken, it is one of the most remarkable reproductions of the writings of any modern author.

But notwithstanding all this, only three of his pieces have any promise of permanence—"Maggie," "The Red Badge of Courage," and "The Open Boat." His admirers have rated him too high. He led his own generation into strangenesses. He was the first to drop everything like plot from his stories. But according to H. D. Traill, the English critic, he was unable to tell a story: he "can only string together a series of loosely cohering incidents." He created atmospheres rather than stories. He brought emphasis to bear on unique impressions; he was an exhibitor adept in throwing the spotlight upon selected areas to the exclusion of other areas. His truth therefore is but half truth. And totally does he lack pathos. He was an inspired reporter who wrote as he ran his picturings of the moment.

Any implication that he had been influenced in his style by the French naturalists angered Crane. He could not read French, he declared, and what he had read in translations of Zola and the "naturalists" filled him with disgust. He had never heard of Zola's "Le Débâcle," he insisted, when he wrote "The Red Badge of Courage." Undoubtedly he was right, yet somewhere one feels he must have come in contact with French influences. It was impossible to escape them if one read the current magazines. Yet, granting this to the full, one is compelled to pronounce his work original—strangely original.

One is impressed first of all in reading it by certain unique mannerisms. His characters have no names, his tales no plots. "The Red Badge of Courage" has the distinction of being a best seller in the America of the mid-nineties with no slightest trace in it of love interest. Again, he wrote gaspingly in short sentences—a staccato style— detail after detail added as in a catalogue, and often without sequence. His one desire, it would seem, was to make his reader see as he saw. Everywhere comparisons: the scene is made vivid by telling how each object impressed him as it flashed before his eyes. One opens "The Red Badge of Courage":

A yellow fog lay wallowing on the treetops.

The fire crackled musically. From it swelled light smoke. Overhead the foliage moved slowly. The leaves, with their faces turned toward the blaze, were colored shifting hues of silver, often edged with red. Far off to the right, through a window in the forest, could be seen a handful of stars, lying like glittering pebbles on the black level of the night.

He now sprang to his feet and, going closer, gazed upon the paste-like face. The mouth was open and the teeth showed in a laugh.

As the flap of the blue jacket fell away from the body, he could see that the side looked as if it had been chewed by wolves.

The youth turned, with sudden, livid rage, toward the battlefield. He shook his fist. He seemed about to deliver a philippic.

"Hell—"

The sun was pasted in the sky like a wafer.

Always images, always a straining for words, for flashes that would convey the vitalizing principle underlying the scene or the action. Says H. J. Mankiewicz in a review of the book:

It can certainly be no accident that there is not a drop of human blood to this book that deals with the reddest of all affairs. Crane was uninterested, supremely, in the flesh and blood of such characters as he was here forced to create to carry on his words. Rather was he gloriously concerned with the letters he could pin to them, their thoughts, their squirmings, their arbitrary manœuvres. Even the central character of *The Red Badge of Courage* is a bloodless creature, a literary device. . . . There he is, that the red sun might be pasted in the sky like a wafer, that the distance might splinter and blare with the noise of fighting, that the moon might be lighted and hung in a tree-top.

That American literature at the moment when it was almost entirely bare of originality, hardened down into monotonous conventionality, trained to believe that all newness and all genius must be imported from Europe, should lose all in a moment four of its most gifted young men, original, daring, impetuous souls—geniuses, all of them, namely Frank Norris, Stephen Crane, David Graham Phillips, Paul Leicester Ford—seems indeed hard. And yet perhaps all of them stand higher in literary esteem than would have been the case had the candle of their lives burned to the dismal socket. Crane's peculiar genius had expressed itself. With his rebellious soul, his original viewpoints, his temperament, his headlongness, his journalistic philosophy of life, he could have added little more.

BIBLIOGRAPHICAL REFERENCES

The standard, indeed the only, biography of Crane is "Stephen Crane, A Study in American Letters," by Thomas Beer, with an Introduction by Joseph Conrad, 1923. It is a most helpful volume, though inclined to over-estimate Crane at times, and—in the modern manner—tending too much to impressionistic treatment and the dramatic staging of picturesque episodes. The definitive edition with its introductions to the various volumes is an indispensable guide.

Most of the magazine articles concerning Crane are unreliable.

"Stephen Crane, a Bibliography," Vincent Starrett, 1923.
"A Study of the Modern Novel," Annie Russell Marble, 1928.
"American and British Literature Since 1890," Carl and Mark
    Van Doren. "Modern American fiction may be said to
    begin with Stephen Crane."

STEPHEN CRANE, 1871–1900

"Maggie: a Girl of the Streets," 1892, 1896; "The Black
Riders and Other Lines," 1895; "The Red Badge of Courage:
an Episode of the American Civil War," 1895; "George's
Mother," 1896; "The Little Regiment, and Other Episodes of
the American Civil War," 1896; "The Third Violet," 1897;
"The Open Boat and Other Tales of Adventure," 1898; "The
Monster and Other Stories," 1899; "Active Service: a Novel,"
1899; "War is Kind," 1899; "Whilomville Stories," 1900;
"Great Battles of the World," 1900; "Wounds in the Rain:
War Stories," 1900; "The Collected Poems of Stephen Crane,"
1930.

A. list of his Works

CHAPTER VI

THE EMERGENCE OF INDIANA

I

FROM the earliest years of the settlement, Indiana in liter-ary and cultural development led the other states of the Ohio valley. She was fortunate in her early settlers. Men like George D. Prentice came early. The pioneer ministers were many of them men of culture with dominating personalities. More than the usual number of colleges sprang up early in the State. The larger towns all had newspapers with literary pages and poets' corners. Crawfordsville became known as "the Hoosier Athens." Meredith Nicholson, literary historian of the state, makes much of this:

The successes of several Indiana authors were a great stimulus to literary ambition in Indiana; and the literary clubs were an additional encouragement. Poetry seems to the amateur much more easily achieved than prose, and poets rose in every quarter of the State in the years following the general recognition of James Whitcomb Riley and Maurice Thompson. There was a time in Indiana when it was difficult to forecast who would next turn poet.[1]

The period before 1890 had produced a remarkable group of writers. There was Lew Wallace, born 1827, author of that best seller of the eighties, "Ben Hur"; Edward Eggleston, born 1837, declared by Nicholson to be with his "Hoosier Schoolmaster" "the pioneer provincial realist"; John Hay, born 1838, poet and novelist and biographer of international fame; Maurice Thompson, born

[1] "The Hoosiers," Meredith Nicholson, 1900, p. 27.

73

1844, author of nature books and of "Alice of Old Vincennes," one of the most successful of the historical romances; and, best-loved of all, James Whitcomb Riley, born 1849, whose birthday in later years was to be made forever a State holiday.

Riley lived well into the new period, to 1916 in fact, and his poetry issued in small booklets, usually in Christmas dress and by an Indiana firm, was for years a part of every publishing season. Distinctly however was he part of the period before. He worked in homely native stuff at the level of all his people, and he throve. He had humor, he had sentiment in abundance even to sentimentality, and he had moral basis. He was handled by a vigorous Indiana publishing house which advertised him freely. Even before he died he had been clothed in myth and reverence like an old bard from earlier years, and it became *lèse-majesté* in Indiana circles even to intimate that he was not one of the major poets not only of his own State but of America and the world. And who may question his position? To be the loved and reverenced poet of the people of a great state, of *all* the people—what more may one ask?

II

The typical Indiana writer of the later period, the typical Westerner, perhaps the leading American novelist of his generation, is Booth Tarkington, born in Indianapolis in 1869 and resident there all of his working years. Unlike the majority of the younger Westerners—the prairie poets and the corn-belt novelists of the new century—Tarkington was reared in a home of ideal surroundings if not of affluence. His father, a prosperous lawyer of the city, sent him East to Phillips Exeter Academy to prepare for college. Two years at Purdue University followed, and then at the beginning of the junior year removal to Princeton where he completed his college work. Like Norris, therefore, he approached literature from the standpoint of the college classics.

The atmosphere of the Eastern university stimulated greatly the young midlander. He was popular at once; he was the best solo-singer in the university—his rendition of "Danny Deever" is still vividly remembered; he was a play-actor of parts and a writer of all things including poetry. He was more than all this—he was a man with a fixed purpose: he would be a novelist.

An influence from his earlier years cannot be passed over lightly: he was a near neighbor and playmate and admirer of Riley in the days when the poet was at the high tide of his fame. It is the approach to the early work of the young novelist: Tarkington was a James Whitcomb Riley with a college education, writing prose fiction instead of verse. Seldom, save in his first romantic days, did he wander far from his boyhood Indiana. His characters, as Meredith Nicholson has observed, depict "the semi-urban type that Mr. Riley so often celebrates in verse." And always is there sentiment in abundance, usually directed at the remembered romance of adolescent days, as was Riley's—think of the word "old" in Riley's titles: "The Old Swimmin' Hole," "An Old Sweetheart of Mine," "The Boys of the Old Glee Club."

His apprenticeship was severe and long: seven years it was before work of merit from his diligent pen appeared in print. "Monsieur Beaucaire" was the first. Repeatedly had it been rejected, but at last came the bolt out of clear sky: S. S. McClure accepted the tale, and issued it in "McClure's Magazine," and with so much success that he was emboldened to attempt the young author's novel "The Gentleman from Indiana" also as a serial. Its instant popularity—the title itself was a winning coup—not only brought Tarkington into the main current of the literary times but brought new emphasis upon the fact that there was a peculiarly Indiana school. In reality it was nothing new. "The Gentleman from Indiana" in char-

acters and plot and even in style is Egglestonian from beginning to end. Instead of the schoolmaster fighting to
victory against the hoodlum settlement, we have the young
editor who has taken the dying local paper and made it a
power, smashed the local vice ring, and defied the local
boss, and is finally killed in true "movie" fashion by the
crossroads white caps. But right triumphs; grit and courage are rewarded. The hero comes to life, marries the
heroine, and—can we believe so marvelous a tale?—is
actually nominated for Congress. In this unbelievable blaze
of glory ends the novel. E. P. Roe has no ending to match
it. But there are times when the young writer forgets his
proper models and his sentimentality, and becomes alive.
The mob is skilfully pictured; it carries conviction for
pages:

> "We want to get into some sort of shape," cried Eph.
> "Shape, hell!" said Hartley Bowlder.

That in the mid-nineties, in a magazine "for all the
family"!

But not often did the young author let himself go.
Fundamentally in the beginning he was a romanticist.
Youth eternally is romantic. "Monsieur Beaucaire" pleased
him at first far more than the depicting of the raw Indiana
crossroads types. Clearing his desk of his apprenticeship
pieces—"Cherry," which had long sought a publisher, and
"The Two Vanrevels"—he wrought with diligence, in the
materials which seemed most in demand at the time, stuff
of the "Monsieur Beaucaire" type. The high-tide period
it was of the doublet-and-hose romance. Recipes for
sugared layer-cakes like "When Knighthood Was in
Flower" and "The Ladder of Swords" were being everywhere studied by young writers who would make their way.
"Monsieur Beaucaire" is in the list of thirty-two historical
romances written by Americans in six years, and in artistry
and lightness of touch perhaps it is the best of them all.

It is usually classed with the short stories, though Tarkington speaks of it as a romance: "It was a romance in miniature, no longer than a long short story."

Romanticism was the fashion then; a romanticism somewhat sentimental, but more concerned with the continuous movement of incredible "characters" than with sentiment. What the action of my own small outright romance in the fashion required was that nearly all the secondary characters should be inimical to the principal figure; and I had happened to conceive this principal figure as a sympathetic French gentleman, sojourning in England. Therefore the inimical characters were all English, and, as the action was based upon snobbery, all the English depicted were shown to be virulent and ruthless snobs except one.[2]

In other words, the piece is a melodrama, with action supreme—reason enough for popularity. But in addition it has a lightness of touch, a Gallic deftness of phrase and *finesse* that must have come from much revision.

In 1913 came a second period in his literary life. He fell in step with the new realism, he would abandon his "Monsieur Beaucaire" stuff. The new century was in its teens and bursting with newness: why follow old leaders? Why use "plot" in fiction? Scrap it: it was a thing outworn. No more romances. He would simply present his old neighbors, even as Riley had done. "The Gentleman from Indiana" after all was the genre that displayed his best powers: real life presented in a real way. In the "Saturday Evening Post"—inspired common denominator of American literature—he published "The Flirt," a photograph of adolescence. Next came "Penrod," "Penrod and Sam," and "Seventeen"—humorous picturings of the tragedy of adolescence in a main-street western town. Tenderness is in every line of the comic strip of episodes through which he puts his victims, and the suspicion finally becomes conviction that like Judge Henry Shute's contemporary "Real

[2] "The World Does Move," Booth Tarkington, 1928, p. 70.

Diary of a Real Boy" it is all autobiography touched undoubtedly with the romance of memory. High spirits on
every page. He is working with joy, with humor at full
tide—again one thinks of Riley. Nothing else that he has
written is so spontaneous and so genuine. For most readers
the books belong on the same shelf with "Huckleberry
Finn" and "Tom Sawyer."

With 1918 came the period of his three most ambitious
studies of American life: "The Magnificent Ambersons,"
"Ramsey Milholland," and "Alice Adams," the first and
the last of which brought the author the Pulitzer Prize
for two years in succession. He had reached the height of
his powers. His characters, drawn wholly from American
life, he knew were true to fact, alive and compelling. He
had striven for popularity. The work at every point was
pitched for the enjoyment of the many, not for the Henry-
James few inured to art and the tonal and architectonic
perfection of the finished classic.

And here must come the first severe criticism of the
man's work. From the first he has been a follower rather
than a pioneer leader. Like Davis he has retuned his instrument to echo every newness. And he has flourished.
To do this is not at all a literary crime, but it puts him who
does it forever in second or third place in the final reckon-
ing. Not a happy thing this to record, for in passages and
chapters and even in certain completed stories Tarkington
has shown unquestioned power. Never, however, can one
lay down one of his books completely satisfied. One feels
as one reads on and on that it is the work of a professional
bookmaker, who sits at his desk like any other business
man and finishes daily his stint.

Consider, for a single example, one of his latest efforts,
"The Plutocrat," a tale that undoubtedly was planned to
be a setting forth of the Midwestern barbarian Tinker,
first in all his vulgarity and then in all his genuineness and
power. It was to be a sharp antidote for Sinclair Lewis's
"Babbitt" and for the whole Main Street school of be-

littlers of Midwestern life. As a novel it starts with power. A bloodless esthete, a "high-brow" playwright from the esoteric circles of New York is introduced for contrast with the wild Midwestern Goth Tinker, president of companies and master of men in masses, men who look to him for very life. With all his loudness and coarseness we are made to feel that the man is a man. Europe bows to his money first and then bows to him. For a third of the book he is as alive as Babbitt. Then the author nods, becomes interested in the New York esthete who has found a queen of the desert. He has been reading, we feel, "The Garden of Allah." Tinker and the rebuke to Babbitt are forgotten. For chapter after chapter we have a reversed sheik tale, pure melodrama, with a heroine like the dream of a caliph. And the ending is like the ending of an E. P. Roe creation: the esthete marries the plutocrat's daughter, the desert goddess is appeased with a king's ransom, and they all live happy ever afterwards. It is the "movies" put within covers. It is for the entertainment of "the general," that vast middle class who makes best sellers possible, that peculiarly American type described by Ogle in "The Plutocrat":

They belong to an objectionable bourgeoisie with which we ourselves avoid contact. We are never conscious of them unless we travel and then we are but too unhappily made aware of their existence. They swarm in politics and in business; they thrive upon a horrible ceremonial known as the Great American Banquet; they read mystery stories, buy maroon velours furniture, call their advertisements "literature," and speak of a tragic drama as a "show." They are blissful when a brass band plays "In The Gloaming." If it plays "Suwanee River" they cry. Their religion is to pay for their wives' pews in expensive stone churches full of "art glass," and their patriotism is to bellow at a cultivated Chinaman that they are one-hundred-per-cent Americans.

Thus Booth Tarkington, purveyor of entertainment to the commonalty—not a bad achievement, but nevertheless an achievement destined to bring nothing save temporary emoluments. Never a newspaper man he was nevertheless a journalist, a worker always in accurate step with his times. Mr. Boynton in a review of one of Tarkington's volumes humorously recalls hearing once that an editor had "just made a contract with Booth Tarkington's agent for half a dozen 'Tarkingtons' [not a line of them written yet], at $2,000 per. The agent had held out for that price, and there was nothing for it but to pony up. Otherwise the agent would have peddled his Eminent Author elsewhere." When the literary artist becomes a manufacturer with a product for the market thoroughly up to date to be delivered to an agent in stated quantities at stated times, classics cease to appear.

After all, his literary world has been a small one and his literary box of make-up and his properties very few. To turn out "Tarkingtons" is not a hard task. Mr. Boynton has said the final word:

Tarkington, with all his virtues, belongs to the order of story-tellers with only a few people in his cast, a few ideas, a single setting, and handful of dramatic-humorous situations. Problems of the time, of social or intellectual conflict, of the new relations and manifestations of sex, hardly exist for him. He has been quoted as saying something to the effect that there is enough disagreeableness in real life, without a novelist's rubbing it in. An attitude which the tired housewife thoroughly approves and shares.

The fact is this writer's imagination has never gained entrance to the twentieth century. A few times it warmed to the past, as in "The Two Vanrevels" and "Monsieur Beaucaire." For the rest it early settled down, and has continued to dwell in the land of the Nineties, where the author first came to his full literary stature.

III

Equally fluent and versatile, but more original and more distinctive in style and diction, is George Ade, born in

Kentland, Indiana, in 1866 and educated, like Tarkington, at Purdue University. Newspaper work became his profession, first in his home environment, then in Chicago on the "Record," which held him for ten years. The details of this apprenticeship he has told in his autobiography:

In 1893 I was put in charge of a department called "Stories of the Streets and of the Town." I was not exactly a columnist. They were generous and let me have two columns on the editorial page. The task meant from 1200 to 2000 words a day. If the pictures provided by John McCutcheon could be made to enlarge obligingly, I would cheat a little on the text. In the next column to me were the "Flats and Sharps" of Eugene Field. He wrote one full column every day with a fine steel-pointed pen. The type was nonpareil and his average was 2700 words. He never solicited or accepted contributions —wrote everything himself. He was known the world over, but did not sign his stuff. He never referred to himself except by an occasional playful use of the editorial "we." He threw fire-crackers at the pompous millionaires and noisy politicians, but he always hid back of the fence.

I kept my two-column department going for seven years. Before I retired to the clover pasture and began to steal money by syndicating, I had published four books, all of the material having first appeared in the paper.

The books he refers to were the "Fables in Slang" series issued under various titles, sketches soon taken over by a syndicate to the immense financial profit of their author.

Then had come the second phase of his literary career: his emergence as a popular playwright. Rollicking comedies like "The Sultan of Sulu" (musical), "The College Widow," and "The County Chairman" were soon everywhere on the American stage and he was prospering more abundantly than Tarkington who also had essayed stage comedies.

In many ways the man has been the leader of the Indiana group. He has been original, spontaneously humorous, and gifted with the powers of caricature and gentle satire in high degree. His mastery of the drolleries of current slang has been unique. He is to be rated as a humorist, working in the ephemeral materials of his little hour, and destined therefore to be quickly forgotten, for humor in its usual forms is the most volatile of all literary stuff. But in Ade's work one feels an element that is more than mere buffoonery. Behind all his slang and his fun there is a philosophy of life, there is depth and perspective. The characters too who mouth his amazing argot are really no automatons: they are as alive as the characters of Dickens and as permanent.

His comedies too, ephemeral it would seem as a "movie" film, have qualities at times that make one pause before consigning them to the limbo of things that perish with their day, qualities that one looks for in vain in the work of his fellow dramatist Clyde Fitch. In dialogue they are distinctive, vivid, witty, seemingly spontaneous; and in characterization they stand high.

Despite the handicap of seeming triviality of materials, of excessive use of the slang that perishes over night and thereafter can be read only with copious foot-notes, the "Fables in Slang," a goodly number of the earlier ones and to some extent the comedies, seem destined to survive— at least for a time. No American humor—most ephemeral of all ephemerae—has in it more of seeming vitality and promise.

IV

The rest of the Indiana group so carefully listed by Nicholson in his history, one may dismiss with a paragraph. Meredith Nicholson himself may detain us for a moment. Once he seemed a novelist of promise. His "House of a Thousand Candles," 1905, serialized in a major magazine, attracted wide attention, as did his "Port of Missing Men," two years later. But time has shown already that as a novelist he was but a passing show. He has done far better with his historical studies like "The Valley of Democracy," and his really distinctive volume "The Hoosiers."

With the poems of Riley quoted from all platforms, with "Tarkingtons" in all the magazines, with "Fables in Slang" syndicated in all the newspapers, with comedies like those of George Ade in all the theaters, and with best sellers like "The House of a Thousand Candles" and the volumes of David Graham Phillips on all the book-stands, surely Indiana during the *fin de siècle* was entertaining America.

BIBLIOGRAPHICAL REFERENCES

"The Hoosiers," Meredith Nicholson, 1900.

"Indiana Authors," M. O. Williams, 1916.

"Old Familiar Faces," Meredith Nicholson, 1929. A charming set of studies of the Indiana of the author's boyhood. "Without Benefit of College" is especially revealing.

"Booth Tarkington," Robert Cortes Holliday, 1918. The only biography of the novelist at present. Highly unsatisfactory. Written without perspective and everywhere too laudatory.

"The World Does Move," Booth Tarkington, 1928. A capital study of "the good old gay nineties" with comparisons constantly with present conditions. One of the best things Tarkington has done.

"Some Contemporary Americans," Percy H. Boynton, 1924. The best critique of Tarkington's work thus far.

"Booth Tarkington: a Sketch," Asa Don Dickinson, 1925.

"Contemporary American Novelists," Carl Van Doren, 1922.

"Our American Humorists," Thomas L. Masson, 1922.

"George Ade," in "Prejudices," First Series, H. L. Mencken, 1919.

"Totaling Mr. Tarkington," in "American Nights Entertainment," Grant Overton, 1923.

BOOTH TARKINGTON, 1869–

"The Gentleman from Indiana," 1899; "Monsieur Beaucaire," 1900; "The Two Vanrevels," 1902; "Cherry," 1902;

"In the Arena," 1905; "The Conquest of Canaan," 1905; "The Beautiful Lady," 1905; His Own People," 1907; "The Guest of Quesnay," 1908; "Beauty and the Jacobin," 1911; "The Flirt," 1913; "Penrod," 1914; "The Turmoil," 1915; "Penrod and Sam," 1916; "Seventeen," 1916; "The Magnificent Ambersons," 1918; "Ramsay Milholland," 1919; "Alice Adams," 1921; "Gentle Julia," 1922; "The Fascinating Stranger," 1923; "The Midlander," 1924; "Women," 1925; "The Plutocrat," 1927; "Looking Forward and Others," 1927; "Claire Ambler," 1928; "The World Does Move," 1928. (Plays not listed.)

GEORGE ADE, 1866–

"Artie," 1896; "Pink Marsh," 1897; "Doc Horne," 1899; "Fables in Slang," 1900; "More Fables," 1900; "Forty Modern Fables," 1901; "The Girl Proposition," 1902; "People You Know," 1903; "Circus Day," 1903; "In Babel," 1903; "Breaking into Society," 1904; "True Bills," 1904; In Pastures New, 1906; "The Slim Princess," 1907; "Knocking the Neighbors," 1912; "Ade's Fables," 1914; "Hand-Made Fables," 1920; "Single Blessedness," 1922; "Bang! Bang!" 1928. (Plays not listed.)

CHAPTER VII

THE INDIAN SUMMER OF WAVERLEY ROMANCE

I

ROMANCE never dies. It flames up at times in special brilliancy because of some dominating creator, but always is it present. That it flourished so decidedly in the eighteen nineties, despite the increasing trend toward realism, can be accounted for in part by the work and the personality of Robert Louis Stevenson. By 1890 his romances in England had become a recognized force, one that was influencing strongly, as we now realize, the younger group just coming into power—A. Conan Doyle, Stanley J. Weyman, J. M. Barrie, Quiller-Couch, Maurice Hewlett, and the rest—but it was his death in 1894 that made him a "world figure." Never was romancer's passing more appealingly staged: the winsome soul in the clutch of incurable disease; the plucky fight, with its shifting battle-grounds—the Adirondacks, California, and the South Sea island where he ruled like a Crusoe; then his death, and his burial on the lonely mountain-top while was sung the "Requiem" from his own pen:

> Under the wide and starry sky
> Dig the grave and let me lie.
> Glad did I live and gladly die,
>   And I laid me down with a will.

It was front-page news in all the journals of the English-speaking world, especially in America. For a decade and more, Stevensoniana—articles, biographies, reminiscences, journals, editions—flooded the papers and news-stands.

The initial number of the "Bookman," February, 1895, issued as a supplement an illustrated brochure dealing with the man's life and work. "R.L.S." memorabilia and the growing "R.L.S." myth became at length a nuisance.

He was Scotch, son of "The Keeper of the Northern Lights," and romance was in his blood. "For my part," he had once written, "I liked a story to begin with an old wayside inn where, 'towards the close of the year 17—, several gentlemen in three-cocked hats were playing bowls." And again, "Dumas I have read and re-read too often, Scott too, and I am short. I want to hear swords clash. I want a book to begin in a good way; a book, I guess, like 'Treasure Island.'" With Scotch positiveness and temperament he fought the new and advancing realism. At Howells, mildest of realists, he could discharge a bolt like this:

None ever couched a lance with narrower convictions. His own work and those of his pupils and masters singly occupy his mind; he is a bond-slave, the zealot of his school; he dreams of an advance in art like what there is in science; he thinks of past things as radically dead; he thinks a form can be outlived; a strange immersion in his own history; a strange forgetfulness of the history of the race. Meanwhile, by a glance at his own works (could he see them with the eager eyes of his readers) much of this illusion would be dispelled. For while he holds all the little orthodoxies of the day—no poorer and no smaller than those of yesterday or to-morrow, poor and small, indeed, only so far as they are exclusive—the living quality of much that he has done is of a contrary, I had almost said of a heretical, complexion. A man, as I read him, of an originally strong romantic bent—a certain glow of romance still resides in many of his books, and lends them their distinction. . . . The obvious is not of necessity the normal; fashion rules and deforms; the majority fall tamely into the contemporary shape, and thus attain, in the eyes of the true observer, only a higher power of insignificance; and the danger is lest, in seeking to draw the normal, a man should draw the nil, and write the novel of society instead of the romance of men.[1]

[1] "Longman's Magazine," December, 1884.

Other romantic forces not Stevensonian were influencing America. In 1896 Felix Gras's "Reds of the Midi" was among the best sellers, and the same year Gilbert Parker's "Seats of the Mighty" ran as a serial in the "Atlantic." Then had come—curious importation—a mass of historical romance by the Lithuanian romancer Sienkiewicz: "With Fire and Sword," "The Deluge," "Pan Michael," "Quo Vadis?"—all of them brilliantly translated by Jeremiah Curtin. In 1897 "Quo Vadis?" headed for months the lists of our best sellers. A year later came the stampede to "The Prisoner of Zenda" and a resulting deluge of Zenda books—imitations like George Barr McCutcheon's "Graustark" and George Ade's travesty "The Slim Princess." Romance was running wild. The publishers, even as far west as Indianapolis, were flourishing. "Literature" had become a "big business." Francis W. Halsey late in 1901 estimated the sales to date roughly as follows:

David Harum, 520,000; *Richard Carvel,* 420,000; *The Crisis,* 320,000; *Janice Meredith,* 275,000; *Eben Holden,* 265,000; *Quincy Adams Sawyer,* 200,000; *D'ri and I,* 100,-000; *To Have and to Hold,* 285,000; *Black Rock* and *The Sky Pilot,* together nearly 500,000.[2]

"David Harum" excepted, almost every one of the books was a historical romance. And the exception was caused by a seemingly trivial matter: "David Harum" had nothing at all in it noteworthy save David Harum, the droll old rascal who beat the deacon in a horse-trade. For that single horse-trade—"he'll stand without hitching," this of the balky horse he was selling—a half-million persons in a single year spent a dollar and a half, not to mention those hundreds of thousands who went to see the delicious episode reproduced in the theater.

But the prevailing literary tide was strongly toward

[2] "Our Literary Deluge," Francis W. Halsey, 1902, p. 24.

"Waverley" romance. Professor Richard Burton in 1902 saw danger in the situation:

It is hardly too much to say that in the present year of grace the general public is fairly rabid for heroic stories of the past. Publishers are suggesting historic themes to novelists, who, on their side, are grubbing in old records and furbishing up their memories of bygone centuries. Booksellers buy their wares, keenly cognizant of this popular appeal.[3]

The enormous sales were turning the heads of even the standard old novelists. Sarah Orne Jewett left her Maine coast natives and wrote a romance of the Revolution *à la mode*—"The Tory Lover"—and Mary E. Wilkins, grim realist, repressed depicter of the New England decline, blossomed suddenly into a romancer of Old Virginia with her "The Heart's Highway," flamboyant with adjectives. Richard Harding Davis trimmed most prosperously his sails to the new breeze, as did the Philadelphia neurologist Dr. S. Weir Mitchell, whose "Hugh Wynne, Free Quaker," was for a few weeks hailed as a classic. The inanity of the criticism of the time exceeds belief. At every publishing season there were novels advertised as superior to Thackeray's or Scott's. Anna Robeson Burr in her recent "Weir Mitchell: His Life and Letters" (an excellent account of Dr. Mitchell's literary work) offers this pungent criticism: "Who can blame the man for his self-conceit when critics so lost their heads as to assure him that 'Hugh Wynne' far surpassed 'Esmond,' that 'François' gave a far better idea of the French Revolution than 'A Tale of Two Cities,' or that his 'Ode on a Lycian Tomb' was finer than 'Lycidas'? Aldrich went so far as to write him that there were two great American novels, 'The Scarlet Letter' and 'Hugh Wynne.'" And she adds: "the long, slow, stiff novel." A Saturnalia of sentiment and bathos, of manufactured archaisms, theatric settings, and imagined history.

[3] "The Cult of the Historical Romance," in "Forces in Fiction," 1902.

In every novel sword-play, the hero victorious always, whatever the odds.

Even Mark Twain caught the literary measles of the hour and essayed anonymously in "Harper's Monthly," beginning in May, 1895, a romance entitled "Personal Recollections of Joan of Arc." His disguise was quickly recognized: even in medieval French recordings, Mark Twain was Mark Twain. His volume, though highly praised by many, falls inevitably into the enormous limbo of his later inferiorities. Let me fortify myself with W. P. Trent's estimate of the book, which must be taken as definitive:

A large piece of mosaic work: first we have a slab of history and then a slab of fiction. . . . The fusing process has not taken place, and the history and the fiction are separate, though in juxtaposition. Such was not the method of him who was at once the first and greatest of historical novelists—that Sir Walter who, whatever certain modern critics may say, grows greater with the years both as a writer and as a man.

Joan he pronounced a shadowy figure, "not really human and alive. . . . Too often he has to content himself with that most disappointing form of description, to wit, exclamatory comment"; and to this he added "lack of timbre in the adjectives" and "lack of imagination in the descriptions."

It is criticism that applies to most of the historicated romance of the period—"lack of timbre in the adjectives," "lack of imagination." Very little of it has survived its decade. It was artificial, it was over-sentimental, it was keyed to costume, to sword and velvet; its world was as false to actuality as was that of Sylvanus Cobb, the extravagant romancer of Bonner's "New York Ledger" which ruled the sixties; it was made to sell. Wilson Follett, in "Some Modern Novelists," dismissed the whole "school" with a phrase: "After Stevenson a flock of writers who debased and all but destroyed the form." The verdict is a just one, and it stands.

Carl Van Doren limits the period of this "most active school of historical romances the United States has produced" to the six years between 1896 and 1902, and wisely.[4] Romance of the same classification undoubtedly there had been all through the period after 1870;[5] one needs but cite Cable's "Grandissimes" and Mrs. Catherwood's works as examples. But during the six years after 1896, it dominated all other fictional forms. The more successful performances of the period may be limited to some thirty-one volumes:

1896. "King Noanett," Frederick J. Stimson.
1896. "Personal Recollections of Joan of Arc," Mark Twain.
1897. "The Choir Invisible," James Lane Allen.
1897. "Soldiers of Fortune," Richard Harding Davis.
1897. "Hugh Wynne," S. Weir Mitchell.
1898. "The Adventures of François," S. Weir Mitchell.
1898. "When Knighthood was in Flower," Charles Major.
1898. "Red Rock," Thomas Nelson Page.
1898. "Prisoners of Hope," Mary Johnston.
1898. "Via Crucis," F. Marion Crawford.
1899. "To Have and to Hold," Mary Johnston.
1899. "Janice Meredith," Paul Leicester Ford.
1899. "Richard Carvel," Winston Churchill.
1900. "In the Palace of the King," F. Marion Crawford.
1900. "Monsieur Beaucaire," Booth Tarkington.
1900. "Alice of Old Vincennes," Maurice Thompson.
1900. "Eben Holden," Irving Bacheller.
1900. "The Heart's Highway," Mary E. Wilkins (Freeman).
1900. "The Duke of Stockbridge," Edward Bellamy.
1901. "The Tory Lover," Sarah Orne Jewett.
1901. "D'ri and I," Irving Bacheller.

[4] "The American Novel," Carl Van Doren, 1921, p. 248.
[5] See "A History of American Literature since 1870," Fred Lewis Pattee, Chapter XII.

1901. "The Crisis," Winston Churchill.
1901. "Graustark," George Barr McCutcheon.
1901. "Cardigan," Robert W. Chambers.
1901. "The Cavalier," George W. Cable.
1901. "Lazarre," Mary Hartwell Catherwood.
1902. "The Virginian," Owen Wister.
1902. "The Conqueror," Gertrude Atherton.
1902. "The Battleground," Ellen Glasgow.
1902. "The Valley of Decision," Edith Wharton.
1902. "Audrey," Mary Johnston.

The materials and backgrounds in these novels, as in the dozens of minor romances which imitated them, were for the most part American. Never before such searchings of records and newspapers colonial and revolutionary. Virginia with its Cavalier first families was a rich hunting ground: duels had actually been fought in Old Virginia and always with opponents of romantic quality. And in Virginia could be found conditions tapestried and medieval: demesnes of baronial magnificence unknown to barren New England—vassals, slaves, traditions, manners, heroines, chivalry.

The heavy emphasis upon American backgrounds and materials undoubtedly came as a prolongation and variation of the "local color" régime of the previous decade. It was local color in harmony with the new times. A younger generation, born after the close of the Civil War, was coming into power, a generation to whom the grim conflict of the sixties was romance rather than the ghastly reality their fathers had experienced. America for over thirty years had been without war—a generation reared in prose and dullness. Then suddenly had come bloody insurrection in Cuba. The doctrine of frightfulness so utterly new, the newspaper exaggerations of the military horrors attending the revolt, jangled hideously upon American nerves unused to war and strife save as depicted by Stevenson and Scott:

Old, unhappy, far-off things,
And battles long ago.

America sympathized with the under dog—the Cubans, who seemed to be fighting for independence as America had fought a century before. Filibustering lawlessness furnished food for a time to the yellow journals, and then suddenly like a fire gong at midnight came news of the sinking of the battleship *Maine* in Havana harbor. And the whole American nation arose like a single individual inebriated with rage. They demanded war, and war was declared with Spain. Spain!—war in the romantic old Spanish Main!—war to free the brutally oppressed Cubans struggling as America had struggled in '76!—this was romance! Volunteers rushed to the colors as they had done in 1861. Theodore Roosevelt sent into the wild cowboy areas and recruited his regiment of "Rough Riders"—it keyed perfectly with the emotions of the time. The young men of the land were in uniform again as in '61 marching to war—heroes. The young women went into excited raptures: they cut buttons from the uniforms of their heroes and dreamed of returning colonels and generals— heroes, the proud winners of laurels plucked in the romance lands of the old Spanish Main.

Read Sherwood Anderson's chapter in his autobiography and note the end of the adventure. In a few weeks—days, really—the war was over and the heroes were no longer heroes. "All dressed up and nowhere to go." But the girls and the older matrons who had kissed the soldier boys so fervently—at least they could *read* of heroes. In "When Knighthood Was in Flower" or "Monsieur Beaucaire" or "To Have and To Hold" the hero could hold at bay two and three of the best swordsmen of the land and win the beautiful heroine in the end. And then again the prowess of the early American heroes—Paul Jones in "Richard Carvel," John Rogers Clark in "Old Kaskaskia," and the like—was in full key with the patriotic emotions which had been stirred by the war.

The sudden ending of the hectic Indian summer of romance is not easily explained. One may note that the year 1902 was the opening year of the Roosevelt period in America, the era of "red blood" and "the strenuous life." The word "mollycoddle!" was hurled now in masculine contempt. Historical romance vanished from the lists of the best sellers over night. A stubborn or a serene few, like Mary Johnston or the young Virginian Cabell, went on with tales of a romanticized past, but the era of romance modeled on Scott or Dumas or Stevenson was over.

II

Viewed in the perspective of thirty years, only a few of the volumes have escaped the oblivion that overtakes all work that merely copies the fashions of its day. Winston Churchill's trilogy, "Richard Carvel," "The Crossing," and "The Crisis," to enumerate them in the order in which they should be read, survives and doubtless will survive.

Churchill was a Westerner, one of the vigorous trans-Allegheny group that became so increasingly evident during the mid-nineties and beyond. Born in St. Louis of New England parentage, reared in the romantic newness of the city that had once been the starting-point of all the cavalcades which broke into the savage areas beyond the Mississippi, educated in the East—at the United States Naval Academy, most practical of institutions—he was peculiarly fitted for the literary task which later became his life-work. First of all he was a romancer, an epic "seer" like Frank Norris, a product of the new West. At Annapolis, city of traditions, of decaying mansions that whispered of a great past, of an aristocratic old régime like nothing he had ever known in the adolescent city of his youth, he found himself kindled to romance of gentler texture. In a history class at the Naval Academy he awakened to his life-work. Like Roosevelt he too would write the saga of America, the romance of the winning of the western world.

Finishing his course at the Academy, he resigned from the navy, and for a year, gravitating to the literary East, engaged in journalistic work. His marriage the next year, however, to the daughter of a wealthy St. Louis family gave him the opportunity to devote himself to his romance. Never was there a more conscientious literary worker. For his first volume, "Richard Carvel," he gathered materials as if he were to write the history of a period. As he himself has expressed it, "I prepared myself by visiting all the places concerned in the story, and by reading biographies, histories, memoirs, letters, old newspapers— in fact, everything which could give me an insight into the life of those days or into the character of the people like John Paul Jones and Charles Fox, whom I desired to introduce." The result was a romance founded on facts, so far as facts can be found after a century of silence— facts seen through the temperament of one reared near the American frontier and educated amid the antiquities of the lands that had seen colonial days. "What I wanted to do in 'Richard Carvel' was to give a picture of the life of Colonial Maryland and Virginia, with special reference to Annapolis, and to contrast the people who made it with the corresponding element in England."

Never romance more timely. It chorded with the excited patriotism of the Spanish war period, the popular demand for heroes. All in a moment the obscure young toiler found himself a celebrity, everywhere lionized, even in England, where they detected his likeness to Thackeray. Sensational offers came from all the publishers, but he refused to be hurried. On each of his romances, even to the last, he worked at least two years. The making of the American republic from Yorktown to Appomattox, from Washington to Lincoln, was the work of three distinct generations, and to each he gave a volume, each centering in a crisis. "Richard Carvel" was centered about the Revolution, though everywhere it suggested the American origins; "The Crossing" told of the savage middle period, the winning of the great West; "The Crisis" brought to a focus the spirit of the Lincoln era that culminated in the Civil War.

The three volumes are more than mere romances: they are interpretations of America and Americanism. Centering in each of them is a philosophical explanation of the era, an interpretation. "The Crisis," for example, has as its chief background the city of St. Louis, and this is the reason:

This old city became the principal meeting place of the two streams of emigration which had been separated more or less since Cromwell's day. To be sure, they were not all Cavaliers who settled in the tidewater Colonies. There were Puritan settlements in both Maryland and Virginia. But the life in the Southern States took on the more liberal tinge which had characterized that of the royalists, even to the extent of affecting the Scotch Calvinists, while the asceticism of the Roundheads was the keynote of the Puritan character of New England. When this great country of ours began to develop, the streams moved westward; one over what became the plain states of Ohio, Indiana, and Illinois, and the other across the Blue Ridge Mountains into Kentucky and Tennessee. They mixed along the line of the Ohio River. They met at St. Louis and farther west, in Kansas.

If Sienkiewicz with his trilogy "Fire and Sword," "The Deluge," and "Pan Michael" wrote the national epic of Poland, then Churchill with his three romances has written the epic of the American Republic. Only Mary Johnston has done work to compare with it. In ability to concentrate areas of space and time into a unity, to compel from them an explaining philosophy, and yet at the same time to keep moving the current of his narrative and to present with vivid lifelikeness a gallery of characters, many of them historical; then at the same time to bring the feeling of actuality into his scenes of action as in the historic fight of John Paul Jones in "Richard Carvel"—in all this he is the equal of the Polish master. His characters include nearly all of the American founders and besides them many of the English statesmen and generals; and they are not names merely, marionettes moved by wires: they are almost without exception compellingly alive. Only a single fault can be found in his portrayal of them: they talk for the most part a manufactured argot true only to the world of historical romance. The death scene of General Whipple in "The Crisis," to cite but a single instance, becomes ludicrous in our realistic day: the dying man speaks his last words in rounded Johnsonian periods like a Webster addressing the United States Senate.

It is conventional to speak of the influence of Thackeray's "Henry Esmond" upon the "Richard Carvel" romance, and even more upon the others, but it is not here that criticism should begin. The influence of the Polish romancer and of the Russians is far more apparent. National romantic epics were best sellers in America when "Richard Carvel" was making, and the young author was conscious of the literary currents of the time. He had not acquired the historical romancer's last gift: the ability to divest himself completely of his own day. There are times when the narrative breathes the odor of the musty volumes consulted. Then, too, one may criticize him for his squeamishness, his shrinking from the repulsive and horrible so inseparable from the battle areas he has dealt with, a squeamishness found not at all in the Polish and Russian recorders of their national history. Too often, also, is he sentimental in his love scenes. The feminine characters lack red blood and vitality. For the most part they are eighteenth-century marionettes, like Cooper's "females," and they lead their heroes into E. P. Roe wooings that fill the younger critics with nausea and rage.

The final volume of the trilogy was not ready until 1904, and upon its publication Churchill awoke to find himself all but alone. Over night historical romance had become a commodity outmoded and unsalable. No one was reading it. The era of "the strenuous life" was on.

Churchill had taken up his residence in New Hampshire, in the summer colony at Cornish soon to be famous, and he had established there a distinctive home, Harlarkenden Hall. He had, moreover, become interested in the local political situation. When the new "Bull Moose" season opened, he joined the Roosevelt party, sought the nomination for Governor of New Hampshire, and conducted for months a Bull-Mooselike campaign. The political organization of the State he attacked with Rooseveltian fury, stumping personally all the leading towns in a whirlwind campaign.

Failing of the nomination by a narrow margin, he continued his campaign by means of propagandist novels. By birth and training the man was Puritanic. He was of old New England stock. His first novel, "The Celebrity," like most first novels, discloses fundamental characteristics; it was a biting satire upon what he considered current literary abuses—a lampoon, some declared, upon a contemporary novelist. He would continue in step with Rooseveltism: he would uncover the concealed corruption, he would show it up in all its foulness. He had awakened from his romantic dreamings of the past to find himself in a "muck-rake" era—everywhere exposure.

His first volume was "Coniston," which had as its central figure an actual personage, one Ruel Durkee of Cornish—introduced in "Coniston" as Jethro Bass—the rural boss who for years "had carried the State of New Hampshire in his vest pocket." Following this came "Mr. Crewe's Career," dealing with the railroad domination of the State. Then, leaving the political field, in "A Modern

Chronicle" he criticized American social conditions, his action centering about the thesis that masculine absorption in mere business and feminine absorption in the excitements and activities outside the home were undermining the foundations that alone were safe. Following it came "The Inside of the Cup," another propagandist novel, criticizing the established church. Muck-raking exposure was not, however, its primary design. To quote its author's words, it was written as "a setting-forth of a personal view of religion."

Of all this later work "Coniston" ranks first in value—first, perhaps, even if we include in the comparison the volumes of the early trilogy. In novelistic technique, in realistic rendering of dialogue, in characterization, even in the case of the feminine characters, the volume surpasses all else he has done. Its chief glory is the character Jethro Bass, a real addition to the gallery of original American characters. The episode of "the woodchuck session" of the Legislature is unique.

III

The sudden decline in popularity of historical romance sent Churchill into other literary fields, but not Mary Johnston, who had come into prominence at the same moment: the two romances, "Richard Carvel" and "To Have and To Hold," together with Ford's "Janice Meredith," had furnished an article for the "Atlantic," entitled "Three American Historical Romances," in March, 1900.

Miss Johnston was a Virginian, daughter of a Confederate officer, a man of culture with an unusual library. Of frail physique, she received most of her education at home, largely in the paternal library, which was rich in Virginia chronicles. Early she was forced upon her own resources by the death of her father, and—like Mary E. Wilkins, her contemporary in the North, whose life has so many points of similarity with hers—turned to fiction for support. That she chose this literary field for a life-work was inevitable. She was history-minded, an antiquary by instinct and by early surroundings. Moreover, her dreamings among her records of the Virginia origins had made her a romanticist—unalterably a romanticist. Her temperament, too, threw her into Waverley fiction. Like Miss Wilkins she was lyrical, intense, impulsive, dramatic. She would reproduce in prose the lyric drama of the Virginia settlement.

For a long period she lived outside the bounds of her native State, in Alabama and then for a time in New York City, thereby gaining the perspective necessary for realistic romance. Her first volume, "Prisoners of Hope," was only fairly successful, but her "To Have and To Hold" placed her at once near the leadership of the current romantic school. Her materials were even in their bare prose verity highly romantic: the episode of Captain John Smith, of the shipload of wives sent the settlers, of the fiery Roundhead proprietors with their intrigues and their duels—the whole history of the State, in fact. But to Mary Johnston Virginia was *alma mater* and she threw all this into lyric passion, idealizing it and stripping it of everything not picturesque and moving and dramatic.

Her volume "Audrey" came next, and then one by one other historic episodes centering in the Old Dominion. That the historical romance régime was all but over, that "Oddsfish!" romances seemed now as absurd to the younger critics as did even Little Lord Fauntleroy dresses, troubled her not at all. During the Roosevelt period she was no longer prominent, but still she grubbed in her Virginia history and found romance and published steadily on.

Then in 1911 and 1912 came what perhaps is her most significant addition to the literature of her period, her two novels of the Civil War, "The Long Roll" and "Cease Firing." Again she was writing from the depths within her. The story of the war had come to her in childhood from the lips of her relatives, a sacred myth which had grown more and more golden with the years. She wrote it with knowledge, with conviction, with sympathy, with almost total submergence of the present. The result is a dramatic presentation of the great struggle from the Virginian standpoint. It is better than a history of the war, for it re-creates for its reader the very spirit of the great tragedy. One emerges from the volumes with the feeling of having one's self been an actor in the drama. The characters, especially Jackson and Lee, she vividly realized. They become saga heroes, colossal, compelling. She has done nothing better than these two volumes.

Her chief rival during the period of her power was Churchill, though Churchill's product is small in quantity as compared with hers, and the two were widely different in object and in methods. Churchill was panoramic and discursive; she was intensive and dramatic. Churchill was leisurely of movement, save at times in his battle scenes; she was nervous, rapid, even headlong at times in her action. His eye was telescopic, able to sweep within its focus an era and a continent; hers was microscopic, dwelling upon the concentrated area of a single State, and even upon a minutely studied section—Jamestown, Williamsburg—during a brief moment. Both at times were over-sentimental, at times even melodramatic, and both were unable to conceal a certain straining for archaic effect, especially in their dialogue, which is bookish, sometimes mawkish. Of the two Miss Johnston is the better historian, the more intense presenter of her material, the better story-teller; Churchill the more philosophic observer, the more epic, the more interpretative.

Her later novels need not detain us. No novelist more industrious—twenty-two titles in nineteen years, most of them historical romances; but, viewed in the light of "To Have and To Hold" and "Cease Firing" and even "Lewis Rand," they have, most of them, but ephemeral value.

BIBLIOGRAPHICAL REFERENCES

The first aid of workers in the field of historical fiction is Jonathan Nield's "Guide to the Best Historical Novels and Tales," new revised edition, 1929.

An excellent bibliography of works dealing with historical romance is in Dorothy Dondore's "The Prairie and the Making of Middle America," 1926, p. 450.

Articles worth reading are Paul Leicester Ford's "The American Historical Novel" in the "Atlantic," December, 1897; Marie Thérèse de Solms Blanc's "Le Roman Historique aux Etats-Unis," in the "Revue des Deux Mondes," April, 1906; and E. A. Bennet's "The Craze for Historical Fiction in America," in "Fame and Fiction," 1901. Richard Burton's "The Cult of the Historical Romance" in his volume "Forces in Fiction," 1902, was timely and helpful; as was Brander Matthews's essay in his volume "The Historical Novel and Other Essays," 1901.

WINSTON CHURCHILL, 1871–

Chapter 7 of John Curtis Underwood's "Literature and Insurgency" deals with Churchill as a fighter for "civic righteousness." Much of the chapter is a refuting of the critical estimates of Frederic Taber Cooper in the volume "Some American Story Tellers," 1911.

See also Charles Crittenton Baldwin's "The Men Who Make Our Novels," 1919; "Famous Authors" (Men), E. F. Harkins, 1901; and "Contemporary American Novelists," Carl Van Doren, 1922.

"The Celebrity," 1898; "Richard Carvel," 1899; "The Crisis," 1901; "The Crossing," 1904; "Coniston," 1906; "Mr. Crewe's Career," 1908; "A Modern Chronicle," 1910; "The Inside of the Cup," 1913; "A Far Country," 1915; "The Dwelling-Place of Light," 1917.

MARY JOHNSTON, 1870–

"Mary Johnston: America's Foremost Historical Novelist," advertising brochure issued by her publishers. "The Women Who Make Our Novels," Grant Overton, revised edition, 1928; "Cargoes for Crusoes," Grant Overton, 1924.

"Prisoners of Hope," 1898; "To Have and To Hold," 1900; "Audrey," 1902; "Sir Mortimer," 1904; "The Goddess of Reason" (poetic drama), 1907; "Lewis Rand," 1908; "The Long Roll," 1911; "Cease Firing," 1912; "Hagar," 1913; "The Witch," 1914; "The Fortunes of Garin," 1915; "The Wanderers," 1917; "Foes," 1918; "Pioneers of the Old South," 1918; "Michael Forth," 1919; "Sweet Rocket," 1920; "Silver Cross," 1921; "1492," 1922; "Croatan," 1923; "The Slave Ship," 1924; "The Great Valley," 1926; "The Exile," 1927.

CHAPTER VIII

THE DECADE OF THE STRENUOUS LIFE, 1901–1909

I

THE entry of the new century was all that the men of the *fin de siècle* dreamed it was to be. It came in like a tropic storm. All in a moment America awoke to the fact that she was facing not only a new century, but a new era. Yesterday she was a world by herself, provincial and satisfied, built solidly upon Washington's Farewell Address, which frowned upon foreign complications: now she was an empire, with control over vast areas of the Asiatic and the Caribbean worlds. It divided sharply the American people. William Vaughn Moody, laureate of the decade, voiced in lyric anger the forces of the opposition:

> Tempt not our weakness, our cupidity!
> For save we let the island men go free,
> Those baffled and dislaureled ghosts
> Will curse us from the lamentable coasts
> Where walk the frustrate dead.

But the islands were held.

Then suddenly in 1901—called to the presidency by the assassination of William McKinley—came into power Theodore Roosevelt. It was like the rising of the curtain for a new act. Never President more positive, more impetuous. In the words of a contemporary, for eight years America viewed "a continuous performance staged from the White House." John Morley, visiting the United States in 1904, declared, "I have been chiefly impressed in this country by two things, Niagara Falls and the President of the United States." The era of the "strenuous life" had opened:

I preach to you, my countrymen, that our country calls not for the life of ease, but for the life of strenuous endeavor. The twentieth century looms before us big with the fate of many nations. If we stand idly by, if we seek merely swollen, slothful ease and ignoble peace, if we shrink from the hard contests where men must win at the hazard of their lives and at the risk of all they hold dear, then the nobler and stronger peoples will pass us by, and will win for themselves the domination of the world.[1]

For the first time in decades America had a man of letters in the White House. He was a Harvard man, a scholar finished by residence in Europe, a biographer who had written lives of Oliver Cromwell and of Senator Benton, a historian who had issued "The Naval War of 1812" and four volumes on "The Winning of the West." But he was more than a scholar: he had ridden with cowboys on western ranches, had captured desperadoes on the border, had shot grizzlies and mountain lions and elks, and had won the admiration of the elemental men who respect only forceful ability and courage. And for the war with Spain he had organized these men of the ranches into his Rough Riders regiment and had led them personally in the battle of San Juan Hill.

Everywhere a new atmosphere. World dominion was in the air of Europe. Rudyard Kipling was broadcasting his imperialistic gospel, "Take up the White Man's Burden." The German army was increasing daily in numbers and efficiency, and plans were ripe for a navy to surpass England's. The young men of the Fatherland were quoting Nietzsche's "the will to power" and the "Übermensch," and were awaiting the word of their war lord

[1] The "Strenuous Life" speech was delivered in Chicago in April, 1899. With other pieces it was issued in book form in October, 1900.

who posed as the superman of Europe. In England there was George Bernard Shaw with his "Man and Superman" and there was the insidious drama played in London and elsewhere that pictured the total destruction of the city by the German air-fleet. It was the period of the "blond beast" to come. Over everything the shadow of the inevitable conflict.

The literature of the first decade of the twentieth century was more thoroughly and obviously influenced by the war than will be that of the decade following. Think of that amazing quickening which found expression in the novels of René Bazin, and the immortal ballads of Francis Jammes, and the work of countless other writers. These people were preparing themselves and their fellow-countrymen for the mighty ordeal which was before them. . . . The war held me in its spell long before the German troops crossed Belgian soil.[2]

In America romance changed its background over night. No more historicated dreamings: the demand now was for actuality. Theodore Roosevelt was in power, a strenuous young school was shouting the new gospel: Why locate all your romance in the dead past? Talking of heroes and supermen, you can find them alive. Did you ever know the boss of a river drive in the wilds of the Michigan lumber-camps, or the tyrant who rules the crew of a deep-sea sailing vessel, or the trapper who spends his winters in the northern muskeg, or the man and the squaw who mush all day with a dog-team in the intense cold of the Klondike and then dance all night to harmonica music on the log floor of an Arctic fur station? All at once fiction began to be talked of in terms of "red blood," "men with the bark on," supermen, and their deeds in the wild areas of actual adventure. Alfred Henry Lewis's "Wolfville Stories" of the melodramatic Southwest now awoke. Soon Jack London was a best seller—London, the typical

[2] "The Heresy of Supermanism," Charles Rann Kennedy, in "Literature in the Making," Joyce Kilmer, 1917.

literary man of the decade, brutal prophet of the "Pentecost of horror" to come. Then a flood of such volumes as Frank Norris's "A Man's Woman," Seton's "The Biography of a Grizzly," White's "The Blazed Trail," Charles D. Stewart's "The Fugitive Blacksmith," London's "The Call of the Wild," "The Sea Wolf," and "The Mutiny of the Elsinore," and Upton Sinclair's "Manassas" and "The Jungle." Actuality was the word now, red-bloodedness, truth to life as life is lived in the actual *now*.

It was the golden age of the war correspondents, young reporters sent to the ends of the world by the metropolitan newspapers to gather materials in the very atmosphere of the happenings. A vigorous, headlong group it was, men like Richard Harding Davis, Stephen Crane, John Fox, Jr., Julian Ralph, Jack London, Ralph Paine, and Frederic Remington, and they sent home stirring stuff. Remington especially is a noteworthy figure. To the flying leaves of the correspondent he added a permanent element: he was a draughtsman with unique powers—a genius in fact. Wherever there was "news" in the wild areas of the world there was Remington with pen and pencil. Especially was he at home in the frontier areas of the American Northwest, where were to be found what he termed "men with the bark on." With the Indian he worked always with genius.[3] His fellow-adventurer in the wilds, Owen Wister, has penned this tribute:

A monument to Frederic Remington will undoubtedly rise some day; the artist who more than anyone else has gathered up in a grand grasp an entire era of this country's history, and handed it down visible, living, picturesque, for coming generations to see—such a man will have a monument.

II

The spirit of the President influences the decade like a fortissimo *motif*. From his pen came a steady output of

[3] Hamlin Garland has gathered the best of these Indian sketches into his volume "The Book of the American Indian," 1923.

volumes. He would be included in a literary history of the period even had he never achieved the presidency. His early studies in American history and biography are vigorous in style, and carefully documented, though often marred by prejudice and party blindness. They emphasize the striking and the picturesque, and they pause at heroic figures. Intensely are they American; on every page there is emphasis upon the national glory, the national responsibilities, the civic duty of the citizen. Particularly did the President's wild life on The Bad Lands ranches endear him to the West. He was a hunter: he issued "Hunting Trips of a Ranchman"; and he was a soldier, he had been leader of a unique regiment. He wrote the history of the campaign himself—a rough-and-ready volume, journalistic in style as if dictated to a stenographer, but intensely Rooseveltian. Mr. Dooley reviewed it with unholy glee:

If I was him I'd call th' book "Alone in Cubia." At another place he suggested as titles "Th' Biography iv a Hero, be Wan Who Knows"; "Th' Darin Exploits iv a Brave Man, be an Actual Eye-witness"; "Th' Account iv the Desthruction iv the Spanish Power in th' Ant Hills, as it Fell from th' Lips iv Teddy Rosenfelt an' Was Took Down be His Own Hands." [4]

From 1901 to the end of the decade is the era of Theodore Roosevelt. He dominated the whole decade like a major chord.

III

Finley Peter Dunne, Chicago-born and Chicago-retained until he was famous enough to be called to New York at thirty-three, was the philosopher of the war era and indeed of the whole Roosevelt period. America from

[4] "The Turn of the Century," in "Our Times" by Mark Sullivan, 1928. The treatment of Roosevelt in chapters 4, 10, and 13 is delightful reading.

the days of Seba Smith and Jack Downing has had its court jester, its mentor with cap and bells, and with whip also to be cracked about the ears of even the highest, always, however, with hilarious good humor. One thinks of the Civil War lampooners like Nasby and Bill Arp, and, to pass over two generations to our own time, of Ring Lardner and, later still, Will Rogers.

Like all others of the Chicago group, Dunne for years was connected with the city newspapers, but like Field and Ade he was more than a mere reporter. While Field was scribbling at his "Sharps and Flats" and Ade was working at his "Fables in Slang," he was evolving for his paper a humorous character, one Martin Dooley, Irish philosopher, who read the newspapers religiously and discussed the news each day with his neighbor Hennessey. His articles were syndicated, and soon the whole nation was seeing the world daily through the comically focused glasses of the old Irish sage, and was laughing and quoting; no one else during the decade, not even Roosevelt, was so widely quoted.

To Mr. Dooley nothing was sacred. In politics he had his favorites, but he was no stand-patter. From reading his lampoonings one can hardly tell whether he was a Democrat or a Republican—he was a Dooleyite, with a club for sham and trickery. During the Bryan split in the Democratic party this was his version:

"No, sir, th' Dimmycratic party ain't on speakin' terms with itsilf. Whin ye see two men with white neckties go into a sthreet-car and set in opposite corners while wan mutthers 'Thraiter' an' th' other hisses 'Miscreent,' ye can bet they're two Dimmycratic leaders thryin' to re-unite th' gran' ol' party."

He became a power in the muck-rake era—his philosophy changed votes—but he was no reformer. He could reprove the holy muck-raker as harshly as he did the muck-raked sinner. His inimitable "Crusade against Vice" is the antidote for Upton Sinclair.

Nothing escaped him. The rising tide of Christian Science, for instance, he explained learnedly to Hennessey; and he had opinions even upon college athletics:

"Did ye iver hear of Grant wearin' anny medals f'r a hundherd yard dash? Did anywan iver tell ye iv th' number iv base hits made be Abraham Lincoln? Is there anny record iv George Washington doin' a turn on a thrapeze or Thomas Jefferson gettin' th' money f'r throwin' th' hammer?"

His philosophy was never radical. Always was he "a pourer of oil" upon dangerous waters. When Roosevelt invited a Negro as a guest at the White House, he was inclined to be sarcastic, but this was his conclusion:

"They'se nawthin' wrong in him havin' me frind Booker T. up to dinner. That's a fine naygur man, an' if me an' th' Prisident was in a private station, d'ye mind, we c'ud f'rget th' color iv th' good man an' say, 'Booker T., stretch your legs in front iv th' fire—while I go to th' butcher's f'r a pound iv pork chops.' But bein' that I—an' th' Prisidint—is public sarvants an' manny iv our customers has onrais'nable prejoodices, an' afther all 'tis to thim I've got to look f'r me support, I put me hand on his shouldher an' says I: 'Me colored friend, I like ye an' ye're idjacation shows ye're a credit to th' South that it don't desarve, an' I wud swear black was white f'r ye; but swearin' it wudden make it so, an' I know mos' of me frinds thinks th' thirteenth amindmint stops at th' dure shtep, so if ye don't mind, I'll ast ye to leap through th' dure with ye're hat on whin th' clock sthrikes siven."

Satire, however, no matter how biting or sparkling, perishes with its own generation. It is aimed at its own times, and its later reprintings more and more must be supplied with explanatory notes. Moreover, the slang or the dialect in which often it appears grows old-fashioned and unintelligible. Humor in its popular varieties, like fashion in dress, changes completely from decade to decade, even from year to year. A generation has come that does not read Mr. Dooley; long ago was he outmoded, but he will not pass completely into the limbo where most of the American comic entertainers have gone. Like Josh Billings he was an original philosopher, a genius in his way, the leading humorist of his period.

IV

"Steam and electricity make short work of epochs," wrote Owen Wister in 1911.[5] He was but fifty, yet, so far as American fiction was concerned, he had seen two epochs and had been the transition figure leading to a third. He had seen "local color" blaze into historical romance, and he had stood with Roosevelt and had been brought to realize that autumnal colors are but symptoms of decay.

Wister was an Easterner, the son of a distinguished family of Philadelphia, Harvard-educated, destined for the law. Rare good fortune, as earlier in the case of Roosevelt, broke him physically two years after his graduation and sent him for recuperation to Wyoming and Arizona. That was in 1885, the golden age of the cowboy and the desperado. To the city-reared student the experience from the first moment of it was romance. In his own words, "Wyoming burst upon the tenderfoot resplendent, like all the story-books, like Cooper and Irving and Parkman come true again. . . . Here was what the boy runs away from school to find . . . here was Saturday eternal where you slept out of doors, hunted big animals, rode a horse, roped steers, and wore deadly weapons."

Fifteen trips he made first and last into the wonderland thus early discovered. His Eastern law studies, and later his law practice, became more and more his avocation. His heart was in West with the men of the frontier, men whose qualities were genuine and unmistakable. It added him distinctively to the new young Western group. There

[5] To the second edition of "Lin McLean," 1908, to "The Virginian," and especially to his collection entitled "Members of the Family," Wister has supplied autobiographical prefaces. My quotations are from these prefaces.

was, he felt something vital, "something of promise in the air, promise of a democracy which the East had missed." Just as it had struck Garland and Norris and David Graham Phillips, the East was more and more impressing him as something effete, outworn, dead, something to be reformed, revivified, brought again into the real spirit of democracy. In the preface of one of his earliest volumes, there is a note of real Western insurgency:

We Americans, judged not hastily, are sound at heart, kind, courageous, often of truest delicacy, and always ultimately of excellent good sense. With such belief, or, rather, knowledge, it is sorrowful to see our fatal complacence, our as yet undisciplined folly, in sending to our State Legislatures and to that general business office of ours at Washington, a herd of mismanagers that seems each year more inefficient and contemptible, whether branded Republican or Democrat. But I take heart, oftener and oftener. I hear upon my journey the citizens high and low muttering, "There's too much politics in this country," and we shake hands.

The East, he felt, knew nothing of the West in its actuality. As late as 1885, he declared, "the Eastern notion of the West was 'Alkali Ike' and smoking pistols. No kind of serious art had presented the frontier as yet." As for himself, "repeated sojournings in camp, ranch, and military post" throughout the whole Rocky Mountain area had, to use his own expression, "saturated him" with the West, and in 1890 "this saturation ran over in the form of fiction."

His first distinctive volume was "Red Men and White," 1896. It was no "tenderfoot" in literary composition that was writing even at that early date. He had served a careful apprenticeship. Ever since his college days at Harvard, he declares, he had written constantly and read constantly:

In 1884 Mr. Howells (how kind he was!) had felt my literary pulse and pronounced it promising; a quickening came from the pages of Stevenson; a far stronger shove next from the genius of *Plain Tales from the Hills;* during an unusually long and broad wandering through the Platte Valley, Powder River, Buffalo, Cheyenne, Fort Washington, Jackson's Hole, and the Park, the final push happened to be given by Prosper Mérimée; I had the volume containing *Carmen* with me. After reading it in the Park I straightway invented a traveller's tale. . . . A second followed, both were sent to Franklin Square and accepted by Mr. Alden. Then I found my pretty faithfully kept Western diaries (they would now fill a shelf) to be a reservoir of suggestion.

He classed himself not as a realist, but simply as another historical romancer. He insisted, however, on his own definition: "Any narrative which presents faithfully a day and a generation is of necessity historical; and this one presented Wyoming between 1874 and 1890." A romanticist he was unquestionably, but not at all of the Hugh Wynne–Richard Carvel school. He dealt with a dead past, to be sure: "Where is the buffalo and the wild antelope, and where the horseman with his pasturing thousands? . . . He rides in the historic yesterday. . . . You will no more see him gallop out of the unchanging silence than you will see Columbus on the unchanging sea come sailing from Palos with his caravels." And yet he could study this antiquity from his own diaries. It was utter romance, yet he could record it with utter realism. Romance indeed is the soul of "The Virginian." Its hero is as swashbucklingly perfect as Richard Carvel, as melodramatic even and immune from disaster as any movie hero, and he works to a climax as sentimental as an E. P. Roe. But "The Virginian," be it remembered, was dedicated to Theodore Roosevelt, who had caused one of its chapters to be rewritten, and who we suspect served as model for the hero. All four of the volumes are Rooseveltian in flavor, episodes illustrative of the strenuous life, true despite their melodrama to the actual West that both men knew. It was the land of supermen—the superman alone could survive. And it was the land of efficiency and genuineness. The Virginian explained it in terms of things done *well*:

"Now back East you can be middling and get along. But if you go to try a thing on in this Western country, you've got to do it *well*. You've got to deal cyards *well*; you've got to steal *well*; and if you claim to be quick with your gun you must be quick, for you're a public temptation, and some man will not resist trying to prove he is quicker. You must break all the Commandments *well* in this Western Country."

Much has been made of the fact that the novels are made up of independent episodes, first published, many of them, as short stories. With Bret Harte the short story measured the length of his literary stride; with longer units he could not work. In Wister's fiction, however, this relay structure, this episodic presentation, was a deliberately worked out design. "It was my aim," he has explained in the preface to "Lin McLean," "to tell a long story, not through a series of chapters in the usual way, but through a chain of short stories, each not only a complete adventure in itself, but also a fragment of an underlying drama." And again, "The West was nomadic in essence and called for a nomadic art form to express it most adequately."

Always has he been the artist, working invariably with full knowledge of his art. To one who has read all of his fiction it is not surprising to have him say: Henry James "of all living authors has influenced me most. His art makes most other fiction look only half grown up." One finds this influence most complete in the exquisite "Lady Baltimore" romance of his later period, and in his humorous Harvard novelette "Philosophy 4." It is his earlier work, however, notably in "The Virginian," that is most sure of permanence.

V

Quickly followed "the red-blood school of writers," all of them actual adventurers in the regions they described, all their work seemingly realistic, yet glamorous with romance. Contemporaneous with "The Virginian" and with London's "The Call of the Wild," came "The Blazed Trail" by Stewart Edward White.

White was from Michigan—born at Grand Rapids in 1873; at twelve, like Frank Norris, removed to California with his father. No more restless soul—Jack London excepted—in the whole history of our literature. As a boy he had penetrated into the Michigan wilds, eager in his study of birds, and had prepared a series of papers, later published, on "The Birds of Mackinac Island." In California for four years he had all but lived in the saddle. When the Black Hills gold stampede came he was among the foremost stampeders. Then had come four years in the University of Michigan, with frequent vacation trips into the forests of the upper peninsula; then the beginnings of a law course at Columbia. But everything within the lad called out against the law as a life-work. He wanted to write, and he wandered into the class-room of Professor Brander Matthews, who advised him with rare wisdom. He had material in his hands, this critic declared, worth its weight in gold. He should go back and study still more his men of the Michigan frontier. And the young man went back, became a lumber-jack for a whole winter, holding his own with ax and peavey with a wild crew. And he emerged with materials unique. His first published books were "The Westerners" and "The Claim-Jumpers," 1901, but the following year there appeared as a serial in "McClure's" a story based on his experience in the lumber camps. When issued in full as a volume with the title "The Blazed Trail" it leaped at once into best-seller popularity. Here indeed was something new. Here was actuality, yet it read like romance. And its major character was strenuous enough even for a Roosevelt—a superman, "hard-boiled," triumphant over seeming impossibilities, the embodiment of the new American gospel of "Get there!" An episode in the hero's love life gives us the measure of the man:

> "I have seen a vision," said she simply, and lowered her head to conceal her eyes. Then she looked at him again. "There can be nothing better than love," she said.
> "Yes, one thing," said Thorpe, "—the duty of success."

It is the atmosphere of the new America of the opening century, the America that founded the magazine "Success," that inspired Orison Swett Marden, that started the "American Magazine" with its emphasis always upon successful achievement. Moreover, it dealt with the new American idea of "big business"—great corporations built up by crushing rivals. "The Blazed Trail" is the story of a fight between two lumber companies seeking absolute control, and it is a warfare between Titans, relentless, knowing no quarter.

Following the volume came "The Riverman," "The Blazed Trail Stories," and "The Rules of the Game," epic tales of the Michigan forests. In all of them action, headlong and impetuous, and in all of them the wilderness made a living thing, mysterious, alluring, arousing in the reader primal urges and dreamings. A love element there is, but it is negligible—put in, one feels, solely because demanded by the general reader. Seldom is there sentimentality; the forest, the wild things, the elemental men, the action, these for the author are sufficient.

"The Blazed Trail" series has perhaps been the most influential of White's volumes. Yet in another field he has done work as distinctive. His "Conjuror's House" and "The Silent Places," written after long residences in the muskeg areas of British Columbia with trappers and Indians and Hudson's Bay Company agents, are among the great books of the period. Many have placed them even above "The Blazed Trail." In the opinion of Churchill Williams: "What this wilderness of the North means Mr. White comes nearer to giving us a conception than any-one who has yet written of it." And according to John Curtis Underwood: "One may go so far as to say that it is more than American; that it is cosmic; and that equally with *The Octopus,* it belongs indisputably to the irredu-cible medium of human interpretation through fiction that the centuries retain in the literature of the world at large." [6]

In his later journeyings White has broken always into the unknown and unrecorded. He followed Roosevelt into Africa, penetrated the wildest areas of the Black Conti-nent, killed big game, lived among the fiercest blacks, and recorded his impressions and adventures in "The Land of Footprints" and the inimitable "Simba." Again he pene-trated the African jungles after lions, armed only with bow and arrows. Surely no author of the period has of-fered stranger literary materials gathered more conscien-tiously in unrecorded areas, or has presented his work more vividly and compellingly.

VI

The eighteen nineties were the period of the bird-books, of John Muir and the later John Burroughs, of the new out-of-doors movement and of Nature study in the schools.[7] It was a phase of the general swing of the period toward realism and "naturalism," terms so widely dis-cussed for years. The culminating story of the movement belongs to our present study; an episode it was decidedly of the Bull-Moose decade.

Ernest Thompson Seton was a Canadian naturalist who for years had studied wild life in the upper Manitoba for-

[6] "Literature and Insurgency," John Curtis Underwood, p. 271.

[7] "The History of American Literature since 1870," Fred Lewis Pattee, Chapter 10.

ests and then for five years had continued his studies in the wild areas of the western United States. He had been trained as an artist and had followed his birds and animals into their natural habitats. His abilities were soon recognized. The "Century Dictionary" employed him to draw the pictures of American birds and animals, some two thousand of them, and he was soon honored everywhere as an authority. It was not, however, until the appearance in 1898 of "Wild Animals I Have Known" that he was known to the reading public. His "Biography of a Grizzly" which followed, two years after his first volume, first as a serial in the "Century Magazine," became at once a best seller. Then had come his "Lobo, Rag and Vixen," and in 1901 his "Lives of the Hunted," volumes unique. The animals were presented with their minutest habits and all the characteristics of their psychological operations almost as if they were human. Old Silverspot, the Crow, he studied as a real personality as also he did Lobo the wolf, and Vixen the fox. No one ever wrote of animals with fuller knowledge, and no one had ever made them so real.

The lead given by these books was quickly taken by others. Volumes began to multiply with titles like "Little Brothers in Feathers and Fur." One writer especially became voluminous, the Rev. William Joseph Long, who began a series with such titles as "Ways of the Wood Folks," 1899, "Wilderness Ways," 1900, "Secrets of the Woods," 1902, and "Following the Deer," 1903. When Long touched upon the habits of the deer, however, Theodore Roosevelt, himself a hunter and a naturalist, awoke with a roar of protest. "Nature-faker!" he shouted, and for a decade the phrase was a bone of contention. The veteran John Burroughs sided with the President, and in a series of articles settled the question to his own satisfaction. Animals have no thinking powers, he declared, in the sense that human beings have them, and to read human-like mentality into their actions is most assuredly nature-faking, even as the President had maintained.[8]

The close friendship of the two men, made much of by all the newspapers of the period, added greatly to the growing interest in out-of-door life and to all that pertained to Nature study generally.[9]

VII

The later writers who have followed in the train of these pioneers have been too numerous even to mention. Wild western novels have come as a flood from such writers as Rex Beach, James Hopper, Zane Grey, Eugene Manlove Rhodes, Clarence Mulford, George Pattullo, and dozens of others. The cowboy theme has been chased in every direction until it has found final refuge in the vast swamp of the "movies." Nature study has even been sentimentalized. Gene Stratton Porter's volume "A Girl of the Limberlost," a skilful blend of extensive and exact knowledge with flattest sentimentality, became for months and even for years a best seller on all the news-stands. Sentiment in America never dies: it is the sugar that must be sprinkled even upon science and realism.

BIBLIOGRAPHICAL REFERENCES

THEODORE ROOSEVELT, 1858–1919

"History of the Naval War of 1812," 1882; "Hunting Trips of a Ranchman," 1885; "Life of Thomas Hart Benton," 1886; "Life of Gouverneur Morris," 1887; "Ranch Life and the Hunting Trail," 1888; "The Winning of the West," 1889–1896; "History of New York," 1890; "The Wilderness Hunter," 1893; "American Ideals and Other Essays," 1897; "The Rough Riders," 1899; "Life of Oliver Cromwell," 1900; "The Strenuous Life," 1900; "Outdoor Pastimes of an American

---

[8] "Ways of Nature," John Burroughs, 1903.
[9] "Camping and Tramping with Roosevelt," John Burroughs, 1907.

Hunter," 1906; "European and African Addresses," 1910;
"African Game Trails," 1910; "The New Nationalism," 1910;
"Through the Brazilian Wilderness," 1914; "Works, Elkhorn
Edition," 28 vols., 1906.

FINLEY PETER DUNNE, 1867–

"Mr. Dooley in Peace and War," 1898; "Mr. Dooley in the
Hearts of His Countrymen," 1899; "Mr. Dooley's Philos-
ophy," 1900; "Mr. Dooley's Opinions," 1901; "Observations
by Mr. Dooley," 1902; "Dissertations by Mr. Dooley," 1906;
"Mr. Dooley Says," 1910; "New Dooley Book," 1911; "Mr.
Dooley on Making a Will," 1919.

OWEN WISTER, 1860–

"The New Swiss Family Robinson," 1882; "The Dragon
of Wantley—His Tail," 1892; "Red Men and White," 1896;
"Lin McLean," 1898; "The Jimmy John Boss," 1900; "U. S.
Grant, a Biography," 1900; "The Virginian," 1902; "Philos-
ophy 4," 1903; "Journey in Search of Christmas," 1904;
"Lady Baltimore," 1906; "The Simple Spelling Bee," 1907;
"Mother," 1907; "The Seven Ages of Washington," 1907;
"Members of the Family," 1911; "The Pentecost of Calam-
ity," 1915; "The Ancient Grudge, or a Straight Deal," 1920;
"Indispensable Information for Infants," 1921; "Neighbors
Henceforth," 1922; "Watch Your Thirst," 1923; "Roosevelt:
the Story of a Friendship, 1880–1919," 1930.

STEWART EDWARD WHITE, 1873–

"The Westerners," 1901; "The Claim-Jumpers," 1901;
"The Blazed Trail," 1902; "Conjuror's House," 1903; "The
Forest," 1903; "The Magic Forest," 1903; "The Silent
Places," 1904; "The Mountains," 1904; "Blazed Trail Sto-
ries," 1904; "The Pass," 1906; "The Mystery" (with Samuel
Hopkins Adams), 1907; "Arizona Nights," 1907; "Camp and
Trail," 1907; "The Riverman," 1908; "The Rules of the
Game," 1909; "The Cabin," 1910; "The Adventures of Bobby
Orde," 1911; "The Land of Footprints," 1912; "African
Camp Fires," 1913; "Gold," 1913; "The Rediscovered Coun-
try," 1915; "The Gray Dawn," 1915; "The Leopard Woman,"

1916; "Simba," 1918; "The Forty-Niners," 1918; "The Rose Dawn," 1920; "Daniel Boone," 1922; "On Tiptoe," 1922; "The Glory Hole," 1924; "Credo," 1925; "Skookum Chuck," 1925; "Lions in the Path," 1926; "Back of Beyond," 1927.

CHAPTER IX

JACK LONDON

I

THE leading writer, however, during the strenuous era, the typical figure, in many ways perhaps the most remarkable personality produced during the whole period since 1890, was Jack London. One may go further: weighed in the scales of European popularity, he overbalances even Emerson and Whitman and Poe. No life more paradoxical, more upsetting. From the first year of the new century, when he burst upon the consciousness of the reading world, until the year before America entered the World War, he shocked and thrilled and horrified the American people. No literary success more colossal than his, and more spectacular. From 1902 until the year of his death a stream of checks from more than eighty different magazines and from six leading publishing houses poured in upon him. In sixteen years he issued—not counting his plays—forty-six books many of them heading the lists of the best sellers. The sixteen years were his. He was the startling figure in the colorful decade before the European explosion, the voice in the wilderness crying "Make ready for the reign of the brute!"

To study the man is to be impressed first of all with his inherent Americanism. He was as autochthonic as Mark Twain, the culmination of a century and a half on American soil, a New World product impossible of growth in any other soil than that of California in the opening decade of the century. He was of primitive American stock—English adventurers, Welsh settlers of

New Jersey, Teutonic refugees in Pennsylvania. A restless breed: they abode nowhere long. Steadily they gravi-
tated to the West, always in the van of the settlement.
They lived in emigrant wagons, they were massacred by
Indians, they excelled as trappers. One of them, "Priest
Jones," tarried behind in Ohio as a circuit rider through
regions where physical prowess was the chief prerequisite
for spreading the Gospel, and he became the grandfather
of the novelist. By 1860 both branches of the family had
reached the Gold Coast, but they had found no gold. With
riches everywhere about them to be had for the taking,
they were still pressing restlessly on for something better.

Over and over in his novels has London pictured this
breed from which he sprang. "The Valley of the Moon"
is the epic of the descendants of the "Argonauts" halted
in their westward march by the Pacific, too restless to
settle down, and allowing their hard-won prize to be taken
from them by the more patient tribes of the toilers and
grubbers who had followed their lead. And the iron race
of "frontier chasers" had gradually degenerated into
dreamers, revolutionists, aimless adventurers, settled down
to rot along the waterfronts of the continent, the end of
the frontier. The father of the novelist, instead of clinging to lands that easily would have brought him wealth,
had turned northward from the ended frontier and had
spent his young manhood as a trapper and adventurer in
the raw Canadian hinterland.

By 1873 he was back in San Francisco, a member of the
police force, and here, three years later, was born his
tenth child, Jack London, most restless soul of all his restless breed. And his rearing was in a hotbed of restlessness
and of nourished individualism. When he was four his
family was living on a truck farm in Alameda; three years
later they were on a desolate ranch in San Mateo County.
His whole boyhood was a procession of movings from
squalid ranches to ranches more squalid. Until he was eleven

there was nothing in all his surroundings to refine him or to elevate his thinking. Forced to a round of labor he hated, driven in upon himself, starved in his imagination, he became dwarfed in all save the physical; but this, as if to compensate, became at length all but perfect. Of the religious and moral there was nothing in his surroundings —worse than nothing. "All the inconceivable filth a child running at large in a primitive countryside may hear men utter was mine."

When he was ten came the final move of the family, this time to Oakland, a veritable new world to the starved lad. Now he could attend the public schools, though not as the children of the well-to-do. Poverty flung him literally into the streets. Before and after school hours he sold papers, and on Saturdays and Sundays he set up pins in bowling alleys, swept out saloons, and helped behind the bar. When he was eleven he was given a newspaper route along the city waterfront, then the "tenderloin" district. His education now was rapid. He was a member and then the leader of a boys' gang, gaining his place by a fight with a slum gamin, "Cheese-face," which, as described in "Martin Eden," was utterly primitive in its brutality. Speedily he became learned in the lore of the street and saloon. After a time he was all but living in the notorious waterfront dives, the last frontier of the continent, where, halted by the Pacific, the tide of the westward march had settled into rottenness and despair or had turned men's restlessness into lawlessness and piracy.

At fourteen the boy ran away from home and school and lived as a free lance.

"My head filled with the tales of the old voyagers, my visions with tropic isles and far sea-rims, I was sailing a small centreboard skiff around San Francisco Bay and the Oakland estuary. I wanted to go to sea. I wanted to get away from monotony and the commonplace. I was in the flower of my adolescence, athrill with romance and adventure, dreaming of wild life in the wild man-world. . . . And the winds of ad-

venture blew the oyster pirate sloops up and down San Francisco Bay, from raided oyster beds and fights at night on
shoal and flat, to markets in the morning against city wharves
where peddlers and saloon-keepers came down to buy."

With money lent him by a colored mammy from her
savings, he bought himself a sloop, the *Razzle-Dazzle,*
hired a crew of one man, "Spider Healey," "a black-
whiskered wharf-rat of twenty," and joined the poachers
who lived from raids on the oyster beds. Again his progress was rapid. In dime-novel fashion he became the
leader of the gang. "When I was sixteen I had earned the
title of 'Prince,' but this title was given me by a gang of
cutthroats and thieves, by whom I was called 'The Prince
of the Oyster Pirates!' " He was sailing partner now of
the heroes of the last frontier, men like "Clam" and
"Young Scratch Nelson." "Clam was a dare-devil, but
Nelson was a reckless maniac. He was twenty years old
with the body of a Hercules. When he was shot in Berni-
cia a couple of years later, the coroner said he was the
greatest-shouldered man he had ever laid on a slab." It
was fame to be the leader of men like these. After a mad
exploit—a fight won at midnight on the oyster beds—he
was invited to the bar as an equal by the father of "Young
Scratch" himself. Fame indeed! " 'Old Scratch' was a blue-
eyed, yellow-haired, raw-boned Viking, big-bodied and
strong-muscled despite his age. And he had sailed the seas
in ships of all nations in the savage sailing days. . . .
His nickname 'Scratch' arose from a Berserker trick of
his, in fighting, of tearing off his opponent's face."

To get the full madness of this period in London's life
one must read his alcoholic autobiography "John Barleycorn." The mad exploits of the young oyster pirate are
still remembered in the dives of the last frontier. "Along
the Oakland waterfront," writes one who knew him at
that period, "the old salts will even now be recounting
ripping tales of the 'young dare-devil London,' who could
drink any man down at the bar, and knock any two of

them down at once who had the temerity to refuse his invitation to 'line up.' "

At seventeen, to quote his own words, he was "a drunken bum." "I practically lived in saloons, became a bar-room loafer and worse. For weeks at a time I did not draw a sober breath." His philosophy was the philosophy of the waterfront saloon: "Better to reign among booze-fighters, a prince, than to toil twelve hours a day at a machine at ten cents an hour." The earnings of a night on the oyster beds, whatever their amount, he "blew in" during the day. One raid netted him $180. "There are no purple passages in machine toil, but if the spending of $180 in two hours isn't a purple passage, then I'd like to know what is."

A road like that is short. All that saved him from the fate that overtook "Clam" and "Young Scratch" and the rest was an accident. Into the Oakland saloons that winter came "the skippers, mates, hunters, boat-steerers, and boat-pullers of the sealing fleet wintering in San Francisco Bay." Their tales of adventure fired his besotted imagination, and in January, 1893, when he was seventeen, he signed for a voyage in the three-topmast sealing schooner *Sophie Sutherland* to the North Pacific and Japan. It was a turning point in his career. Returning in August, the liquor driven from his system by the seven months' cruise, he was horrified to find his old boon companions all either dead or in prison. Moved by his mother's advice "to consider his wild oats sown," he found a job and plunged into it with characteristic intensity. Work in the jute mill he soon found intolerable, and he became a coal-heaver; but one day in the springtime he suddenly dropped everything and boarded a freight car as "blind baggage" with General Kelley's "Army of Protest" bound East; but he soon deserted. He was too completely an individualist to keep step even with an army of protest. "I became a tramp, begging my way from door to door, wandering over the United States and Canada, sweating bloody sweats in slums and prisons. I was in the pit, the abyss, the human cesspool, the shambles and the charnel-house of our civilization."

The Jack London that the world knows dates from this experience: it was while tramping with tramps that Jack London awoke. He was in his nineteenth year; his whole life had contained nothing that had not fed his rampant individualism. "I could see myself only raging through life without end like one of Nietzsche's *blond beasts,* lust-fully roving and conquering by sheer superiority and strength." But now he found himself in a world of which he had never dreamed. "On rods and blind baggages I fought my way from the open West, where men bucked big and the job hunted the man, to the congested labor centers of the East where men were small potatoes and hunted the job for all they were worth. On this new *blond beast* adventure I found myself looking upon life from a new and totally different angle." He was converted —"reborn" as he expressed it—to the doctrine of Social-ism. In his contacts with worn-out laborers on city benches, men who had once been just as "blond beastly" as he and who now were mere rubbish on the dumps of a city, he made the discovery that the rewards of the world go, not to the muscle-workers, but to the brain-workers. It stirred his imagination: something awoke within him. "I resolved to sell no more muscle, but to become a vendor of brains. Then began a frantic pursuit of knowledge. I returned to California and opened the books."

For a year he was a student in the Oakland High School, paying his way by working as janitor. The slow pace of the school disgusted him: it would be two years more before he could enter the University of California, and characteristically he wanted to enter at once. To think was to act. "I gritted my teeth and started to cram myself. There were three months yet before the university en-trance examinations. Without laboratories, without coaching, sitting in my bedroom, I proceeded to compress that two years' work into three months and to keep reviewed on the previous year's work. Nineteen hours a day I studied. For three months I kept this pace, only breaking it on several occasions." And he passed the examinations and was matriculated in the fall. He has told the story in his novel "Martin Eden." The feat seems incredible, but the records sustain it.

He remained in the university a little more than a semester, leaving in January, 1897. "The pressure from lack of money, plus a conviction that the university was not giving me all that I wanted in the time I could spare for it, forced me to leave." He had determined to make a writer of himself, and with characteristic impetuosity he chose the nearest way. By sheer main force he would master the writing art and enroll himself in the ranks of the literary creators, as he had entered the university—perchance in three months. He would take the kingdom of letters by storm. "Heavens, how I wrote! The way I worked was enough to soften my brain and send me to a mad-house. I wrote, I wrote everything—ponderous essays scientific and sociological, short stories, humorous verse, verse of all sorts from triolets and sonnets to blank-verse tragedy and elephantine epics in Spenserian stanzas." His manuscripts were returned as regularly as they were sent out, but like Martin Eden, he toiled on.

Then suddenly as he worked, like a repetition of the wild days of '49, came the news of a gold strike in the Klondike region of Alaska, and as impulsively as he had joined the Army of Protest he was off with the first wave of adventurers. A year later, compelled by an attack of scurvy, he fought his way out of Alaska, making a 1900 mile trip down the Yukon in an open boat in nineteen days. Arriving in Oakland he found that his father had died and that the care of the family had shifted to his own shoulders. Work was hard to find; in desperation he turned again to writing, and during the following three or four years fought the battle which he has described, undoubtedly in heightened terms, in his "Martin Eden." Whatever one may think of his literary product, one can but admire the pluck and the perseverance that brought his final success. No one ever succeeded with heavier odds, and no one with more of toil.

His first recognition came in January, 1899, when the "Overland Monthly" of San Francisco published his first story, "The Man on Trail," following it during the year with seven other Alaska stories. Then the "Atlantic Monthly," repeating the Bret Harte episode of thirty years before, accepted his story "An Odyssey of the North," and early in 1900 the nine tales were issued under the title "The Son of the Wolf." Success, however, was far from won: his first five books were published by five different houses. It was not until 1903, with his sixth book, "The Call of the Wild," that he may be said fairly to have arrived as a writer of fiction.

II

The fullness of biographical detail is necessary if one is to realize the paradox of the man, his development in the one era of the world's history that could have produced such a figure, his training which made him the typical voice, the prophet, indeed, of the hectic days before the German explosion. Never life, even the strenuous President's, more strenuous. Now he is in the slums of London, "the abyss," in rags and without money for weeks, that he may know and describe conditions in the underworld of the modern Babylon; now he is in the Far East as a war correspondent; now he is in Mexico among the revolutionists. When his writings had brought him the means, he caused to be built for himself a ship after his own specifications and actually started out, himself the captain and for the most part the crew, to make a tour of all the oceans. And to pay for the dream world which his imagination bodied he poured out feverishly story after

story. He started a ranch that was to be a veritable kingdom; it was planted with thirty thousand eucalyptus trees;
there were to be vast herds of cattle and of horses; and in
the midst of all was to loom the big house with the one
lady of all the world its queen.[1] And again the feverish
writing of books and stories and magazine articles and letters sent hot-footed to his publishers for advances upon his
royalties. In mere quantity the work he did staggers the imagination. In the sixteen years of his literary life he wrote
nineteen complete novels, eighteen short-story collections
with a total of 152 stories, three plays, and eight other
books, autobiographical or sociological—some fifty volumes, with others perhaps still to be published from his
manuscripts.

After the quantity one is next surprised by the hetero-
geneousness of his output, its unevenness of texture and
content, its vagaries, its wide area covered. To read Jack
London straight through is to emerge in confusion: a
swift-running film of highly colored pictures; hobbies
furiously ridden; headlong narratives; wild snapshots of
jungle and borealis, of naked head-hunters and fur-muffled
dog-drivers. Everywhere extremes, superlatives, antithe-
sis: soap-box shrillness and soft harmonies; vulgarity and
sublimity; realism and romanticism; schoolboy cheapness
and sonorous ornateness; brutality and weltering sentiment—and always superlatives, always exaggeration in
utter riot—the astonishing hodge-podge we call Jack London.

If we do not understand him it is not because he has not
put himself on record. He has told us everything. His confessions bewilder us by their quantity and by their brutal

---

[1] "The Little Lady of the Big House" is undoubtedly semi-autobiographical, as is also "The Valley of the Moon." At least they present
London as he dreamed himself to be. His autobiographical writings,
all of them doubtless much exaggerated, are voluminous. "People of
the Abyss," "The Road," "John Barleycorn," "Martin Eden," "The
Cruise of the 'Snark,'" and probably others record more or less truthfully his own experiences.

frankness—can we believe all he has told about himself? As egocentric was he as Byron. All his characters—Jacob Wilse, Wolf Larsen, Martin Eden, Burning Daylight, Billy Roberts, Dick Forest—are Jack London himself in various costumings and make-ups. To create a character he must project himself into his foreground, and draw from the picture his imagination bodied forth, not the actual Jack London but the superman he himself was in his dreamings.

It was the Alaska stories that gave him his first hearing. He had the amazing good fortune to be able to write at the one moment when all readers were eager to listen. In 1898 the imagination of the world had been stirred by the Klondike gold strike, and everywhere was demand for literary material concerning it, material that was concrete, circumstantial, hot from first-hand observation. Of London's first six books all save one, a juvenile in "St. Nicholas," were tales of the Alaska gold fields, vivid with pictures, and seemingly everywhere alive with actuality. It is upon these five—"The Son of the Wolf," "The God of His Fathers," "A Daughter of the Snows," "Children of the Frost," and "The Call of the Wild"—that his ultimate fame must rest. All are of short-story texture: even the novel "A Daughter of the Snows" is a series of episodes, and "The Call of the Wild" might have for its subtitle "Seven Episodes in the Life of the Super-Dog Buck."

His method was the method of Kipling, as Kipling's had been that of Bret Harte. He would present a field new to literature by means of dramatic episodes: swift scenes flashed upon a screen with emphasis, even to exaggeration, upon the unusual and the unique. Everywhere the Bret Harte paradoxes: the seeming villain proves to be a saint, the holy man of God turns out to be a blackleg and a murderer. Everywhere the rush of the narrative is compelling and the seeming fidelity to the minute facts of the background convincing. The opening chapters of "A

Daughter of the Snows," picturing the landing in Alaska of Frona Wilse—the baggage-strewn beach, the excited mob gathering for the march, the horrors of the long trail, the discarded dunnage and the crippled victims strewn along the miles, the squalid night camps, and over it all the madness and lure of the goal that stripped men to the primitive elements of character—all this the reader accepts without question. Had not London himself fought his way over the Chilcoot?

We are won at the start by the positiveness of the man. We must take him on faith, however: few of us know just how civilized men behave beyond the bounds of civilization, how men die of starvation, and how dogs deport themselves in the Arctic night. He tells us all this in minute detail with a Defoe-like piling of detail upon detail. Can we trust him? It seems like utterest realism, but is it true? Like Bret Harte he was writing always from memory, without notebooks, with imagination at fullest stretch, the story of a vanished period, a brief and picturesque day in a new environment, where youth is supreme and alone, and his fancy hovers over it fondly, and heightens and exaggerates and colors it even to romance. His characters are not actual men whom he has himself seen and known: they are supermen, demigods, the unsung heroes of a heroic age now for the first time put into epic setting.

Moreover to this he adds the romance of a fading race. He dates "The God of His Fathers" at "the moment when the Stone Age was drawing to a close." His Indian women are convincing, a remarkable group: Ruth, wife of Mason in "The White Silence," Madeline in "An Odyssey of the North," Unga in "The Wife of a King," Passuk, wife of Sitka Charley, Zarniska, wife of Scruff Mackensie, Sipsu, the Chief's daughter in "Where the Trail Forks," and Killisnoo, wife of Tomm, introduced with the remark: "Takes a woman to breed a man. Takes a she-cat, not a cow, to mother a tiger." By no means are they realistic studies. They were drawn from imagination rather than from notes made after observation; they are blood-sisters to the heroines of the dime novels of their creator's boyhood, better drawn, but of the same stuff. Romanticized and overdrawn though they be, however, nevertheless these women are vital and compelling. They are his only additions to the gallery of original characters in American fiction. Their doglike fidelity and honesty, their loyalty and self-sacrifice, their primitive resourcefulness in danger and privation excite unconsciously our admiration and our pity.[2]

It is not too sweeping to say that the primary purpose of all London's early fiction was pictorial. He would reproduce for us the White North. Everywhere moving pictures, flashlights. His affinity is with Conrad: with him he might have said, "My task which I am trying to achieve is, by power of the written word, to make you hear, to make you feel—it is, before all, to make you *see*."

"The Call of the Wild," the crowning work of his earliest period and indeed of his career, perfectly illustrates his methods when at his best. His zest of life is in it and the undiminished enthusiasm of youth. It is evenly balanced between the realistic and the romantic. There are no digressions; no social philosophy, and no propaganda. One who reads it surrenders to the romance of the North as completely as one surrenders to the romance of medievalism when one reads Scott. Its success was instantaneous, as it should have been; from the moment it first appeared its author's literary place was secure. Jack London had arrived; and yet, even as we say this, we must add that the very year of his arrival is the date of the beginning of his literary decline.

The causes of this decline lay, first, in his own temperament, and secondly in the nature of his literary field. His

---

[2] It is interesting to note how the Indian woman in White's "The Silent Places" resembles London's various squaws.

first five books exhausted the gold in his Alaska claim: his lode petered out. Harte and the local colorists of the eighties and even the later Kipling had discovered that to confine one's self to the recording of a primitive area is ultimately to run out of material—and soon. London had added nothing to Harte's outfit save a new set of drop scenery, a new, fresh vigor of treatment, and a Gogol-like gruesomeness of detail, and these quickly lost their startling newness.

The enormous success of "The Call of the Wild" gave him new latitude. Publishers now deluged him with offers. He cleared his desk of the early manuscripts which had been nearly worn out in their travels from office to office—"The Faith of Men," "The War of the Classes," "Moon Face," and the like, and began to write as he pleased. By nature and training he was a revolter, a propagandist, a preacher: the blood of "Priest Jones," the circuit rider and revivalist, was in his veins—nothing delighted him like the haranguing of a soap-box audience in a park on Socialism and the rights of the under-dog. More and more he began to ride hobbies, some of them furiously. He had discovered in his tumultuous reading the evolutionary theory, the recapitulation theory, Gogol, Spencer, Karl Marx, Nietzsche; and they filled him with materials. This world so new to him he exploited with the unction of a novitiate. He would reform his readers without their knowing they were being reformed. They would think they were playing. This was his theory:

Apparently it was to be a rattling sea story, a tale of twentieth century adventure and romance, handling real characters, in a real world, under real conditions. But beneath the swing and go of the story was to be something else—something that the superficial reader would never discern and which, on the other hand, would not diminish in any way the interest and enjoyment for such a reader. It was this, and not the mere story, that impelled Martin to write it.

That the theory is totally wrong, one needs but to read "The Sea Wolf" to realize. It is a story that begins tremendously: the opening chapters are as moving as anything in all American fiction, but before it has reached its middle point its failure is so apparent that it may be used in college classes as a specimen of what a novel should not be. So it was with all his later fiction. "Burning Daylight," though often brilliant in episode, is a mass of materials for fiction rather than a novel. "The Valley of the Moon" is three stories superimposed: how Billy Roberts, prize-fighter, wooed and married Saxon the laundry worker—excellent; the story of the Oakwood strike and the brutalization of Billy—propaganda; and the flight from the city and the idealization of the country—nauseatingly sweet romance.

London was not a novelist: he was too impatient, too headlong to round out a large plan. He had not the time to revise—what he wanted was quantity, material for sale like the output of a factory. He had, moreover, no patience for revision: he refused to read his earlier chapters as day by day he proceeded with his plot. As a result his novels grew by accretion, and became, like "The Little Lady of the Big House," masses of loosely bound materials for fiction.

His range was small. Of one whole rich area of society he knew only the surface. The sordid misery of his childhood and the brutal education on the waterfront during his adolescence had warped his sense of values and narrowed the circle of human characters that he knew intimately enough to portray with sympathy and insight. His world, therefore, is amazingly lopsided and misleading.

Moreover, within his own chosen field he was limited in range. After the voyage of the *Snark* he added the South Seas to his literary area and tried to do for them what he had done for Alaska, but it was only a changing of the drop-scenery and the make-up. Instead of intense cold, intense heat; instead of the aurora, the glamour of the tropic night. Of the real life of the South Sea islands he had little knowledge. He had seen the picturesque surface and he now sought to make his reader see it by means of colorful superlatives. Sadly was there a falling-off from the Alaska zest and thrill. To him the South Seas were merely background for startling picturings of the loathsome, the sensational, the unique. One feels that he has chosen them for background simply because he must have an unfailing supply of salable copy.

It is revealing to compare his work in this area with that of Conrad, his contemporary. At many points there is parallelism. Both dealt largely with outcasts; both exalted their leading characters into supermen—Captain MacWhir in "Typhoon," Razumov with his "men like us leave no posterity"; both tell graphically of typhoon and violence; both are sonorous and gorgeous of diction. But Conrad is objective while London is prevailingly subjective; Conrad knew the sea better and he loved it. He was more human than London. To him sailors were "an organized brotherhood" of which he was a member: in such work as "The Nigger of the Narcissus" there is almost a grotesque display of tenderness. London could never close a novel or a short story with a passage like this: "Goodby, brothers! You were a good crowd. As good a crowd as ever fisted with wild cries the beating canvas of a heavy foresail; or tossing aloft, invisible in the night, gave back yell for yell to a westerly gale."

In the depicting of action, however, he was the equal of Conrad. Few have surpassed him in power to present vivid moving-pictures: records of fights—dog-fights, prize-fights, bull-fights, the fight of a bull moose with a wolf pack, the battle of a Scruff Mackensie with a whole Indian tribe for the chief's daughter whom he wins and finally carries away, the single-handed battle of a Wolf Larsen with a whole mutinous crew, the stand of a band of island lepers against the authorities. Scenes of battle and typhoon kindle his imagination with power: typhoons in the Solomon Islands, races with the Yukon mail, mutinies at sea, Arctic supermen conquering single-handed a whole firm of Wall Street sharpers. Chapter 38 of "The Mutiny of the Elsinore," where Pike single-handed fights the ship off the Horn, surpasses Cooper in his own field, is, indeed, as stirring a bit of adventure as there is in the whole literature of the sea.

At one time—about 1903 it was—O. Henry's influence is to be detected in London's work, notably in such stories as "The Faith of Men" and "Moon Face," but between London and O. Henry there was a vastness of difference. London was passionately in earnest; he wrote without humorous intent; he wrote with a *motif,* often propagandist, and this *motif* he never forgot even in his most headlong moments of copy production. Behind his fiction was a principle that he fought for, a conviction that was Puritanic in its intensity. But, like Bret Harte, O. Henry lacked this principle, and lacking it both he and Harte are in danger, despite their literary cleverness and their humor, of falling into the ranks of the professional entertainers, useful people, but not a class to be placed high in the major scale of values.

III

Were it not for this element in London's work, we might dismiss him at this point, contending that he was merely a picturesque incident in the history of his period; but, like Mark Twain, he must be considered as the interpreter of his times and of his region. In his underrunning *motifs* we find the underrunning *motifs* of his period. He was not an entertainer *merely,* any more than Mark Twain was a humorist merely: he was a voice, the voice of the new America emergent beyond the Rockies, the first really Californian writer worthy of our study, for Harte and his circle were Easterners who were temporarily in the West. London was indigenous, a voice Californian. He was from the pioneers and the Argonauts, the blond race in the first van of the march into the unknown. And when the mirage of the golden West had disappeared, when the frontier ceased, with them he lifted his voice decrying the decadent days that had followed the age of the heroes who had gambled with the horizon. "The Valley of the Moon" is a sermon with this text:

Whenever a man lost his stake, all he had to do was to chase the frontier west a few miles and get another stake. They moved over the face of the land like so many locusts. They destroyed everything—the Indians, the soil, the forests, just as they had destroyed the buffalo and the passenger pigeon. Their morality in business and politics was gambler morality —the loser chased the frontier for fresh stakes. The winner of to-day, broke to-morrow, on the day following might be riding his luck to royal flushes on five-card draws. So they gobbled and gambled from the Atlantic to the Pacific.

This almost a decade before Turner's "Frontier in American History."

In all the man wrote was the spirit of the new world beyond the Rockies, its magnificent distances, its recklessness and exaggeration, its adolescent dreams. In atmospheres like this are born the giants of the race. London's supermen are only Californians as Californians dream of themselves. They came from his Western expansiveness, his life in camp and forecastle where the masculine predominated, and from the romance of the border that creates from the material about itself its own mythology. On the westward-looking borders always iconoclasm, always fierce individualism that erects self-reliance into a religion. Consider the philosophy of Jacob Wilse:

"Conventions are worthless for such as we. They are for the swine who without them would wallow deeper. The weak must obey or be crushed! Not so with the strong. The mass is nothing; the individual everything; and it is the individual always that rules the mass and gives the law."

All of London's leading characters are of this type: supermen, superwomen, dreams of their creator, half-mythical. All of them are blonds even to the golden degree. They have blue or gray eyes and bodies that are perfect. His men have muscles that creep and knot like living things, and skin like silk. His women are mates for his men, women of the border type, the half-mythical idealizations of a young man whose life has been passed largely in masculine groupings.

Youth is the key to it all. In the glorious youth of his native region he was adolescent, driven, as he has said of one of his own heroes, by "the urge of life healthy and strong, unaware of frailty and decay, drunk with sublime complacence, ego-mad, enchanted by his own mighty optimism." When London died at forty he was still, like his California, in the "flower of his adolescence." Romance is in all he wrote, the thrill of romance like that he put into the climax of his "The Call of the Wild." The super-dog Buck evolved from the weakness of civilization into the glory of the utter wild:

When the long winter nights come on and the wolves follow their meat into the lower valleys, he may be seen running at the head of the pack through the pale moonlight or glimmering borealis, leaping gigantic above his fellows, his great throat a-bellow as he sings a song of the younger world, which is the song of the pack.

It is the soul of Western individualism, the spirit of the young, free West of our America.

IV

But not only was the man the embodiment of the spirit of a vibrant locality, he was during a brief period a voice that was national and international, the most arresting literary voice of the decade preceding the World War. He was swept first into notice upon the crest of the Kipling wave, that reaction of the nineties against Tennysonian sentiment and sweetness, against Pre-Raphaelitism, Oscar-Wildeism, Aubrey-Beardsleyism. In 1903 when Kipling seemed for a time to be suffering eclipse, Jack London—taking as a text the pronouncement of a Chicago reviewer that Rudyard Kipling, "prophet of blood and vulgarity, prince of the ephemerals, and idol of the non-elect," was dead—hailed him as the most living writer of the nineteenth century: "When the future centuries quest back to the nineteenth century to find what manner of century it was, to find not what people of the nineteenth century thought they thought, but what they really thought; not what they they ought to do, but what they really did do, then a certain man, Kipling, will be read and read with understanding."

It was inevitable that he should take his own stand with the prophets of blood and vulgarity: his birth and his training had fitted him for nothing else. Moreover, it was his good fortune that the time was ripe for such prophets. Most perfectly did he key with his times. Roosevelt, ranchman of the Northwest, wilderness hunter, Rough Rider, apostle of the free air and the out-of-doors and the strenuous life, was in the fierce light of the presidency. "The Call of the Wild" was a bugle note that was in key. At the one moment in our history when it would have been possible, London seized the bâton and for a moment led the orchestra.

It was as if he foresaw the reign of savagery that was to come with the German uprising. His cry was: Face the truth. Why refuse to see what is straight before your eyes? Soft-living peoples have always been awakened by the blond ones of the North:

Civilization has spread a veneer over the surface of the soft-shelled animal known as man. It is a very thin veneer; but so wonderfully is man constituted that he squirms on his bit of achievement and believes he is clad in armor-plate. . . . Yet man to-day is the same man that drank from his enemy's skull in the dark German forests, that sacked cities, and stole his women from the neighboring clans like any howling aborigine. The flesh-and-blood body of man has not changed in the last several thousand years. Nor has his mind changed. . . . Starve him, let him miss six meals, and see gape through the veneer the hungry maw of the animal beneath. Get between him and the female of his kind upon whom his mating instinct is bent, and see his eyes blaze like any angry cat's, hear in his throat the scream of wild stallions, and watch his fist clench like an orang-outang's. Maybe he will even beat his chest. Touch his silly vanity, which he exalts into high-sounding pride, call him a liar, and behold the red animal in him that makes a hand clutching that is quick like the tensing of a tiger's claw, or an eagle's talon, incarnate with desire to rip and destroy.

And the same rule, he believed, applied to nations:

The Anglo-Saxon is a pirate, a land robber and a sea robber. Underneath his thin coating of culture, he is what he was in Morgan's time, in Drake's time, in William's time, in Alfred's time. The blood and the tradition of Hengist and Horsa are in his veins. In battle he is subject to the blood lusts of the Berserkers of old. Plunder and booty fascinate him immeasurably.

London out-Kiplinged Kipling for the simple reason that he knew more than Kipling. The author of the "Plain Tales" is as brutal and as vulgar as the life he describes, but London had been into depths that Kipling was ignorant of. He has seen the naked truth, he has seen with his own eyes what men become when all restraints are off, and he has told his generation in words and pictures as strong as his generation would bear. To the last he complained that he was not allowed to tell the whole truth. Even when he was at the height of his fame he had stories rejected by magazines because the editors considered them too brutal for their readers to bear. We can imagine his sardonic chuckle when the "abysmal brute" broke loose in

Europe and reigned for a season like the sea wolves and the *Elsinore* crews of his own novels.

V

The influence of London in Europe during his decade cannot be overlooked. In Sweden translations of twenty-four of his books were sold to the number of 230,000 in nine years. Many editions of his later Socialistic books were taken by Russia before the revolution: the number is uncertain. When he died in 1916 more space was devoted to him in the European papers than to the Emperor Francis Joseph who died at the same time. His Socialism was undoubtedly taken more seriously abroad than at home. We tolerated his pictures of the burning and rape of Chicago in "The Iron Heel," and of the blotting-out of American civilization in "The Scarlet Plague," as graphic bits of imaginative picturing, but Bolshevist Europe accepted them as solemn prophecy and as all-but-accomplished facts. For Jack London in these volumes spoke with no peradventures. To him Socialism meant war to the utter limit: "It is its purpose to wipe out, root and branch, all capitalistic institutions of present-day society." And only shortly before his death he resigned from the society in disgust, because of its lack of fire and fight, and its loss of emphasis on the class struggle.

Richard Henry Little, who was with the Russians during the period after the fall of Germany, when the Red Army was coming into power, has given a glimpse of the influence of Jack London upon the Russian people.

I wasn't left in doubt as to whom the Russians considered the greatest living American. It was "Yakclunnen." For the life of me I couldn't figure out for a while just who Yakclunnen was, although I eagerly agreed that he was the greatest American of them all. Then they brought out a great many treasured and tattered volumes, and I realized that they were talking of Jack London.

Never was an author so idolized as Jack London is among the Russians. Apparently all his works have been translated into Russian, and I found them everywhere. Officers passed them around from one to another, and I often have seen little groups of soldiers sitting in the woods, while the man who could read was doing so aloud to the eager delight of the awestruck group around him. At every mess the officers wanted me to tell them all I knew about Jack London. I wanted to talk about Lenin and Trotzky, but they wanted to talk about "Yakclunnen."

A widely disturbing element undoubtedly he has been, but his influence cannot be enduring. His philosophy was materialistic, based upon the Nietzschean doctrine of the omnipotence of force; and the World War, if nothing else, has shown its fallacy. Undoubtedly he will be rated as a picturesque incident of a stirring era. His social philosophy and his pseudo-science will disappear early. If anything of his writings is to survive its own day, it will be a few fragments from his novels, a dozen or two of his short stories that are wholly American in scene and spirit, and "The Call of the Wild" volume which has in it not only the freshness and the realism of the living North, but the atmosphere and the thrill of romance, which is the eternal spirit of youth.

BIBLIOGRAPHICAL REFERENCES

JACK LONDON, 1876–1916

"The Son of the Wolf," 1900; "The God of His Fathers," 1901; "A Daughter of the Snows," 1902; "The Children of the Frost," 1902; "The People of the Abyss," 1903; "The Kempton-Wace Letters," 1903; "The Call of the Wild," 1903; "The Faith of Men," 1904; "The Sea Wolf," 1904; "The Game," 1905; "The War of the Classes," 1905; "Tales of the Fish Patrol," 1905; "Moon Face and Other Stories," 1906; "White Fang," 1907; "Before Adam," 1907; "Love of Life," 1907; "The Iron Heel," 1907; "The Road," 1907;

"Martin Eden," 1909; "Last Face," 1909; "Revolution," 1910; "Burning Daylight," 1910; "Theft," 1910; "When God Laughs," 1910; "The Cruise of the Snark," 1911; "South Sea Tales," 1911; "Smoke Bellew Tales," 1912; "The House of Pride," 1912; "A Son of the Sun," 1912; "The Night Born," "The Abysmal Brute," 1913; "John Barleycorn," 1913; "The Valley of the Moon," 1913; "The Strength of the Strong," 1914; "The Mutiny of the Elsinore," 1914; "The Scarlet Plague," 1915; "The Star Rover," 1915; "The Cruise of the Dazzler," 1916; "The Little Lady of the Big House," 1916; "The Turtles of Tasman," 1916; "Jerry of the Islands," 1917; "The Human Drift," 1917; "Michael, Brother of Jerry," 1917; "On the Makaloa Mat," 1919.

For biographical and critical details see "The Book of Jack London," Charmian London, 1921; "Our Short Story Writers," B. C. Williams, 1920.

CHAPTER X

THE MUCK-RAKE SCHOOL

CRITICISM of executives and men in power generally has always in America been free and caustic. Washington was vilified beyond belief, as were Jackson and Lincoln and all others who have dared run the gauntlet of a presidential campaign. It has been a thing inseparable from the American idea of liberty: it is free speech without which there is no true freedom. The newspaper in America has never been censored, never been checked indeed save by some outburst of public opinion which has affected the journal's subscription list or its advertising.

Another phase of our Americanism has been what Europeans have called "the habit of washing dirty linen in public," a result, say our younger critics, of the inherited virus of Puritanism. Always they contend has there been a dour squad of reformers who have pointed with horror at every lapse in public morals or private manners, not only publishing it to the world but starting crusades to make it emphatic. It is a land, they declare, of periodic outbursts of righteousness.

One such outburst was the so-called "muck-rake" campaign of Roosevelt days. The prime mover of it undoubtedly was S. S. McClure, who was struggling to float his fifteen-cent magazine. Utterly unconscious that he was inaugurating a new *genre* that was to receive a name, he commissioned Ida Tarbell to study the oil trust and prepare for him a series of articles exposing to the full their shortcomings; then he sent Lincoln Steffens to investigate the city government of Minneapolis, which he believed had become a stench and a scandal. And the man produced a series of exposures of city governments—Philadelphia among them, "corrupt and contented"—and he published them under the title "The Shame of the Cities." Young Ray Stannard Baker he set to work on the anthracite coal strike and the beef trust. Other magazines quickly followed. Edward Bok in the "Ladies' Home Journal" began crusades against evils threatening child life and the home, and always with success.[1]

Both editors were quick to realize that to fight powerful organizations like wealthy corporations and corrupt city governments one must have facts, absolutely proven evidence that could not be shaken even in the courts. Mere newspaper methods would not do. To quote McClure:

The fundamental weakness of modern journalism, it seemed to me, was that the highly specialized activities of modern civilization were very generally reported by men uninformed in the subjects upon which they wrote. . . . I decided, therefore, to pay my writers for their study rather than for the amount of copy they turned out—to put the writer on such a salary as would relieve him of all financial worry and let him master a subject to such a degree that he could write upon it, if not with the authority of a specialist, at least with such accuracy as could inform the public and meet with the corroboration of experts.[2]

No series of articles ever caught more quickly or more completely the reading public. During certain months it was impossible to keep the supply of magazines up to the demand. And the articles soon were followed by results. Everywhere "clean-up" campaigns and reorganized corporations. "Mr. Steffens' articles dealt in large part with material that had been brought out in the courts or by grand juries, and were instrumental in the first awaken-

[1] For a detailed account of his work see "The Americanization of Edward Bok," 1920.
[2] "My Autobiography," S. S. McClure, Chapter 8.

ing of the American people to municipal administration." [3]

Unquestionably the various attacks were aimed first of all at the conscience of the nation. They were based on the suppressed premises that "vice to be hated needs but to be seen," that the people, in the great average, are fundamentally good, are horrified at a reign of crime or a miscarriage of justice, that they need only to be awakened, but that once awake, once completely aware of the corruption about them, they will rise in their wrath and smite till their hands cleave to the sword.

It was the last spasm of the Puritan conscience. It was also good business. Fighting for righteousness could be made a sensational thing, and sensational disclosures added circulation to the magazine and increased the advertising profits. The literature of exposure had become a "big business proposition." Startling revelations like Lawson's "Frenzied Finance" were everywhere in eager demand, and a supply naturally followed. Nothing seemed safe, nothing exempt from damning disclosures. Foreign nations read the articles with amusement and profit: this, then, was America; they had long suspected it.

Then it was that Theodore Roosevelt awoke. "Muckrakers," he roared, and the word stuck in the national vocabulary; has clung there even to the present. The allusion, he explained, was to Bunyan's parable, in "The Pilgrim's Progress," of the wretched creature raking for straws in the muck, all unconscious of the glories in the heavens above him. The President had in mind only the commercial crew who were exhibiting the wretched straws of America's failings, completely blind to her strength and glory. Not at all was he aiming at the Tarbell-Steffens group; they were honest workers for a better America. But the burr once thrown made no distinctions: the exposer of evils whatever his purpose was a "muck-raker." The word had a sinister connotation: it classified a man; and as a result the elder workers ceased their investigation

[3] "My Autobiography," S. S. McClure.

and withdrew to other literary areas. Steffens went into newspaper work, Ida Tarbell into the making of biographies and juveniles, and Ray Stannard Baker disappeared as we shall see.

Then came the third stage of the episode: muck-raking for muck-raking's sake, muck-raking debauched into deliberate attack upon the fundamentals of everything established and inviolate, muck-raking with deliberate cynicism and jeers—"debunking"! The "younger generation" was upsetting all the old standards. Disillusion seemed more and more to be in the air like an infectious disease. Some accounted for it as an effect of the disappearance of the American border with its free land and its century-old mirage of a golden West, instancing Mark Twain, who died in 1910 the most embittered man of his generation; Mark Twain, whose early years as revealed in "Tom Sawyer" were a dream of romance. The very brightness of his expectations and his dreaming they declared had been his undoing. And he had written in his last years, instead of romance of the epic West, caustic sagas of disillusion like "A Connecticut Yankee in King Arthur's Court," and muck-raking parables like "The Man That Corrupted Hadleyburg," and finally that embittered diatribe against the whole human race, "What Is Man?"

The disillusion and cynicism increased with the new century. Especially bitter was the attack upon Puritanism, which now seemed to assume the place formerly occupied by the devil. Atheism became blatant, and a young Western editor solemnly "debunked" the Ten Commandments and the New Testament. Partly was it a reflex of European thinking, and a dozen ports were there for the entry of the new gospels. Fitzgerald's version of Omar Khayyam was one. In 1898 John Hay, American ambassador, had said to the Omar Club of London: "In the cities of the West you will find the quatrains one of the most thoroughly read books in every literary club," a fact to thank God for; but, he added, it was not "the exquisite beauty, the faultless form, the singular grace of the quatrains" that was fascinating and molding the young men: far more was it, he declared, "the depth and breadth of their profound philosophy." Sinclair Lewis, in the vernacular of his generation, said the same thing, right at home:

In nothing do the inarticulate "million hall-room boys who want to be geniuses," the ordinary, unshaved, not over-bathed, ungrammatical young men of any American city, so nearly transcend provincialism as in an enthusiasm over their favorite minor cynic, Elbert Hubbard or John Kendrick Bangs, . . . or Mr. Fitzgerald's variations on Omar.

Other elements were coming across the Atlantic. The young H. L. Mencken was introducing to his generation the new twentieth-century Messiahs, Nietzsche and Bernard Shaw. Graduate students were flocking to the German universities and were returning home upset in their thinking. Then had come the war, but the war created nothing new: it but intensified a condition already present. As expressed by Simeon Strunsky, a younger critic of discernment:

The march away from romanticism to realism and the hard-boiled, from reticence to full self-expression, had begun long before the German armies marched into Belgium. By 1912 in this country the Puritan battle-line was giving way before the pagan assault, if there are no objections to "pagan." At the very least our complacency was yielding before the onset of the "critical spirit."

The amazing extent of this "pagan assault" has been told us by another of the younger generation, Henry Sydnor Harrison, in the "Yale Review," 1928:

In the ten years since the war, to go no farther back, how many books by Americans have devoted themselves, in part or whole, to attacking, exposing, deriding, or just laughing at the Americano (or Homo Americanus, indifferently) and his ignoble ways and scene? Let the reader as an exercise begin, say, with "Main Street" and "These United States," and, computing backward and forward around the six or seven volumes of "Prejudices," try to count his way out to the newest collection of "Americana," "The Great American Band-Wagon," or such later contributions as may by this time have appeared. Let him by no means forget the historical and biographical works of the "debunkers." Let him further try to reckon roughly (for the sands of the sea are no more numerable) the totality of articles, essays, addresses, lectures (how eagerly do we walk miles in the rain, money in hand, and pack the hall to hear them!), symposia, critiques, reviews, skits, skats, squibs and paragraphs, elaborating the same thesis. If he survive his comptometrics, he is not likely to deny that, in a few brief years, we Americans have rolled up a literature of self-depreciation of absolutely staggering proportions.

II

The assault upon manners and the social régime was for a decade—1901–1911—led by David Graham Phillips. Again a revolt from the West; again shrill protest against the evils of Eastern effeteness. He belongs to the Indiana chapter—he was born at Marshall in that State in 1867 and like Booth Tarkington he was sent to Princeton to remove the burrs from his Westernism. He belongs to the journalism chapter—after college he plunged with eagerness into the newspaper game first in Cincinnati then in New York City where he soared high in the esteem of the "Sun" and then of the "World." Still more, however, he belongs to the muck-rake squad that soon was to educate the new era.

Completely did he fit the period in which he found himself, Underwood has called him "the Roosevelt of American literature," and it is wise criticism. The same strenuous plunging into the line of action: in ten years twenty novels each on the average of 100,000 words in length, and in addition a vast bulk of miscellany; the same eagerness for reforming all things—he joined the muck-rakers early and his first tilt was at the windmill of the Senate, published with the title "The Treason of the Senate."

In 1901 he changed his methods. Resigning from the newspaper staff he devoted himself entirely to a battle against what he considered current social evils, using now the cloak of fiction to conceal his weapons—fiction made so popular that it could be published as serials in the "Cosmopolitan" and the "Saturday Evening Post," be rated among the leading best sellers, and yet be in reality camouflaged bombshells for fighting things that should not be. Like the President, he worked always for results, and like him displayed courage verging at times upon rashness. A contemporary estimate of the man, widely copied, had the title "Phillips the Fighter." And it was a fight without reservations and often without tact. He was shot when he was but forty-four by a fanatic who thought he had been used as the model for one of Phillips's characters.

His first muck-rake novel, "The Great God Success," made use of his own experiences in the newspaper world, even to the extreme, it is believed, of using his own employer, Pulitzer, as the villain of the piece. Then had come a series of exposures of political rottenness—"The Golden Fleece," "The Plum Tree," "The Master Rogue," "The Deluge." Always there was the touch of contemporaneousness: they grew out of the problem of the moment like a newspaper editorial. When the life insurance companies were under fire, for instance, he aided the attack with his "Light-Fingered Gentry." Not at all were his methods new; all about him were other novelists either exposing political evils or educating the people to see. But all of them he excelled in his bid for publicity. There were Brand Whitlock's "The Thirteenth District," 1902, Mark Lee Luther's "The Henchman," 1902, Churchill's "Coniston," 1905, and a whole armful of novels similar, but somehow Phillips held the center of the stage.

Political rottenness interested him, but it was at society and its failings that most of his shots were fired, particularly at the conventional woman of the "upper" or wealthier classes. Here he went to extremes. Mrs. Annie Nathan Meyer in a critique of 1911 has this deduction from the series of novels with the titles "A Woman Ventures," "Old Wives for New," "The Husband's Story," "The Second Generation," and "The Grain of Dust":

Unfaltering, mercilessly, Mr. Phillips has exposed the absurd pretentions of the American woman. His heroine and her kind are held up as bungling housekeepers, callous seekers after their own pleasure, ignorant mothers, slave-drivers to their good-natured, indifferent, woman-worshipping, woman-despising, money-making husbands. Furthermore, they are empty-headed and frivolous, both vain and colossally conceited.

On the whole he was pitiless in his realism, but he worked without adequate knowledge. He was prejudiced, he was bound often by narrow preconceptions. His style, too, lacks distinction, lacks verve and lightness and humor. In nearly all of the early reviews of his books there was the charge of hasty composition. Phillips, however, retorted with heat that no other novelist ever surpassed him in revision; that he rewrote his work at least three times and always threw away three-quarters of all he produced. The defense may clear the man, but it does not help him. It illuminates him like a headlight. He was a machine turning out day by day a standard product—on it is the mark of the machine. He was a newspaper reporter, viewing everything he used with the newsman's eye. Like an editorial it was timely, but it was stuff pregnant only with the moment.

The severest criticism of his work, however, is the fact that it has not survived. With his tragic death he dropped completely from the public consciousness. His books are out of print: he is forgotten. The problem novel must carry other freight than its problem if it is to survive at all its day.

III

The culmination of the school, the leader of all muck-rakers, the man indeed who has raised muck-raking to a profession and has practised it with intensity for a life-time has been Upton Sinclair. No book-list so amazing as his in all literature—a five-foot shelf of vehemence, of protest, of shrill invective. Like a Hebrew minor prophet, for a generation he has stood in the market place and poured out doom warnings and denunciation.

He was born in Baltimore of Southern stock in 1878 and lived there until his tenth year, when his parents re-moved to New York City. Intense, precocious, reared in a family unbalanced between father and mother, he lived through all his boyhood in a world of his own construction, a world of poetry and dreams constructed from the ma-terials of his multitudinous reading. Most thoroughly was he schooled, saturated with the "classics" taught under the ancient régime, and graduated from the College of the City of New York before he was eighteen. The world to him was books, and life as he visualized it for himself was to be poetry. Not to him was it a "passion": it was life itself. He was sent to Columbia to study the law; but law is not poetry.

A change in the family fortunes brought practicality with sharpness. There was his mother to support, but he would earn no dollar save with his pen. He wrote dime novels for Street & Smith, in a sixteen-hour day at $70 a week and for years, totaling by his own estimate a final bulk of composition "equal to the complete works of Sir Walter Scott." His autobiographic novels dealing with his early years—"Love's Pilgrimage" and "The Journal of Arthur Stirling"—belong on the same shelf as London's "Martin Eden," on the same shelf indeed as Rousseau's "Confessions." A youth passed among books in a dime-novel world of his own creation, this was his preparation for life—an adolescent Bronson Alcott transferred to the twentieth century. Alcott had as neighbor the shrewd Emerson, philosopher and dreamer, but yet a Yankee; Sinclair, at the climacteric moment of adolescence, found not an Emerson but an idealist with a passion, a militant socialist who set him to reading Karl Marx and all the library that follows. The youth's conversion to socialism was swift and sure. Henceforth was he to be a soap-box crier, a protester, a muck-raker militant, a twentieth-century Amos thundering against the fat cows of plutocracy.

His early novels, published at his own expense, made no impression. They were written by one who knew life only as a dreamer and potential poet. One may linger a moment with his "Manassas," a war piece, his first attempt at realism. Jack London was convinced that it bit more deeply into reality than Crane's "Red Badge of Courage": "The best Civil War book I've read," he declared. Amazing promise there was in the book. It was to be, its author said, volume one of a trilogy, but like Norris's projected "Gettysburg," it was never to be written. A new trail had opened.

The "embalmed beef" scandal of the war days suddenly burst again into the newspapers. A sniff of it reached the young war dreamer, and he was off to Chicago to return seven weeks later outraged and nauseated by what he had seen in the little world of the stockyards. He had seen the cheapness of human life, the wreckage of humanity that had been passed through the most brutal of machines, and he poured his vehemence into a novel which he issued serially in a socialistic journal, "The Appeal to Reason," published in Girard, Kansas. Issued as a volume it created a sensation tremendous and world-wide. The public saw not at all the dominant thesis of the book. As Sinclair himself expressed it, he had "aimed at the public's heart and had hit it in the stomach." To quote his biographer Dell, "His deepest concern had been with the fate of the workers, and he realized with bitterness that he had become a celebrity not because the public cared anything about the workers, but because it did not want to eat diseased meat." [4] It was the best seller of the year, realizing for its author $30,000, a sum in those days colossal; it was more: the President because of it was forced to appoint a commission to investigate the packing-houses, and their report caused reorganization of packing-house methods.

The publication of the book marks undoubtedly the climax of the muck-rake era. Dell in his biography is inclined to side with Sinclair in his contention that following the devastation caused by "The Jungle" the corporations awoke and in wrath put an end to the muck-rake nuisance. Again to quote Dell:

The stage of Upton Sinclair's literary career, immediately ensuing upon his immense celebrity as the author of *The Jungle,* falls within this period when "muck-raking" was being outlawed and editors and writers taught a lesson by those in control of American business. He was one of the few who dared to brave this Thermidorian reaction and he was the chief of those to suffer from it. It is his temerity which explains the fact that his reputation in America as a novelist fell during that period to zero, or lower. He missed, by remaining a "muck-raker," his chance of regaining literary respectability.

From this time on Sinclair's life was hot with warfare. The titles of his books reveal the width of his battle area: "The Moneychangers," (a muck-rake charge upon Wall Street), "The Overman," "The Profits of Religion," "King Coal, a Novel of the Colorado Strike," "The Goose-Step, a Study of American Education," "Money Writes!" "Boston" (based on the Sacco-Vanzetti case). The total list runs into the dozens.

Emerging from his triumph with "The Jungle," the $30,000 in his pocket troubled him: it was unsocialistic. But not for long. Like Alcott and Ripley in the era of

[4] "Upton Sinclair, a Study in Social Protest," Floyd Dell, 1927.

Fruitlands and Brook Farm, he would start a community —"Helicon Hall" on the Hudson, a colony of middle-class intellectuals brought together on the high levels of their ideals. Strongly it started: $30,000 gives impetus, but its life was shorter even than that of Fruitlands. After six months the Phalanstery burned, and the man was a wanderer. He was in California organizing theatrical companies to spread his own gospel as revealed in a series of his own dramas, one of them entitled "Hell"; he was organizing the Intercollegiate Socialist Society, and the Civic Federation Union of California. For seven years he was an inhabitant of the single-tax colony at Arden, Delaware.

He is to be classed as a propagandist rather than as a novelist. The purpose in his work so overrides everything else that one can hardly think it is fiction. It is evidence chaotic: facts hurled with vehemence and rancor. Its one purpose seems to be to plunge its reader into a like heat, and often it succeeds. But even as propaganda it has serious failings. It is unbalanced. He finds what he looks for, but he finds nothing else. In his novel "The Metropolis," for a single instance, he exposes the frightful extravagance of the new-rich of the cities, their "monkey dinners," their expensive clothes worn but once and then given to servants, baths in priceless aromatics used for a moment and then dumped into the sewer. All he tells has actually happened somewhere. It is truth; he can show you the clipping; but it is but half the truth. From a dozen selected instances he lays down a law affecting millions of cases. No one has more sanely summed this up than young Van Wyck Brooks:

It is natural that Mr. Sinclair should be popular with the dispossessed: they who are so seldom flattered find in his pages a land of milk and honey. Here all the workers wear haloes of pure sunlight and all the capitalists have horns and tails; socialists with fashionable English wives invariably turn yellow at the appropriate moment, and rich men's sons are humbled in the dust, Irish lasses are always true and wives never understand their husbands, and all the good people are martyrs, and all the patriots are vile. Mr. Sinclair says that the incidents in his books are based on fact and that his characters are studied from life. No doubt they are. But Mr. Sinclair, naturally enough, has seen what he wanted to see and studied what he wanted to study; and his special simplification of the social scene is one that invariably makes glad the heart of the victim of our system.[5]

One must reckon always with the colossal egotism of the man. His analogue is Jack London—the likeness at times is startling. Both were autobiographic well nigh to the extreme of objective sterility; both were realists because of what may be termed an inverted romanticism: unable to see good in the world, they revenged themselves by exaggerating the bad. At basis it was egotism. What Ida Zeitlin has said of Gogol applies as well to them:

In utter loathing of these imperfections he seized upon them, exaggerated, distorted, and held them up to scorn, made a public mock of them so that, implicitly, their reverse qualities might be exalted and glorified. . . . Every time he damned human greed or hypocrisy or self-love he was, negatively, celebrating generosity and truth and human brotherhood and thus ministering to his own passionate need of reverence.

Only one of Sinclair's novels can hope to survive at all his period. "The Jungle" with its touch of the universal in humanity, its subtle use of suggested horror, its realism, its pathos, is one of the great books of the period. The rest are but abandoned war materials in wars for the most part forgotten.

IV

An illuminating sidelight was the reaction of Ray Stannard Baker. Western-born—Lansing, Michigan, was his

[5] "The Novels of Sinclair Lewis," in "Emerson and Others," Van Wyck Brooks, 1927.

early home—educated in the State university, for five years
a reporter in Chicago on the "Record," not at all a rebel
and a muck-raker. In the whirlpool of a city newspaper
office, he yet kept his soul serene and wrote for the Eastern
magazines quiet little essays and idealistic tales. And once
in a while one of them was accepted. The "Century" and
then "McClure's" published him, and then came the letter
from the East that all Chicago writers toiling in city newspaper offices dreamed of finding in their mail: he was invited to go to New York in the employ of the McClure
syndicate and "McClure's Magazine." It clashed with all
his literary dreams, but he went: he had a growing family
to support, and such offers could not be ignored.

Then had come his muck-rake work for McClure, in-
vestigations of railroad conditions, of negro problems, and
finally of international conditions, which sent him into the
Orient and gave him at least one vivid adventure, a part in
the rescue of the missionary Ellen Stone held for ransom
by Turkish bandits. Constantly his work in muck-rake
vein was appearing under the signature of Ray Stannard
Baker.

But a new writer had appeared, one David Grayson. No
one had ever seen him, no one knew the slightest thing
about him. For years the public had been enjoying his
"Essays in Contentment," the first collection of them as
early as 1907. With the waning of the muck-rake moon,
Baker, like Miss Tarbell and Steffens, found other employment. He went back to Michigan, where his family
still were living, and gradually the name of Ray Stannard
Baker became a dim memory. But the name David Grayson was becoming a familiar one. It connoted love of nature and of country life. It preached the doctrine that for
a moment had been brought to the whole of America by
the French author Wagner in his book "The Simple Life,"
for one season a best seller even in New York City. "Adventures in Friendship" came in 1910, "The Friendly
Road" in 1913; others followed. Who was David Gray-

son? Perhaps even to-day we should not know had not another claimed the authorship. David Grayson was Ray Stannard Baker: it was as if he feared that the muck-rake soil had saturated his name until forever it would connote only muck-raking stuff. And he would begin utterly anew.

The David Grayson books, sweet, gentle, wise, have been a quieting influence in a turbulent, headlong era. A few others have joined him in his anti-muck-rake adventurings, notably Dallas Lore Sharp, whose quiet nature observations, published often in the "Atlantic" and elsewhere, have been quiet zones in an age too much given to the artificial and the excitedly urban, to muck-raking recriminations and newspaper headlines.

BIBLIOGRAPHICAL REFERENCES

DAVID GRAHAM PHILLIPS, 1867–1911

There is as yet no biography of Phillips. An excellent study of his work and his personality, though perhaps at times too extravagant in its estimates, is "David Graham Phillips, The Greatest American Novelist," Chapter I in "Latest Contemporary Portraits" by Frank Harris, 1927.

"The Great God Success," 1901; "Her Serene Highness," 1902; "A Woman Ventures," 1902; "Golden Fleece: the American Adventures of a Fortune Hunting Earl," 1903; "The Master-Rogue; the Confessions of a Crœsus," 1903; "The Cost," 1904; "The Deluge," 1905; "The Plum Tree," 1905; "The Reign of Gilt," 1905; "The Social Secretary," 1905; "The Fortune Hunter," 1906; "Light-Fingered Gentry," 1907; "The Second Generation," 1907; "Old Wives for New," 1908; "The Worth of a Woman," 1908; "The Fashionable Adventures of Joshua Craig," 1909; "The Hungry Heart," 1909; "The Husband's Story," 1910; "White Magic," 1910; "The Conflict," 1911; "The Grain of Dust," 1911; "George Helm," 1912; "The Price She Paid," 1912; "Degarmo's Wife, and Other Stories," 1913; "Susan Lenox: Her Fall and Rise," 1917.

UPTON SINCLAIR, 1878–

"The Journal of Arthur Stirling," 1903, is Sinclair's nearest approach to autobiography. "The Novels of Upton Sinclair," in "Emerson and Others," 1927, Van Wyck Brooks. For a bibliography of Sinclair see Manly and Rickert, pages 286–288.

CHAPTER XI

O. HENRY

I

THE second original force that entered the new century—Jack London was the first—was a man whose pseudonym, like Mark Twain's, obliterated his original name. The first work of "O. Henry" appeared along with London's in the closing months of 1899. It was the era of "red-blood literature," of "men with the bark on," and he burst into it in full costume—first as a tramp, then as a cowboy of the Southwest, or, in his own vernacular, as a "knight errant of the chaparral." His magazine stories had Bret Harteness in them—original idioms, humor, strange localism, gusto, action. They were felt instantly. Bored copyreaders, handling with apathy their daily stint of dullness, awoke with a start. Who wrote this? Who is this O. Henry? And the public excitedly echoed them.

The publishers told all they knew. His real name, they said, was William Sydney Porter; he had come originally from Greensboro, North Carolina; he had been sent to Texas because of threatened tuberculosis. That he had lived the wild life he described, they said, was evident on the face of the tales. Whoever he was, they had unearthed the literary "find" of the decade. Here indeed was a man to delight the Rooseveltian heart, and, marvel of marvels, he could write. Gradually there filtered in other details, most of them sheer inferences from his stories. He had vagabonded through Honduras; he had been a beach-comber in the Spanish American tropics; he had led revolutions, of course, against Central American presidents; and now he was bringing, what no one had ever brought before, exotic atmospheres and unholy adventure from uncharted realms to the west and the south of the Caribbean. He was hailed as Kipling had been hailed in the nineties, the bringer of wild exotic atmospheres, a new sensation in a jaded age—surely "Cabbages and Kings" would have brought sensation to any age.

So much we knew of O. Henry in 1902. Then had come the second chapter of the wild harlequinade: this vagabond "bull-whacker" of the Southwest, this South American play-boy, consorter with Al Jennings, with beach-combers and yeggs, had appeared suddenly in the East, as interpreter—amazing metamorphosis—of "little old Bagdad on the Hudson." "McClure's Magazine" had discovered the man, and at length all the wood-pulp magazines of America were upon him. The New York "World" made the landing, announcing its catch with loud trumpetings. He was to be a member of the staff, a reporter-at-large, with the single requirement that he furnish to the Sunday edition a one-page story every week. The outpouring that followed was like nothing else in American literature, a potpourri of sketches and stories and anecdotes and modern instances syndicated at once in all the major newspapers everywhere. Never such an amazing outpour—then all of a sudden it stopped. Death had caught the creator in full career—death at forty-eight after a literary life of but ten years. He had come like a comet; he disappeared like a comet.

That was in 1910. But the paradox of O. Henry had only begun. Stories written for the Sunday supplement are as ephemeral as the comic section they neighbor, but these ephemeræ from the very first were treated as classics. Some of the tales had been swept into volumes even during the headlong six years of his greatest fecundity, but the man was scarce buried before every one of them had been ferreted out for a complete set of his works. He had been enormously creative, it was found. During the two years following "Cabbages and Kings" he had produced one hundred and fifteen stories, and his total output, almost all of it created during six years, was two hundred and fifty pieces not counting the scraps gathered later in the final volume of his "remains."

Then had come the second stage of O. Henry—O. Henry as a set of books, O. Henry thrown at the American people with all the devices of modern advertising. "The Yankee Maupassant," "England has her Dickens, France her Hugo, and America her O. Henry," "a collection of thrills unparalleled in literature"—such catchwords and "blurbs" caught the eye in every magazine. The set, with the first ebbing of the tide of orders, was sold with the complete works of other authors thrown in free, Kipling, E. Phillips Oppenheim. And amazingly the public responded, for years they responded. In 1919 the publishers claimed that "up to the present time about four million, one hundred thousand of O. Henry's books have gone to the public," or about one volume to every twenty-five of the population. And during the ten years that have followed the sales have steadily continued.

Six years after his death came the next anticlimax: the man's very biography, it seemed, was an O. Henry tale with a surprise ending. In 1916 Dr. C. Alphonso Smith, a scholar of international standing, a man of the South and hence presumably sympathetic with his subject, issued a life of the novelist. For the first time appeared the real story of William Sydney Porter—a startling revelation. He had not been a cowboy at all—at least, not a rider of horses. During his eleven years in Texas he had lived most of the time in the larger cities, had been successively reporter, clerk, joke-writer for northern papers, editor of a magazine of humor, bank teller, and finally fugitive from justice. Charged with appropriating bank funds, he had in sudden panic made a plunge into South America by way of New Orleans. For months he had been a vagabond in non-extraditionary ports, living the Bohemian life described with impressionistic detail in "Cabbages and

Kings." Learning of his wife's critical illness, he had plunged as temperamentally back into the North again, had reached home before she died, had then been arrested, convicted, and sentenced to prison. Nearly four years he served of his sentence, the greater part of it as a "trusty" in charge of the prison drugstore. Freely was he allowed to draw upon the little library of the institution, which was rich, if in nothing else, in works by Bret Harte and Kipling.

To secure money for birthday presents for his little daughter, who knew nothing of her father's imprisonment, he began to write stories, modeling them at first upon the fiction at his command, then marketing them through a friend in New Orleans. His pen name he had assumed necessarily, for was not William Sydney Porter a convict? When "Whistling Dick's Christmas Stockings" appeared in "McClure's," its author had two and a half more years to serve on his sentence.

So much for the man: what of the two hundred and fifty tales and sketches in the thirteen volumes of his literary remains?

II

Conservative criticism has been inclined to withhold its verdict and wait. Perspective is needed. A comet, be it ever so brilliant, will fade and disappear if but given time; but in the case of O. Henry the critic has not been allowed to wait. He has been forced to render judgment. It has been impossible to ignore the voices that have poured in upon him from university and barber-shop, from rural home and public library, from rotary club and sacred desk, from reviews in town weeklies and critiques in scholarly journals. Dr. Smith sent forth his biography with the solemn dictum: "O. Henry's work remains the solidest fact to be reckoned with in the history of twentieth-century literature." Again, at the dedication of the Raleigh, North Carolina, memorial to Porter he added the man to the quartette of great American short-story writers: Irving, Hawthorne, Poe, and Harte. "O. Henry," he declared, "has given the American short story a new reach and a widened social content . . . he has socialized the short story." The Canadian humorist and critic, Stephen Leacock, published an essay entitled "The Amazing Genius of O. Henry" and in it dared to go to such extremes as "The time is coming, let us hope, when the whole English-speaking world will recognize in him one of the great masters of modern literature." One might multiply such superlatives and from men as fastidious even as the late William James. Few authors have ever so won the general public and at the same time the critical few. O. Henry, approach him as you will, is paradox.

To read the thirteen volumes of his set—and I have done it—that strange harlequin epic of incongruous shreds, that amazing salmagundi concocted of every condiment for compelling the palates of an over-stimulated generation, is to emerge at the end, unable for a time rightly to evaluate anything, condemning the whole thing one hardly knows why, yet at the same time inclined greatly to praise. Taken as a condiment, a single taste of the mixture affects one like a shake of tropic spicery: a sensation unique, a new thrill; but to swallow a whole volume, the whole thirteen volumes, is like making a dinner on *hors d'œuvres*. Where else in all literature can one find such a mélange—stories bedeviled and made into fire-crackers; travesties on all things holy and unholy; sermons in motley and the ten commandments of yeggdom; fun like "Alice in Wonderland" ending in a barbarous caper as primitive as the Sunday comics; short stories that violate every canon of their art yet so effective that they are printed as models in school text-books; serious sketches somersaulting in topsy-turvy: philosophizings through a horse-collar, doxologies through a saxophone? Everywhere everything too much. What spirits! What abandon! What zest in life! What curiosity concerning all things human! What boyish delight in the

great show we call life! Not much muck-raking here, no
concealed sermonizing; no shouting of "moron" because
the crowd's unlike yourself. He is an entertainer, and he
has a show. Not a paragraph that does not rebound upon
the reader like a peal of laughter, or startle him, or challenge him, or prod him unawares, and then roar at his
surprise. No repose in these books: they are deviled meat
for jaded palates. No subtle nuances, no refined atmospheres of style. The tones are loud, the humor is of the
slap-you-on-the-back order, the characters are as theatric
and as exaggerated as any in "Boz"—Smike, or Nicholas
Nickleby, or Mr. Pickwick. No realism here. It is pitched,
all of it, for men, for healthy, elemental men, men of the
bar-room and the club foyer and the barracks. In no writings since Dickens does liquor flow so freely. The dominant
note of "The Rubaiyat of a Scotch Highball" he strikes
at the start: "drink shall swell the theme and be set forth
in abundance." "The Fourth in Salvador" is the most besotted tale in our literature. And yet, despite the fact that
the stories, whole volumes of them, record life on isolated
masculine ranches, in vice-sodden tropic towns, and in the
submerged areas of New York City, at every point that
touches the feminine, the work is as chaste as Emerson.
No Zola here, no Frank Norris, no Stephen Crane even.
Enter vaudeville—vaudeville with genius, stories to snatch
you out of yourself for a moment that is different: "as
new as a trellis of sweet peas and as rollicking as a clarinet
solo."

Before one has spent an hour with the volumes one is
aware of a strange duality in the work, one that must have
had its origin in the man himself. It is as if Hawthorne had
sold his pen to Momus. There are pages where the style
rises to distinction. One might cull extracts that would
imply marvelous wholes. We realize before we have finished a single tale that we are dealing with no uncouth
cowboy who has literary aspirations and who writes in
slang because slang is all he knows. It is the work of a

creator, exhilaratingly original, yet of one who has read widely: his quotations and allusions cover an area most surprising. And a vocabulary he has of wide compass. He is, when he wishes it, as accurate in his usages and as rich in his variants as a Henry James. His biographer records that for years the dictionary was his favorite reading, that he pored over it as one pores over romance. In his descriptions of the tropics he can be as richly impressionistic as Lafcadio Hearn. There are paragraphs that catch the very soul of the West Indies—"the fetterless, idyllic round of enchanted days; the life among this indolent romantic people—life full of music, flowers and low laughter; the influence of the immanent sea and mountains, and the many shapes of love and magic and beauty that bloom in the white tropic nights."

But one catches only fitful glimpses of this other O. Henry. The Momus that ruled his pen snatched him always away in the very midst of his seriousness. A sentence may begin like Emerson—beware: it will close with a pigeon-wing. Never can we trust him. His tale of southern life "The Guardian of the Accolade," let us take as an instance. Its opening beguiles us. For paragraph after paragraph it rings true; it is exquisitely told. Uncle Bushrod is as feelingly, and as perfectly presented as Uncle Remus. We have discovered a classic: at last from O. Henry a work of serious art with no harlequin tricks and no vaudeville capers. Then comes the final sentence: Pshaw! we have been fooled, we have been played with. The master was not absconding after all; the faithful old negro had not, as he so proudly supposed, rescued the family from the gulf of disaster and shame. All he had done had been to prevent his master from taking with him on a fishing trip his favorite handbag, and that handbag—not full of stolen bonds as the old darky believed—surrendered after piteous pleading for the family honor, and returned by the old man to the bank he supposed his master had robbed. There was nothing in that bag but "two quarts of the finest old silk-velvet Bourbon . . . you ever wet your lips with." We have been trifled with. We no longer think of the piece as an exquisite tale of the old South. The author has prostituted his art: he has been watching his reader all the time and grinning in his sleeve at the thought of what he is going to do with him. Deliberately has he fabricated the whole story for no other purpose than to serve as an ambush for this single moment of vulgar surprise. One begins the next piece, however fine its opening, with watchful caution. We have been trifled with. This is not a maker of literature: it is a little devil with a bean-shooter luring you into range of his infernal machine.

III

Vaudeville is seldom literature; why go on with the man; why analyze with seriousness mere vaudeville? Because O. Henry was a mirror held up to the period: it was the age of O. Henry. To neglect him in a history of the literature of the twentieth century would be like omitting the dime novel from a comprehensive literary history of the eighteen fifties and sixties. To know O. Henry is to know the age that considered him a classic. Let us analyze, therefore, this amazing pepper-pot and isolate the components.

First of all, there is humor. If we are to label the man, the general label must be Humorist. He is the twentieth-century successor of John Phoenix and Artemus Ward. To consider him long from any other point of view is to be confronted with a *non sequitur*. He had been trained as Phoenix had been trained, as Mark Twain and Artemus Ward and Bill Nye had been trained and all the other comedians. To produce American humor there must be schooling on the frontier, in some remote area of America where individualism is religion and where men are living under primitive conditions in the rush and excitement of moving enterprise. Before he was twenty-one O. Henry had observed for some months, never however as an active participator, the rough life of a sheep-ranch in the wilds of the Southwest, and he had learned, among other things, how the primitive man laughs—and at what. Then for twelve years he had lived in Texas cities—Austin, Houston —surrounded by men who had seen the early lawless days' of the State. Western breeziness there was in these little cities, boundless spirits, hilarious optimism, and sentiment in abundance, even sentimentality, a frontier element. To the Southern youth, by nature as sensitive to the incongruous as even Artemus Ward, it was school and college.

Humor was a birthright of the lad. Incongruity as with Mark Twain sat upon him like a garment. To look at him, to be with him only for a moment, was to laugh. He was a mimic, a caricaturist, a punster, a practical joker: always he moved in a gale of laughter. He was a professional humorist for years before the kindly tragedy that precipitated him into fame. As early as 1887 he was contributing a regular budget of jokes to the "Burlington Free Press" and by 1895 he was editor and proprietor of a humorous journal of his own, "The Rolling Stone"—"out for the moss." It was a year before it ceased to roll, and then, as a variant to his work as bank teller, he conducted a "column" in the Houston "Daily Post" under the heading "Tales of the Town." And there he might have remained the rest of his life, pouring his newspaper column into the bottomless pit of a Texan daily, had not the kindly hand of what at first seemed annihilating disaster rescued him for fame. At thirty-five then O. Henry was a professional "columnist" of the frontier type.

It was this element of humor that gave the man his first readers. He was classed from the first as humorist. When in 1903 "Harper's Magazine" accepted his genre story "The Whirligig of Time," they printed it in "The Editor's Drawer." It is American humor: it is as autochthonous as Mark Twain. Through and through is it shot with Americanism. To translate it into another language would be impossible. What would a German savant make of a sentence like this:

The common people walked around in barefoot bunches, puffing stogies that a Pittsburgh millionaire wouldn't have chewed for a dry smoke on Ladies' Day at his club.

His allusions are lost on all but ingrained Americans. Even our own younger generation is begining to require footnotes:

They became inebriated with attention, like an Atlanta Colonel listening to "Marching Through Georgia."
He first saw the light of day in New York at three years of age. He was born in Pittsburgh, but his parents moved east the third summer afterwards.

Original as he was, however, he added few devices to those already associated with distinctively American humor. He used exaggeration as outrageously as did Phoenix or Mark Twain. No one, indeed, has ever pressed the device to deeper abysses of absurdity. After a political gathering many cigar "stubs" undoubtedly are to be found scattered in the vicinity, but when O. Henry tells the story the cigar "stubs" are knee-deep for a quarter of a mile about. A man has chills and fever: "He hadn't smiled in eight years. His face was three feet long, and it never moved except to take in quinine." In the originality and unexpectedness of his exaggerations he has never been equaled. His comparisons are unique. One may open his volume at random and find specimens:

She had hair the color of a twenty-dollar gold certificate, blue eyes, and a system of beauty that would make the girl on the cover of a July magazine look like the cook on a Monongahela coal barge.
Her eyes were as big and startling as bunions.
He loosened up like a Marcel wave in the surf of Coney.
He had a voice like a coyote with bronchitis.

Again there is in his work the American fondness for epigram. He is as pregnant with quaint wisdom as a Josh Billings. His philosophy, however, is redolent completely of O. Henry and his period. This for instance concerning the muck-rake school:

A story with a moral appended is like the bill of a mosquito: it bores you, and then injects a stinging drop to irritate your conscience.

Pessimistic he seems, but never is he bitter:

A straw vote only shows which way the hot air blows.
What a woman wants is what you're out of.
There ain't a sorrow in the chorus that a lobster cannot heal.

Words are as wax in his hands. He works with precision. One feels the glow that only the perfect can give when one comes upon felicities like these:

She was as tidy as a cherry blossom.
At length he reached the flimsy, fluttering little soul of the shop-girl. Tremblingly, awfully her moth wings closed and she seemed about to settle on the flower of love.
Something mushy and heavily soft like raised dough leaned against Jim's leg and chewed his trousers with a yeasty growl. [This of a pug dog.]

No device for raising a laugh but he has used it to the utmost and for the most part with a zest that is primitive. He uses irreverence as startlingly as John Phoenix. Nothing to him is sacred. His most prominent mannerism, however, the one that runs like a falsetto motif through all of his work, is a variety of euphemism, the translating of simple words and phrases into resounding and inflated circumlocutions. John Phoenix invented the device but O. Henry gave it circulation. So completely did the trick take possession of him that one may denominate it almost as a *cliché*, the trademark of O. Henry. All of his characters make use of it as a dialect. Sometimes it is even funny. A waiter in a German restaurant is not a waiter but a "friendly devil in a cabbage-scented hell"; a tramp becomes a "knight on a restless tour of the cities"; a remark about the weather becomes "a pleasant reference to meteorological conditions." Mr. Brunelli does not fall in love with Katy: "Mr. Brunelli, being impressionable and a Latin, fell to conjugating the verb *amare* with Katy in the objective case." A reasonable amount of this is tolerable, perhaps, but the man wears the device threadbare. One feels at length that he is straining constantly for bizarre effects, for outrageous circumlocutions, for unheard-of methods for not calling a spade a spade. A plain statement like "the woman looked at him, hoping he would invite her to a champagne supper" becomes with O. Henry "she turned languishing eyes upon him as a hopeful source of lobsters and the delectable, ascendant globules of effervescence." It is too much.

And at this point lies O. Henry's failure as a humorist. Mark Twain was laughable even when he was not trying to be humorous. He was born with a drawl both in his voice and in his pen, humor with him was a spontaneous thing. So it was with Artemus Ward. But the humor of O. Henry seems to have been deliberately manufactured, the humor of a man who is ingenious and professionally funny like a "blacked up" endman. The artificiality of it is sometimes painfully obvious. One of his mannerisms, for instance, is the use of incongruous mixtures, in a series of three items, the third item a preposterous addition: "He was a mixture of Maltese kitten, sensitive plant, and a member of a stranded 'Two Orphans' company." Still another mannerism, overworked to the bounds of boredom for the reader, is his use of incongruous association: "She possessed two false teeth and a sympathetic heart," "They took me by surprise and my horse by the bridle."

O. Henry then is a humorist, a John Phoenix up to date, a wood-pulp comedian whose sketches should be illustrated by the creator of Mutt and Jeff.

IV

If his admirers would only accept him as a comedian, one of the Artemus Ward and Bill Nye school, one might agree even with their superlatives, but to label him "comedian" does not satisfy: he must be ranked with Poe and Hawthorne and Maupassant; he must be added to the great story-writers of the world; he must even be credited with inventing a new short-story genre. And the voices that demand this are voices not to be disregarded. What then of O. Henry as a writer of fiction?

A study of his short stories in the order in which they were written, the first twelve of them produced while in the Ohio prison, makes clear the fact that the transition from Sydney Porter, the Texan newspaper columnist, to O. Henry, the short-story writer, came through Bret Harte. His opening effort, "Whistling Dick's Christmas Stocking," would pass anywhere as a Harte creation. It is a story of sentiment, theatric rather than realistic, theatric indeed to the point of melodrama and falseness to life. Its central incident and its title character are both impossible. And the same criticism applies to "An Afternoon Miracle," "The Sphinx Apple," "Christmas by Injunction," and all the stories of the Southwest. They were molded by Harte just as Harte's tales were molded by Dickens. The West is used simply as scenery and setting to his stage; the characters are the conventional ones of Western melodrama, all of them redolent of the paint-box and appropriately bedecked from the costume-room. Like Harte, and his California "School," the writer had no enthusiasm for the West and no story burning within him that *must* be told. A few times the glow of insight and sympathy hovers over the fifteen studies he made of his native South—by all means the best part of his fiction—but rarely does one find it elsewhere.

The external manner of Harte he outgrew, but never

did he free himself from the less obvious faults that make the work of both men inferior when compared with those absolute standards that time has decreed a work of art must have if it is at all to endure. Neither of the men had a philosophy of life, and neither of them presented humanity as humanity actually is or as sane idealists dream that humanity should be. Neither of them told the truth. Both worked with fragments of life, anecdotes, striking incidents rather than with rounded wholes. Their catastrophes are coincidences, accidents, not like Maupassant's inevitable dooms, deliberate workings out of the ironies or the perversities of fate. Of the two Harte is the greater. His work is single; never is it mixed with buffoonery; and a few times in his long career he *did* succeed in creating an individual human soul rather than a marionette or a caricature.

In the second group of O. Henry's tales fall the South American sketches and "The Gentle Grafter" skits that fill up two entire volumes and overflow into most of the others. Despite much splendid description and here and there the display of marvelous skill in the reproduction of atmosphere and the spirit of the tropics, they are literature at its lowest levels. Without a doubt the character in "The Gentle Grafter" had prototypes. The stories may even be founded on actual incidents, yarns told their author by voluble convicts in the Ohio prison. All his materials for the tales of bank-breaking and highway robbery may have come from first-hand reports. Al Jennings's amazing book, "Through the Shadows with O. Henry," throws much light here; but nevertheless, the tales are false. They are not life: they are *opéra bouffe* with characters no more alive than are Punch and Judy. Examine the dialogue: it is on the face of it a manufactured argot unknown outside the comic theater and the Sunday supplement. Imagine a common Indiana hotel-keeper who has been asked casually concerning the ownership of a house replying in this lofty strain:

"That," says he, "is the domicile and the arboreal, terrestrial, and horticultural accessories of Farmer Ezra Plunkett."

Again, imagine an Irish farmer bidding a perfect stranger who has ridden up to his door on a mule to dismount in terms like these:

"Segregate yourself from your pseudo-equine quadruped."

The sheep-herder Paisley Fish and his companion talk always at this astounding level:

"I reckon you understand," says Paisley, "that I've made up my mind to accrue that widow woman as part and parcel in and to my hereditaments forever, both domestic, sociable, legal, and otherwise, until death do us part. The smiles of woman," goes on Paisley, "is the whirlpool of Squills and Charlybeates, into which vortex the good ship Friendship is often drawn and dismembered."

This is not an occasional pleasantry for humorous effect: it is the everyday speech of all the characters. They talk nothing else from the beginning to the end of "The Gentle Grafter" volume and the "Heart of the West" collection, and not one of the other volumes is free from it. It is a mannerism.

Art is truth, truth to facts, truth to actual human nature; and art is based upon the presumption, fundamental at least in civilized lands, that truth is superior to falsehood, that right is superior to wrong, and that actual crime is never to be condoned. Despite his freedom from salacious stain, O. Henry must be classed as an immoral writer: immoral not because he presented vulgarly picaresque material or because he recorded the success of villainy; immoral he is because he sympathized with his law-breakers and bandits, laughed at their crimes, and commended their philosophy of the underworld. It does not excuse Jeff Peters to explain that he fleeces only those who have fleece to spare, or those rich ones who really enjoy the fleecing because it affords them a new sensation.

V

The last period in O. Henry's life began in 1904 with his work for the New York "World." He had been in the city for two years and had supported himself by writing for the popular magazines. He had studied the demands of the time from the New York point of view. The city had laid hold of him, infected him, molded him into new patterns. Moreover, he had discovered Maupassant. His biographer records that during his later years he kept the work of the great *conte*-writer always within reach. His style began to change : more and more he used the surprise-ending trick, more and more he put on the Sunday supplement style, attuning his work to the level of the newspaper mass.

The newspaper—the word brings illumination. When asked his profession in the Ohio prison, he had replied "newspaper reporter." With the exception of a single story in "Harper's" and another in the "Century" all his work was first printed on wood-pulp stock. His "World" stories make up more than one third of his entire written product. What the paper really did was to engage him as reporter— a highly privileged reporter at large, told to roam the city and to bring in one entertaining "story" each week.

The requirements of the newspaper "story" are exacting. It must be vivid, up to date, and condensed, and it must have in it the modern quality of *go*. It is usually an improvisation by one who through long practice has gained the mastery of his pen ; and it must be made by one, moreover, who has been in living contact with that which he would portray. It is written in heat, excitedly, to be read in excitement and thrown away. There must be no waste material—no "lumber," no "blue-pencil stuff," and there must be, so far as possible, "punch," a constant bidding for attention.

The complaint has come that one does not remember the stories of O. Henry. Neither does one remember the newspaper "stories" one reads from morning to morning, brilliant though they may be. The difficulty comes from the fact that the writer is concerned solely with his reader. The dominating canon of his art is—Anything to catch the reader. He is catering to the blasé, he is mixing a condiment for palates gross with sensation. If a story is to be printed as fiction, wider latitude is allowable. Humor is the surest bait for Americans, but it must be American humor, grossly strong, stingingly piquant, sensationally new. The soul of the Sunday supplement is the unexpected; its style is an exploitation of the startling—New York City, electric advertising, radios, Coney Island, jazz bands, Boob McNutt, Bringing up Father, the "movies," the "talkies," O. Henry.

On the mechanical side of the short story O. Henry has rare skill. He possessed the rare power of gripping his reader's attention and holding it to the end. He worked with *finesse:* he could turn every element of the seemingly careless narrative to a single surprising focus. It is this architectonic quality of his work that has endeared him to the makers of short-story handbooks and correspondence courses. His technique is peculiar. He began always at the end of his stories and worked back to the beginning. With him it was primarily an intellectual problem. A typical O. Henry tale begins with seemingly random remarks of a facetiously philosophical nature illustrated at length with an example apparently improvised. The example widens into a rather interesting situation. The reader unconsciously begins to speculate as to the solution of the problem that is fast becoming complicated. He sees clearly at length how it is to be ended, and is about to turn the page to the next story, when suddenly an unlooked-for turn, an ending totally different from anything expected, comes like a jet of water in the face. Note the mechanism of such tales as "Girl," "The Pendulum," "The Marry Month of May," and the like. The whole narrative is built up solely to bring the final sentence startlingly into focus.

Intellectually brilliant as all this may be, however, one must not forget that it concerns only the externals of short-story art. His failures were at vital points. A short story must have characterization, portrayed individuals—and O. Henry deals in caricature, with types. And we seldom see even his types: we see only the externals of costumes and masks and exaggerated physical peculiarity. Try to visualize a creation like this: "She was looking like a bulbul, a gazelle, and a tea rose, and her eyes were as soft and bright as two quarts of milk skimmed off the milky way" —original, but vaudeville.

He writes much of the New York shop-girls but never convincingly. They are literary materials. One never sees in his stories *a* shop-girl: always it is *the* shop-girl described in generalities, a mere marionette, carefully costumed.

VI

His influence upon the short story during the decade since his death has been remarkable. More than any one else he helped to turn the tide of short fiction in the direction of manner. The ghost of O. Henry even now flits hoveringly over the magazines. Examine any file of the "Saturday Evening Post" during the early years of Sherwood Anderson, Irvin Cobb, Edna Ferber, and dozens of others. The trail of the man over later fiction has been broad.

His clientele has been most loyal to his memory. The Society of Arts and Sciences at a dinner given in April, 1918, in honor of "the genius of William Sydney Porter," voted to award $250 as a prize yearly for the best short story published during the twelve months. Moreover, the best of the stories of each year were to be issued as an annual with the general title of the O. Henry Memorial Award volumes. Edited by Blanche Colton Williams, the series, beginning in 1919, has continued to the present. Instead of characterizing the general content of the average of these volumes, let me quote a review of one of them by Vera Gorden:

On the whole it is manner and not matter, treatment and not theme that counts. Realistic handling and semi-slangy, pseudo-epigrammatic style will excuse any theme, however slight. . . . There is everything in this remarkable book: slap-stick farce, sob stuff, melodrama, coincidence, and *Grand Guignol* horrors. There are also three or four good stories. The collection has only one thing in common—good craftsmanship.

It is a fair summary of all the collections; it characterizes with insight the legacy left to the American short story by William Sydney Porter.

VII

He admitted his failure. In the last weeks of his life, the power of wizard expression gone forever, the physique which he had so fearfully abused sinking into collapse when it should have borne him through thirty years more of creative work, came his pathetic cry: "I want to get at something bigger. What I have done is child's play to what I can do, what I know it is in me to do." And again, in connection with "The Dream," that last story of his, a creation never finished: "I want to show the public I can write something new—new for me, I mean—a story without slang, a straightforward dramatic plot treated in a way that will come nearer my ideal of real story-writing." He was planning a novel, "the story of a man—an individual, not a type," as he expressed it, but it was too late. What he had written he had written.

We may explain O. Henry best perhaps in the terms of his own story "The Lost Blend" : a flask of Western humor —John Phoenix, Artemus Ward; a full measure of Bret Harte—sentiment, theatricality, melodrama; a drop or two of Maupassant—constructive art, brilliancy of diction, *finesse;* a dash of journalistic smartness and of after-dinner wit; a generous pouring of slap-stick farce and end-man jugglery; and then—insipid indeed all the blend without this saving addition—a bottle of the Apollinaris of the man's own peculiar genius, and lo! the astonishing blend that intoxicated a generation—"elixir of battle, money, and high life"—O. Henry.

BIBLIOGRAPHICAL REFERENCES

O. HENRY (WILLIAM SYDNEY PORTER) 1862–1910

"Cabbages and Kings," 1904; "The Heart of the West," 1907; "The Gentle Grafter," 1908; "The Voice of the City," 1908; "The Four Million," 1906; "Roads of Destiny," 1909; "Options," 1909; "Whirligigs," 1910; "The Trimmed Lamp," 1907; "Strictly Business," 1910; "Let Me Feel Your Pulse," 1910; "Sixes and Sevens," 1911; "The Gift of the Wise Men," 1911; "Works," 12 vols., 1911; "Rolling Stones," 1912; "O. Henry Biography," C. Alphonso Smith, 1916.

"Selected Stories from O. Henry," edited by C. Alphonso Smith, 1922.
"The Complete Works of O. Henry," in one volume, 1396 pages, 1926.
"The Emperor of Bagdad; the Life, Letters, and Works of O. Henry," Robert H. Davis and Arthur B. Maurice, 1930.

CHAPTER XII

THEODORE DREISER

I

To follow the advancing tide of realism as it left the boundaries set by Howells and Frank Norris and Stephen Crane, and, with the new century in its 'teens, submerged all landmarks, is to come ultimately upon the Caliban figure of Theodore Dreiser, just as in our poetry we come at length to the colossal stumbling-block Walt Whitman. With no thought of founding a cult, or of organizing a rebellion, he became the central figure in what is now recognized as a "school of fiction," the synonym in the popular mind of that literary something called "extreme realism" or "naturalism."

The man's novels of disillusion and gloom undoubtedly were bound to come from some pen or other. The time was ripe. The American period of adolescence had reached the doubt-everything stage in its evolution, and the expression of it in fiction was inevitable. From earliest times the attitude of America toward all things had been optimistic. Romanticism is the spirit of youth, and the atmosphere of the frontier, the dreamings of immigrants, the coming into new lands of vast numbers of the most adventurous and idealistic souls of their generation, the opening of the unimagined richness of the new West, all this had fostered to the extreme the romantic spirit. Thinness of population played its part; provincialism is ever to romanticism a nursing mother. In lonely farmhouses where books are the only human contacts, in

Gopher Prairies where life and beauty seem located somewhere beyond the narrowing horizon, it creates a world
of its own.

Disillusion came first to the East, to the growing cities
which as the nineteenth century drew to its close had increased to surprising masses of population, to the pinched
by financial panics, to the victims of growing industrialism. There was perforce a facing of material facts of a
new order, the growing domination of the machine, the
concrete reality for the first time keenly felt of crowded
urban areas. But the West still overflowed with the spirit
of youth, and daily it was crowding into the overpopu-
lated East where—as they dreamed—lived opportunity,
culture, romance. There had been the young Mark Twain
in the squalid river-town watching the daily steamboat
as it disappeared down the river into the vast "world";
there had been the young Howells in the crossroads printing office dreaming of Boston and the "Atlantic
Monthly"; and there was now the young Lochinvar
group of the opening new century—Garland, Ade, Tarkington, Phillips, Masters, Sandburg, Anderson, Lewis,
Cather, Gale, Dreiser, and the rest, all of them utter
romantics. And with their contact with the East, with
the new urbanism, with all the conditions of the new rising industrial age, their optimism, their romanticism was
utterly to vanish. The first thirty years of the century
may be denominated The Age of Growing Disillusion.

To understand the forces that worked the transforma-
tion, to realize the elements in the evolution, one can do
no better than to study the life of Theodore Dreiser in
his own record of it to be found in the three or four volumes of his autobiography, volumes which throw most
illuminating flashlights into the heart of the America of
the new century. For the young Dreiser had gone to seek
his fortune in Chicago a youth of dreams and idealism all
compact. Honestly he had believed that the world was
good, that it was fundamentally kind, that the meek in-

herited the earth, and that God's in his Heaven: all's right with the world.

As a boy in the small towns of the middle West I had no slightest opportunity to get a correct or even partially correct estimate of what might be called the mental A B abs of life. I knew nothing of history, and there was not a book in any of the schools which I attended, labeled either history or science or art, containing the least suggestion of the rationale which I subsequently came to feel to be relatively true, or at least acceptable to me.[1]

After disheartening preliminaries he had found his desire, a job as reporter on a great daily newspaper, first in Chicago, then in St. Louis, and in Pittsburgh and New York, a four years' course in disillusion, a four years' apprenticeship as inspector and recorder of the human garbage of a city's day. The romanticist sickened in Chicago and St. Louis, and finally died in New York City. Read "A Book About Myself" which tells with minute details the story of the four years. The idealist died and was buried. In after years, after a visit to his fiancée on a Missouri farm, he could write a passage like this:

To me it seemed that all the spirit of rural America, its idealism, its dreams, the passion of a Brown, the courage and patience and sadness of a Lincoln, the dreams and courage of a Lee or a Jackson were all here. The very soil smacked of American idealism and faith, a fixedness in sentimental and purely imaginative American tradition in which I, alas, could not share—I had seen Pittsburgh.

He was in the grip of a new age: everywhere a revision of valuations. The industrial revolution was changing the whole spirit of American life. The natural wealth of the nation, increased beyond all calculation by new industrial processes, was being poured out in floods and for the

[1] "Hey Rub-a-Dub-Dub," Theodore Dreiser, 1920. Read Chapter 19 entire.

most part was being absorbed by the competent few. Materialism was in the saddle. It was the age not of science in the abstract, but of "applied science," pragmatism—will it work? The demand was for the concrete thing: in literature "realism"—no more romanticizing, God's Truth: life as it is actually lived in the here and now.

II

The man Dreiser illustrates a new element in the American literary problem, the infusion of new blood that came with the tide of European immigration following the fifties of the nineteenth century. His parents were immigrants from central Europe, utter bourgeoisie: in them no trace of Briticism, no conception of Puritan ideals. The youth, number twelve in a brood of thirteen, was reared with English not the mother-tongue, in a home pinched by poverty and strenuous in the steady demand for toil. Absence of Puritanism, however, implied no lack of religious training: there was an overflow of it even to abnormality. Of his father Dreiser has written:

I never knew a narrower, more hidebound religionist, nor one more tender and loving in this narrow way. He was a crank, a tenth-rate Saint Simon or Francis of Assisi, and yet a charming person if it had been possible to get his mind off the subject of religion for more than three seconds at a time. He worked, ate, prayed, slept and dreamed religion. With no other thought than the sanctity and glory and joy of the Catholic Church, he was constantly attempting to drive a decidedly recalcitrant family into a similar point of view.

But it was the mother whose impress sank deepest into the boy's young life, "a pagan mother taken over into the Catholic Church at marriage, because she loved a Catholic and would follow her love anywhere. A great poet mother, because she loved fables and fairies and half believed in them, and once saw the Virgin Mary standing in our garden, and was sure it was she. . . . An open, un-educated, wondering, dreamy mind."

The father disappeared early from the story, but not the mother. Despite poverty and severest toil the children were cared for and sent to school. Dreiser was even able to work his way into the local university, but not for long. No awakening here. The opening paragraph of "A Book About Myself" records the real beginnings of his literary life:

During the year 1890 I had been formulating my first dim notion as to what it was I wanted to do in life. For two years and more I had been reading Eugene Field's *Sharps and Flats,* a column he wrote daily for the Chicago *Daily News,* and through this, the various phases of life which he suggested in a humorous though at times romantic way, I was beginning to suspect, vaguely at first, that I wanted to write, possibly something like that. Nothing else that I had so far read—novels, plays, poems, histories—gave me quite the same feeling for constructive thought as did the matter of his daily notes, poems, and aphorisms, which were of Chicago principally, whereas nearly all the others dealt with foreign scenes and people.

As a result he moved to Chicago and after long waiting found a job on one of the papers. The grilling, pitiless machine took the lad as rawest of raw material and in four different cities ground him to its remorseless patterns. He blundered and lost jobs, he walked blindly into "scoops," he lived in close intimacy with the trained men of the force—youngsters with literary ambitions, men who had written novels and talked Balzac, "ancients" who had seen everything and sneered at everything. And pitilessly, constantly, was it driven in to him that he must learn to write. Listen to the lecture by the experienced old editor Wandell:

"A good story, is it?" I can see him smirking and rubbing his hands miser or gourmet fashion, as over a pot of gold or a fine dish. "She said that, did she? Ha! ha! That's excellent, excellent! You saw him yourself, did you? And the brother, too? By George, we'll make a story of that! Be careful how you write that now. All the facts you know, just as far as they will carry you; but we don't want any libel suits, remember. We don't want you to say anything we can't substantiate, but I don't want you to be afraid either. Write it strong, clear, definite. Get in all the touches of local color you can. And remember Zola and Balzac, my boy, remember Zola and Balzac. Bare facts are what are needed in cases like this, with lots of color as to the scenery or atmosphere, the room, the other people, the street, and all that. You get me?"

In Pittsburgh he was able to sample in the public library the Balzac and the Zola, up to then mere names, and they stirred him to the depths, especially the Balzac. He read all he could find of "The Human Comedy," often a book at a sitting. And vague, chaotic longings began to shake him. He too would be a novelist and do for an American city what Balzac had done for Paris, "for the romance of my own youth was still upon me, my ambitions and my dreams coloring it all." And he moved on to New York, the center of all literary dreamings, and flung himself into the maelstrom of the city press. As reporter on the "Sun" his disillusion became total. He could endure no more, and he left it. That was in 1895. Then came a period of hack editorships of minor magazines, work in the major magazine offices, and then for some years the editorship of the "Delineator" and its associated journals. And now with all the patience of his peasant soul he sought to make of himself a novelist. Through the ten years of the nineties that shaped him, he read omnivorously—Kipling, Hall Caine ("a novelist of the quack order," he calls him), Mrs. Humphry Ward, Howells, Warner, Cable, Page, and the rest. "I read, and read, but all I could gather was that I had no such tales to tell, and, however much I tried, I could not think of any."

You could not write about life as it was; you had to write about it as somebody else thought it was, the ministers and farmers and dullards of the home. Yet here I was busy in a profession that was hourly revealing the fact that this sweetness-and-light code, this idea of a perfect world which contained neither sin nor shame for any save vile outcasts, criminals and vagrants, was the trashiest lie that was ever foisted upon an all too human world. Not a day, not an hour, but the pages of the very newspaper we were helping to fill with our scribbled observations were full of the most incisive pictures of the lack of virtue, honesty, kindness, even average human intelligence, not on the part of the few but of nearly everybody.

No use to write a novel of life as he knew life to be: "The publishers wouldn't stand for it." Young Jack London was making the same complaint: whenever he had told the plain facts about life as he had lived it, his manuscripts, he declared, had come back marked "too strong." Garland's innocuous "Rose of Dutcher's Coolly" was being ruled from the libraries even of Chicago; Hardy's "Jude the Obscure" was being reviewed under the title "A Novel of Lubricity": "The naturalistic school of France regards life from the point of view of a theory in which morals in the Anglo-Saxon sense of the word have no place whatever . . . 'Jude the Obscure' is a moral monstrosity and an outrage on art . . . the studied satyriasis of approaching senility." That was in 1896. In England Sir Theodore Martin was damning with scarlet ink the whole "new literature of the Boulevards . . . the school of a debasing animalism, thinly veneered with specious sentimentalism."

But young Dreiser was not Anglo-Saxon; there was in him not a shred of Puritanism; nothing was farther from his mind than the leading of a revolt. He was honestly perplexed. By and by he wrote his novel in the only way he could write it—wrote it as his old editor had told him to write a news story. He called it "Sister Carrie" and sent it on its forlorn journey through the publishing houses, and by rare good fortune it came to the Double-days and their manuscript-reader the young Frank Norris. His superlatives swept the firm for a moment off their feet and they accepted the thing and put it into type. And well might the young reader commend the book: it was a bog-fire of his own setting, companion volume to "McTeague" and Crane's "Maggie," though in Balzac-like comprehensiveness and honesty of presentation it was worth a whole shelf-full of these immaturities. But the time was not ready in America for Gallic frankness. The publishers regained their senses and sent copies as "feelers" to selected critics. So unanimous was the report of these specialists in the condition of the public pulse that they withdrew at once the entire edition from circulation. They were right: a publisher is in business to watch the market and sell books. But this also can be added: Norris too was right. The result was the first battle in the war against Dreiser.

It was eleven years before the next novel appeared, "Jennie Gerhardt," a more mature and more epical treatment of the same theme as that in "Sister Carrie." Again the guns opened fire; all excellences and all defects in the novel were lost sight of in the hot discussion of its treatment of sex. He worked steadily on, however, refusing to be moved from his foundations or to be hurried. Like Norris and Phillips he began upon a trilogy, a series which was to picture the conditions resulting from the new era of industrialism. Two of them he finished, "The Financier" and "The Titan," each of them a portrait from the life of a nationally known traction magnate of Philadelphia and Chicago. Then in 1915 came "The Genius," which was so frank in its sex-picturings that it was suppressed for a year. The battle now began in earnest: the heavy artillery awoke. First, there was Stuart P.

Sherman's volley, which instantly was countered by H. L. Mencken's,[2] though the technique and the artistry of the book violated all his literary ideals. Lesser guns began to crackle along the literary front. Again nothing was settled save the fact that Dreiser had become during the conflict enormously a best seller. It was ten years before the next novel (and the next battle)—"An American Tragedy."

In the meantime he had poured out a copious mass of autobiography and self-explanation: "A Traveller at Forty," "A Hoosier Holiday," and "A Book About Myself." With tremendous seriousness have the younger group taken themselves: autobiography at forty—one hundred and twenty thousand words in a single volume covering but four years of life. Four volumes also there were of short stories and sketches: "Twelve Men," "Free," "Chains," "A Gallery of Women." He had resigned his editorships and was devoting himself entirely to literature. The product was voluminous.

III

To weigh the man as a force in the period one must begin with his six novels; the rest of his output is but chips and explanations and excursions. All of them are analyses of failure, all of them are picturings of the darker and more sodden areas of life. To Dreiser environment is the dominant molding force—mere physical contacts. Of the forces of the unseen he tells us nothing. He will show us only "the disintegration of a character under the pressure of environment," and always in its material forms. So careful is he in his presentation of evidence that he begins his story with a study of the earliest environments of his subjects, even of childhood. To

2 "The Barbaric Naturalism of Theodore Dreiser," in "On Contemporary Literature," Stuart P. Sherman, 1917.
"Theodore Dreiser" in "A Book of Prefaces," H. L. Mencken, 1917.

turn this method upon Dreiser himself with the abundance of information he has presented is to understand his novels.

First of all, one finds a childhood sordid, savagely repressed, dominated by a growing inferiority complex from which he never entirely escaped. Note his own diagnosis:

> I was a weakling of the worst kind. Nearly everybody could do these things, and nearly all of the youths were far more proficient in all the niceties of life than was I: manners, dancing, knowledge of dress and occasions. Hence I was a fool. The dullest athlete of the least proficiency could overcome me; the most minute society man, if socially correct, was infinitely my superior. Hence what had I to hope for? And when it came to wealth and opportunity, how poor I seemed!

It accounts for his literary gaucherie, his clumsiness with words and sentences. The awkward lad learning penmanship bears on too hard, uses too much ink, smears his page. The "writing game" he never fully learned. No novelist of modern times has climbed to fame over such an amazing mass of redundancy, elephantine sentences, left-handedness of expression, pleonasm, even solecisms sophomoric, as has Dreiser. Everything too much. To tell the story of a youth who got a girl into trouble and then murdered her, he uses four hundred thousand words, two volumes each the size of a Waverley novel.

The environment of his newspaper training was the next dominating force. Never a brilliant reporter, he was gradually hammered into mannerisms that became to him clichés. A newspaper "story" is facts, facts without embroidery or implication, facts without humor or comment. The writing of novels, therefore, was to him but the continuation of his reporter's methods. All of them smell of newspaper rooms. Wanting facts for his novel "The Financier," he hunted for weeks through the files of the Chicago papers. Always must he face the concrete thing. For his collection "Twelve Men" he took as models twelve men whom he knew. "An American Tragedy" was suggested by an actual case reported by the press. Such a "story" in the newspaper drags day after day, sometimes week after week. There is no plan for the ending—always it ends with a sprawl. Though Michaud in the most brilliant study yet made of the man [3] classifies his "great social novels 'The Financier' and 'The Genius'" as "dramatized pieces of muck-raking," I find little evidence of purpose on the part of the author other than the newspaper one of record. The novels are good reporting. Their object primarily is not to preach or condemn, but to hold the mirror up to the facts of a day. A poorly ground mirror it may be, one held up, it may be, to selected areas, yet the intent of the holder has been an honest one. He is not a showman like Lewis nor a man with a panacea like Sinclair: he is a newspaper man.

And within certain limits he has done remarkable work. He can handle a canvas as broad as Balzac's. No other novelist during the period, English or American, has been able to marshal facts and groupings of characters with more skill. If one can read straight through one of his colossal reportings there will emerge a situation and characters that burn themselves into one's memory. Moreover, there remains for days an atmosphere one cannot clear one's self from, like the odor from a morgue. It is good reporting.

It is too early to attempt definitive judgments or to make predictions as to the future of the man's work. The strange Caliban personality of the novelist, like Whitman's in our poetry; his daring; his static leadership in a campaign that perhaps gave him more prominence than he deserved; his continued triumph in spite of clumsy technique and inferior materials, complicate the problem. This, however, may be said with certainty: the weaknesses of the man's work are at fundamental points.

[3] "The American Novel To-Day," Régis Michaud, 1928.

His point of view is strabismic. Externally a realist, he is congenitally a romantic. One feels it in all his work. Naturalism is to him an artificiality, a forced thing. He is ironic, one feels, yet wistful. The revolt from his father's theologic standards, we believe, went to extremes fully as radical on the other side. His reaction from Howells also led him to extremes. He lacks poise, he lacks balance; but greatest of all his failings, he lacks conviction, and without conviction there can be no greatness, no permanence in art. "I am," he says, "one of those curious persons who cannot make up their minds about anything."

I accept now no creeds. I do not know what truth is, what beauty is, what love is, what hope is. I do not believe any one absolutely, and I do not doubt any one absolutely. I think people are both evil and well intentioned.

Life he views with bewildered helplessness, or, as expressed by Van Doren, with "the true peasant simplicity of outlook—the peasant's confusion in the face of complexity." [4] We demand leadership of our literary men, positiveness, clearness of vision, a point of view. "The trouble with most realism," said Sarah Orne Jewett, "is that it isn't seen from any point of view at all, and so its shadows fall in every direction and it fails of being art." Perfectly does this describe the work, for the most part, of Theodore Dreiser. In a review of his latest book, "A Gallery of Women," Thayer Hobson has this illuminating passage:

Portrayer of fact. Dreiser is absorbed in fact, and dominates the reader with fact. He filters life and character drop by drop, and then describes with deadly authenticity. He leaves nothing more to say, nothing else to say. He is, above all, the great portrayer of fact. Search in vain through these two volumes for any imaginative flight, beyond an occasional expression of beauty, for any abstract reflection or groping among the

[4] "Contemporary American Novelists," Carl Van Doren, 1922.

mysteries of life. The most you will find is a conjecture, tentative, almost apologetic.

One may follow this with a quotation from Emerson, who in a moment of self-depreciation wrote this to Carlyle: "I do not belong to the poets, but only to a low department of literature, the reporters, suburban men." Dreiser has been a reporter of mere fact, a photographer rather than a painter, and Emerson's estimate holds. A few times he has forgotten his disillusion, his tremendous pose of seriousness, his dismal journalizings, and has been joyously spontaneous. In a book like "A Hoosier Holiday," in some of the parts of "Hey, Rub-a-Dub-Dub," and in his "Twelve Men" sketches he has revealed what might have been his contribution to art had his environment not cramped him to its will. His autobiographies too are full of valuable material: picturings that undoubtedly are to have value in process of time as first-hand documents for those who would study our period.

BIBLIOGRAPHICAL REFERENCES

"The Barbaric Naturalism of Theodore Dreiser" in "On Contemporary Literature," Stuart P. Sherman, 1917.

"Theodore Dreiser," in "A Book of Prefaces," H. L. Mencken, 1917.

"Portraits, Real and Imaginary," Ernest Boyd, 1924.

"Theodore Dreiser" (Modern American Writers Series), Burton Rascoe, 1925.

"The Frontier in American Literature," Lucy L. Hazard, 1927.

"Theodore Dreiser," in "Spokesmen: Modern Writers and American Life," T. K. Whipple, 1928.

"The American Novel To-Day, A Social and Psychological Study," Régis Michaud, 1928.

"Theodore Dreiser," Milton Waldman, in "Contemporary American Authors," J. C. Squire and associated critics of "The London Mercury," 1928.

THEODORE DREISER, 1871–

"Sister Carrie," 1900; "Jennie Gerhardt," 1911; "The Financier," 1912; "A Traveller at Forty," 1913; "The Titan," 1914; "The Genius," 1915; "A Hoosier Holiday," 1916; "Plays of the Natural and Supernatural," 1916; "Free, and Other Stories," 1918; "The Hand of the Potter," 1918; "Twelve Men," 1919; "Hey, Rub-a-Dub-Dub," 1920; "A Book about Myself," 1922; "The Color of a Great City," 1923; "An American Tragedy," 1925; "Moods" (verses), 1926; "Chains," 1927; "Dreiser Looks at Russia," 1928; "A Gallery of Women," 1930.

CHAPTER XIII

THE TRANSITION POETS

THE twenty years following 1890 produced little of distinctive verse. Near the end of the eighties, Edmund Clarence Stedman in an article on "The Twilight of the American Poets" had announced that the silence was the moment of hush before the matin song of a new chorus, but the twilight proved to be of the evening rather than the morning. The singers he prophesied did not come. More and more the age was voicing itself in prose and in newspaper forms.

Was prose after all not the literary medium of a machine age? "Is it possible," asked the young Richard Hovey, "to write poetry with a stylographic pen? Is the steam-engine radically inconsistent with the epic?" There were those who argued that poetry was an outgrown thing; that an age of science had opened and that science is the antonym of poetry. Advancing science meant advancing realism, and what had realism to do with poetry? Woodrow Wilson, then a professor at Princeton, upheld the negative of the debate, maintaining with logical analysis that science and "mere literature" belong to different worlds. "Literature in its essence is mere spirit, and you must experience it rather than analyze it." [1] But the debate created no poets.

In Europe, too, poetry had seemingly gone upon the rocks. A school of young French decadents all through the eighties were playing ducks and drakes, so it seemed, with the old conceptions of poetic art, and the young

[1] "Mere Literature and Other Essays," Woodrow Wilson, 1896.

English decadents of the "Yellow Book" were now following them. In 1895 an article in the New York "Bookman" by Adolph Cohn essayed a diagnosis of the French epidemic with its rash of "French forms"—of symbolism, of decadent yellowness generally—declaring that France was now full of young rebels, that the bookstands were covered with strange poetic *feuilletons,* "Le Chat Noir," "Le Décadent," "La Plume," "Le Scapin," and the like. But, he added, "in addition to their revolt against the trammels of the old versification what was these young men's message? Alas! few were those who could understand their lines."

Revolt against the trammels—this became a war-cry for the young men of America, especially for those still in their college classes. Young Richard Hovey at Dartmouth poured out a flood of villanelles and rondeaux. America, as we have seen, was showered with decadent little pamphlet periodicals stuffed with versicles—the "Chap Book," the "Lark," the "Purple Cow." The laureate of the decade was Masters's "Petit, the Poet," embalmed forever in "The Spoon River Anthology":

> Triolets, villanelles, rondels, rondeaus,
> Seeds in a dry pod, tick, tick, tick,
> Tick, tick, tick, what little iambics,
> While Homer and Whitman roared in the pines!

The poets of the older school were adding nothing of note. Harte, vocal in the seventies, dropped out in 1902; Hay, long silent as a poet, in 1905; Aldrich in 1907; Joaquin Miller in 1913; and Riley in 1916. Many young voices that had been thought promising were breaking into falsetto. Madison Cawein, discovered by Howells, and loudly trumpeted by him as a Nature poet of coming powers, faded out in mere voluminousness. The leading magazines made little of poetry. Braithwaite in 1904 prefaced his annual summary of the year's poetry for the Boston "Transcript" with the statement that, so far as poetry was concerned, he considered only six magazines worthy of notice —the "Atlantic," "Harper's," "Scribners's," the "Century," "Lippincott's," and "McClure's." Nine years later, in 1913, he had found only three more to add to his list, the "Forum," the "Smart Set," and the "Bellman." Even to these select few, it must be said, poetry was for the most part a supernumerary thing convenient for filling semi-blank pages at the close of articles or stories.

I

The most noteworthy poet of the period was one who, strangely enough, died four years before the period opened. Like Melville and Whitman, Emily Dickinson made a small impression on her own generation: her message, so far as she delivered one, was for the generation that followed. She was a New Englander, a "daughter of the campus," her father an official of Amherst College. Nearly all her life she lived in seclusion well-nigh complete, her one diversion, as revealed after her death, being the recording of her inner life, her whims, her conceits, her Puritanic philosophy touched at times with rebellion, in a series of compressed lyrics created, like Thoreau's journal, with no thought of publication—her day-book kept for herself and the gods. These poems were to be burned after her death; but through the influence of Thomas Wentworth Higginson, a life-long friend of the poet, they were at her decease kept from the flames and a few of them published in the "Independent." Encouraged by the reception of these samplings, in 1890 Higginson issued a small volume with a glowing introduction. The surprising fact that six editions were demanded in a few months brought out a second series in 1891 with an introduction by Mabel Loomis Todd, and a third, and seemingly final, gathering of fragments in 1896. This, however, was but the beginning of the Emily Dickinson chapter. Through the efforts of Martha Dickinson Bianchi, niece of the poet, there have come other editions, a biography, a collection of her letters, and in 1929 the publication of a volume of her lyrics newly discovered.

She wrote, it seems, no poetry at all before she was thirty. One will look, therefore, in vain through her verses for adolescent *sturm und drang*. A love affair when she was nearly thirty—apparently an *impasse*—tremendously affected her. One gets a glimpse in a confession like this, jotted down we know for no eyes but her own, and for years withheld from publication by her sister Lavinia:

> I got so I could hear his name
> Without—
> Tremendous gain!—
> That stop-sensation in my soul,
> And thunder in the room.
>
> I got so I could walk across
> That angle in the floor
> Where he turned—so—and I
> Turned—how—
> And all our sinews tore.
>
> I got so I could stir the box
> In which
> His letters grew,
> Without that forcing in my breath
> As staples driven through.

She retired, as we know, into a seclusion almost complete, mastering her passion with Puritanic rigor so thoroughly that, although her verses are her journal, one finds hardly a trace of it even in the final long-withheld portions. Everywhere in these little jottings there is a serene aloofness from the world of the physical, a shrinking from the vulgarity of the actual. To quote a figure from William Vaughn Moody, her verses are like forgotten potatoes in a cellar "that sprouted toward the crack of sunshine with a wan maiden grace not seen above." Completely was she in control, forcing always contemplation upon the generalities under which Higginson and all the later editors have classified her poetry: "Life," "Love," "Time and Eternity."

Judged by the Victorian standards under which the lyrics were written, there is in them everywhere scorn of conventional technique, a "revolt against the trammels" of fixed forms and canons. She was not consciously in rebellion. She was jotting down in verse form the introspection, the contemplation, the attempts at constructive thinking that came with each new day. Her ear was childlike in its demand for sharply emphasized rhythm, even at times for jingle, but rhyme was always secondary to thought. Rather than modify her original flash of poetic expression she would allow slovenly rhyming to a degree bordering upon the ludicrous. *Gown* she rhymes with *on* and *done, endure* with *door, loveliness* with *vase.* For the most part she deals with the abstract. Local color, contemporaneousness, realism, one seeks in vain in these virginal poems, Puritanic, cold for the most part as borealis gleamings on a winter night. Often they are Orphic utterances, compressed, Emersonian, mere fragments:

> A toad can die of light!
> Death is the common right
>   Of toads and men,—
> Of earl and midge
> The privilege.
>   Why swagger then?
> The gnat's supremacy
> Is large as thine.

Ever before her was the baffling mystery of life and death:

> Down Time's quaint stream
> Without an oar,

We are enforced to sail,
Our Port—a secret—
Our Perchance—a gale.
What Skipper would
Incur the risk,
What Buccaneer would ride,
Without a surety from the wind
Or schedule of the tide?

She was brought like a phonograph record into the period that needed a poet, and to a degree she influenced the new "school" of young innovators that came when the new century was thin-sickled in its first quarter, but she influenced them in nothing save a rebellion against law and order in versification. Her transcendental glimpsings, her Emersonian flashes, her uniqueness of imagination, her visionings, her Orphic obscurities sometimes packed with wisdom for the careful seeker, they did not, perhaps could not, see or feel. It was only her lofty carelessness with the materials of poetry, her seeming revolt against the trammels of the older forms, that made her for them an inspiration. Her final place among the poets is still open to question. The sensation occasioned by the discovery of her work has hardly yet subsided enough to allow cold analysis. Already is it seen that the enduring part of her poetry is embedded in much that is childish, much that must be dismissed as jingling nonsense.

II

The leading younger poet of the transition was William Vaughn Moody, born in Indiana in 1869. No other Western youth, not even the young Hamlin Garland, was ever more eager for the "culture" which, as he dreamed of it, lay in the East, in the Boston of Emerson and Longfellow and Lowell; and none ever was more handicapped by what in the older college argot was denominated *res angusta domi*. The death of his father, a river-boat captain, threw him at seventeen wholly upon his own resources, yet by teaching rural schools and by utilizing every moment he not only fitted himself for Harvard, but worked his way to a degree in the university in three years. Influenced profoundly by the Greek and Latin classics, he continued his studies abroad, in Germany, Switzerland, Italy, and Greece. On his return to America he accepted an instructorship in English at Harvard, and then in 1895, a similar position at the University of Chicago, where he remained until 1903, resigning to devote his time wholly to literature. He died in 1910 at the age of forty-one. This is the biography, in its externals, of William Vaughn Moody.

As a poet his work, like that of Lowell's musing organist, began "doubtfully and far away," a "bridge from dreamland." The Greek mythology first ruled his imagination, then Milton; he edited the poet's works for the Cambridge Edition. Early he conceived the idea of a trilogy of poetic dramas dealing with the ways of God, and gods, with man, and painstakingly he worked at it for years. In logical order the three dramas composing the trilogy are "The Fire-Bringers," "The Masque of Judgment," and "The Death of Eve," the last of which he left unfinished. It is a poet's dream, Hellenic, Hebraic and Puritanic by way of Milton, and touched often with recollections of Shelley—a poem for poets. Everywhere, in Moody's own words, "the vagueness of youth." His own explanation of it is as mystical and as medieval of atmosphere as the trilogy itself:

Of course I didn't intend my "strangely unpleasant" God to be taken seriously. To me the whole meaning and value of the poem lies in the humanistic attitude and character of Raphael, the philosophic outlook of Uriel, and the plea for passion as a means of salvation everywhere latent. The rest of it is only mythological machinery for symbolizing the opposed doctrine—that of the denial of life.

Hardly in key with the spirit of the coming new century, and yet he is quick to add to his explanation that—

. . . as Christianity (contrary of course to the wish and meaning of its founder) has historically linked itself with this doctrine, I included certain aspects of it in this mythological apparatus—always with a semi-satirical intention.

Everywhere this strange duality. A Janus figure he is in the period, looking dreamily back into the old poetic world and at times hopefully into the coming new century—a personality unsettled, neither one thing nor the other. In one of his letters he wrote: "I am an ancient and—as I thought—irreconcilable enemy of the Whitman verse-mode, but your handling of it goes far to prove me wrong and baptize me into the new dispensation."

Never, however, was he of the new dispensation so far as verse-modes were concerned. In his polishings and rejectings and tonal testings he was as fastidious a lapidary as Aldrich. A complete classicist, and yet when the Spanish War brought the Philippines as spoils, he could let himself go in unclassic rage. His "Ode in Time of Hesitation," and "On a Soldier Fallen in the Philippines" and "The Quarry," aimed at the attempted dismemberment of China, are no longer vague and dreamy idlings; they are alive with the thrill of a present crisis: they are of "the new dispensation."

The hesitant, dual nature of the man one finds in his attempts to blend the spirit of the East with that of the West. A Hoosier born, he found himself, like Howells, more at home in the East. His residence in Chicago he considered as exile. Again and again he condemned the place with superlatives—"Chicago is several kinds of hell"—and yet from the first he felt the strange new tonic of its atmosphere. In 1896 he could write:

As for Chicago, I find that it gives me days, or at least hours, of broad-gauge Whitmanesque enthusiasm, meagerly sprinkled over weeks of tedium. The tedium is not of the acid-bath sort, however. Genuinely, I feel mellower, deeper-lunged, more of a lover of life, than I have ever felt before.[2]

And again:

Cambridge and her elegiac air seems still lovely and of good report. But these chaps here, though very moderately elegiac and of dubious report, are splendidly American and contemporary; and I feel convinced that this is the place for young Americans who want to do something.

Not cold and classic was this vast newness:

I find that the West cries out with one voice for the feathers and furbelows of feeling that you Cambridge mode-makers consigned to the garret decades ago. They are a little bedraggled at times, but we wear them with an air! Rousseau would weep over us—Châteaubriand would call us brother. I wonder if Rousseau and Châteaubriand were as ridiculous after all as they seem from the serene middle of Harvard Square?

The West was reclaiming him. In 1901 he spent some weeks in the Rocky Mountains with Hamlin Garland, who imparted to him a bit of his own enthusiasm. In later excursions he explored Arizona alone, and the West over wide areas. The literary result was "The Great Divide," a prose drama which in 1906 had the great good fortune to be adequately staged. It was the sensation of its season: it was keyed to the general. Gilder, writing from New York, declared "it has taken the town with a vengeance." It was for its author a new start in a new direction. Always a transition figure, he stood now on the boundary line between the old and the new, on "the great divide" which is neither East nor West, and recorded the clash between two phases of American democracy, the headlong, buoyant, flamboyant, iconoclastic West dashing itself against the Puritanism, the rock-

[2] The quotations are from "Some Letters of William Vaughn Moody," edited by Daniel Gregory Mason, 1913.

bound New Englandism, the conscience, the orderliness, the culture, of the East. In "The Faith Healer," the drama that followed—less successful on the stage—he dipped over to the Californian side of the line and revealed again the heart of the West, its youthful daring even to extremes of Messiah-like leadership, its self-consciousness, its adolescent dreamings and yearnings. Had the poet now found himself at last? The question will never be answered. Suddenly came the end—death at forty-one, his trilogy incomplete, his one popular triumph written in prose, his poetic fame largely dependent on half a dozen lyrics, the most noteworthy the three lyrics of the Spanish War period, mere spontaneous cries forced out by circumstance.

His fame ultimately must rest upon this small anthology of selected lyrics. They have been highly praised. Said Marguerite Wilkinson, "In my opinion 'Pandora's Song' from 'The Fire Bringer' is the finest short lyric ever written by an American." Others have made a claim as extreme for "Gloucester Moors." Unquestionably for twenty years he was the leading American poet, the laureate of "the time of hesitation," the poet hesitant. The poet, a victim of an uncertain day, must always take secondary place, and be dismissed as one who, perhaps, in more confident days might have risen to the heights of song.

III

The second original voice in the period of hesitation was that of another Westerner, Richard Hovey, born in Illinois in 1864, but so early saturated with the East as to show in his work nothing of Westernism save in breeziness and rebellious demands for a freedom which at times lapsed into license. Educated in the Washington schools and later at Dartmouth College, he thought first of theology as a profession, but he was too headlong, too lyric, too vagabond of soul to settle as yet into the humdrum of conventional work. He was off to Europe, where he found Maeterlinck whom later he translated for American publication; then he was in New York City fighting for recognition as an actor, translator, dramatist, lecturer, poet. There he met the Canadian lyrist Bliss Carman, a congenial spirit, with whom he vagabonded in lyric brotherhood, and with whom he poured out as the fruit of their Bohemian *Jugendzeit* three series of "Songs from Vagabondia." Divinity studies still clinging in his memory, he lectured for Alcott in his Concord School of Philosophy, and just at the ending of his life he secured a lectureship on literature in Barnard College, New York City.

But poetry, at first an outpouring of excited lyrics haphazard along a vagabond trail—college fraternity odes with "stein song" refrains, Spanish War rouses, sonnets and ballades and villanelles, whole canto additions to "Don Juan" with the very soul of Byron—

> For Eleanor, the maiden's name was Eleanor,
> Had four and twenty different kinds of Hell in her—

But poetry must be of more serious stuff to be an enduring contribution. He began therefore a series of poetic dramas on the Arthur theme, a modernization of the message of the old legend, making of it a living thing for the day and period. It was to be a cycle complete in nine parts; but like Moody's trilogy, the whole was never to be: five of them he wrote, and then—he was dead, at the Byronic age of thirty-six, another thwarted poet in an era sadly needing poetic leadership.

Hovey's poetical "remains" may be considered under three classifications: his occasional poems, his Vagabondia lyrics, and his poetic dramas. In the first he was at his best. The song in his Psi Upsilon banquet ode entitled "Spring," as set to music by Bullard, is the best convivial lyric yet produced in America. It has in it the very soul of youth and of *fin de siècle* America.

For we're all frank-and-twenty
　　When the spring is in the air,
And we've faith and hope a-plenty,
　　And we've life and love to spare;
　　　And it's birds of a feather
　　　When we all get together,
With a stein on the table and a heart without a care.

The lyric "Unmanifest Destiny," acclaimed by many as the best poetic voicing of the spirit of the Spanish War, has in it a buoyant optimism that is primitively Western rather than Eastern of the new twentieth century:

　　　I do not know beneath what sky
　　　　Nor on what seas shall be thy fate;
　　　I only know it shall be high,
　　　　I only know it shall be great.

And there was his response when his college, Dartmouth, sought a lyric voicing of her soul for an "Alma Mater." His "Men of Dartmouth" is the best college song of its kind yet produced in America.

Concerning the rest of his poetic product one can be more sparing of superlatives. In his Vagabondia lyrics there is an affected rowdyish spirit, a Bohemianism hardly spontaneous. One feels that for the series Hovey furnished the hobo make-up and Carman the trippingly voiced lyricism. Marvelously brilliant are they in their technique, but their materials are worthless—paste diamonds.

And Hovey's poetic drama work, fine as are passages of it, one feels is on the whole a *tour de force*. It owes its inception undoubtedly to Lanier's volumes, the source of his first inspiration. The manner and the motif of much of the work suggest also Maeterlinck. It arrives nowhere, and whole acts in it mean little save that they are nimble exercises in poetic gymnastics. Hovey's conception of Guenevere is original, all his own, but to bring the Queen to the twentieth century accomplished nothing: again we must say, it is a *tour de force*.

One final piece of Hovey's work, however, is of different texture, his "Seaward," an elegy on the death of the elder poet Thomas William Parsons, first published in the "Independent." In the number containing it, the editor devoted to it nearly a page of editorial comment:

We admire in the poem a lofty conception, a large and free execution, a clear plan, and a firm execution. It is a poem of noble structure. There is about it not the mere mechanical excellence of academic verse-writers, but thought and power as well. It is not easy for us to foretell what may be in the future for a young man who can do such work as this. It is certainly one of the most memorable poems which have been published for many a day, and will, we think, be numbered among the great elegies of the language.

Time has modified this extreme verdict, but it has not disproved the fact that "Seaward" must be ranked with the great elegies in English. The poet who could do such work was indeed a loss when he dropped his pen just as he was beginning to settle into what must have been strong leadership.

IV

Moody and Hovey and Carman were college men who built their poetic world more from books than from the observed actualities of life. To the Oregon laureate, Edwin Markham, however, born in 1852, poetry was what it was to an earlier Oregon singer, Joaquin Miller: a thing of Byronic resonance, or reverberating periods, of turgidness of feeling. Markham was born and was reared to manhood on a frontier ranch, a life bare of art, primitive, unintellectual. Inspired somehow with the wish to create poems, he wrote an amazing amount of poetastic worthlessness, much of which he sent to the newspapers.

Then at forty-seven, when he saw for the first time a reproduction of Millet's painting "The Man with the Hoe," he burst out in genuine poetic passion, just as Miller had done once and once only in his lyric "Columbus." The poem—with the same title as the painting—was first published in the San Francisco "Examiner" on January 15, 1899, but soon it was scattered as widely and as excitedly as was Harte's slapstick ballad of the seventies, "The Heathen Chinee." Despite its grandiose diction it was, and is, a truly stirring lyric, a call to action, a Marseillaise in the new war of labor against industrial unfairness. Never again did its author reach anything like its lyric fire and expressiveness. His "Lincoln, the Man of the People" comes nearest to it in excellence, but it lacks the final touch of great poetry. The man, despite his voluminousness, must be rated as a single-poem poet. Once and once only at a vital moment he spoke the needed word in adequate tones: the rest must be forgotten.

V

Of a multitude of twittering little singers all through the two decades of this era of hesitation one need not speak. They helped not at all the progress of poetry during the period, and their conventional little songs are as dead and forgotten as are the poetical "remains" embalmed in earlier years by the Reverend R. W. Griswold. A passing mention, perhaps, is due to Katharine Lee Bates for one single poem from her voluminous collections, "America the Beautiful," which has doubtless won a place among our national anthems. John Bannister Tabb (1845–1909), too, cannot be passed over unmentioned —a maker of exquisitely finished quatrains and moral observations expressed with epigrammatic distinction. Within a narrow poetic area he stands alone.

A negro poet, Paul Laurence Dunbar, whose parents had been slaves, for a time engrossed the attention of the period, became in fact for a decade or more an international figure. His dialect lyrics presented in the Riley manner brought out often exquisitely the pathos and reality of the lowly life of the negro. But there was little of moral or intellectual stability in the strangely gifted youth. Too much was made of his poetic powers—too much was made of *him*. He ceased to write of negro life and began to work "in straight English in the white-man manner." There was secured for him a position in the Library of Congress, and he was universally fêted. It was too much: he became dissipated and died at the age of thirty-four. Howells did much to make the youth's work known: his estimate of it is doubtless not at all too strong:

> So far as I could remember, Paul Dunbar was the only man of pure African blood and of American civilization to feel the negro life æsthetically and express it lyrically. . . . His brilliant and unique achievement was to have studied the American negro objectively, and to have represented him—with humor, with sympathy, and yet with what the reader must instinctively feel to be entire truthfulness.

VI

A few there were of the older choir, poets who had had lyrics in Stedman's "Anthology" of 1900, poets of the nineteenth century strayed into the twentieth, and singing serenely on in the old measures oblivious of the youngsters. They were born for the most part in the decade beginning with 1852:

    1852. Edwin Markham, Henry van Dyke
    1853. Robert Underwood Johnson
    1854. Edith M. Thomas (died 1925)
    1855. George Edward Woodberry (died 1930)
    1856. Lizette Woodworth Reese
    1859. Katharine Lee Bates (died 1929)

1860. Clinton Scollard, Frank Dempster Sherman (died
    1916), Harriet Monroe
1861. Louise Imogen Guiney (died 1920), Bliss Carman
    (died 1929)

The lyric genius of Edith M. Thomas I have treated in
my earlier history.[3] Next in order in lyric intensity is
Lizette Woodworth Reese, a native of Baltimore and for
forty-five years a teacher in a high school there. In workmanship she resembles Aldrich, never permitting in her
poems word or line that was not weighed with utmost
care. In her six small volumes of lyrics her sonnets are
uniformly her best work. One of them, "Tears," belongs
in the small list of American sonnets universally accepted
as classic:

When I consider Life and its few years—
A wisp of fog betwixt us and the sun;
A call to battle, and the battle done
Ere the last echo dies within our ears;
A rose choked in the grass; an hour of fears;
The gusts that past a darkening shore do beat;
The burst of music down an unlistening street,—
I wonder at the idleness of tears.

Ye old, old dead, and ye of yesternight,
Chieftains, and bards, and keepers of the sheep,
By every cup of sorrow that you had,
Loose me from tears, and make me see aright
How each hath back what once he stayed to weep:
Homer his sight, David his little lad!

"At least a dozen of her brief songs and lyrical sonnets,"
says Untermeyer, "will find a lasting niche in American
literature." A collection of her selected poems was issued
in 1926. In 1929 appeared her prose work, "A Victorian

[3] "A History of American Literature since 1870," Fred Lewis
Pattee, p. 341.

Village," an autobiography with especial attention to the atmosphere of old Baltimore.

Another of the group is Clinton Scollard, who since his first book of poems, "Pictures in Song," 1884, has issued some forty-five volumes, mostly poetry, not to speak of hundreds of poems never republished from the magazines. Like Solomon's as recorded in I Kings, "his songs were a thousand and five." And always they have been written with sincerity and with keenest appreciation of the beautiful. Fastidious in technique, quiet, he has been a stabilizing influence in an age of riot and experiment. Opening at random, one finds a lyric like this, "Of Parson Herrick":

> Where Parson Herrick lies none knows
> Who sang of Julia and the rose;
> There is no grim stone to deface
> His grassy final resting-place.
>
> What though no marble marks the spot,
> No effigy the quiet plot,
> He rests serenely and content;
> His verses are his monument.

Fit epitaph for Scollard himself. The loud horn never has trumpeted his work, but he helped to keep real poetry alive during an arid winter. His edition of Frank Dempster Sherman with memoir is worthy of note.

Harriet Monroe has been a more active influence; first as a poet, her supreme moment coming on October 21, 1892, when her "Columbian Ode" was read at the dedication ceremonies at Chicago, preparatory to the Exposition; and second as the founder of the magazine "Poetry," which was to become the rallying center of the new Prairie School. Her "New Poetry, An Anthology," edited with Alice C. Henderson, shows the limits of her influence. As a poet she has been in her own work conservative and regular, but in her editorial supervision she has been quick to see genuine originality and to reward it with liberality.

VII

All through the decade of the nineties a poetic renaissance seemed imminent, but never fully did it come. For a brief moment it seemed as if Stephen Crane might be the Whitman of the new century that was opening. In the first number of the "Bookman," February, 1895, appeared this significant jotting:

"The Black Riders and Other Lines," by Stephen Crane, to be issued soon by Messrs. Copeland & Day, contains some bright, original work. Piquancy, satire, and an odd pleasantry characterize the specimens we have seen, one of which we are permitted to quote. They are to be printed in capitals throughout, in green ink, on Japan paper.

> Three little birds in a row
> Sat musing.
> A man passed near that place,
> Then did the little birds nudge each other.
>
> They said: "He thinks he can sing."
> They threw ·back their heads to laugh.
> With quaint countenances
> They regarded him.
> They were very curious,
> Those three little birds in a row.

The quaint booklet was followed soon by another as unconventional—with wide meadows of margins, formless and unrhymed pastels, suggested perhaps by Emily Dickinson's lyrics, perhaps by the decadent versifiers of France and England. But to Crane they were a mere creative impulse, a moment's whim. They kindled no new poetic fires.

Again, Bliss Carman, born in Fredericton, New Brunswick, in 1861, educated in the University of New Brunswick and abroad, seemed fitted for leadership. Trained for three years in the office of the New York "Independent," which for years contained the best contemporary poetry in America, he suggested to the new firm of Stone & Kimball, Chicago, the publication of the "Chap Book," and he served as editor of the adventurous little magazine until its early death. After the publication of his distinctive volume, "Low Tide on Grand Pré," he was recognized widely as a lyrist of promise. In the first volume of "Songs from Vagabondia," done in partnership with Hovey, was an opening lyric cry for freedom, Hovey's and his own:

> Off with the fetters
> That chafe and restrain!
> Off with the chain!
> Here Art and Letters,
> Music and Wine
> And Myrtle and Wanda,
> The winsome witches,
> Blithely combine.

It was a hobo call for Bohemianism, for poetic vagabondage, but it led nowhere to firm ground. After the death of Hovey, Carman settled into less excited lyricism. His "Pipes of Pan," five volumes, contain his best offerings in his later manner. But perhaps with the spirit he caught from Hovey he is at his best in such vagabondings as are expressed in outpourings of nature-love like this:

There is something in the autumn that is native to my blood—
Touch of manner, hint of mood;
And my heart is like a rhyme,
With the yellow and the purple and the crimson keeping time.

The scarlet of the maples can shake me like a cry
Of bugles going by.

And my lonely spirit thrills
To see the frosty asters like a smoke upon the hills.

There is something in October sets the gypsy blood astir;
We must rise and follow her,
When from every hill of flame
She calls and calls each vagabond by name.

The early rebellion seemed to die with the nineties; perhaps it was because the rebels themselves died. An ominous fatality seemed to be the price of literary rebellion during the early years of the period—Crane, Moody, Hovey, Norris, Phillips, Paul Leicester Ford, Dunbar, Cawein, Harold Frederic, Wolcott Balestier—America could hardly spare so heavy a toll in a time that was sadly in need of new creative power.

BIBLIOGRAPHICAL REFERENCES

EMILY DICKINSON, 1830–86

"Poems of Emily Dickinson," edited by two of her friends, Mabel Loomis Todd and T. W. Higginson, 1890; Second Series, 1891; Third Series, 1896; "He Ate and Drank the Precious Words," 1900; "The Single Hound: Poems of a Life Time," 1914; "The Letters of Emily Dickinson," 1845–1866, edited by M. L. Todd, 1906; "Complete Poems of Emily Dickinson," with an introduction by her niece Martha Dickinson Bianchi, 1924; "Further Poems of Emily Dickinson," withheld from publication by her sister Lavinia. Edited by her niece Martha Dickinson Bianchi and Alfred Leete Hampson, 1929; "Emily Dickinson, the Human Background of her Poetry," Josephine Pollitt, 1930; "The Life and Mind of Emily Dickinson," Genevieve Taggard, 1930.

"Emily Dickinson," MacGregor Jenkins, 1930.

WILLIAM VAUGHN MOODY, 1869–1910

"Poems," 1901; "Poems and Plays," with an introduction by J. M. Manly, two volumes, 1912; "The Masque of Judgment," 1900; "The Fire Bringer," 1904; "The Great Divide," 1909; "The Faith Healer," 1910.

RICHARD HOVEY, 1864–1900

"Poems," 1880; "The Laurel: An Ode to Mary Day Lanier," 1889; "Launcelot and Guenevere: a poem in Dramas," 5 vols. 1907: I. "The Quest of Merlin," 1891. II. "The Marriage of Guenevere," 1895. III. "The Birth of Galahad," 1898. IV. "Taliesin: a Masque," 1900. V. "The Holy Graal," 1907; "Seaward: Elegy on the Death of Thomas William Parsons," 1893; "Along the Trail: a Book of Lyrics, 1898; "The Holy Graal and Other Fragments," edited by Mrs. Richard Hovey with a preface by Bliss Carman, 1907; "Dartmouth Lyrics," edited by Edwin Osgood Grover, 1924; "To the End of the Trail," edited with notes by Mrs. Richard Hovey, 1908.

With BLISS CARMAN

"Songs from Vagabondia," 1894; "More Songs from Vagabondia," 1896; "Last Songs from Vagabondia," 1900. Collected Edition, three volumes, 1903.

BLISS CARMAN, 1861–1929

"Low Tide on Grand Pré," 1893; "A Sea Mark," 1895; "Behind the Arras," 1895; "Ballads of Lost Haven," 1897; "By the Aurelian Wall," 1897; "St. Kavin, a Ballad," 1894; "At Michaelmas," 1895; "The Girl in the Poster," 1897; "The Green Book of the Bards," 1898; "The Vengeance of Noel Brassard," 1899; "Ode on the Coronation of King Edward," 1902; "From the Book of Myths," 1902; "Pipes of Pan," 1902, 1903, 1904, 1905; "Poems," Collected Edition, 2 vols., 1905; "Kinship of Nature," 1903; "Friendship of Art," 1904; "From the Book of Valentines," 1905; "The Making of Personality," 1907; "The Gate of Peace," "The Rough Rider," 1909; "A Painter's Holiday," 1911; "Echoes from Vagabondia," 1912; "April Airs," 1916; "Far Horizons," 1925; "Wild Garden," 1929.

CHAPTER XIV

THE *ÉMIGRÉ* WRITERS

To an esoteric few, America with its democratic level-ings and its lack, on the whole, of the calm and the poise of civilizations long worn in traditional groovings, America has been intolerable, and (when possible) they have escaped from it. With the exception of Whittier and Whitman and Thoreau, all of our major authors have lived much in Europe, returning there again and again to renew their grip upon the fundamentals of "culture," like missionaries returning home for a year of recupera-tion after exile in heathendom. And the list is by no means a roll-call of New England Brahmins. To begin with modern times, there was Bret Harte, who escaped from America and lived the last twenty-five years of his life in Europe, never once returning; and there was Mark Twain who, despite his ingrained Americanism, pre-ferred to live thirteen years of his literary life in foreign lands. Of Henry James, the classic example of *émigré* American, we need not speak, or of Whistler the artist, or of F. Marion Crawford, born abroad, son of an Ital-ianated American sculptor.

I

The period opening with the nineties had as its most sensational *émigré* author, at least for a moment, Henry Harland, a man so completely in key with his times that migrating to London he was entrusted by John Lane with the associate editorship of the new "Yellow Book." So far as his American career is concerned he belongs in the period of the eighties. He was a New York City product, born there in 1861, and educated at New York University. Later he was at Harvard and then in Rome and London doing graduate work. In America again in 1883, he accepted a position in the Surrogate's office in New York City, a position he held for three years. His novel "As It Was Written," 1885, with the pseudonym "Sidney Luska," an intense, grim picture of seemingly new areas of New York City life, caused a flurry in literary circles. Here was a new voice and a new manner. Then had come "Mrs. Peixada," 1886, "The Yoke of the Thorah," 1887, and in 1889 a collection of short stories and sketches original, colorful, with the title "A Latin-Quarter Courtship and Other Stories." There was newness in the man, unusual brilliancy, power enough, it might seem, to have asserted itself in the leadership of a new American school. But suddenly he disappeared from American literary circles. His English work does not concern us. He died in England in 1905 at the age of forty-four.

Richard Le Gallienne, who was himself of the "Yellow Book" group, has given us a vivid picture of the man in his prime:

Harland was one of those Americans in love with Paris who seem more French than the French themselves, a slim, gesticulating, goateed, snub-nosed, lovable figure, smoking innumerable cigarettes as he galvanically pranced about the room, excitedly propounding the *dernier mot* on the build of the short story or the art of prose. He was born to be the life and soul of one of those *cénacles* which from their café-tables in "the Quarter" promulgate all those world-shaking "new movements" in art which succeed each other with kaleidoscopic rapidity. The most vivacious of talkers, "art" with him, as with his Parisian prototypes, was a life-and-death matter. Nothing else existed for him.[1]

Harold Frederic, local colorist and historical romancer, an *émigré* for professional reasons, after 1884 London correspondent of the "New York Times," also belongs

[1] "The Romantic 90's," Richard Le Gallienne.

for the most part to the decade of the eighties. A single volume of his, however, "The Damnation of Theron Ware," 1896, made him, at least in America, one of the forces in the *fin de siècle* decadence. The novel was, for its day, a daring criticism of an American Protestant religious denomination, and everywhere it was labeled dangerous. The English publishers, afraid of its startling title, issued it as "Illumination." Parts of it are excellently done. Its opening chapters, picturing a Methodist conference in its last hours before and during and after the reading by the presiding bishop of the ministerial "appointments" for the year, is vivid realism. The young radicals of America were overjoyed. Booth Tarkington records how his Bohemian group of young garret starvelings in New York, working feverishly for recognition, whooped their joy. Here is a fragment of their conversation:

"I'm going to take you to dinner at the Lantern Club," he said. "Irving Bacheller's the toastmaster; Steve Crane's a member and he knows Harold Frederic. Has anybody ever written a better novel than Frederic's *Damnation of Theron Ware?*"
"No, it isn't possible to write a finer novel but . . ."

That was in 1896. The novel is still read, reissued only recently in new dress, a statement that can be made concerning little of the fiction of the nineties. Frederic was, unquestionably, a man of real powers, but, like so many others of his time and since, he was borne away from all safe landmarks of literary artistry by the demands of his profession. The headlong, excited world of journalism produces no enduring art. Frederic died in England in 1898, after an exile of fourteen years.

II

But the leading *émigré* writer of the period, indeed of all periods, is that strangest of literary comets ever shot into our literary system, Lafcadio Hearn. A full half of his work belongs to the period before the nineties, most of it to the eighties. The man's life was in two distinct chapters, divided sharply by the year 1890, as sharply indeed as if he had died and had transmigrated into another existence which we have been enabled to know.

Years ago E. C. Stedman dropped this into one of his letters: "Hearn will in time be as much of a romantic personality and tradition as Poe is now." Time has confirmed the critic. In the more than a quarter of a century since the man's death there has grown up a veritable Hearn myth, and the end is not yet.

First, there was the man himself. Certainly American literature in all its picturesque annals has produced no more romantic specimen. Mystery, doubtless never to be penetrated, covers many areas of his early life. Poe's story is prose compared with the wild arabesque skeins that make up Hearn's biography. Strange mixtures were in the man: Irish with a dash of Gypsy blood; Ægean Greek inflamed with mad Arab and Moorish lawlessness. Born on an island of the Cyclades, of British soldier father and native mother, he was a hybrid, an exotic in whatever land he might be, a man unstable, unpoised, a man without a country, and at last a man without a race. And his rearing had been as irregular as his origin—Ireland at first, where he received as a mere lad a second insuperable handicap, for while playing a rough game he lost the sight of one eye. The strain upon the other eye weakened it permanently, and caused it at length to bulge into a prominence that to the sensitive youth, and later man, seemed a thing of horror.

The effect of all this upon his temperament and his attitude toward life cannot be overestimated. He ran away from the school where he was to be fitted for the priesthood, and for a period followed the steps of the young De Quincey. For a year he was adrift in the Bohemian areas of Paris where he learned French, then in the slums of London for one knows not how long. In the late eighteen sixties he had reached New York City a penniless waif, and for two years again darkness. Seeking his brother-in-law, he went at length to Cincinnati, where for years again he lived a hobo life sleeping in packing boxes and livery-stable lofts, barely subsisting until at last he found work on one of the newspapers. His lurid account of a local murder established him. Then during some six years in Cincinnati he produced an amazing amount of work—literary articles for the Sunday edition, which have recently been found by careful detective work and republished in several volumes.

The wanderlust upon him, he drifted to New Orleans, where he spent nearly ten years. And here it was that for the first time he discovered to the full his peculiar powers. The romantic old city, itself an exotic, a hybrid mixture of elements, semi-tropic, yet held by strange northern inhibitions, chorded completely at first with his temperament, fed completely at first the starved side of the man, so eager, sensuous, pryingly curious, hungry for the voluptuously beautiful, the side that had so languished in the drab environment of Cincinnati. The strange old Gulf city—"the Marseilles of the new world" he called it—was like Bagdad after Edinburgh. He threw himself with eagerness into the exploration of its exotic recesses and un-American uniquenesses. One can hardly bring into relief this picturesque area of the man's development without lapsing unconsciously into Hearn's own manner, with his own tropic vocabulary, colorful of adjective. To read what he wrote during this era of his excitement is to be perpetually in the languorous Creole atmosphere of a romanticized South. Whether his picturings and colorful studies are true or not, only natives born may say, but to the reader they carry complete conviction.

The gathering into volumes of all Hearn's American writings, including even the scraps of his newspaper work, has permitted for the first time a critical study of the man's personality and his early sources. First, we note the influence of Poe, the Poe of the horrific and the morbidly ghastly areas. The authorship of any disputed article of his early period, declares his editor, can almost surely be attributed to Hearn if it is found to contain such characteristic words as *spectral, elfin, phantom, grotesque, arabesque, eldritch, ghoulish, weird, ghastly, lurid, fantastic, phosphorescent, hideous, dismal,* and the like. Everywhere horrible subjects like "The Utilization of Human Remains," or "The Poisoners"; or murder tales like the news story that first made him famous in Cincinnati—"The Tan-yard Cremation," ghastly in its realistic details. He delighted too, in this early period, in essays implying much curious research—ghost studies, essays in bizarre linguistics, nightmare legends, picturings of New Orleans uniquenesses, studies of negro life, the sensations of steeple-climbers and the like. Everywhere the unusual, the unique, the extreme.

From Poe it was but a step to Baudelaire, the French Poe, and then to Gautier, whom he translated in all his voluptuous bareness, a translation impossible of publication in the America of the eighties. A part of it, savagely "Comstocked," he finally did publish as "One of Cleopatra's Nights," but he was ahead of his times.

It was New Orleans and later the French West Indies that awakened to the full his De Quincey-like, his Gautier-like, imagination. Nowhere else in English such a jungle of exotic flora—in diction, in imagery, in startling impressionism. Note this wild description of one of his dreams:

Dust! dust!—noisome, fetid, pungent!—quagmires of phosphoric rottenness—and the million mushroom growths of disintegration. Dust, dust, dust!—vapid, peccant, dreggy, pestiferous, fermenting. And always the Unknown Impluse prevailed, drawing me on as with some intangible but unbreakable thread—with mingled mesmerism of desire and loathing . . . into the blackness I fell. . . . I fell and continued to fall, sometimes rolling, sometimes rebounding, but softly, lightly—as a pellet rustling with dry elasticity. For hours, for days, did I seem to fall. Then a sudden shock of stoppage in dust—a dust more clammy and more ancient than all other dust, old dust of dead men!—and I stifled in it, and I gasped in phosphor-light, while a voice seemed to command me: EAT!

The dream undoubtedly of one who went to sleep over Poe's "Berenice" and De Quincey's "Opium Eater," but all the same original and blood-chilling, giving an impression unique in all the later literature in English.

His tropic vocabulary he stretches to its full richness when he would describe the feminine types that peopled his imagination. Like Baudelaire, like Dumas, he found more of lure and voluptuous sensuousness in the colored races. Here is his picture of an octoroon:

That word reminds one of a celebrated and vanished type— never mirrored upon canvas, yet not less physically worthy of artistic preservation than those amber-tinted beauties glorified in the Oriental studies of Ingres, of Richter, of Gérôme! Uncommonly tall were those famous beauties—citrine-hued, elegant of stature as palmettos, lithe as serpents; never again will such types reappear upon American soil. Daughters of luxury, artificial growths, never organized to enter the iron struggle for life unassisted and unprotected, they vanish forever with the social system which made them a place apart as for splendid plants reared within a conservatory. With the fall of American feudalism the dainty glass house was dashed to pieces; the species it contained have perished utterly. . . . What figures for designs in bronze! What tints for canvas!

No one like Hearn, either, has caught the mystery, the shuddery meaning of the African with his Voodoo soul and his race memories. This of the jungle music:

The first time you hear it you will certainly rein in your horse to listen. It is the beating of an African drum, the tapping of a ka or tamtam by fingers of iron. As you draw nearer, the sense of a marvellous rhythm bursts upon you—a rhythm unlike anything you ever heard or imagined before. It brings to you a singular shock—the sudden knowledge that you have entered into a world not your own and that a soul is speaking in that savage rhythm, uttering syllables of a tongue which you do not know but which stirs something ghostly within you like a thought forgotten for a million years. And at last when the full sound storms and bounds in beating eddies about you, you feel a wild excitement of which you are almost ashamed; all your animal life struggles and throbs in response to that exultant barbaric measure. . . . If you could fully know why, you might know also the mystery of a race.

His novel "Chita" and his "Two Years in the French West Indies," a throwing of the Gulf islands and the Caribbean tropics into pastels drenched with vermilion and ochre, are like nothing else in English. They add color and Gautier-like brilliance to our all-too-drab American literature. In our Puritan age Hearn was a man emotional, unanchored, a bundle of jangling nerves, moody, sullen, sensuous, with little of vision save for physical beauty and the voluptuousness of external colorings. The Oriental strain that came with his mother's blood was forever at war with her Hellenic classicism; and this in turn was made revolutionary by his Gallic imagination, and still again by the Gypsy urge that also was a part of his birthright: strange apparition in the morning twilight of our prosaic America. Nowhere indeed could such a personality be at home. Surfeited with the Nordic and the blond, he escaped at last into the strangeness of an alien race—alien even to him, foreign indeed to every shred of inheritance within him—and began again with new eagerness, newly aroused emotion, to record his impressions. He had escaped forever, he believed, to use his own words, "the sterility of that American atmosphere in which the more delicate flowers of thought refuse to grow," and at last had found the land of his dreams.

III

And yet it must be recorded that the Japan chapter in Hearn's life was none of his own making. It came almost by accident. He had been sent to the Orient by the Harpers to gather materials for publication, but upon his arrival in Japan he had fallen out with his employers, and had cut loose to see the land for himself. Instantly he was carried off his balance, just as he had been in the West Indies, by the quaintness, the strangeness, the alien beauty, the impenetrable mysticism of everything he saw. Read "My First Day in the Orient" in "Glimpses of Unfamiliar Japan." Again roseate illusions in this soul so susceptible to illusions. He saw the new land through the cloud of unreality that always enveloped him. This first volume in the new portfolio differs little from those in the old—save in background. The typical book of the earlier period might have been called "Glimpses of Unfamiliar Caribbean Islands." A theatric phantasmagoria it was, rather than a realistic picturing; a gorgeous inventory of exotic drop-scenes, of painted side wings and colored lights. Always the surface, always sensuousness, always blended pigments—words mixed like paints on a palette, words chosen and applied with infinite care. "For me words have color, form, character; they have faces, ports, manners, gesticulations;—they have moods, humors, eccentricities:—they have tints, tones, personalities." Humanity, if any obtruded into his canvas, had been simply a part of the spectacle—everything to him, indeed, was a spectacle to be viewed objectively through the emotions, never with humor, never with pity, never with isolation of the individual soul. He was as impersonal an impressionist as Turner, who made sunsets overglorious because with myopic vision he saw them so.

Dealing only with surfaces, he had exhausted for himself the tropic islands of the Gulf, and old New Orleans, and the drabness of headlong, practical America. But as he was eagerly painting his first impressions of Oriental strangeness, something new awoke within him. More and more he saw not Japan but the Japanese. These strange little people with their smiling faces, their unfeigned hospitality, their genuineness, their perfect at-homeness in the environment that ages had made for them—everything appealed to a something new within him. He married at length a Japanese lady, marvelously poised, marvelously self-effacing, noble beyond adjectives, the culmination of generations of good breeding; it brought the human element emphatically into his life, as did the birth of children into his home. He was a father now, with love in his heart and pity. For their sakes he settled into a fixed orbit, gave up all plans of returning to the Western world and to his own race, changed his very name, was naturalized with the name Yakumo Koizumi, adopted the Buddhist religion; lived his last years and died as a Japanese.

His books of this last period belong on a different shelf from those created during his American apprenticeship. He was seeking now the soul not of a place but of a people and a race, and so far as it was in him to do so he succeeded.

He was not in the least equipped for realism, and he was not at all a scientist. Though saturated with the current French writings he was an ingrained romantic. To Hearn, Flaubert for example exemplified the "extravagance of the romantic laboriousness of art—the exaggerations that preceded the realistic reaction"; and to him Zola was a thing of horror. "Zola," he said, "represents the extreme swing of the pendulum between severe reserve and frantic license. His school must die with him." Nor was Hearn in sympathy with the "Decadents," who were in full career when he was learning his art. "The new poetry," he declared, "is simply rotten!—morally and otherwise. . . . A splendid something entirely absent from the new poetry—the joy of life. There is no joy in this new world—and scarcely any tenderness: the language is the language of art, but the spirit is of Holbein and Gothic ages of religious madness. I do not know that poetry ought to be joyous, in a general way; there is beauty in pain and sorrow. Only,—is ugliness or pain, without beauty, a subject worthy of poetry?"

Pity and tenderness came now into the art of the man, so far as he was permitted by his nature to feel it. So incurably was he a romantic, however, that everything he touched he romanticized. Undoubtedly the characteristic was partly physiological. His biographer, Miss Kennard, has told how "when undergoing any severe mental or physical strain Hearn was subject to periods of hysterical trance." His widow in her memoir has dwelt upon this characteristic of the man. His blindness, all but total at times, explains much. Said one who visited him:

I was still more surprised when I discovered how extremely near-sighted he was. His impressions of scenery or Japanese works of art could never have been obtained as ordinary people obtain them. The details had to be studied piece by piece with a small telescope, and then described as a whole.

Moreover he never mastered the Japanese language thoroughly. Most of what he got concerning Japan and the Japanese came from interpreters: Orientalism in every way came to him through a glass darkly. He delighted in the tiny bits of arc that came within his observation—manners, religious rites, superstitions, ceremonials, survivals of mystic attitudes, tribal lays, habits of thought—and he sought with intuition and imagination to deduce complete circles. Yearningly he analyzed for inner meanings, for the soul of Japan, even for the mystery of the unfathomable East, but always his quest led him into romantic emotionalism. It is not the East we see: it is Hearn projected against the East. The unsolvable problem—unsolvable at least by Occidental mathematics—he never solved.

There were moments when he penetrated deeply—more deeply, perhaps, than any other Occidental—but his ten Japanese volumes must on the whole be classed as intuitive impressionism. The titles themselves are revealing: "Shadowings," "In Ghostly Japan," "Exotics and Retrospectives," "Japanese Fairy Tales," "The Romance of the Milky Way," "Japan: an Attempt at Interpretation," "Some Chinese Ghosts," "Gleanings in Buddhafields." Such a sketch as "The Dream of a Summer's Day" in "Out of the East" is poetry pure and simple. The man was a stylist inevitably, incorrigibly, like a Walter Pater or a Ruskin. This he wrote in a letter to his half-sister, Mrs. Atkinson:

I am only beginning to learn; and to produce five pages means to write at least twenty-five. Enthusiasm and inspirations have least to do with the matter. The real work is condensing, compressing, choosing, changing, shifting words and phrases,—studying values of color and sound and form in words; and when all is done, the result satisfies only for a time. What I wrote six years ago, I cannot bear the sight of to-day.

During the closing years of his life in Japan he was given a lectureship in literature in the University of Tokyo. Again a new world opened to him: he was to interpret to these Orientals the soul of Occidentalism, the poetry and romance of Europe. He solved the problem in the light of his own personality. He determined to speak not to the intellect of his class but to their emotions; not to explain technique and forms, but to penetrate to the inner meanings of the classics and to work out the common denominator, to render them capable of universal comprehension. And, amazing as it may seem, this work which he never wrote still survives. Some of his students captured his words by shorthand, and the results have been published, a unique work. It places Hearn among the literary critics as does the volume of critical essays collected by Albert Mordell and issued with the title "Essays in European and Oriental Literature." Hearn's treatment of literary tendencies current in the eighties and the nineties—"Idealism and Naturalism," "Decadence as a Fine Art," and "Literary Pessimism"— his elucidation of Zola, Maupassant, Baudelaire, and Loti, and his studies in Russian realism form a brilliant introduction to the literary period we are studying now.

The last years of the man, despite an ideal home life with wife and children, were inwardly tragic. More and more the realization was burned into his soul that he was not only a man without a country but a man without a race; more and more he felt the force of the impenetrable wall that separated him even from his own half-Japanese children. In one of his letters—always his letters are his most distinctive, perhaps his best, literary product if spontaneity be the criterion—he struck this pathetic chord:

You talk about being without intellectual companionship. O YE EIGHT HUNDRED MYRIADS OF GODS! What would you do if you were me? Lo! the illusion is gone! Japan in Kyushu is like Europe—except I have no friend. The differences in ways of thinking, and the difficulties of language, render it impossible for an *educated* Japanese to find pleasure in the society of a European. My scholars in this great government school are not boys, but men. They speak to me only in class. The teachers never speak to me at all. I go to the college and return after class,—always alone, no mental company but books. But at home everything is sweet.

In his efforts to make a Japanese of himself he had erased so much that it was impossible ever to return to the Occidental world of his birth and training. He had obliterated his very self: he was neither Occidental nor Oriental. He died the loneliest death in the whole history of romanticism.

Such men leave no posterity, found no schools, establish no system. And yet his genius, more eccentric in its way even than Poe's, his uniqueness, his De Quincey-like word-buildings, make him a borealis illumination that streams with fantastic waverings, pallid light, without heat, and yet one that does not fade out nor die. His reputation, says John Erskine, "is as securely fixed as that of any man who has written in English in the last quarter century."

More so, indeed, if we are to judge by the increasing stream of material concerning him that has been issuing from the presses during the twenty years since he died. A new literary myth has been growing. As in the case of Poe, elements have been added gradually but surely. Instead of Mrs. Whitman and Mrs. Osgood, we have had Elizabeth Bisland and Miss Kennard—feminine glorification; instead of Dr. Moran, there has been Dr. Gould—medical diagnosis and explanation; instead of Ingram, Y. Noguchi—exotic interpretation and defense; instead of Woodberry and Stedman and Harrison, a modern group increasing steadily—his Japanese widow, Hutson, Henry Watkin (of the "Letters from the Raven"), Krehbiel, Thomas, and his Japanese students. In addition to all this there have been issued his letters, his lectures rescued by shorthand, his editorials, and finally four large volumes of his contributions to Cincinnati and New Orleans newspapers. Walt Whitman ten years ago passed through this critical stage; Poe even yet is in transition.

IV

Another *émigré,* Edgar Saltus, born in New York in 1858, was a stylist as phantasmagoric and as lurid at times as even the earlier Hearn. His education, amazing in its comprehensiveness and its impracticality, was gained for the most part abroad—in German universities, in France where he fell in with the "decadents," in England, where he was boon companion with Oscar Wilde, rivaling him in epigram and caustic wit, and at Columbia University where he attained to the Ph.D. and LL.D. degrees.

His personal life, some of it scandalous, we need not dwell upon. Neurotic, temperamental to the last degree, erotic, *parisien,* he was rated from his first work, "Balzac," 1884, as a decadent influence. The approach to him is from France. His novels, dealing with the field covered by Mrs. Wharton, were exquisite in finish and epigrammatic sparkle, but totally untrustworthy as fact. He was a stylist, a literary decorator with bizarre tastes. According to his widow, who in 1925 published a biography, his toil over his work was always extreme. First there was a rough draft.

The next writing put it into readable form, and on this second he always worked the hardest, transforming sentences into graceful transitions,—injecting epigrams, witticisms and clever dialogue, and penetrating the whole with his personality. The third writing (and he never wrote a book less than three times) gave it its final coat of varnish.

"In literature," he wrote, "only three things count, style, style polished, style repolished." One fundamental fact he seems to have neglected in his definition: there must be something to polish. First, of all, substance. One may scour pumice into brilliance, but yet it is pumice.

His later years he spent for the most part abroad. During the war he became a British subject, but he was never rooted anywhere. Says his widow, he was a man "with no home, no anchor," and she might have added "no country." Following his death in 1921 there was a vigorous attempt by younger critics to rehabilitate him and establish him as one of the major forces of the period. According to Carl Van Vechten, "The neglect of this man is one of the most astounding phenomena in the scoriac history of American literature." Charles Honce in an introduction to a reprint of "The Uplands of Dream," with a bibliography of Saltus, gave this critical estimate:

He could be brilliant over a trifle, he illumined everything he touched, he dealt in glamour. It is not so much the subject matter which charms, but rather the witchery of words, the cadence of phrases, the mighty roll of sentences that mount step by step, lightly yet irresistibly, to a star-spangled climax, the apogee of syntax.

But the attempt to resurrect Saltus, to galvanize life into his volumes twenty and thirty years out of print, has been a failure. There was lack of genuineness in the man, of humankindness, of truth. Like Bierce, he was a conscious cynic, a professional sneerer at life, a reducer of all things revered by the commonalty to caustic epigrams. He was akin to Oscar Wilde: full of smart saws—"Love is a fever that ends in a yawn," "A man who is always right is a bore." From the wit in his volumes one might compile another "Devil's Dictionary," but why compile it? He was a wit, and wit dies with its generation; he was a stylist, and style is a garment, the fashion of which totally changes with the years.

v

The roll of American authors who have left their country to live abroad permanently because of conditions more favorable to their artistic lives has been a long one. We need but call the roll of such expatriates as Ezra Pound, John Gould Fletcher, Louise Imogen Guiney, Hilda Doolittle, T. S. Eliot, Anne Douglas Sedgwick, Conrad P. Aiken, and Ernest Hemingway.

Several brilliant birds of passage have flitted in and out of the American scene during the period. The most notable was Rudyard Kipling, who settled down at Brattleboro, Vermont, for some two years, married a Vermont lady, collaborated with her brother Wolcott Balestier on a novel "The Naulahka," and wrote some of his early novels there, notably "Captains Courageous," the materials for which he obtained during visits to the fishing fleet at Gloucester, Massachusetts. Another visitant, George Santayana, remained longer. Born in Spain in 1863, he came to America in 1872 and studied philosophy at Harvard, taking his Ph.D. in 1889. From 1907 to 1912 he was a professor in the University. He was a poet of distinction during the transition years of the period, and an essayist with rare beauty of style. His most influential work, however, has been in his own special field—philosophy. Of late he has made his home in England, which now claims him as a maker of English literature.

BIBLIOGRAPHICAL REFERENCES

LAFCADIO HEARN, 1850–1904

"One of Cleopatra's Nights and Other Fantastic Romances," Théophile Gautier, translated by Lafcadio Hearn, 1882; "Stray Leaves from Strange Literature," 1884; "Gombo Zhêbes," "Little Dictionary of Creole Proverbs," 1885; "Chita: A Memory of Last Island," 1889; "Two Years in the French West Indies," 1890; "Youma," 1890; "Glimpses of Unfamiliar Japan," 2 vols., 1894; "Out of the East: Reveries and Studies in New Japan," 1895; "Kokoro: Hints and Echoes of Japanese Inner Life," 1896; "Gleanings in Buddha-Fields: Studies of Hand and Soul in the Far East," 1897; "Exotics and Retrospectives," 1899; "In Ghostly Japan," 1899; "Shadowings," 1900; "Japanese Miscellany," 1901; "Kottō: Being Japanese Curios with Sundry Cobwebs," 1902; "Japanese Fairy Tales," 1903; "Kwaidan," 1904; "Japan: an Attempt at Interpretation," 1904; "The Romance of the Milky Way and Other Studies," 1905; "Some Chinese Ghosts," 1906; "The Temptation of St. Anthony," Gustave Flaubert, translated by Lafcadio Hearn, 1910; "Fantastics, and Other Fancies," edited by Charles Woodward Hutson, 1914; "Books and Habits, from the Lectures of Lafcadio Hearn," edited by John Erskine, 1921; "Writings of Lafcadio Hearn," 16 vols., 1922; "Essays in European and Oriental Literature," edited by Albert Mordell, 1923; "An American Miscellany, Articles and Stories Now First Collected," Albert Mordell, 2 vols.; "Occidental Gleanings," collected by Albert Mordell,

1925; "Editorials of Lafcadio Hearn," edited by Charles Woodward Hutson.

"Shelburne Essays," Second Series, P. E. More, 1905; "Letters from the Raven: the Correspondence of Lafcadio Hearn with Henry Watkin," 1905, 1907; "Life and Letters of Lafcadio Hearn," 2 vols., Elizabeth Bisland, 1906; "Concerning Lafcadio Hearn," G. M. Gould, with bibliography by Laura Stedman, 1908; "Japanese Letters of Lafcadio Hearn," edited by Elizabeth Bisland, 1910; "Leaves from the Diary of an Impressionist," introduction by Ferris Greenslet, 1911; "Lafcadio Hearn in Japan," Y. Noguchi, 1911; "Lafcadio Hearn," E. Thomas, 1912; "Lafcadio Hearn," Nina H. Kennard, 1912; "Reminiscences of Lafcadio Hearn," Setsu Koizumi (Mrs. Hearn), 1918; "Lafcadio Hearn's American Days," Edward Larocque Tinker, 1924.

EDGAR SALTUS, 1855–1921

PARTIAL LIST

"Balzac," 1884; "The Philosophy of Disenchantment," 1885; "The Anatomy of Negation," 1886; "Mr. Incoul's Misadventure," 1887; "Tales Before Supper," from Théophile Gautier and Prosper Mérimée, 1887; "The Truth about Tristrem Varick," a novel, 1888; "Eden: an Episode," 1888; "A Transaction in Hearts," 1888; "The Pace that Kills: a Chronicle," 1889; "The Transient Guest," 1889; "Love and Lore," 1890; "Mary Magdalen: a Chronicle," 1891; "A Story Without a Name," translated and introduced by Edgar Saltus, 1891; "Imperial Purple," 1892; "The Facts in the Case of H. Hyrtl, Esq.," 1892; "Madam Sapphira. A Fifth Avenue Story," 1893; "Enthralled," 1894; "When Dreams Come True: a Story of Emotional Life," 1895; "Purple and Fine Women," 1903; "The Yellow Fay," title changed later to "The Perfume of Eros," 1904; "Vanity Square," 1906; "Historia Amoris," 1906; "The Lords of the Ghostland," 1907; "Daughters of the Rich," 1909; "The Monster," 1912; "The Paliser Case," 1919; Barbey d'Aurevilly's "A Story Without a Name," with impressions of the author by Edgar Saltus, 1919; "The Imperial Orgy," 1920; "The Ghost Girl," 1922.

CHAPTER XV

THE RISING TIDE OF FICTION

I

BEFORE 1890, at any given time one might trace with confidence the main stream of American fiction, ignoring the casual tributaries; but in the new period the main stream became lost in a veritable Everglades. During the eighteen eighties localized picturesqueness had dominated American fiction, and the genre had by no means died during the decade of the nineties, the decade so influenced by the rising young Kipling. The gentle rebellion led by Norris and Kipling and aided all unconsciously by Mary E. Wilkins and others was still insistent on local color. And there were survivals from even the sixties and the seventies still working on as if the *fin de siècle* had not arrived.

Among the survivals were four cheery mid-Victorian women who refused to change to the modern fashions but wrote on to the end as if the Civil War, even, had never been: Amelia E. Barr, 1831–1918; Harriet Prescott Spofford, 1833–1919; Marietta Holley ("Josiah Allen's Wife"), 1844–1926; and Anna Katharine Green, 1846—.

The last of these, Anna Katharine Green, cannot be passed over even in a history of contemporary literature. Her "Leavenworth Case," a detective story written at a period when it had nothing to compete with save Poe's "The Murders in the Rue Morgue," had made her famous despite the fact that it was crude work from every literary standpoint. A new variety of novel it was, thrilling, mystifying, compelling, and it called for more of its kind. Dozens of volumes in similar key followed it, and her name, even down to the days of her grandchildren, was fairly synonymous with detective story. Many of her latest creations like "The Filigree Ball," 1905, "The Woman in the Alcove," 1906, and "The Step on the Stair," 1922, were best sellers in their season, competing in popularity even with the Sherlock Holmes tales and the more modern work of Mary Roberts Rinehart. Her strength as a storyteller lay in her ability to invent and manipulate situations and to hold her reader breathless to the moment of the solution of the mystery. She failed, however, in characterization. Had she possessed mastery at this one point she might have claimed equality with the best masters of her art; but failing here she becomes one who has distinction simply because she was a pioneer.

Still another survivial from the earlier period, a transition figure, his most distinctive work done in the eighties and yet a writer through all the forty years after 1890, was E. M. Howe of Kansas. Born in 1854, educated at the printer's case, for nearly half a century editor of a single Main Street newspaper, he is known the world over to-day for two things: his novel "The Story of a Country Town," a novel that was so advanced in 1882 that no publishing house would issue it, and that came into print only because its author put it into type with his own hands and printed it on his own press; and his later syndicated column published in many of the leading newspapers. The novel was so original, so realistic, so true to the life it depicted that for a time there was hope that America was to have a Thomas Hardy of her own. Completely was it made from life and not from books:

Had I lived in fifty different, widely separated towns or countries from 1877 to 1929, I do not believe I would have had better opportunity to know life and human nature. In every town there is material for the great American novel so long expected, but no one appears to write it. If I chose I could tell of three or four happenings in Atchison [Kansas] and without varying a hair's breadth from the truth, that most readers would characterize as the most surprising they had ever heard.

His volume "Plain People," 1929, is as remarkable in the field of autobiography as was his "Story of a Country Town" in the field of realistic fiction. The two volumes are his contribution to American literature, though during fifty years he was the beloved editor of a country paper universally read in its own area. Of his town he could say, "I knew every man, woman and child black and white in Atchison."

The order in which the major writers of the earlier period dropped from the scene is noteworthy:

1900. Charles Dudley Warner.
1902. Bret Harte, Frank R. Stockton, Mrs. Catherwood, Edward Eggleston
1904. Kate Chopin.
1905. Lew Wallace.
1907. Thomas Bailey Aldrich.
1908. Joel Chandler Harris.
1909. F. Marion Crawford, Edward Everett Hale, Sarah Orne Jewett.
1910. Samuel L. Clemens.
1911. Elizabeth Stuart Phelps Ward.
1915. F. Hopkinson Smith.
1916. Henry James.
1920. William Dean Howells.
1922. Mary N. Murfree, Thomas Nelson Page, John Kendrick Bangs.
1924. Frances Hodgson Burnett, Kate Douglas Wiggin.
1925. George W. Cable.

II

The revolution of the nineties which expressed itself in so many diverse ways was fundamentally associated with publishing changes, themselves a revolution. The improved mechanics of book-making, the growing facilities for distribution, the new methods of advertising, the amazing multiplication of newspapers and magazines—by-products, in a way, of the new advertising—all these made radical changes in the whole area of book-making. The old idea of a publishing house as a happy family of authors and publishers associated to advance the great cause of literature and to be of mutual service—the idea made so much of by the Fields and Osgood firm, by the Harpers, and the Putnams and the Ticknors—was giving way now to the one idea of a publishing house organized for business only. Concentration more and more now was upon the production of a manufactured product that could be marketed with profit. Quantity now became a ruling element in publishing organized as "big business"; emphasis was upon single products, individual books, intensively advertised and pushed into the hundreds of thousands, rather than upon long lists of "ordinaries," each selling but a single edition. The era of the best seller had opened, the book advertised with intensity like a soap or a patent medicine for a few weeks or months, then dropped entirely, and the plates sold to a firm organized for the purpose—a Grosset & Dunlap company, which would issue a second run of the book in a cheap edition, and then drop it forever. In the old publishing days books were held for years on the shelves of a company and sold, a few copies now and then, to readers of the company's catalogues; but now there was a house-cleaning after every publishing season, the unsold copies were disposed of as "remainders" to companies organized to peddle them out at cut prices— what was a $10 set last summer becomes now a $3.50 bargain.

With the new century there began to appear vigorous young publishing houses, most of them founded by college men who had had training with the older firms. One notes the names of Doubleday and Page, of Alfred Knopf, of

Boni and Liveright, of Harcourt and Brace. The vigorous personalities of these young men—more and more a veritable army of them—have in this single field of book-selection and book-publishing caused what may be called a revolution. The thing they have done is worth a book rather than a paragraph. The best study of their work thus far is a series of articles in the *"Literary Digest* International Book Review" of 1914, under the title "With the Makers of Books in America."

The emphasis everywhere was upon books that were alive, books and sets that possessed irresistible "talking points," books to handle in vast quantities like a manufactured product from a mill. Now as never before, fiction was pressed into huge editions. Every publishing hook was baited for marvelous best sellers; every publishing season brought a new one, and every one apologized if caught out in company with this latest book unread. The new literary magazine, the "Bookman," first issued in 1895, acted as self-constituted Nilometer of the rising flood. Its monthly list of the "six best sellers" unquestionably helped to swell the rising tide of fiction that soon submerged all the old landmarks.

A study of the entire thirty-five years of this "Bookman" list—for it has persisted without a break to the present time—is food for pessimism: every year new novels—often of flimsiest texture—blazed into comets that for a moment filled the whole sky; multiplied to the hundreds of thousands by quantity processes, with flamboyant "blurbs" upon their elaborate jackets declaring them to be classics surpassing Dickens and Thackeray; and then abandoned after a few months for others advertised in precisely the same way.

The volleys of superlatives that made up the book-review sections in the earlier years of the period, seen in the perspective of to-day, seem incredible. Concerning James Lane Allen, for some years on every list of best sellers, James MacArthur, editor of the "Bookman," could say:

Like Minerva issuing full-formed from the head of Jove, Mr. Allen issues from his long years of silence and seclusion a perfect master of his art—unfailing in its inspiration, unfaltering in its classic accent. . . . It would be difficult to recall another novel [He was reviewing *The Choir Invisible*] since *The Scarlet Letter* that has touched the same note of greatness, or given to one section of our national life, as Hawthorne's classic did to another, a voice far beyond singing.

And Mr. Hamilton W. Mabie, writing in the "Outlook" of Allen's novel, could say that in comparison with his art "one recalls only Mr. Hardy's three classics of pastoral England, and among French novelists George Sand and Pierre Loti." In the light of to-day this is not criticism: it is humor. My own estimate of the man's art in my "History of American Literature Since 1870," an estimate angrily protested against by Allen himself, I still maintain. The disappearance of Allen from all the book-lists of the later period has been complete.

Of the meteoric shower of historical romance near the close of the century we have already spoken. Fundamentally it was a best-seller phenomenon. The greater mass of it was preceded by what is perhaps the most sensational piece of book-exploiting that had been done in America up to that time, the marketing in 1898 of "David Harum," a volume that in three years sold 520,000 copies. The story of this amazing *coup* throws light upon its times. The author, a non-literary man and an invalid, had written the book as a diversion during the progress of what proved to be a fatal illness. The manuscript, written in long hand and nearly two feet high, went the round of all the publishers and was promptly rejected until, in the office of the Appletons, it encountered a bright young reader who discovered in the mass the one delicious fragment in the volume, the horse-trade with the deacon, with its "he'll stand without hitching" motif. This, he thought, could be placed early in the story, carefully "featured" and made the "talking point" of the advertising. There was no objection:

the author had died, and the house made the change. The result we know. There is nothing worth while in the book except David Harum, the central figure. Technique, style, good taste at times, plot, diction—everything was wanting, and yet the book sold. It was because David was alive. His aphorisms for a time were on all lips:

Do to the other feller what he'd like to do to you, and do it first.

A reasonable amount of fleas is good for a dog: it keeps him from brooding on being a dog.

The book became in its way a classic: it "started something." It was discovered that the American reader, the buyer of best sellers, wanted first of all characterization—strong, vigorous, dominating characters, crude if need be, with a dash of humor and a plentiful supply of sentiment. From this moment characterization became more and more a dominating demand of the makers of fiction. For years the David Harum influence was everywhere visible. For a single example note its effect upon a later best seller, Irving Bacheller's "Eben Holden."

III

The first real literary discovery of the period had been Mary E. Wilkins of Massachusetts and Vermont.[1] The story of her literary "arrival" is significant. Harper & Brothers had been the first to recognize the worth of her crude but intensely original short-story work and had issued in "Harper's Magazine" a number of her pieces, carefully supervised by Mr. Alden, and in 1887 had published them in a volume entitled "A Humble Romance." In the flood of local-color fiction it was unnoticed, as was her later and stronger collection "A New England Nun," 1891,

[1] See "A History of American Literature since 1870," Fred Lewis Pattee, p. 235, and "On the Terminal Moraine of New England Puritanism" in "Sidelights on American Literature," Fred Lewis Pattee.

the year of "Main-Travelled Roads," "Gallegher," and "Flute and Violin." But suddenly had come the unexpected: the book was discovered in England and was praised by English critics as a new and significant note in fictional realism. The response in America was instant and emphatic. Soon reviewers were comparing her stories even with Hawthorne's.

Time has modified these early superlatives, but it has not, as in the case of so many other popular best sellers of the period, dropped her from modern consideration. Her "A New England Nun" collection, the novel "Pembroke" which followed, and several of her later collections like "The Wind in the Rose Bush" cannot be neglected in any history of the period since 1890.

An Emily Brontë personality, frail of body, intense, sensitive, retiring, she had learned little of life from actual contacts. Much of her life she had lived in a world of her own creating, compact of fairies and imagination. Of English or French or Russian realism she knew nothing, read nothing. Her conceptions of living were as lyric of texture as Emily Dickinson's. When she cast them into the short-story mold they were prose ballads. Her theme the New England decline, repressed lives, personalities in some way warped by their inheritance or their environment, lives compelled by Puritanic standards, lives cheated by a sinister Nemesis that held them, as Egdon Heath did in Hardy's "Return of the Native": maidens held to an iron home régime until withered by age. Always repression; passion and passions held in check by stoic pride until repression no longer was possible, and then the flood, like a Vermont river on the rampage for the first time in a generation, destroying all landmarks. And the style was completely in harmony: staccato, Saxon of diction, unadjectived, unconnected. The originality and spontaneousness of it was recognized, but always in the first reviews there was complaint of crudeness, of lack of flowing beauty, of intolerable grimness of style.

And from this point came the first cause of her decline. She obeyed her critics and worked for ornament, even to the writing of a historical romance of early Virginia, flamboyant with adjectives; she furnished serials to the popular magazines keyed to best-seller demands.

IV

It is impossible to trace the literary currents of the period and not be aware at every point of this tremendous main stream in the fiction of the time, the all-dominating best seller. A list of representative American best-seller novels since 1900 is suggestive.

1899. "David Harum," Edward Noyes Westcott.
1900. "The Reign of Law," James Lane Allen.
1901. "Alice of Old Vincennes," Maurice Thompson.
1902. "Mrs. Wiggs of the Cabbage Patch," Alice Hegan Rice.
1903. "The Virginian," Owen Wister.
1904. "The Little Shepherd of Kingdom Come," John Fox, Jr.
1905. "Freckles," Gene Stratton Porter.
1906. "The House of Mirth," Edith Wharton.
1907. "The Lady of the Decoration," Frances Little (Fannie C. Macaulay).
1908. "The Shuttle," Frances Hodgson Burnett.
1909. "The Trail of the Lonesome Pine," John Fox, Jr.
1910. "The Prodigal Judge," Vaughn Kester.
1911. "The Sick-Abed Lady, and Other Stories," Eleanor Hallowell Abbott.
1912. "The Harvester," Gene Stratton Porter.
1913. "V. V.'s Eyes," Henry Sydnor Harrison.
1914. "The Inside of the Cup," Winston Churchill.
1915. "The Turmoil," Booth Tarkington.
1916. "Seventeen," Booth Tarkington.
1917. "Mary 'Gusta," J. C. Lincoln.
1918–20. Foreign Novels—Wells, Bennett, Blasco Ibañez.
1921. "Main Street," Sinclair Lewis.
1922. "Babbitt," Sinclair Lewis.

1923. "Black Oxen," Gertrude Atherton.
1924. "So Big," Edna Ferber.
1925. "The Perennial Bachelor," Anne Parrish.
1926. "The Private Life of Helen of Troy," John Erskine.
1927. "Elmer Gantry," Sinclair Lewis.
1928. "The Bridge of San Luis Rey," Thornton Wilder.

One notes that the majority of these writers were traffickers in simple emotion; sometimes, as in the case of the John Fox novels, of "V. V.'s Eyes," and "The Shuttle," of sentiment pressed to the limits of mawkishness. James Lane Allen, all of whose novels reached best-seller prominence, worked with more carefully selected pigments. Though undoubtedly the best technician in the whole list of best-seller leaders, he had no story to tell that compelled him, he had no power to make his personalities alive, he had no vision he must share: he worked coldly and by rule; he was not an artist—he was an artisan.

A study of the list reveals other characteristics. Humor embodied in a broadly characterized central personage like David Harum, or the youth in "Seventeen," or Mrs. Wiggs of the "Cabbage Patch," has usually been a successful talking point for those who sell commercial fiction; so, too, has been the atmosphere of specialized knowledge, as in "Caleb West, Master Diver" and "Tom Grogan," by F. Hopkinson Smith, or in the romances of Gene Stratton Porter where it is compounded of entomology, Nature adoration, and sentimentalism.

During the third decade of the period there came into best-seller leadership more and more the novel dealing with some subject taboo to the ordinary, or "pussy-footed about" for the easily shocked. Churchill's "The Inside of the Cup" dealt smashingly with the shortcomings of the modern church, as did Lewis's "Elmer Gantry" some years later. Mrs. Atherton's "Black Oxen" had gland-transplanting and sex-renewal as its central motif, and John Erskine drew upon the classic Helen of Troy, Galahad, and

Uncle Sam myths for titles and motifs for his best-seller dollar-makers, advertised like breakfast foods or soaps.

To reprehend those authors who deliberately chose to turn their artistry into the easy channels leading to quick and abundant cash returns is not the business of the historian of literature. One may deplore, however, the prostitution of genius. Consider John Erskine, for example— or better still, Robert W. Chambers, born in 1865 in Brooklyn. From 1886 to 1893 he was a student in the Académie Julian, Paris. Returning to America, his volumes "In the Quarter" and "The King in Yellow" had in them a Gallic fineness and finesse that in the opinion of many gave richer promise than anything else in the new nineties. But New York City is a sirocco, it is a death blast to the genius it imports; it withers everything it touches. The Gallic deftness and lightness of touch of Chambers, the poetic soul of the later Erskine, were sold deliberately. Let Mencken tell the story: there are moments when Mencken is inspired. Referring to a favorable estimate of Chambers by Percival Pollard, he wrote in 1919:

He saw the shoddiness in Chambers, the leaning toward "profitable pot-boiling," but he saw, too, a fundamental earnestness and a high degree of skill. What has become of these things? Are they visible, even as ghosts, in the preposterous serials that engaud the magazines of Mr. Hearst and then load the department stores as books? . . . Chambers grows sillier and sillier, emptier and emptier, worse and worse. Was he ever more than a fifth-rater?

The artist in the long average of his creation discloses his real self. The genuine artist soul is an artist soul, and it refuses at any price to prostitute its artistry. If it has genuine power, it compels the times to its own standards.

There is hope, however; a single gleam at least. Young Thornton Wilder has kept his art at high levels. "The

Bridge of San Luis Rey" led the entire best-selling group for a year. Wilder then followed it with a volume after still more classic models. One does not have to surrender to the baser elements.

CHAPTER XVI

THE FEMININE NOVEL

I

THE growth of the novel in America has been for a century *per saltum:* advance not by slow increment but by explosions. At first every novel was fired upon. Even "The Scarlet Letter," as late as the eighteen fifties, was branded as dangerous to youth. With the opening of the new period in the nineties it was French realism and French morals that troubled the guardians of the young. An awful something like a contagion was coming, they felt, and it must be stopped. A whole decade before Crane's "Maggie, A Girl of the Streets"—1888 it was—four novels, all of them by women, were marked "unsafe," even "scandalous" and "immoral," and thus, despite their feebleness, were elevated into the ranks of the best sellers:

"The Quick and the Dead," Amélie Rives
"Eros," Laura Daintry
"Miss Middleton's Lover," Laura Jean Libbey
"What Dreams May Come," Gertrude Atherton

The first of these created a sensation. It was even parodied at book length: "Be Quick and be Dead." Its author, however, like the author of "Eros," held the stage center only for a moment. Laura Jean Libbey lived into the second decade of the new century as a synonym for over-sweetness and lightness, but Mrs. Atherton had powers that were to develop and make her one of the forces in the new period. Her work along with that of Mrs. Wharton, who was soon to appear, became strong enough to force its way and help overthrow the barriers of narrowness, prudishness, and timidity. Both are transition figures, both moved for a time from novel to novel through a barrage of criticism, both are veterans from the no-man's land of a war even now not entirely won.

Gertrude Atherton was born precisely where she should have been—in California; and at the moment most appropriate—eight years after the gold discovery, the era of Bret Harte and Mark Twain and Joaquin Miller. To be a child in this atmosphere bred fearlessness and originality and nerve. Another element came early: she was sent to a select school in Kentucky where she saw—and felt—the romance and the spirit of the Old South. The ghost of it was to flit through all her work. It is needless to add more details to her biography. Following an early and distinguished marriage, she was left a widow at thirty, and since has lived a cosmopolite in many lands, always, like Mrs. Wharton, among what she herself has termed "The Aristocrats."

Next her fiction. The approach to it is through a single gate marked *Californian*—originality, profusion, richness, independence. She will stand on her own feet; she will brook no master; she will be starred with no "school." Early she issued her *salut au monde*. It is in the "North American Review"—here is a paragraph:

Great original genius is only recognized and admired after a desperate fight, because there is no greater coward than the intellectual public. . . . Think of the monopoly of the world's letters if no original minds had ever come to break loose from traditions, inaugurate new schools, and plant new ideas! Suppose the glorious galaxy now illuminating our past had succumbed to the inevitable fire of public protestation—what sort of literature would we have today?

Knowledge of European literature and long residences abroad have stimulated her genius for originality and enabled her to be a pioneer in many fictional areas. She wrote Van Dine detective stories before Van Dine; and in her novel "The Conqueror," issued as far back as 1902, she became the pioneer in the later "Maurois school" of biographical fiction.

To be at all with her novels is to be impressed with her daring, with her recklessness at times. Often for chapter after chapter she invites opposition—she stalks through paragraph after paragraph with visible chips upon her shoulders. It becomes a defect. Take for instance what we consider her best work, "The Conqueror." It is a masterpiece. It is a life of Alexander Hamilton classified in many libraries as biography, and yet it is a novel. For her materials she worked with all the methods of a modern historian, even to the visiting of the West Indies for data. The blending of the two elements is brilliantly done, it is unique—one finds oneself using superlatives. But a second reading inclines one to modify one's judgments. Hamilton is too perfect; he is a hero of the old romantic type, and Jefferson is the foil, the villain, with Washington little better. And the purpose of it all soon appears: Hamilton was a love-child— illegitimate, yet a demigod as contrasted with the blue-blooded Washington.

It takes courage in America to disparage the god-like Washington, but in Mrs. Atherton the pussy-foot element never was. Too fastidious to soil herself with mere nastiness for nastiness' sake, she can yet handle sex, when needful, with European frankness. Her best-seller triumph "Senator North" deals with a subject few Americans would dare to touch, a theme which five years later Thomas Dixon was to handle in his "The Clansman" at the risk of his life—the theme of marriage between whites and negroes. With almost every novel she has met with opposition, often severe. She has a genius for finding bloody angles. Even her titles are provocative: "American Wives and English Husbands," "The Californians," "The Aristocrats," "The Splendid Idle Forties," "Perch of the Devil," "Black

Oxen." Thirty-seven novels she has written, many with California backgrounds, some with international motifs, some wholly unusual. She can make her reader follow to the end, and she can create for him characters that seem alive, Californian in their vitality. This she can do.

But her defects are at times appalling. She is too headlong often for mere technique; with feminine perverseness and whim she gallops often from the main road into attractive side-paths. Often she turns her novel into what is really a treatise. "American Wives and English Husbands" is an essay on American and English traits—excellent analysis. She is a journalist. She is vibrantly sensitive to news values, to every wave of contemporaneousness. She knows every nerve in the modern body and can touch it when she wills. Her up-to-dateness has elements in it akin to genius, but genius without a governor.

So near the line of permanence has she come at times that her failure is tragic. As a single concrete instance, consider her novel "Black Oxen." Its theme Hawthorne might have made into a classic. "Doctor Heidegger's Experiment" brought back with his magic liquor the whole of youth without impairment; Mrs. Atherton's narrative of gland-transplanting brought back only the outward and physical youth. The soul of man keys only with its own generation, she implies. Her victim, physically a youth, now is inwardly senile, with loneliness unutterable. A youthful body and an aged soul: a theme for a master, but it is lost in a jungle of otherness. She is too prone to free her mind, too likely to lapse into melodrama and extravagance. Style, finish, artistry are not hers—save in patches. She has what Mrs. Wharton has not: passion, femininity, appeal. Mrs. Wharton has what she has not: technique, poise, permanence. She will survive longest in "The Conqueror." Next, perhaps, come those children of her old age, studies in classic history like "The Immortal Marriage," a romance of the Greece of Pericles and Aspasia.

II

The work of Mrs. Wharton centers in the second decade of the new century. From her first novel it was realized that a new craftsman had appeared, vibrant, Gallic in art mastery, fitted to bring into the opening century what Henry James had brought into the seventies and the eighties a generation before—technique, European fastidiousness in style, and, more than all this, the cultivated viewpoint, exotic, aristocratic atmosphere. The decade overflowed with her. In the ten years after 1899, the date of her first volume, she published three major novels, three novelettes, and five collections of short stories, most of the parts of which had appeared previously in the magazines. "Scribner's" for a decade was full of her serials, her short stories, her travel sketches. As with Mrs. Atherton, after each of her major works of fiction came blasts of criticism: the European morals of her tales, the seeming overdoneness of her picturings, the cold-bloodedness of her revelations; and as promptly came forces of defense which poured forth barrages of superlatives as vigorous. Sex problems in her fiction she handled with Old World freedom and thoroughness, but never, it must be added, with nastiness.

Edith Newbold Jones, later Mrs. Wharton, was born in 1862 in the Washington Square area she has used so often in her novels. Her family, wealthy, ancient (as American antiquity is reckoned), of "Old World gentility" as she herself would phrase it, gave her every advantage—education by private tutors, long residences in Europe, contact everywhere with what on the Continent is supposed to make for "culture." French and Italian and German became to her as mother-tongues, and with them she secured a knowledge of European literature comparable only with that secured by an earlier American similarly educated, Henry James. Her later biography need not detain us. She was married at twenty-three to Mr. Edward Wharton of

Boston; she lived in New York, in Newport, in Lenox, with frequent and long visits to Europe, and in 1904 with her husband she took up her residence permanently in France. It need be added only that her work during the period of the World War, extensive and distinctive, brought her from the French government, as similar work did to Mrs. Atherton and Mrs. Deland, the Cross of the Legion of Honor.

Turning to her literary career, one notes that her first volume appeared when she was thirty-seven years of age. She started on her wingings full-fledged: she needs blush at no surviving awkwardness. Again it is noteworthy that her first major novel was an attempt to catch the trade winds of a popular fictional movement. "The Valley of Decision," 1902, is a historical romance, laid in medieval Italy, a volume upon which she expended much labor in research and revision, a remarkable volume, one that may be ranked even with George Eliot's "Romola." The historical fiction period produced nothing better done. Buried in the rubbish of the flood that for a time blotted out all landmarks, it has never received, doubtless will now never receive, the attention it deserves.

Then in 1905 came "The House of Mirth," published first as a serial in "Scribner's Magazine," then brought into prominence as the best seller of its year. It was the beginning of what may be called the first phase of her art: a dissection of the so-called idle-rich class of New York. Eleven major novels she has written, most of them revolving in one way or another about this single area. Excluding her "The Valley of Decision," these novels are:

"The House of Mirth," 1905
"The Fruit of the Tree," 1907
"The Reef," 1912
"The Custom of the Country," 1913
"The Marne," 1918
"The Age of Innocence," 1920

"Glimpses of the Moon," 1922
"A Son at the Front," 1923
"The Mother's Recompense," 1925
"Twilight Sleep," 1927

To these one may add five novelettes, perhaps nine, Henry-James-like in length yet single of situation, short stories in everything save shortness,—transitional creations between two *genres:* "The Touchstone," 1900; "Sanctuary," 1903; "Madame de Treymes," 1907; "Ethan Frome," 1911; "Summer," 1917; and the four parts of "Old New York," 1924.

Artistry first of all. In technique and finish all she has touched is distinctive. Edged with satire, pointed with wit, they are French rather than American or English. To compare them to the work of Henry James is conventional, but it is also unavoidable. The tap-roots of the art of both pierce through the Anglo-Saxon into Gallic strata. Only in her materials is she American. She can make a volume on "The Writing of Fiction," noting all forces and all writers that have contributed to the evolution of the novel, and allude to only three Americans: Poe, Hawthorne and Henry James, in the section treating the short story, noting only that their work was really not of short-story texture. Both James and Mrs. Wharton must be classed as virtuosi trained in the school of Stendhal, Balzac, Flaubert, and Turgeniev. Both must be classed as intellectuals, concerned fundamentally with form, with manners, with art.

One does not read long in a volume like "The House of Mirth" without being impressed with its atmosphere of artificiality. In technique it is near perfection, but one cannot breathe. It is the artificiality of the city as contrasted with the naturalness of the country. Its author is dealing with metropolitan society, with vast wealth, monstrous personalities, vain, empty of all save selfishness. All her women are parasites, cruel as leeches and as soulless. To be good in this Vanity Fair, this sleek den of leopards, is impossible. Lily Bart, the best character in her novels, elaborated with all the detail of a Becky Sharp, attempted morality in its polluted circle and failed. The ball-and-chain of her inheritance dragged her down to its level.

Her novels are not muck-rake work though they came, the earliest of them, in "the shame of the cities" era, and though they lay bare social evils with the unction of an Upton Sinclair. Never is she furnishing propaganda, with a vision of reform. Her function is diagnosis of the diseases incident to the artificiality of modern civilization, diagnosis clear and positive. Not for her the surgery.

Of her major novels after her first venture the best is "The Age of Innocence," New York society as she knew it in the seventies, New York with the Indian summer light upon it of remembered childhood. After it in value come "The House of Mirth" and "The Custom of the Country." "Ethan Frome" in its brevity seems more perfect, but the novel is a structure with complexities; its difficulties are architectonic—the difference between a villa and a cathedral. It centers in the portrayal of character, whereas the short story centers about a situation. In a novel we live long with the characters and learn to know them intimately, so intimately indeed that, if the work be well done, we close the book with a sigh and awake as from an experience that has taken us from the actuality of our own living. But the short story is a flash, a glimpse, a humor, a situation not lived with. It is a moment of feeling, like a lyric.

Like Henry James, Mrs. Wharton has carried parallel with her major pieces of fiction numbers of these shorter-length works—more than fifty in all. They have been praised more than her novels have, and they deserve praise. Nowhere can one find in English better models for study, better illustrations of all the devices of the modern and complicated art of short-story creation. Yet, as we have seen, they must not be rated above her major novels, which are architecturally as perfect. Artistry reveals itself more readily always in the small-wrought area than in the large.

Her success with a small canvas like "Ethan Frome" we can account for. The *conte,* the modern short story, is an art form: technique is its life-blood, and Mrs. Wharton first of all is a craftsman.

And here again we must note that her art is fundamentally intellectual, just as Mrs. Atherton's is emotional. It is at this point that she fails of reaching the heights where the great masters stand. Her works are mere *works.* Great art must have in it more than faultless technique: it must have something that lifts it into the realm of the spiritual, it must have *soul*—that which one may feel but no man define. This final touch she has seldom been able to give. Even in so perfect a bit of artistry as "Ethan Frome" it has all but escaped her. Let an English critic sustain me:

It is a tale with a beginning and a middle and an end. It is dramatic and arresting. It is simple. As a work of art it can be compared with *Silas Marner,* and that is high praise. But just as *Silas Marner* was, even in its title, too literary to be great literature, too like a study of peasant life from a scholar's window to be a living image of the countryside, so *Ethan Frome* . . . is a structure rather than a creation. The very virtues in which such constructions abound are betrayals of their origin. We must admire, we hesitate to love them.[1]

Despite her artistry, therefore, Mrs. Wharton has failed, as the eighteenth century failed, by her insistence upon definitions of life in terms of the artificial, in terms of civilization rather than in the fundamentals of Nature. Of the great quivering, suffering, laboring human mass she knows little. "The World of Labor," says Boynton, "is mentioned in but one of her novels, and in this for the sole purpose of supplying an added ground for a marital misunderstanding." Nature unadorned she views with all the horror of an Addison or a Pope. She is at home only in landscaped grounds with topiary-bordered walks and green

[1] Osbert Burdett in "Contemporary American Authors," originally published in the "London Mercury," 1928.

lawns, with mansion houses and servants, where perfectly dressed drones take tea. Within this area she is perfectly at home. Choose at random from her lists of novels: you will not go far wrong.

III

It must not be forgotten that alongside the newnesses of the younger novelists the placid stream of fiction from the survivors of the earlier period still flowed on. Sarah Orne Jewett was first to go, in 1909. Kate Douglas Wiggin was a cheerful soul with her witty and sunny "Penelope" volumes. She lingered till 1923. Mary N. Murfree ("Charles Egbert Craddock") died a year earlier. Her later years were pathetic: she outlived her materials. Who deals with stuff as limited in range as the social system of a Tennessee mountain cove must simply repeat and repeat. Frances Hodgson Burnett, busy to the end, lingered on until 1924 and Clara Louise Burnham until 1927.[2]

The work of Margaret Deland[3] belongs, as does that of Mary E. Wilkins, to both periods. They were forces in the transition; they grew with their times, they were vibrant with their day. Mrs. Deland's earliest novel, "John Ward, Preacher," 1888, published when the reaction to the findings of modern science was violent in all religious circles, placed her work in comparison with the English sensation of the year, Mrs. Humphry Ward's "Robert Elsmere," best seller on both sides of the water.

"John Ward, Preacher" was daring work, but with the new century Mrs. Deland changed her key from the religious motif to others as daring in social and humanistic areas. Always she faced the actual and revealed it. Her two novels "The Awakening of Helena Ritchie" and "The Iron

[2] A literary incident worthy of record is the fact that Mrs. Burnett's son, the original Little Lord Fauntleroy, has written the biography of his mother, entitling it "The Romantic Lady."

[3] See "A History of American Literature since 1870," Fred Lewis Pattee, chapter XVII.

Woman" are documents in the history of their times, strong novels of the transition period. Perhaps her best claim to remembrance, however, is her series of short stories, "Old Chester Tales," and the volumes which followed. In them appears Dr. Lavender, her best creation—a character to add to the small gallery of fictional personalities uniquely American. The old clergyman is a philosopher, a father to his people, a pastor of the old type—intensely human, kindly at heart, and wise with the Benjamin Franklin wisdom beneath his piety. And in the solution of his parish problems he threw light upon many contemporary questions. The short story "The Stuffed Animal House," with its motif the question of ending painlessly the lives of the hopelessly sick, created long-drawn-out discussion, and even consternation, but when has feminine fiction not been an explosive?

IV

During the post-Civil War period the South was central. Its fiction—despite Miss Murfree, who would conceal her sex with a pseudonym and an attempted masculinity of style—was written by men. And the whole of it was romance. Cable when he tried to work with honesty and actuality was compelled to flee to the North. For a generation there was negro dialect, "befo' de war," moonlight on the cottonfields, banjos and spirituals, "the old régime." In Thomas Nelson Page, it was Cavalier chivalry completely destroyed by the war, blooded aristocracy like Old World nobility forever gone. The new realism of youngsters to whom the Civil War was apparently as far away as the Revolution, had little sympathy with this romance. It threw overboard the dialect and branded such revered classics as Page's "Marse Chan" as bosh; it was false on the face of it, for the old negro tells the whole tale in artistically handled dialect and with careful observance of all the short-story rules.

The time was ripe for a new voicing of the South. Enough material was available to satisfy a Fielding or a Dickens or a Hardy. The only man of the younger generation seemingly capable of handling this wealth was James Branch Cabell; but he resigned, ran away from the actual about him, and built himself a playhouse in a fantastic world of his own invention.

But there was a woman. Ellen Glasgow was to attempt the work, and to become one of the major forces of the new period. She emerged with the incoming century and grew in power with every succeeding book, until with her novel "Barren Ground" she was recognized as a leading American novelist, one to class with Mrs. Wharton and Willa Cather.

She was born in Richmond, Virginia, in 1874, and was almost exclusively self-educated. She taught herself to read by spelling out the words in Scott's novels. Her dreams of a literary life began to shape themselves during the early years of that decade so dominated and all but damned by the mania for historical and historicated fiction. No literary contagion has ever surpassed it. What novelist escaped?

Miss Glasglow's approach to literature, unlike that of most of her contemporaries, was old-fashioned in its setting. No cosmopolitanism, as with Mrs. Atherton and Mrs. Wharton; no old-home dreamings after transplantation into alien soil, as with Mrs. Deland; no apprenticeship in journalism as in the case of Dreiser and Miss Cather and Lewis. She remained in her native Richmond and wrote of Virginia. And she began early: twenty-three she was when her first novel appeared. The title was good—"The Descendant,"—ominous: she would deal not with the romantic old régime, but with the descendants, the actuality of *now*.

Her literary "arrival" was in 1900. After "The Voice of the People," issued when she was twenty-six, readers in the North realized that a new literary force had awakened in what Mencken later was to call "the Sahara of the Bozart." In step with the times, she began with actual history as background. To know the Virginia of to-day it was necessary, she believed, to know the old régime from which it was evolved, the Virginia destroyed by the Civil War. The approach to her seventeen novels is a trilogy of historical romances to be read in order thus:

> "The Battle-ground," 1902
> "The Romance of a Plain Man," 1909
> "The Voice of the People," 1900

These constitute a tragedy in three acts: (1) the old régime and the whirlwind that destroyed it; (2) the agony of Reconstruction; (3) the new régime. The first act is in the sixties, the second in the seventies, the third in the eighties. Her later novels for the most part have been studies of two social classes in Virginia since the nineties: the war-wrecked aristocracy, and the semi-aristocrats who are not F.F.V.'s and not "poor whites."

James Branch Cabell, himself a Virginian, has been specific as to her work with the materials of her State:

You have in the works of Ellen Glasgow something very like a complete social chronicle of the Piedmont section of the State of Virginia since the War Between States, as this chronicle has been put together by a witty and observant woman, a poet in grain, who was not at any moment in her writing quite devoid of malice, nor of an all-understanding lyric tenderness either, and who was not through any tiniest half-moment deficient in a very consummate craftsmanship. What we have here, to my first finding, seemed a complete natural history of the Southern gentlewoman, with every attendant feature of her lair and general habitat most accurately rendered. But reflection showed the matter to be more pregnant than I had at the outset suspected; for the actual theme of Ellen Glasgow, the theme which in her writing figures always, if not exactly as a relentless Frankenstein's monster, at least as a sort of ideational King Charles's head, I take to be The

Tragedy of Everywoman, as it was lately enacted in the Southern States of America.

Such work has been akin to that done by Mary E. Wilkins Freeman in New England: analysis of the ruins left by the tornado of the sixties. Both have dealt with survivals. In four volumes, "Virginia," "Life and Gabriella," "The Builders," and "Barren Ground," Miss Glasgow has dealt with the chief victims of the tragedy: the women—last social area unreconstructed; as in Miss Wilkins, impoverished *grandes dames* maintaining with rigor the old distinctions, pathetic old maids who dream, poor whites admirable but ineffectual, and always among them and of them, eager youth rushing toward life.

She is a realist, as pitiless in her picturings as Dreiser, but, totally unlike him, she has humor, and she has values other than news recordings: she is a painter, not a photographer. She has a pen, too, as sharp for satire as is Lewis's; "blood and irony" is her motto. But she is not a showman, nor is she a cynic. She loves her people—all of them—and if there is harshness in her treatment it is the harshness of the surgeon.

A realist she is, but yet a poet. It is noteworthy that all the feminine realists of the period have issued volumes of poetry, these at the head of the list:

"The Old Garden, and Other Verses," Margaret Deland, 1886.
"The Freeman," Ellen Glasgow, 1902.
"April Twilights," Willa Cather, 1903.
"Artemis to Actæon," Edith Wharton, 1909.
"The Secret Way," Zona Gale, 1921.

It explains much: the lyric note, the inevitable word, the swallow flights above the sordidness and prose of realism, the picturings of sun-lighted backgrounds:

She delights by her talent for presenting the wonder and bloom of Virginia gardens and countryside. Go where you will in her Southern world, there is perfume in the sunlit air, hyacinths and the scent of wild grapes and microphylla roses; there are the budding sycamore and the foam of dogwood and redbud; sparrows rustle among the Virginia creepers, thrushes sing, bluebirds and red-winged blackbirds flicker over the pastures; sunsets glow behind dark pines; there is the sound of water flowing.[4]

She has wit, moreover, as rapier-like in its flash and parry as Agnes Repplier's. It saves her pages from Dreiser-like heaviness and gloom. With a single volume she has made herself one of the leading humorists of the period: "The Romantic Comedians" is redolent of Virginia and of human nature the world over. "I'm a bird with a broken wing," sighs the old Judge, left a widower at sixty-five, but after a year he began to detect "odd palpitations within the suave Virginia depths of his being, where his broken wing was helplessly trying to flutter." And of the fluttering of this broken wing she makes her novel. Nowhere more practical wisdom, more genuine humor, more of human nature.

Her novels contain a philosophy of life that is never Puritanic. Indeed, she has her fling at Puritanism:

You are all tainted with Puritanism, even down here in Virginia, where, Heaven knows! you ought to have escaped the blight. But America is an American nation, and the danger with national anæmia is that it runs to fanaticism in the brain. You are so harassed by the ideas of indecency that when you can't find fresh food for scandal, you resort to the canned variety.

It is wider than Virginia, wider than America. Her novel "Barren Ground," with its broom-sedge symbolism— "broom-sedge is fate"—is not alone Virginian. One thing, she finds, can conquer even broom-sedge, one only: it is courage. The word rings through volumes of her work.

[4] "Ellen Glasgow: The Fighting Edge of Romance," in "Critical Woodcuts," Stuart P. Sherman, the best treatment of her work so far.

Profuseness is her major defect; she draws out her situations at times to weariness. Sherman advised a twenty per cent cut in bulk when her final set is issued. Not all her books would bear such mutilation, but there are chapters in all of them that would be improved by even more drastic surgery than that suggested by Sherman.

v

In a recent symposium participated in by thirty-two "outstanding critics," each critic rendering his verdict independently, two women, Willa Cather and Edith Wharton, were adjudged to be the leading American fiction-writers at the present time. And near the head of the list were two other women, Zona Gale and Ellen Glasgow.[5]

Miss Cather was the latest arrival in the major feminine group. Though but two years younger than Ellen Glasgow, her first significant work was issued a decade later than the Virginia novelist's. As late as 1912 she had done nothing significant. It is noteworthy at the start that she too was of old Virginian stock and that she spent her early childhood not far from where Miss Glasgow spent hers. There are no other resemblances. At the age of eight Willa Cather was taken by her parents to Nebraska, and until late girlhood was reared amid frontier conditions—everywhere the open prairie unfenced to the horizon, with herds of half-wild cattle, immigrants (totally un-English) the only neighbors, and horseback riding the only means of travel. Six or eight years of wild freedom in the open erased all memories of Virginia. She was a transplanted thing, but in the new soil of the West she flourished, she became a Western product, for a time utterly Western. High school life at Red Cloud occupied her for a time, and then for four years the University of Nebraska. She was nineteen when she graduated, and here for a moment it is well to pause.

[5] "American Novelists Ranked: A Psychological Study," by John M. Stalnaker and Fred Eggan. "The English Journal," April, 1929.

Willa Cather was the first recognized literary product of a new force in American life: the Western university. Soon were to come Zona Gale, Dorothy Canfield, Fannie Hurst, and a score of others.

Restlessness was upon her from the first. Nowhere has she ever been rooted, nowhere at home as Miss Jewett was at home in her Berwick, Maine, or as Miss Glasgow is at home in her Richmond, Virginia. Her first venture was in Pittsburgh where she found employment as a reporter on one of the papers—perfect schooling for a novelist if early dropped. Her dream from college days had been literature—fiction: she had written it as theme work in her freshman English courses, descriptions of prairie life, especially of the picturesque immigrant families that took up the land about her father's ranch.

From Pittsburgh she escaped early. She was in New York writing for recognition, poetry, short stories, fiction. Suddenly came unbelievable good fortune: S. S. McClure discovered her work, felt the promise that was in it, accepted her stories for "McClure's Magazine," added her to his magazine force, and then after two years made her his managing editor. For four years she conducted the magazine, four years of most valuable literary contacts, of growing experience with literary values, of knowledge of the demands of the reading world. She resigned at length to follow the star of her early dream: she would write a novel.

Her literary life falls into three distinct periods. In the first came her apprentice work: a book of poems published at her own expense by Badger, then a reissue in book form of her magazine stories, "The Troll Garden"—arresting title. And then had come a silence of six years—the years of the "McClure's" editorship. Even in her first novel, "Alexander's Bridge," her first work after resigning her editorship, work influenced by Henry James and Edith Wharton, there was little save promise. Then in 1912 had come to her a vision, one that opened to her a new period in her literary life: she came in contact with Sarah Orne Jewett: in her own words:

I had the good fortune to meet Sarah Orne Jewett, who had read all of my early stories and had very clear and definite opinions about them and about where my work fell short. She said "Write it as it is, don't try to make it like this or that. You can't do it in anybody else's way; you will have to make a way of your own. If the way happens to be new, don't let that frighten you. Don't try to write the kind of short story that this or that magazine wants; write the truth and let them take it or leave it." It is that kind of honesty, that earnest endeavor to tell truly the thing that haunts the mind, that I love in Miss Jewett's own work. I dedicated "O Pioneers!" to her because I had talked over some of the characters with her, and in this book I tried to tell her the story of the people as truthfully and simply as if I were telling it to her by word of mouth.

The result was the Nebraska pictures of her second period, three novels.

"O Pioneers!" 1913
"Song of the Lark," 1915
"My Ántonia," 1918

Published in Boston, conservatively advertised, the novels made little stir at first. Mencken was one of the first to discover their real worth. Of "My Ántonia" he wrote:

That pure prose is a great deal more than simply a good novel. It is a document in the history of American literature. . . . No romantic novel ever written in America is one-half as beautiful as "My Ántonia."

That was the early twenties. Curiously enough, a bit of doggerel, a parody of a "Mikado" lyric, helped bring publicity.

Blithe Mencken he sat on his Baltimore stoop
Singing "Willa! git Willa! git Willa!"

The red-headed Lewis joined in with a whoop,
    Singing "Willa! git Willa! git Willa!"
They woke every bird from the Bronx to the Loop
    Singing "Willa! git Willa! git Willa!"
So we willy-nilly, got Willa and read,
And Willa proved all that the booster birds said.

Then came the third "break": a New York publisher of the new school advertised widely and in modern manner his re-publication of her early volumes in attractive new dress, and then a new novel keyed to the times—the new post-war times—"One of Ours." The result was the Pulitzer Prize, and an avalanche of superlatives. It was a moment fraught with peril for the author. Necessarily she changed her background: no more Nebraska—though rich soil, it was capable of only a limited number of crops. She was strong enough to refuse to be hurried, strong enough to put forth this limited product in seven years, all of it exclusively finished, all of it at the height of her powers:

"A Lost Lady," 1923
"The Professor's House," 1925
"My Mortal Enemy," 1926
"Death Comes for the Archbishop," 1927

The last of these four was the sensation of its year, the leader of the best sellers.

Before studying her novels individually it is necessary to note the six years of silence after her second volume. One should compare, too, the magazine versions of her early tales with their final form in the "Youth and the Bright Medusa" collections, 1920. Everywhere evidence of growing fastidiousness in style and technique, everywhere evidence of grinding toil. She made herself an artist; intellectually brilliant, she mastered her brushes, her colors, her perspective, her lines. Nothing too much. Her prototype is James Lane Allen, also an artist, also one who made of art the dominating motif of his life.

Her work for posterity is undoubtedly in her three Nebraska novels with their atmosphere of remembrance. Of "My Ántonia" she wrote:

"It was a story of people I knew. I expressed a mood, the core of which was like a folk-song, a thing Grieg could have written. That it was powerfully tied to the soil had nothing to do with it. Ántonia was tied to the soil, but I might have written the tale of a Czech baker in Chicago and it would have been the same."

It is not realism that colors these volumes, it is youth seen through the golden haze of later years, in far exile. She has given us the Nebraska of the eighties and nineties as it lies rich and warmly lighted in her memory. Here she is autobiographical—her best work centers about moments in autobiographical art. "The Song of the Lark"—the story of the woman who sacrificed everything for her art—is her own story:

This story attempts to deal only with the simple and concrete beginnings which color and accent an artist's work, and give some account of how a Moonstone girl found her way out of a vague, easy-going world into a life of disciplined endeavor. Any account of the loyalty of young hearts to some exalted ideal, and the passion with which they strive, will always, in some of us, rekindle generous emotions.

In most of her own fiction, however, there is mere intellect. She is rooted in no soil, she is centered in no emotional home. In all her later years she has been metropolitan and therefore solitary. As with James Lane Allen, art has taken the place of the old home concepts, and one asks: what of Allen's work to-day?

Patiently, with toil, she evolved an original method, just as Sarah Orne Jewett did. Plot in its old formulæ she has all but discarded. It is useless to turn to the last chapter of a tale of hers to solve the mystery, for there is no mystery; useless to turn there to find who married, for marriage is not always the climactic motif in the novel.

It is her work to present to you characters that you can see, sharp-cut as cameos, with minimum of line and no fili-gree, characters that compel and linger.

But her art, satisfying though it is to the eye, leaves no glow. There is little of warmth in her cameo cuttings. The secret of Miss Jewett she never really caught. For Miss Jewett's characters steal subtly into the realm of one's feel-ing. She loved her own and we love them; she painted not with intellect only, but with emotion. With Miss Cather, save for a few glowing moments where she dreamed of her girlhood on the Nebraska prairies, there is little of that subtle something that makes the heart flutter a bit and the breath come short. We see, but we do not share. A subject to be attractive must be a measurable thing with outlines and dimensions—a thing for T-square and compass. There are no blurred moments in her work, when intuition takes the pencil and dreams—when shadows enter that she cannot explain—when the unseen glimpses itself, the soul beyond all realms of the eye—the glow that some call religion, that some call soul, that some call the divine moments of art.

VI

The stronger feminine writers of the period, with the exception of Edith Wharton and Ellen Glasgow, all came from the trans-Allegheny regions, especially from the ris-ing Midlands. Boston and New York lapsed into complete sterility. Mrs. Wharton survived only because she escaped to Europe. The second and third decades of the new cen-tury are vibrant with the excited voices of new Western women, most of them graduates of the newly established and tremendously earnest colleges and universities of the recent frontier. There was Mary Austin, graduate of Blackburn University, pioneer because of broken health into unfrequented regions of the Southwest, even at length beyond the borders of the Mojave Desert. As early as 1903 she sent East her "The Land of Little Rain," a book in which the Desert is the principal character, alive, sinister lovable, death-dealing, irresistible, beautiful. No stronger book of its variety exists in our literature. And she followed it with "The Basket Woman," "Lost Borders," "The Flock," "The Land of Journeys' Ending," and twenty others, vivid, vital, permanent.

From the State universities came more and more vigorous new voices. From Nebraska, Willa Cather; from Ohio, Dorothy Canfield Fisher; from Wisconsin, Zona Gale; from Missouri, Fannie Hurst. Dorothy Canfield (now Mrs. Fisher) was the scholar of the group. After her graduation from Ohio State University, of which her father was president, she earned her Ph.D. at Columbia University and then took courses in the Sorbonne in Paris. She is a linguist and a specialist in comparative literature. Since her marriage in 1907 she has made her home in Vermont, where now she is greatly beloved. Her first novel, "The Squirrel Cage," 1912, was in key with the Midwestern chorus of the decade: a novel primarily of protest against the narrowness of village conceptions and the dwarfing influences of the Puritan heritage. But unlike Sinclair Lewis and Masters and Anderson, she is never wholly pessimistic. In her later writings—and her volumes of fiction now number eighteen—she has stood for the old fundamentals of home life and training, for the wholesome and the uplifting, for the rights of womanhood in its struggle for existence in the world of modern business. "Doubtless it is to go too far to claim, as certain of her critics do," says Van Doren, "that she has made a counter-attack upon the assailants of the village and the established order, but it is sure that she gave comfort to many spirits disturbed by the radical outbursts of 1920." She has been a wholesome influence upon her period, a period sadly needing such guidance as hers. Her strongest novel—phenomenon most unusual—is her latest, "Her Son's Wife," 1926, a novel of power that for an instant touched the sensitive nerve of an insensate age.

Strongest novelist of the latest group, however, is Zona Gale, born in Portage, Wisconsin, and reared in the environment she has so graphically depicted in her novels and sketches. Feminine novelists seem to come in pairs—in 1857 Mrs. Atherton and Mrs. Deland, in 1874 Ellen Glasgow and Zona Gale. Like so many others of the younger group, like Willa Cather and Edna Ferber and Fannie Hurst, Miss Gale's approach to fiction was by way of journalism—a grilling, discouraging apprenticeship: two years on Milwaukee newspapers, three years on the New York "World." For nine years she besieged the magazines with stories but with no acceptances. Then she went back home to Portage and, all undismayed, worked steadily on. Two years later came her first novel, "Romance Island," 1906. It was insignificant. "The Loves of Pelleas and Etarre" came a year later, and in 1908 her "Friendship Village," the first work to attract general attention. Arresting but not strong: too much of mere sentiment. Seven volumes of fiction were to come and ten years were to elapse before she completely found herself and gained recognition with her strong novel "Birth," 1918, followed two years later by her most popular creation, "Miss Lulu Bett." Publicity came in a flood now, with dramatizations and even movie-izations, but her work steadily gained in power culminating in her strong novel "Preface to a Life," 1926, and her "Yellow Gentians and Blue," 1927, tales and sketches, etched in acid, mordant, arresting, realistic.

Miss Gale is the recorder of inhibited lives, but never with complete cynicism or futility. Like all her Western compeers she is in revolt, but like Willa Cather she leaves hope in her diagnosis. She is original, tireless in her artistry, often disconcerting in her newness, but never discouraging. "The function of the novel," she herself has said, "is to reflect the familiar as permeated with the unfamiliar, to reflect the unknown in its daily office of permeating the known." According to Mr. Mencken, her work lies in two distinct areas: her earlier "Friendship Village" popularities, "intrinsically as worthless as a treatise on international politics by the Hon. Warren Gamaliel Harding"; and her later and more mordant criticism. "Of a sudden, for some reason quite unknown to the deponent, she threw off all that flabby artificiality, and began describing the people about her as they really were. The result was a second success even more pronounced than her first, and on a palpably higher level." Never, however, has she reached the fine artistry of Willa Cather, or of the later Ellen Glasgow.

VII

The work of these women marks the highest reach to which the novel of characterization and manners has attained in America during our period. Perhaps no literary phenomenon in our history has been more noteworthy than this feminine assumption of leadership. The creation of fiction in most of its areas has proven to be an art adapted peculiarly for the powers of women. Feminine success has, however, come also from another peculiar fact: woman has surpassed her male competitors in workmanship, in artistry, in the quality of work toiled over and finished—she has been compelled to do this because of an age-old conception or prejudice. Her success has raised fiction-writing during the period to the rank of a new regular profession for women.

BIBLIOGRAPHICAL REFERENCES

"The American Novel To-Day," Régis Michaud, 1928.
"The Women Who Make Our Novels," Grant Overton, 1928.
"Is There a Feminine Fiction?" in "The Modern Novel," Elizabeth A. Drew, 1926.
"A Study of the Modern Novel," Annie Russell Marble, 1928.
"Contemporary American Novelists," Carl Van Doren, 1922.
"Our Short Story Writers," Blanche Colton Williams, 1922.
"The Novel of Tomorrow and the Scope of Fiction," Studies by Twelve American Novelists, 1922.

"The Writing of Fiction," Edith Wharton, 1925.

"Contemporary Novels and Novelists: a List of References to Biographical and Critical Material," H. L. Wheeler, 1921.

"The American Novel," in "Prejudices," Fourth Series, 1924, H. L. Mencken.

"The Feminine Note in Fiction," W. L. Courtney, 1904. Excellent treatment of Mrs. Atherton.

"Edith Wharton," Robert Morss Lovett, 1925.

"Bibliography of the Collected Writings of Edith Wharton," L. M. Melish, 1925.

"The New American Type," H. D. Sedgwick, 1908.

"Voices of Tomorrow," E. A. Björkman, 1913.

"More Contemporary Americans," Percy H. Boynton. (Margaret Deland.)

"Ellen Glasgow: the Fighting Edge of Romance," in "Woodcuts," 1926, Stuart P. Sherman.

"Ellen Glasgow," in "Virginia Quarterly Review," Vol. V, page 182.

The Old Dominion Edition of the Novels of Ellen Glasgow, is now in progress of publication. Four volumes: "The Battle-ground," "The Deliverance," "Virginia," and "They Stooped to Folly" have been issued, 1930.

"Ellen Glasgow," Dorothea Lawrance Mann, 1927.

"Willa Cather" in "Spokesmen," T. K. Whipple, 1928.

"Willa Cather and the Changing World," in "Woodcuts," 1926, Stuart P. Sherman.

"Zona Gale," Wilson Follett, 1923.

CHAPTER XVII

THE PRAIRIE POETS

THE sudden outburst of poetry during the second decade of the new century was a phenomenon spontaneous, unprepared for, and, in its beginnings, uncommercial. The decade after the death of Hovey in 1900 had been one of the most unpoetic in American literary history. The age of the strenuous life voiced itself prevailingly in prose. Always at every publishing season poetry was present, sometimes in quantity, always a score or more of pleading little volumes, exquisite in binding and print, reviewed, when reviewed at all, in dozen lots and forgotten. Badger of Boston printed them for a reasonable consideration. But suddenly after 1912 poetry began to pour out a flood of volumes and to compete even with the novel as a marketable commodity. For the first time since "Hiawatha" a book of poems entered the list of the best sellers. Seemingly a poetic renaissance had opened, and everywhere it was hailed with enthusiasm. All at once new shibboleths were heard: "free verse," "vers libre," "imagism," "vorticism," "polyphonic prose." A new "school" of poets had arrived, over night, and never school so voluble, so self-conscious, so self-explanatory, so contemptuous of all work save its own. Stedman's "American Anthology," a gathering in some 900 pages, by an accepted critic of the older period, of the best that America had produced up to 1900, was branded at the start as a "Gargantuan collection of mediocrity and moralizing," with "no more than ten pages of what might be considered genuine American poetry." Such was the feeling of the new renaissance.

The causes of the outburst, as we view it now with two decades of perspective, were many. The Irish renaissance of the nineties led by Yeats and sponsored by Lady Gregory was an awakening thing, especially after the American visit of Yeats. Then had come a second international poetic event: the arrival of the much-heralded Bengal poet Rabindranath Tagore. The "decadent school" of the *fin de siècle* had expired early, but it had left as a legacy to the new century a formidable pack of poetic "isms," discussion of which filled the critical journals and overflowed even into the newspapers. Chief of the legatees of this heritage was Ezra Pound, who hastened early to Europe to be in touch with the bizarre remnants of the movement. His erudite outpourings concerning "Imagism" and other isms trickled back to his native land and were discussed by the esoteric.

Other causes, most of them minor events in themselves, contributed to the explosion: the vaudeville chantings of Nicholas Vachel Lindsay [later he dropped the "Nicholas"]—it was impossible to be unaware of them, especially after the publication of his "Adventures" in the "Forum"; the burst of publicity given to Edwin Arlington Robinson's third volume by President Roosevelt's sudden laying-on of superlatives; then the founding of Harriet Monroe's magazine "Poetry" in Chicago; the "Hog Butcher for the World" line in Sandburg's poem "Chicago"; and finally the arrival of the Lady Gregory of the movement, Amy Lowell, sister of the President of Harvard University, rich, scholarly, poetic, a personality, a driving force.

Miss Lowell considered the movement a by-product of the World War period: "The so-called 'new movement' in American poetry," she wrote, "is evidence of the rise of a native school. The welding together of the whole country which the war has brought about, the mobilizing of our whole population into a single strenuous endeavor, has produced a more poignant sense of nationality than has recently been the case in this country of enormous spaces and heterogeneous population. Hyphens are submerged in the solid overprinting of the word 'America.' We are no more colonies of this or that other land, but ourselves, different from all other peoples whatsoever." [1] Sound criticism. From the old home area of Emerson's "American Scholar" oration a new declaration of American literary independence.

Back of the whole new movement lurked the ghost of Walt Whitman. The new young poets everywhere looked upon him as the Moses of their new movement. Fully now did the old pioneer come into his own. Had he not as early as 1872 in his Dartmouth College poem, "As a Strong Bird on Pinions Free," formulated the new free-verse prosody?

The conceits of the poets of other lands I bring thee not,
Nor the compliments that have served their turn so long,
Nor rhyme—nor the classics—nor perfume of foreign court,
    or indoor library;
But an odor I'd bring to-day as from forests of pine in the
    north, in Maine—or breath of an Illinois prairie,
With open airs of Virginia, or Georgia, or Tennessee—or
    from Texas uplands, or Florida's glades.

I

That this new spirit of independence, of originality, of Americanism expressed in poetry, divorced from the old poetic vocabulary and connotations, began in the prairie regions of the Middle West is significant. It was a part of the realistic movement of the age. The first significant singer in the new choir unquestionably was Vachel Lindsay, most picturesque figure of them all, twentieth-century gleeman, the last of the scops. Springfield, Illinois, produced him and reared him to manhood within sight of the Lincoln mausoleum. Hiram College schooled him for three years but could not hold him for the full course.

[1] "Tendencies in Modern American Poetry," Amy Lowell, 1917.

He was off on an excited tour of his own that was to last for years, first as an art student for a period in Chicago and then in New York. The impression that he is an artist, perhaps longest to be remembered for his drawings has never left him.

In the intervals of his art-student career came excited ventures, avocations, hobo-wanderings, attempts to find himself, to reform the world, to evangelize art. A list of his ventures is illuminating: he was a Y.M.C.A. worker, then a Socialist soap-box campaigner. During his early period, the period of his walking tours through the South and the West, he thought of himself as a Saint Francis—the comparison comes again and again in his volume entitled "Adventures While Preaching the Gospel of Beauty." No "soldier of the Cross" missionary in a foreign land ever was more in earnest, more impressed with the importance of his mission. His equipment for his journeys was suggested by that which Christ outlined for His disciples. He was to have nothing to do with money, was to carry no baggage, travel always alone, "be neat, truthful, civil, and on the square, and preach the Gospel of Beauty." This Gospel printed as a broadside for posting in farmers' kitchens and on billboards had in it this paragraph:

I come to you penniless and afoot to bring a message. I am starting a new religious idea. The idea does not say "no" to any creed you have heard. . . . After this, let the denomination to which you now belong be called in your heart "the church of beauty" or the "church of the open sky." . . . We should make our own home and neighborhood the most democratic, the most beautiful, and the holiest in the world.

His intention it was "to carry this gospel across the country beginning June, 1912, returning in due time."

His story of the trip, which took him from Springfield, "across Illinois, Missouri and Kansas, up and down Colorado and into New Mexico," is unique. It was in Kansas that he really awoke to poetry. His apostrophe to the State reveals the meaning of his later chantings:

Kansas, the land of the real country gentlemen, Americans who work the soil and own the soil they work; State where the shabby tenant-dwelling scarce appears as yet. Kansas of the Chautauqua and the college student and the devout school-teacher! The dry State, the automobile State, the insurgent State! Kansas that is ruled by the crossroads church and the church type of civilization. The newest New England!

He would make poetry that would voice the Kansas farmer, the Kansas worker. It should be beautiful, yet within the compass of enjoyment of the plain people of the West. It should be American, unique as the "Jay-Hawk" yell of the University of Kansas. To understand it one must approach it always from the West.

It is fundamentally religious. Not a note in it that was not intended to be evangelistic. The people of his native West were to him the best specimens of humanity the world contained, and he would help them to larger living. "Every time I went on the road in the spring after a winter of art lecturing it was definitely an act of protest against the type of life set forth for all time in two books by Sinclair Lewis: 'Babbitt' and 'Main Street.' "

And his poetry was a part of his campaign. In every household that would admit him he read three poems—"The Proud Farmer," "The Illinois Village," and "On the Building of Springfield." (They are at the end of his first volume "General Booth Enters into Heaven.") In them was his whole gospel. Poetry to him was not for the few, the educated, the esoteric: it was for all America. It was the voice of the average man, of the average town, of the average United States. Especially, however, was it keyed to what Mencken would denominate "the six-day-sock and saleratus Kultur of the Cow and Hog States." Of the Longfellow-Bryant-Lowell traditions there is nothing, of Europe nothing, even of Walt Whitman very little. To win the American people to the beauties of poetry and art, he believed that one must approach them from their own level—jingle in abundance, emotionalism—rag-time, "movie" action,—everything moving and resounding like a marching brass band.

The calliope steam organ at the fair thrills the country crowd, and it thrilled him. To read his interpretation of it while obeying to the full his italic stage directions is an athletic "stunt"; parts of it are to be rendered like a college yell:

"I am the Kallyope, Kallyope, Kallyope,
    Tooting hope, tooting hope, tooting hope, tooting hope.
Willy willy willy wah Hoo!"

For Lindsay the college yell with its rhythmic beat is poetry, the outlet of genuine American emotion expressed in the American way. To hear the man read in his early period "The Kallyope," "The Congo," "General Booth Enters into Heaven," every part of him in action like the cheer-leader at a Hiram game, was a thing to stir the blood. The audience after a puzzled moment was in key, more and more in key, ready to roar with the poet as primitive warriors in Saxon mead-halls clashed their spears upon their bull-hide shields, and along with the excited scop "yelled out the joys of fight." There is a note in it too of the African tomtom music Americanized into the key of the negro spirituals. Often he had his audiences beat time as he read. It is to be rated with the spirituals—folk-song with a fundamental purpose. Whatever it is or is not, it is American and Western.

To him poetry, like music, is for the ear first of all. It is to be read aloud and with action. His poem "General Booth Enters into Heaven," fantastic as it unquestionably is, keyed as it is to African time-beats and imagery, stirs one when one hears it adequately read, like an African Voodoo chorus heard at midnight.

The hosts were sandalled and their wings were fire!
(Are you washed in the blood of the lamb?)
But their noise played havoc with the angel choir.

[*Grand chorus of all instruments. Tambourines in the fore-ground.*]

(Are you washed in the blood of the Lamb?)
Oh, shout Salvation! It was good to see
Kings and Princes by the Lamb set free.
The banjos rattled and the tambourines
Jing-jing-jingled in the hands of Queens.

And when Booth halted by the curb for prayer
He saw his Master through the flag-filled air.
Christ came gently with a robe and crown
For Booth the soldier, while the throng knelt down.
      [*Reverently sung, no instruments.*]
He saw King Jesus, they were face to face,
And he knelt a-weeping in that holy place.
Are you washed in the blood of the lamb?

To poets of the old order this is not high-ranking poetry. This from Edwin Arlington Robinson: "Any poetry that is marked by violence, that is conspicuous in color, that is sensationally odd, makes an immediate appeal, and is likely to be as quickly forgotten." Undoubtedly true, but not all of Lindsay's poetry is in tomtom key. There is a gentle area in his collected "works" that could be admitted even to Stedman's anthology. Heading this list would be "Abraham Lincoln Walks at Midnight," "The Eagle that is Forgotten," "The Voyage," "The Leaden-Eyed," "The Chinese Nightingale," "I Know All This When Gypsy Fiddles Cry."

Always is he American in subject as well as in tone. His very titles lift one into the America of romance and beauty and hope: "The Ghosts of the Buffaloes," "The Golden Whales of California," "The Santa Fé Trail—A Humoresque," "Niagara," "Adventures while Preaching the Gospel of Beauty."

It is easy to criticize him, easy to parody his excesses, easy to detect the swift poetic decline of his later years. His volume of lyrics voiced at his best is not large, and it looks now, despite his present ineffective copiousness, as if we should have no more. This however is sure: the period has produced no more genuine singer, no more original voice.

II

It is food for pessimism to consider that Lindsay was a mere voice in the wilderness until the poet Yeats at the Chicago dinner given him by the Editors of "Poetry," March 1, 1914, addressed "his after-dinner talk primarily to him as 'a fellow-craftsman,' " saying of the poem "General Booth Enters into Heaven," which had been one of the earliest pieces in the magazine—

This poem is stripped bare of ornament: it has an earnest simplicity, a strange beauty, and you know Bacon said, "There is no excellent beauty without strangeness."

I am inclined to date the opening of the new poetic movement October, 1912, the date of the first number of Harriet Monroe's "Poetry, A Magazine of Verse." Poetic forces had been gathering for this culmination ever since the "decadent" days of the nineties. Robinson, Lindsay, Frost, Masters, and Percy Mackaye, had been publishing poetry for years; even Sandburg had issued poetry pitched to the Sandburg key as early as 1902. But with 1912 the movement came to a focus, the new magazine with its insistence upon utter freedom and spontaneousness seemed like the fulfilment of a crying need—its emphasis being upon vital newnesses; whole numbers given to the work and the meaning of a single emerging new poet—culminating in the William Butler Yeats dinner and the coronation of Lindsay—attracted widest attention.

That the magazine was issued in Chicago instead of

New York or Boston shows that the driving power of the new movement was Western. It was a part of the same force that had launched the agrarianism of E. W. Howe, Hamlin Garland, and William Allen White, and the realism of Frank Norris, Theodore Dreiser, and Sinclair Lewis. Out of the new trans-Allegheny West a new Americanism, one, however, soon to be ably reinforced from the East. Perfectly was "Poetry" in key with the times, so perfectly, indeed, that since its first issue in 1912 there have been established, according to Untermeyer, more than thirty poetry magazines modeled on its lines.

Alfred Kreymborg, one of the poets of the new school, a critic with vision, has this inclusive summing-up of the poetic situation after 1912:

With the advent of *The Lyric Year* and *The New Republic* in New York, of *Poetry* and *The Little Review* in Chicago, of *The Poetry Journal* in Boston, supported by the anthological activities of William Stanley Braithwaite (who after 1913 issued a yearly volume devoted to the best poetry produced during twelve months), by Jessie B. Rittenhouse and others, and by the Poetry Society of America and its tributaries, young unknowns were greeted by a growing audience. *The Poetry Magazine,* led by Harriet Monroe, adopted Whitman's maxim: "To have great poets you must have great audiences." This redoubtable woman, more than any other editor, devoted her life to the cause of American Poetry." [2]

III

No "discovery" gave more publicity to the new school than did "Poetry's" discovery of Carl Sandburg in 1914. With fine courage and prophetic judgment Miss Monroe had issued a "bunch" of poems by this totally unknown "rough-neck" Swede, among them a lyric entitled "Chicago" with the terrible opening line, "Hog Butcher for the World." To the whole country the line, everywhere quoted,

[2] "Our Singing Strength," 1929.

came like a blow in the face. The brutality of it! The idea of elevating the hog and hog-butchery into poetry! But at once it was awarded the Levinson prize, $200 for the best poem issued during the year. Carl Sandburg had arrived.

Introduced to Sandburg, we are face to face with a new force in American life and literature. (We had caught a glimpse of it in Willa Cather's "My Ántonia." New England in the seventies moved into the Middle West and was swallowed up, and a non-Puritan race moved into New England and swallowed it up. But in the meantime, to quote from Whitman's "Mannahatta," "Immigrants arriving, fifteen or twenty thousand in a week." Into Wisconsin was pouring a tide of Scandinavians, and into other States a polyglot stream without end. America, especially in its western areas, was no longer English. These men of the new colonial era were picked stock, for only the best, the restless, the daring could break permanently from age-old environments and dare the ocean voyage. The case of the elder Sandburg is typical. He was not a Sandburg at all: he was August Johnson, a hard-working peasant, one of a shipload of immigrants for America. Work he had found in a Western railroad gang. Other "August Johnsons" got his pay envelope, and he changed his name. His son grew up in the prairie town like other Swedish boys. Life meant a job at the earliest possible moment. At thirteen he was driving a milk wagon: it is needless to catalogue his jobs. Later on, in the *wanderjahre* era of his youth, he pushed out for himself into the still farther west, washed dishes in a hotel, stacked wheat in harvest time, worked with a railroad gang, and saw life in other areas of muscular toil. Then came service in the army during the brief Spanish War and final discharge with one hundred dollars in his pocket. Again in Galesburg, his home town, seat of Lombard College, a new ambition came to him: he would get an education. Four years of college, earning his way, and at the end newspaper work: journalism has been his profession ever since. With the college, poetry had come to him: he had been editor of the college "monthly," and had wooed in it most of the muses. As early as 1904 he had poems enough for a volume: but it fell dead from the press.

Newspaper work in every variety. One learns much of life in a year's round of reporting, especially in Chicago. He had socialistic leanings and went on the stump, or rather the soap-box, haranguing nondescript audiences. In 1914 had come his poem "Chicago," and two years later his volume "Chicago Poems." It was a national event. Here was a new atmosphere, totally new save as one found traces of it in Walt Whitman. To those reared on Emerson and Longfellow and Whittier and the English Victorians, the book was a scandal, an insult to the word poetry. Read Tennyson's "Sweet and Low" and then Sandburg's "To a Contemporary Bunk Shooter":

"You come along . . . tearing your shirt . . . yelling about
        Jesus.
    Where do you get that stuff?
    What do you know about Jesus?"

When even the poets of the nation could salt their lyrics with slang and coarseness and not only get away with it but be elevated to seats where they looked condescendingly down upon the "wishy-washy Longfellow," new definitions were demanded. More and more was it realized that the real, the actual, America was something unperfumed and untranscendental, that Chicago was Chicago, and to voice its "rough-necked" virility, its hog-butchering (a thing precisely as needful to humanity as beautiful legends beautifully told), its violent protests against injustice (often punished as crime) was perhaps the real work of poetry. But should not prose do the dirty work? The debate is still on. In the meantime Sandburg the Swede saw hope and beauty even in the maelstrom of Chicago nastiness and crime. The mills of the gods were grinding out a new race, perhaps a Frankenstein conglomeration, but nevertheless one compellingly alive. And he tried to voice it. Nothing unclean of surface repelled him if below the dirt and grime and sin he could see a struggling human soul. Sometimes he let propaganda run away with the muse. He was as democratic as Whitman and as un-squeamish:

I sat with a dynamiter at supper in a German saloon eating
    steak and onions.

Or again:

I drank musty ale at the Illinois Athletic Club with the
    millionaire manufacturer of Green River butter one
    night.
And his face had the shining light of an old-time Quaker, he
    spoke of a beautiful daughter, and I knew he had a
    peace and a happiness up his sleeve somewhere.

A new race with new definitions; life looking *up* from the soil, virile, imperious—iron men from the dragon-teeth sowing of many races in a rich new world.

In Sandburg there was no bitterness, as in Masters and Lewis and Sherwood Anderson; rather a mothering pity especially for the down-and-out and those condemned by the commonalty. His demand from life was freedom and beauty, and he found it in the West which bore him:

I was born on the prairie, and the milk of its wheat, the
    red of its clover, the eyes of its women, gave me a song
    and a slogan.

Three periods there are already in the literary life of the man, perhaps four. There was the period of his first inspiration that voiced itself in "Chicago Poems" and "Corn Huskers"—Walt Whitman plus Chicago socialism, plus the personality of Carl Sandburg. Brutality there was in it, materials condemned—until recently—as totally un-poetical, but there was in them an earnestness and a genuineness the equal of Lindsay's,—the polyglot, the virile newness we call the Great West.

Quickly followed the second period, not so epic in quality: Sandburg with an old banjo about his neck strumming while he chanted his barbaric vaudeville to college boys, who gave him the "locomotive yell" with "Sandburg! Sandburg! Sandburg!" three times at the end. He seemed now to be *cultivating* uncouthness. It brought out the yells. "Slabs of the Sunburnt West"—why slabs? Slabs are waste stuff, worthless. Why sunburnt? Then the third Sandburg, perfumed, struggling toward the esoteric and the vaguely ethereal, the Sandburg of the twenty-six definitions of poetry—flat nonsense (read them some time), unintelligible save to an exquisite few poets. They are the whole diameter of the circle away from all the man's earlier definitions of poetry. Something had happened to him. According to Kreymborg, Sandburg fell under the spell of a comparatively obscure American poet, Wallace Stevens. "As the work of Sandburg grew more esthetic, he came under the influence of this most esthetic American: a glorious dandy who had issued but one volume, with little more than a hundred buyers."

Good-bye, Carl Sandburg. Whitman never deserted. But there is a fourth period in the man's work, the prose period of "Abraham Lincoln: The Prairie Years," and "The American Song Bag." Distinctive work here. He is at work on the second volume of his "Lincoln."

The "Chicago Poems" and the "Corn Huskers" volumes will hold their place in American literature. They are a vital part of their period, rugged shoots from the colossal main trunk of Walt Whitman planted in Western soil. A few lyrics there are of rare beauty: "Lost," "Sketch," "Grass," "Graves," "White Shoulders," "Nocturne in a Deserted Graveyard," "Monotone," and others. As for the rest, I will quote a poet and a critic of Sandburg's own generation, Conrad Aiken:

Has Mr. Sandburg by sacrifice of those qualities of verse which appeal to the ear, and in some measure to the eye, been enabled to say anything that could not have been said more beautifully, or more forcibly, by a keener use of symmetry? For the present critic the answer must, on the whole be negative. In a general sense, Mr. Sandburg's material is the material of Frost, Masters, Gibson, Masefield: the dominant characteristic of all five men is the search for color and pathos in the lives of the commonplace. Mr. Sandburg is less selective, that is all,—he spills in the chaff with the wheat. With much that is clear, hard, colorful, suggestive, there is much also that is muddy, extraneous, and dull. The other members of the realist school use the same material, but, being defter artists, use it better. What Mr. Sandburg adds is the sociological element, which is the least valuable part of his book. Ethics and art cannot be married.[3]

IV

By 1914 the free-verse movement was in full career. Everywhere strangeness, strange names un-Nordic—for instance Emanuel Carnevali signed to a drab pastel like this:

> Out in the hall
> The gas jet
> Doesn't give a damn that it is day already.
> Stench
> Of drenched clothes
> And snore of married men.
> Who shall ask the furnished-room poets to write
> A song for the dawn?

Something had happened to American poetry. Freedom had come, said Miss Amy Lowell of Boston. Verse had freed itself from age-old chains. "Free verse" was now the battle cry, or "vers libre," which was a step beyond in

[3] "Scepticisms: Notes on Contemporary Poetry," Conrad Aiken, 1919.

emancipation. Here were the new rules, the new declaration of poetic independence:

1. To use the language of common speech, but to employ always the exact word, not the nearly exact, nor the merely decorative word.

2. To create new rhythms—as the expression of new moods —and not to copy old rhythms, which merely echo old moods. We do not insist upon "free-verse" as the only method of writing poetry. We fight for it as a principle of liberty. We believe that the individuality of a poet may often be better expressed in free-verse than in conventional forms. In poetry a new cadence means a new idea.

3. To allow absolute freedom in the choice of a subject. . . .

4. To present an image (hence the name: Imagist). We are not a school of painters, but we believe that poetry should render particulars exactly and not deal in vague generalities, however magnificent and sonorous. It is for this reason that we oppose the cosmic poet, who seems to us to shirk the real difficulties of his art.

5. To produce poetry that is hard and clear, never blurred nor indefinite.

6. Finally, most of us believe that concentration is of the very essence of poetry.[4]

Commenting on the first of the rules, Amy Lowell would exclude "old faded expressions" like "battlemented clouds" and "mountainous seas," and all the "old poetic jargon" like

> To ope my eyes
> Upon the Ethiope splendor
> Of the spangled night.

V

Elaborate volumes of the new verse began to pour from the presses so lately obsessed with fiction, some of them approaching best-seller figures. In 1914 came James Op-

[4] "Tendencies in Modern American Poetry," Amy Lowell, 1917.

penheim's "Songs for the New Age," and with it Amy Lowell's "Sword Blades and Poppy Seed," Vachel Lindsay's "The Congo," Robert Frost's "North of Boston," William Rose Benét's "Falconer of God," and Conrad Aiken's "'Earth Triumphant."

Then in 1915 came the sensation of the period, "The Spoon River Anthology" by Edgar Lee Masters, the most talked of, perhaps the most influential, book of poems since "Leaves of Grass." A purely Western thing it seemed, a Chicago thing by a Chicago man.

Its author indeed had been Western-born. Like Sandburg and Lewis and Sherwood Anderson, he had been reared in a prairie town, though not with restricted means. His father was a prominent lawyer, who insisted that his son should abandon the literary foolishness that somehow he had picked up in the public schools and in his reading and go sensibly to work in a man's profession. At twenty-one the boy had broken away for a year and had attended Knox College, where he had read Greek, but it was only for a year. Then the inevitable law again. He had been admitted to the bar in 1891, and after a year with his father had settled in Chicago where during the whole of our period—thirty years—he has been a prosperous barrister.

Masters was forty-five when his "The Spoon River Anthology" appeared: his birth date was 1869, William Vaughn Moody's date and Robinson's. Lindsay's was 1879; Sandburg's 1878. Twenty years of law practice in Chicago would drive, it would seem, even a Milton or a Whitman into brief-case prose—"the law is a jealous dame"—and in addition the young lawyer had entered political life and even run for office. Literary fires, however, still smoldered and even burst out at times in gentle eruption: six or eight volumes of poetry, or drama, all of them unnoticed by public and critics. "I was working under the influence of Poe, Shelley, Keats: sometimes, as to Nature poems, looking to Theocritus. I wrote many sonnets and many vague things in the music of Swinburne." The transition from this material to the "Spoon River" lyrics is as violent a thing as Whitman's sudden jump from sentimental twaddle to "Leaves of Grass," and as difficult almost to explain. Certain external facts we do know.

First, there was William Marion Reedy, publisher of "Reedy's Mirror" in St. Louis, a man of scholarship and critical discernment, unquestionably the godfather of the collection. It was Reedy who suggested to Masters the study of Greek Anthology lyrics as models and the drawing upon the life he knew for materials. Realism was in the air in 1914; Hardy had written "Tess" and "Jude the Obscure"; Dreiser's "Jennie Gerhardt" had appeared in 1911 and "The Titan" in 1914; Miss Monroe's magazine "Poetry" had devoted numbers to Masefield, Tagore, and Pound; imagism, free verse, and vers libre had in places entered even the college curriculum; the poetry of Lindsay and Sandburg was disturbing everywhere the critical standards. As a result of it all, there appeared in "Reedy's Mirror," May 29, 1914, with the pseudonym "Webster Ford," four lyrics: "Hod Putt," "Serepta the Cold," "Amanda Barker," "The Unknown." The series continued weekly throughout the year, and in April, 1915, two hundred and forty-four of the units, each with the name of a person as title, were issued as a volume called "The Spoon River Anthology."

The book was unique, at least in English. It purported to be made up of the epitaphs in a prairie cemetery as they would be written could the persons come back from the dead and tell in briefest compass the actuality of their lives. According to the author, its purpose was "to analyze society, to satirize society, to tell a story, to expose the machinery of life, to present a working model of the big world." Certainly the collection does all this—and more.

The first shock and the first wave of best-seller popularity came from the very realistic sex revelations in the epitaphs. Even Amy Lowell, who had defended Sandburg, had no stomach for realism to this degree: "The pages of Mr. Masters and August Strindberg read like extracts from the Newgate Calendar. Everything that is coarse and revolting in the sexual life is here. 'Spoon River' is one long chronicle of rapes, seductions, liaisons, and perversions. It is the great blot upon Mr. Masters's work. It is an obliquity of vision, a morbidness of mind, which distorts an otherwise remarkable picture."

The second shock came from their ruthlessness, their atmosphere at times of blasphemy, of sneering at the world-law. The dead R. F. Tanner, for instance, returning to compose his epitaph, runs off into a pessimistic bit of philosophy much in the vein of the living Clarence Darrow: Life is a trap, he reveals. The monstrous ogre Life watches you nibble his bait, and when you have sprung the infernal trap, he comes to—

> . . . stare with burning eyes at you,
> And scowl and laugh, and mock and curse you,
> Running up and down in the trap,
> Until your misery bores him.

Then we are told that for some eight years Darrow was a law partner of Masters.

"Here are my two hundred and forty-four men and women," (not Browning's figures) enough people to make up a Main Street village, and like Lewis's work, exhibited to show the rawness and uncouthness of Western life. And yet it is not necessarily *American* life that is exhibited; very little local color here. It is life universal: it is a satire on human life generally. Two-score of these epitaphs illustrate "life's little ironies"—Daisy Fraser's fines, for example, that went toward educating the children of the village; dozens of them are law cases each condensed into ten lines; dozens more are scenarios; many of them are founded on facts brought out in police courts; some are variations of the "Ring and the Book" plan—the wife's story, then the husband's, the murderer's story, and then that of the murdered, the criminal's story and then the town's. Some have a trend of brightness and optimism —especially is this noticeable toward the end of the series; but the accent is strongest on the coarse and the sinful. To live in a town peopled by these two hundred and forty-four would be intolerable.

Little attempt is there at characterization, little at description. It is exposition in story form. Braithwaite, reviewing the volume a few weeks after its first appearance, called it "a novel in verse." Rather is it the fragments of an ◄exploded novel—a novel broken into short-story episodes and each worked into a unity by itself. The epitaph centers always in a single situation: never is it the *whole* life. Seldom is there realistic study—the facing of all the facts and all the phases. These dead are not speaking in character, though they purport to do so. It is Masters who is talking, not Hod Putt. Hod Putt and Daisy Fraser could not talk like this. It is the conception not of a poet but of a legalist. The writer sums up the case like a criminal court advocate stressing only the evidence that he wishes to stress. Many of them are short stories, with what Jack London called a "snapper" at the end; most, however, are briefs of legal cases, mostly criminal cases.

During the early years of the volume praise went to an extreme that, in the light of to-day, seems incredible. A poem addressed to Masters and published early in "Reedy's Mirror" declared that a designated two of the poems outweighed Gray's "Elegy" and Wordsworth's "Intimations of Immortality," and then ended with the colossal simile:

> As the Nile unto Egypt
> So Spoon River to the New World.

Time has not only rebuked such critics, but has made them ludicrous. Masters's fame has been a diminishing thing. One is reminded of Stockton's tale "His Wife's Deceased Sister." At the one moment when such a thing was possible, inspired by a thrill in the air, a moment of expectation, the rush of a great movement, the culmination of a period, he struck thirteen, as it were, and was ruined. For never was he able to do it again, to strike twelve or even eleven. His later poetry has, for the most part, been on the level of his pre-"Spoon River" volumes.

He lacks the singing quality; he lacks the magic, the haunting expressiveness, the tingling atmospheres of poetry on the heights of poetry. He is a man with no "ear" and little voice trying to sing—any choir-leader can tell of that tragedy. Intellectual the poems are, good exposition, excellent narrative—but they are baldly prosaic and should not wear the masks of poetry. And yet one must not be dogmatic: nothing human is so undefinable as poetry. Each soul has its own standards, and perhaps mine are outgrown. Therefore, in perfect fairness, I fortify my judgment again by that of a younger man, a member of the new school, a critic who has written a book with discernment, this time Alfred Kreymborg:

What is any biographer if he fails in artistry? Masters did not fail in all his portraits, but he failed in too many. His book is a remarkable set of documents, far below the poetry it would have become had a genius approached the graves. . . . There is scarcely a poem that does not suffer from some such awkward moment. It is untrue to spontaneous human speech. . . . As a rule, Masters' ear is insensitive. He is a lover of truth, an excellent story-teller without an instinct for beauty. One does not ask for lovely lines liltingly presented. These are untrue and unbeautiful. But, in the light of poems about people in "The Greek Anthology," in English balladry, in Cowper, Burns and Wordsworth, in Robinson, Frost and Sandburg, the "Spoon River" poems sound flat and even unreal. . . . The lawyer-poet has most of the elements of a poet, but few of those essential to an artist.[5]

The value of the "Spoon River" volume lies in its originality of design, its uniqueness, its effect upon its times.

[5] "Our Singing Strength," Alfred Kreymborg, 1929.

Its colossal success started a choir of young poets. Whether we condemn or praise, we must accept it as a major episode in the history of the poetic movement in the second decade of the new century.

VI

Other Western poets contemporary with these three have not been so daring, so willing to snub the elder muses. One of them was John Gneisenau Neihardt, Poet Laureate of Nebraska, given this office by act of the State Legislature in 1921. Born at Sharpsburg, Illinois in 1881, schooled at the Nebraska Normal College, and furnished with peculiarly American subjects by a residence of six years among the Omaha Indians, he was first heard of as a poet in 1907 after the publication of his volume "A Bundle of Myrrh." Another volume, "Man Song," came a year later. Nothing in the pre-Lindsay period, save Robinson's work perhaps, had in it so much of promise. There was virility in the poems, at times even fire. Then had come the Indian epics, narratives founded on actualities, veritable legends,—folk-lore conservation—"The Song of Hugh Glass," "The Song of Three Friends," and others. They are the work of a poet who knows his subject and who has a story to tell. Not for him, however, newnesses and revolutionary ventures. He has taken the wild plains Indian into his professor's study (since 1923 he has been professor of poetry in the University of Nebraska) and has viewed him through an atmosphere of Greek legend. The poems have power at times, movement, descriptive beauty, but they are too often keyed to the merely literary, the rhetorical, the conventional. They are for the older instruments, in the old meters and manners, and so invite comparisons with greater works much better done. Their high promise has not been fulfilled. Out of step they seem now for all save dwellers in Nebraska, where many editions have been prepared for use in the public schools.

A more spontaneous and feeling poet of the West has been Sara Teasdale, sole feminine representative, save Harriet Monroe, of the Prairie School. Though born and reared in St. Louis, she has put little of localism into her lyrics, and not at all has she been in poetic rebellion. Simply, feelingly, she has expressed her own self. She is a lyrist, and only a lyrist, singing harmonies in older forms yet always spontaneously and originally. To understand her, to find the dominant chord of her singing, one must be in sympathy. Feminism in all its phases, the entry of woman into occupations and professions hitherto masculine, feminine enfranchisement, feminine education in practically all the colleges—everything during the period has made what has been denominated "the new woman"—femininity without sentimentality or softness or gentleness of heart. Outwardly yes, fundamentally, however, no: "but yet a woman." In Sara Teasdale is the eternally feminine, expressing its depths of love, its griefs, its fears, its intuitions, its joy. Genuineness of life, ecstasy in living and loving fill the lyrics like a living presence. One need quote but a single lyric—"On the South Downs":

> Over the downs there were birds flying,
>   Far off glittered the sea,
> And toward the north the weald of Sussex
>   Lay like a kingdom under me.
>
> I was happier than the larks
>   That nest on the downs and sing to the sky—
> Over the downs the birds flying
>   Were not so happy as I.
>
> It was not you, though you were near,
>   Though you were good to hear and see;
> It was not earth, it was not heaven,
>   It was myself that sang in me.

There are depths of living in these fragments, these lyric cries, as condensed as Emily Dickinson's and as full of

life and truth and feeling, depths as in this third stanza
of "Wisdom":

> It was a spring that never came;
> But we have lived enough to know
> That what we never have, remains;
> It is the things we have that go.

"Night Song at Amalfi," "I Shall Not Care," "The Solitary," the poems that won the "Brookes More Prize" of
$200 in 1920, and "The Dark Cup" are expressions of her
work at its best. Her first collections "Sonnets to Duse,"
1907, and "Helen of Troy," 1911, were preparatory. Her
full powers came with "River to the Sea," 1915, "Love
Songs," 1917, and "Flame and Shadow," 1920, the last
undoubtedly her best.

BIBLIOGRAPHICAL REFERENCES

A complete bibliography of Lindsay, Masters and Sandburg
    in "Contemporary American Literature," Manly and
    Rickert. Revised Edition, 1929.
"Tendencies in Modern American Poetry," Amy Lowell, 1917.
"Spokesmen, Modern Writers and American Life," T. K.
    Whipple, 1928. (Chapters on Lindsay and Sandburg.)
"Contemporary American Authors," J. C. Squire and Others,
    1928.
"A Note on Carl Sandburg" in "Americans," 1922, Stuart P.
    Sherman.
"Convention and Revolt in Poetry," John Livingstone Lowes,
    1919.
"Present-Day American Poetry," E. H. Peckham, 1917.
"The New Era in American Poetry," Louis Untermeyer, 1923.
"Some Modern Poets," Edward Davison, 1928. (A section on
    Lindsay.)
"From Whitman to Sandburg in American Poetry," Bruce
    Weirick, 1924. (Treats the Prairie Poets at length.)

CHAPTER XVIII

THE NEW ENGLAND POETS

I

IN the opinion of Amy Lowell, the "new poetry movement" began in the East and was simply the culmination of old poetic forces. In her "Tendencies" she devoted ninety-three pages to Masters and Sandburg, and the rest of the volume of 349 pages to Robinson, Frost, "H. D.," and John Gould Fletcher. As seen from the Harvard campus, the Western movement was a vagary, a Wild West variation, to be praised for its suggestiveness and its undoubted sincerity, but by no means to be looked to as a leading force. Leadership always was a thing from the East.

Robinson himself was suspicious of even Amy Lowell, "I can't get over the impression," he told Joyce Kilmer in 1917, "that . . . most of the vers-librists in poetry are trying to find some short cut to artistic success." And as to the Western school, "more than ever before," he said, "oddity and violence are bringing into prominence poets who have little besides these two qualities to offer to the world." He forgot that it was the "vers libre" and the "oddity and violence" that had aroused the current public interest in poetry and had created for him a poetry-reading audience and recognition after many unrecognized years.

For Edwin Arlington Robinson, both in time (he was born in 1869, the same year as Moody) and in early accomplished work (his first volume of poems appeared in 1896), was a poet of the transition era and order, to be studied along with Moody and Richard Hovey. He was of old New England stock, born near Gardiner, Maine, and reared in the old town, the "Tilbury" of his later poetry. For two years he was a student at Harvard, but because of his father's health he did not finish his course. Later he moved to New York City; and for five years—from 1905 to 1910—through the influence of Theodore Roosevelt, he held a position in the Custom House; but since 1910, settled in New York City, he has devoted himself wholly to poetry. Like James Lane Allen, whom in so many ways he resembles, he has lived solitary with but a single thought or aim—his art.

As with Sandburg and Masters, to understand the man's work one must approach it geographically. The approach to Robinson is from the East. Fundamentally he is a New Englander, the last poet of the old New England tradition. His literary kinship is with two makers of prose, two women: Sarah Orne Jewett, also from Maine, and Mary E. Wilkins, both of them workers with the twisted remnants of a great hope, Miss Jewett with cheerfulness making portraits of the last of an aristocracy in the old shipless harbor-towns of Maine, and Miss Wilkins with gloom snapping photographs among the dismal drift on that terminal moraine of humanity left by receding Puritanism. And with them Robinson, with the shrunken inheritance of the latter-day born, has made himself the last laureate of a vanishing race, maker, years before Masters, of the New England Spoon River Anthology. Read at the start "Bewick Finzer," "Aaron Stark," "Reuben Bright," "Miniver Cheevy," "Richard Cory," "Isaac and Archibald," and "Flammonde." Read "The Dead Village":

"Now there is nothing but the ghosts of things."

Read "Calverly's": Over the long miles of deserted lands and homes, once the New Canaan gained after an exodus incredible with toil, already a new race that knew nothing of the old:

> "Poor strangers of another tongue
> May now creep in from anywhere,
> And we, forgotten, be no more
> Than twilight on a ruin there."

"Twilight on a ruin," that is Robinson among the poets.

His first collection, "The Torrent and the Night Before," 1896, and "The Children of the Night," 1897, fell unheeded, but he worked on. In 1902 came "Captain Craig," a book discovered by Roosevelt and praised, but even this tremendous push brought no wide recognition. His poems were completely out of key with "the general" and even with the erudite remnant. "Captain Craig," as defined by Miss Amy Lowell, is "a dreary philosophical ramble," and "The Children of the Night" "one of the most completely gloomy books in the whole range of poetry." But still he worked on.

His poems fall roughly into two classifications: studies of "Tilbury town," its folk and the atmosphere enveloping it, the philosophy of it, and general poems, most of them written with English volumes open all about his writing desk. In both varieties baffled lives, decadence, disillusion. Like Richard Hovey before him and like Tennyson before Hovey, he worked long in the old Arthur legends. Hovey's treatment was ethical, philosophical, esthetic. His epic version of the cycle—in his case left by death unfinished—was a thing of beautiful rhythm, magnificence of setting, with lyric intervals, bursting at times into rapturous voicings that sing like lyrics in the Elizabethan dawn:

> O World! O Life! O City by the Sea!
> Hushed is the hum
> Of streets; a pause is on the minstrelsy.
> I come, I come!
> The sunlight of thy gardens from afar
> Is in my heart.
>
> .   .   .   .   .   .
>
> *I come, I come!*

"While most American poets, says Alexander Laing, "were following a foreign decadence, Hovey used an old garment to clothe the prophecy of a new day." Robinson, on the contrary, mirrored the society of his own day in an antique setting. He did more. In his "Merlin" and his "Lancelot" volumes we have the atmosphere of a beautiful dream at the moment of awakening to dismal reality. The radiant days of the Round Table fellowship are over, the pilgrimages for the Grail have ended in disillusion and treachery and failure. Everywhere a level atmosphere of gloom. The epic "Merlin" ends in gloom and even in darkness:

> Colder blew the wind
> Across the world, and on it heavier lay
> The shadow and the burden of the night;
> And there was darkness over Camelot.

This is greatly significant: Are not these two Arthur poems parables illuminating the wreck of the great dream of the New England Arthur's Court of the early days, with its half-realized vision of the Holy Grail?

If the poet ended always in gloom and disillusion, we might leave him here. But there is New England toughness in the fiber of the man; disillusioned he is, but no "quitter." He is a stoic:

> Life is the game that must be played:
> This truth at least, good friends, we know;
> So live and laugh, nor be dismayed
> As one by one the phantoms go.

But as each phantom departs, he will set it against the sky and view it not realistically but in the light of what it dreamed it would do. His "Man Against the Sky" put him, so far as great vision is concerned, among the greatest of our poets.

Recognition came late. His high tide did not come until nearly a quarter of a century after his first volume—in

1921 it was, after the publication of his collected poems, a volume awarded the Pulitzer Prize and formally pronounced by the American Authors' League "the book of the most enduring value of the year." Among the discerning few, the poetry-minded, he is already crowned as the leading poet of his time.

Never, however, will he be a poet of the people. His lyrics lack the singing quality that most readers demand; they lack emotion. He has written too much. His long poems are full of vast desert areas that can be described by no other word than dull. His sentences oft-times are interminable—one hundred and fifty words in one of them. His vocabulary is for the few; his meanings are often more difficult to find than are Browning's. And when one opens a whole book devoted to a single poem, one thinks of Poe's dictum as to poetic length. One feels too often, also, that this is poetry labored over day after day, returned to day after day as a bookkeeper returns to his ledgers. It is poetry of the intellect rather than the emotions, and to voice my own definition: great poetry bursts out of great emotion and will not be controlled. And great emotion is brief. It captures its reader like life itself: it is human, it is living, it is *you, me*.

To classify Robinson as not of the greatest poets does not debar him from the list of our American greatest. He is the best of our poetic artisans. Nothing he has written falls below his best in diction, in poetic workmanship, in finish. Let me end by quoting the English critic J. C. Squire, who calls him "one of the best writers ever born in America":

Mr. Robinson is usually as quiet as Wordsworth at his quietest, and often makes as great intellectual demands on his reader as did Browning—though not by elusiveness of expression. He is not one of those infectious lyrists who will sing themselves straight into the heart of any age. His musing habit, his interest in the subtler workings of mind and heart, his restraining preference for understatement even of his most powerful emotions, the almost subcutaneous quality of his irony and humour, that uniform quietness which at first glance gives a flat appearance to his work, would always have made him a poet slow to gain his fit audience.

He thereupon considers the positive elements of his poetry and finds them largely in "the consummate triumphs of his craftsmanship," his "detachment," his ability to exhibit "with the most scrupulous fidelity, and with a wide tolerance, the secret thoughts and impulses of his men and women, their most intangible reactions against the codes of themselves and their neighbours." In other words, it is as a literary craftsman and thinker and philosopher that he is to live, rather than as a singer with emotion, as an improviser on the heights of song.

II

Robinson, himself of Puritan stock, born and reared in the heart of the New England tradition, fled from it early and spent his life as a philosopher contemplating it from a distance. Robert Frost on the contrary, equally Puritan and Yankee in his lineage, born and reared outside of the ancestral environment—he spent the first ten years of his life in California—returned to his ancestral New England, and for years, writing as he lived, was in closest contact with its farmland people—purest remnants of the old stock —and its wild beauty of landscape.

Following the death of his father in 1885, the boy Frost had come east to live with his grandfather, overseer of a mill at Lawrence, Massachusetts. A boy in a New England mill-town: it meant high school—he graduated valedictorian of his class. At the age of seventeen he entered Dartmouth College. And now it was that there began to appear the peculiar fiber of the lad, his original bent of mind, his ingrained Yankeeism—the demand for immediate returns. The course he was in, he found, had no practicality, it led to no particular where, it curbed rather than developed his rampant individualism, it trimmed both dunce and genius to the same pattern. Jack London soon was to make something like the same complaint concerning the University of California. College was no place for an original genius. He left Dartmouth after a few months and went into his grandfather's mill for a while, and then he taught school. It is needless to follow his individualism, which included among other things a wife at twenty and then a two years' course at Harvard—1897–1899—a course again suddenly broken off by the conviction that he was getting nothing of real value. Then eight years of farming—his grandfather had given him a farm at Derry, New Hampshire—farming varied by teaching at Derry Academy. Poetry had captured the lad at fifteen. He had eagerly read the English poets, and the American, especially Longfellow, and he had written voluminously but with small published result.

Never soul more restless. For a year he taught psychology in the State Normal School of New Hampshire, in the foothills of the Franconias. Then suddenly, on September 12, 1912, with wife and children he sailed for England. He had sold his Derry farm. "I wanted to go far enough so that my friends wouldn't have to be looking at me with disapproval for pulling up my roots." Recklessly he had determined to stake all in an attempt to achieve success as a poet, and in England money would last twice as long as in America.

Retiring to a small town off the beaten track of tourists, he settled to write poetry. In 1913 the miracle happened: an English publisher issued for him a volume of his poems, "A Boy's Will," and a year later another, "North of Boston." It was a year more before America did what she was bound to do, for when did English acclaim not mean louder American acclaim in due time? Home in 1915, the poet settled on a farm in Franconia, New Hampshire— the heart of the White Hills—and there made a third volume, "Mountain Interval." Since then there has been no question as to his rating.

His biography has not been dramatic, though it has been as vagarious even as Lindsay's. He has been a college instructor for years at a time at Amherst; he has returned to farming in remote districts; he has served as poet-at-large in the University of Michigan with no duties save to be poet-at-large among the students. He has steadfastly refused to be rushed into poetry-making; he has issued nothing that is not at the height of his best. A new volume of his poems is a rare event: "New Hampshire" in 1923, "West-Running Brook" in 1928.

Though his poems at times launch out into what he has called the "world in general," they are prevailingly and unescapably touched with the soil of New Hampshire and Vermont. The two States have enveloped him as completely as Massachusetts and New Hampshire enveloped Whittier. His preliminary poem in the volume "New Hampshire" locates him forever and beyond peradventure:

> Just specimens is all New Hampshire has,
> One each of everything as in a show-case
> Which naturally she doesn't care to sell.
>
> She had one President (pronounce him Purse,
> And make the most of it for better or worse.
> He's your one chance to score against the state).
> She had one Daniel Webster. He was all
> The Daniel Webster ever was or shall be.
> She had the Dartmouth needed to produce him.

It was simply because of these "specimens," these highly individualized men and women, these jumbled mountain "specimens" no two alike, this habit of never repeating herself, making one "specimen" and then breaking the mold, that Frost loved the State and wrote of it. His poems also are "specimens." Certainly his men and women are not conventional. Not at all are they types. Each is a gnarled tree unique, an ancient apple-tree like no other even of its own kind. Read "The Code," "The Death of the Hired Man"—read at random in any of his books. He tells of a lady who could not endure the State,

> But when I asked to know what ailed New Hampshire,
> She said she couldn't stand the people in it,
> The little men (it's Massachusetts speaking).
> And when I asked to know what ailed the people,
> She said, "Go read your own books and find out."

He is entirely different from Robinson. Robinson was born by the Kennebec and reared there, but he left it early. His New Englanders he took with him to his New York laboratory, analyzed them in his accurately scaled test-tubes, worked out with infinite care their formulæ and equations, and presented them to us as epic abstractions— sometimes in parabolic solutions. Frost, born away from his fatherland, returned early, moved into the country, and actually lived with the new dwellers on farms not abandoned; mended wall with them—"good fences make good neighbours"—pitched hay with the hired men, learned to make an axe-helve from a French Canadian who disbelieved in education: his children would be spoiled for the making of perfect helves; and even slept a night with the thick-necked one who had outgrown a hundred collars. As a result, warm human picturings. He knows the New Hampshire of the *now*.

Everywhere external Nature. Nature always has loomed large in American poetry, especially in the poetry of New England. The Puritans, suspicious of all things making for personal adornment, made no Blue Law against Nature's costumings. Therefore Bryant's rapturous worship, and Whittier's and Lowell's. Never is Frost sentimental in his Nature-worship; never does he address individual flowers with gushing words. He works with Puritan restraint, with Yankee parsimony as to epithet and adjective: seldom the superlative. He is simply one "versed in country things," thoroughly in key with "Birches," "Wild Grapes," "Maples," "Oven Birds." His titles reveal him: "Stopping by Woods on a Snowy Evening," "Evening in a Sugar Orchard," "On a Tree Fallen Across the Road," "A Hillside Thaw." Beauty for him has always pathos in it:

> Nature's first green is gold,
> Her hardest hue to hold.
> Her early leaf's a flower;
> But only so an hour.
> Then leaf subsides to leaf.
> So Eden sank to grief,
> So dawn gets down to day.
> Nothing gold can stay.

Simplicity has been his law for poetry: simple, common things in simple, common words. But there must be emotion. "A poem," by his definition, "begins with a lump in the throat; a homesickness or a lovesickness. It is the reaching out toward expression; an effort to find fulfilment. A complete poem is one where an emotion has found its thought and the thought has found the words."

And never does he descend into the grosser areas of the physical for his emotion. To him poetry is a thing to be classed with religion or esthetic beauty:

> Lately in converse with a New York alec
> About the new school of the pseudo-phallic
> I found myself in a close corner where
> I had to make an almost funny choice.
> "Choose you which you will be—a prude or puke,
> Mewling and puking in the public arms."
> "Me for the hills where I don't have to choose."

And again

> Better defeat almost
> If seen clear,
> Than life's victories of doubt

That need endless talk talk
To make them out.

III

With the appearance of Amy Lowell in 1914 the new
poetry outbursts, until then sporadic and scattered, became
an organized movement. There had come a leader. After
her second volume of poems, "Sword Blades and Poppy
Seed" (her first, "A Dome of Many-Colored Glass," 1912,
had been colorless and conventional), she had become an
active propagandist, lecturing before college audiences and
learned societies, pouring out everywhere explanations of
the new poetic art and illustrating everything with specimens of her own creation. She had been in France: "For
the purely technical side I must state my immense debt to
the French, and perhaps above all to the so-called Parnas-
sian School, although some of the writers who have influenced me most do not belong to it."

High-minded and untiring workmen, they have spared no
pains to produce a poetry finer than that of any other country
in our time. Poetry so full of beauty and feeling, that the
study of it is at once an inspiration and a despair to the artist.
The Anglo-Saxon of our day has a tendency to think that a
fine idea excuses slovenly workmanship. These clear-eyed
Frenchman are a reproof to our self-satisfied laziness.

Her volume was a sample-case of the newest Parisian
fashions—lyrics *imagistique,* poems in "polyphonic prose,"
ballads in half-and-half—"I have not entirely abandoned
the more classic English metres. I cannot see why, because
certain manners suit certain emotions and subjects, it
should be considered imperative for an author to employ
no others. Schools are for those who can confine themselves within them."

During the next eleven years—until her death, in fact,
in 1925—she was the Lady Gregory of the new school.

She had brought with her from England the manuscript of an anthology—Ezra Pound had issued the first one in 1914, entitling it *"Anthologie des imagistes"*—and in the spring of 1915 she gave her manuscript American issue with the title "Some Imagist Poets," following it with a second volume in 1916 and a third in 1917. Her elaborate preliminary introductions, especially to the 1916 volume, furnished the text-book to the movement. Within their narrow area they are definitive.

In 1917 came her "Tendencies in Modern American Poetry," a volume that two years earlier had been prepared for by her triangulations of the Gallic Parnassus—"Six French Poets." Another collection of her ballads and lyrics came in 1916, "Men, Women, and Ghosts" (a title, by the way, "lifted" from Elizabeth Stuart Phelps), then a series of collected poems, six of them, the best, perhaps, "Can Grande's Castle," 1918. From this date her poetic decline was rapid. Controversy followed her every utterance, and she was voluble and cocksure,—the "Roosevelt of the new poetry movement," one has called her. "No poet living in America, (possibly no native contemporary writer with the exception of Dreiser)," wrote Mr. Untermeyer in 1919, "has been more fought for, fought against, and generally fought about, than Amy Lowell." Soon he himself was to experience her fighting powers. In an article in the "Nation" in 1922, he had announced a "slump" in the new poetry movement: the vers librists, he believed, were returning to meter and rhyme; whereupon Miss Lowell, in sweeping cavalry-charge articles in the "Literary Review" and elsewhere, rode over all his positions. This was her attitude:

I imagine that no reasonable person would deny that there has been a change in the matter and manner of poetry during the last decade. Granted that, therefore, and granted that this change was itself a reaction, has the pendulum swung backwards? Superficially, it looks as if it had; studied more carefully, we see that we are victims of an optical delusion. For the apparent return, if we examine it, proves to be merely an advance in experimentation.

Nothing could daunt her, nothing disturb the conviction within her that she was leading a growing and victorious host of poets in a renaissance without end. And she died undisillusioned.

A curious duality was in the woman. To her the movement was an American manifestation: "For almost the first time in her history, America has written out of herself," *free* verse, yet verse constantly fitted with European fetters—imagist poetry, poetry as poetry was made in France. Again, this arch-rebel, this apostle of the utter newness—"imagism," "cadenced verse," "polyphonic prose," "vers libre"—for all she was in such rebellion, was the worshiper of John Keats and his biographer *in extenso* with interspersed rhapsodies.

Eight volumes of poetry she wrote in all, some of them with workmanship so patent that we toil with her as we read, poems in every fashion—adaptations from the Chinese, ballads in newest manner, illustrative lyrics; yet for all her scholarship, her championship, her variety, it is now seen in all areas outside of Boston that her poetry for the most part is already outworn. The muse demands the spontaneous, and Miss Lowell's poetry is too often to be admired simply for its finish and its workmanship. A forced thing. Already it is seen that the really valuable part of her work was her critical attacks and her defenses and explanations in the warfare where *dux femina facti*.

She was as radically of New England as were Robinson and Frost:

> Heart-leaves of lilac all over New England,
> Roots of lilac under all the soil of New England;
> Lilac in me because I am New England,
> Because my roots are in it.
> Because my leaves are of it.

But New Englandism, save external touches here and there, is not in her poems. Not often does she deal with native conditions: "Lilacs" comes nearest, and then "Purple Grackles." There are lyrics in Yankee dialect—the Harvard conception of "Yankee patois." Now and then there are touches of landscape, but only a few shadows of the New England tragedy. Poetry to her must "exist simply because it is a created beauty." "I wish to state my firm belief that poetry should not try to teach." To her the soul of poetry was art, manner, workmanship.

She had approached the muse late. Born, like Henry James and Mrs. Wharton, amid refinement and wealth, like them she had been educated by tutors and early sent to Europe for finishing touches. For years she had not discovered herself. She was nearly thirty when finally she determined upon poetry as her profession. No adolescent excitements here, no headlong production, no torrents of emotion in one who deliberately adopts poetry at thirty. Eight years of hard study, years spent largely abroad in contact with the newest matters of her art, years of reading and study and toil. "A poet," she ruled, "must learn his trade in the same manner, and with the same painstaking care, as a cabinet-maker." And her first exhibit of workmanship had been her surprising volume "Sword Blades and Poppy Seed" with its chip-on-the-shoulder preface.

"Imagism" was the magic shibboleth in 1914, and she expounded it elaborately. Not at all did it mean, she said, mere picturings: its warfare was against vague generalities. "For instance, Imagists do not speak of the sea as the 'rolling wave' or the 'vasty deep,' high-sounding, artificial generalities which convey no exact impression." And in illustration she quoted from John Gould Fletcher's poem, "The Calm":

> At noon I see waves flashing,
> White power of spray.

The steamers, stately,
Kick up white puffs of spray behind them.
The boiling wake
Merges in the blue-black mirror of the sea.

Everything in concrete images. In her own work she was always too conscious of manner. Always one is in the presence of mastery of workmanship. It is too perfect. Untermeyer complains that she keeps her reader agitated, that she deals in color, sounds, physical perceptions—always the external—until one cannot follow:

She is, preëminently, the poet of the external world; her visual effects are "hard and clear" as the most uncompromising Imagist could desire. The colors with which her works are studded seem like bits of bright enamel; every leaf and flower has a lacquered brilliance. To compensate for the lack of inner warmth, Miss Lowell feverishly agitates all she touches, nothing remains quiescent. Whether she writes about a fruit shop, or a flower-garden in Roxbury, or a windowful of red slippers, or a string quartette, or a Japanese print—everything flashes, leaps, startles, spins and burns with an almost savage intensity.[1]

Typical of her poems at her best are perhaps these, which have been favorites of the anthologists: "Patterns," "A Lady," "Meeting-House Hill," "Night Clouds," "Lilacs," "Purple Grackles," "Madonna of the Evening Flowers," "Mackerel Sky," "Solitaire," and "The Sisters." Her death in 1925 was recorded everywhere as a national event. Everywhere superlatives. It was as if a new Sappho had come and gone. But as memories of her leadership and her compelling personality fade, and as more and more her place must be determined by her books alone, it is being realized that it was in her abilities as leader that she was greatest. She was a force rather than a poet. The

[1] "Modern American Poetry: A Critical Anthology," Louis Untermeyer, 1919.

"school" collapsed at her death. The youngest generation is not following her.

IV

How utterly the revolution failed, how completely its elaborate theories and its new prosody was to affect nothing save its own little whirlpool of the wartime decade, witness one of the youngest of the new poets, Edna St. Vincent Millay. Born in 1892, her whole life has been within the limits of our period, and graduated from Vassar College in 1917, she has gained her poetic conceptions wholly in the atmosphere of "the new poetry." To the older generations, saturated with Tennyson and Swinburne and Browning, this "new poetry" came as a distinct shock; to like it was an acquired taste, often a taste impossible to acquire. To the susceptible girl, however, from the Maine town—she was a native of Rockland—it was the poetry of the time, the voice of her generation. To learn how little it chorded with her poetic soul read her early lyrics. The college generations of the present day are chording always with the old poetry.

At one point, however, the young Vassar poet was in key with the new: while retaining the old line-lengths, and meters, and stanza forms, and lyrics like the sonnet, she nevertheless avoided the old poetic *clichés,* the stereo-typed linguistic contortions used by the older poets, and expressed herself in the simple and the concrete manner which, as Miss Lowell elaborately explained, had been a requirement of the imagists. She was nineteen when her first poem, "Renascence," appeared in "The Lyric Year" anthology of 1912: she was just out of college when her first volume of poems appeared. Six volumes have followed it, one of them (in 1923) awarded the Pulitzer Prize for poetry.

Her early poems have an intensity, a lyric quality not

often to be found of late in American poetry. Her early sonnets are remarkable, the best perhaps thus far made in the new century. Already, however, it is seen that she is to be classed as a poet whose early poems, a few of them, are destined always to hold a place in the anthologies. She has degenerated into mere cleverness. Her "Buck in the Snow" volume, 1928, deserves very little the superlatives poured upon it by the reviewers.

v

Further consideration of the "free verse" movement takes us quickly out of New England, into a flock of twittering sparrows destined quickly to vanish. Not yet is it time to speak with finality. Even the young poets are in grave doubt as to what really happened in the ten years after 1912.

Alfred Kreymborg, one of them, attempted a history of American poetry from earliest times, and two thirds of his entire volume he gave to the poets who wrote after 1912. "People had written poetry before, but not such poetry as ours." His index is one of the curiosities of the period. It contains literally hundreds of names. Every little spring peeper in twenty years is listed. At the opposite extreme is Conrad Aiken's "Modern American Poets" anthology, which reduces the school to fifteen poets: Emily Dickinson, Edwin Arlington Robinson, Robert Frost, Anna Hempstead Branch, Amy Lowell, Vachel Lindsay, Alfred Kreymborg, Wallace Stevens, William Carlos Williams, John G. Fletcher, "H. D.," T. S. Eliot, Conrad Aiken, Edna St. Vincent Millay, and Maxwell Bodenheim. He omits Sandburg, Ezra Pound, and Masters. "The work of these three poets interests me in the mass, if I may put it so, but disappoints me in the item."

That the movement petered out, ended in a complete débâcle, we shall show in a later chapter.

BIBLIOGRAPHICAL REFERENCES

For Robinson, Amy Lowell, and Frost, "Contemporary American Literature" by Manly and Rickert furnishes complete bibliographies with a tabulated list of authorities.

"Collected Poems of Edwin Arlington Robinson," 1929.

"Edwin Arlington Robinson," Ben Ray Redman, 1925.

"E. A. Robinson and the Arthurian Legend," L. M. Beebe, 1927.

"The Poetry of Edwin Arlington Robinson," L. R. Morris, 1923.

"E. A. Robinson," M. Van Doren, 1927.

"Amy Lowell," R. Hunt and R. H. Snow, 1921.

"Amy Lowell," G. H. Sargent, 1926.

"Amy Lowell," C. Wood, 1926.

"Robert Frost," A. Lowell, 1917.

"Robert Frost," G. B. Munson, 1927.

"Robert Frost," S. Cox.

CHAPTER XIX

THE SHORT STORY

So completely did one literary form dominate the forty years after 1890 that one may christen the period with its name: it has been the Age of the Short Story. To explore the amazing Everglades of it through all its mazes would be work for a volume rather than a chapter. The preliminary surveys already I have made in my "History of the Development of the American Short Story" and in my earlier volume "A History of American Literature Since 1870."

For our present study the first question to answer is: why has the short-story form flourished so abundantly in America, during the last forty years especially, and why with such increasing excellence? We are led at once to England. All through the nineteenth century the leading literary form in Great Britain was the novel. No other nation has ever produced so brilliant a school of novelists and so many novels of dominating excellence. Because of a peculiar combination of conditions, needless at this point to enumerate—the growth of advertising was one of them —American literature during the century has been very largely a matter of magazines and periodicals. In no other country in the world so many periodicals, and nowhere else so amazing a clientele of magazine buyers and readers.

England, dominating Europe with her fiction, held stolidly to one single form, the long novel or romance, in the early years of the century always a "three-decker." The English temperament expressed itself characteristically in long-distance work, fictional "Marathon runs";

the American temperament, more impatient, expressed itself in dashes. This, however, is but half the problem. For years the lack of international copyright laws allowed American publishers to issue without copyright payments any English book they desired to print. Why pay copyright money to American authors when English current classics could be had for nothing? Thus American-made fiction was largely restricted to the shorter forms which were long regarded with contempt by British novelists. American magazines like "Harper's" ran regularly a British serial, one however that they had paid for despite lack of international law compelling it. Dickens, Thackeray, George Eliot, Collins, and Hardy issued much of their work in this magazine. "Scribner's Monthly" began its career with a year-long story by George MacDonald, and the "Atlantic" ran one even longer by Charles Reade. Short stories, however, must be home-made, and there was an increasing demand for them. The reading public found them more enjoyable than the interminable serial to be read in relay heats a month between each two instalments. More and more they crowded out the serial. The "Atlantic" specialized in short-story work; from the first it ran three short stories in every number. The first eleven issues of the magazine contained eight stories by Rose Terry Cooke alone. With the growth of modern advertising methods magazines were multiplied, and each magazine demanded more and more short stories. With the demand came supply, a veritable flood, and the oversupply enabled editors to pick and choose. The standards of short-story excellence rose steadily, and with them rose steadily the powers of the new writers to meet the demand.

Unquestionably it has been the American magazine that has evolved and developed the short-story form. William Dean Howells again and again discoursed on this theme in "Criticism and Fiction" and in The Editor's Easy Chair:

It might be argued from the national hurry and impatience that it was a literary form peculiarly adapted to the American temperament, but we suspect its extraordinary development among us is owing much more to more tangible facts. The success of American magazines, which is nothing less than prodigious, is only commensurate with their excellence. There can be no question that it is one effect of the highest editorial skill when each of the two great illustrated American periodicals attains a currency as large as that of the *Family Herald* in England, or the *Petit Journal* in France.

That was in 1887. As the century turned into the nineties, the creation of short periodical lengths had become well-nigh a new profession. The age of magazines had opened—to a degree undreamed of by the early Howells; magazines soon to be advertised in terms of millions of subscribers, and every magazine insistent in its demand for compelling tales. No literary product, not even verse in the days when it was "free," has ever swept from the presses in such floods. By the mid-nineties the production of the form had become a science, an art, an industry, with handbooks and schools for learners and scholarly courses in the colleges.

Despite the rule-of-thumb dictum in all publishing houses that collections of short stories are financially unprofitable, the decade of the nineties issued a small library of collections. In some publishing seasons short-story volumes even headed the list of best sellers. During three years at the opening of the decade twenty-one collections were issued, each one of them a book of importance. The list is a remarkable one:

1891

Mary E. Wilkins, "A New England Nun."
Richard Harding Davis, "Gallegher."
Thomas Nelson Page, "Elsket and Other Stories."
James Lane Allen, "Flute and Violin."

Joel Chandler Harris, "Balaam and his Master."
Rose Terry Cooke, "Huckleberries Gathered from New New England Hills."
Elizabeth Stuart Phelps Ward, "Fourteen to One."
Richard Malcolm Johnston, "The Primes and Their Neighbors."
Hamlin Garland, "Main-Travelled Roads."
Ambrose Bierce, "In the Midst of Life."

1892

Francis Hopkinson Smith, "A Day at Laguerre's and Other Days."
Bret Harte, "Colonel Starbottle's Client."
Mark Twain, "The American Claimant and Other Stories."
Grace Elizabeth King, "Tales of a Time and Place."
Frederick Jesup Stimson, "In Three Zones."
Henry James, "The Lesson of the Master."

1893

Sarah Orne Jewett, "A Native of Winby."
Robert W. Chambers, "The King in Yellow."
Margaret Deland, "Mr. Tommy Dove, and Other Stories."
Octave Thanet, "Stories of a Western Town."

Alexander Jessup has listed nearly two hundred volumes of collected short stories published during this single decade and in addition to these many individual tales never re-published from the magazines.[1] Almost every writer of the after-1870 period, living during the nineties, furnished at least a volume. Bret Harte, for instance, added sixteen during the decade, and Miss Jewett six. Nearly every member of the new school—Allen, Brown, Chopin, Crane, Davis, Freeman, Garland, King, and the rest—began with short-length fiction.

An examination of the mass reveals the fact that it was

[1] "American Short Stories," edited by Alexander Jessup, 1923. His bibliography at the end of this volume is indispensable for the student of the short story.

for the most part regional picturings, prolongations from the soil-colored eighties. The revolt from romance during the 1870–1890 epoch had been a gentle one, though persistent nevertheless and progressive. First, there had come short-story romance with seemingly realistic background —characters strikingly presented: Bret Harte, Cable, Page, Eggleston; then romance with an attempt at real backgrounds and with apparently realistic characters: Jewett, Harris, Howells; then, crossing the line of the nineties, romance stripped of all its outer costumings and forced to reveal itself not naked yet, but ordinary: Garland, Crane, Wilkins. With the nineties one began to hear of "veritism."

I

In the short-story area this "veritism" centered for a time in Garland and Mary E. Wilkins. During a brief season James Lane Allen of Kentucky was central. To the book-reviewers of the nineties he was the most promising of all the writers of the new generation. For a time he was even hailed as the American Hardy, but removal to New York City smothered whatever genius there may have been in him and he was lost in the wilderness of the new century. The case was a typical one.

The writer who remained longest outside the infected area was Mary E. Wilkins. The bare, Puritanic, Vermont-like quality of her first work promised much. It was grim, and it was first-hand stuff. Two or three characters, always from the life of the everyday round; no description: dialogue bare as the talk of hired men, sentences staccato. Her old maids, her senile survivals, her .balky lovers, her root-bound farmers, grow upon the reader, they become fearfully alive, they grip the throat, then suddenly the story is done, like a ballad. Like Frost, like Robinson, she is face to face with the actuality of the New England *now*. Her characters are alive, specimens she finds on that terminal moraine of human specimens which the New England glacial period has left in its wake.

Her success was her undoing. Little by little she turned from her early style toward sophistication and, during the historical novel period, even toward flamboyancy and over-decoration. Her industry was remarkable: "Edgewater People," 1918, was her thirty-eighth book. Beginning with "Madelon" in 1896, she wrote nine major novels in twelve years, most of them for serial publication in magazines. The total of her short stories in all her collections is one hundred and seventy-three, and she has written some sixty-five others which have never been re-published from the magazines.

She was rushed too fast, she was swept into the maelstrom of New York's publishing area and lost.

II

Throughout the whole period another literary figure has been constant: in short-story fiction, in poetry, in the novel, in drama even, every decade a new phase, Alice Brown. In the nineties with her "Meadow Grass" and "Tiverton Tales" she was local colorist chiefly, depicter of rural New England scenes and characters after the Sarah Orne Jewett patterns. She was intimate with her characters, more witty and sparkling, but never so final in her touches nor so un-studiedly effective. Completing her schooling in a New Hampshire "female seminary," she had taught for a time, and then for years had done magazine hack-work in Boston, chiefly in the "Youth's Companion" office where she had charge of the department edited with scissors and paste brush. It broadened rather than deepened her; it gave her that catholicity and multiplicity of mind that have made her published list such a miscellany of excellence. Hardly a literary form that she has not handled well.

With the next decade her art became broader and deeper. One phase of her powers is well-nigh unique: almost without exception the first collection of short stories by an American writer has been his masterpiece; witness "The Luck of Roaring Camp," "Old Creole Days," "Marjorie Daw," "In the Tennessee Mountains," "In Old Virginia," "Gallegher," "Flute and Violin," "Knitters in the Sun." The powers of Alice Brown, however, have steadily grown; every collection of her short stories has been an advance upon the one before. Nearly thirty years after her first book of tales she could win the distinctive "Harper's Magazine" prize in a contest with nearly every other short-story writer in America.

With advancing powers her art deepened. The tragic began to enter, though never deeply. The imperiousness of the new demand for manner—the O. Henry influence of the new century—compelled her to better workmanship; her early sentimentalism faded and with it her local color of the earlier shades, as in her "Country Neighbors," 1910, and her "Vanishing Points." An element of the dramatic was growing in her work. Several of her early stories she had recast from their primitive forms into one-act dramas, a supreme test for any single tale, an excellent literary exercise for beginners. By 1913 she was able to win the ten-thousand-dollar prize offered by Winthrop Ames of the Little Theatre, New York, for the best drama submitted. From one thousand six hundred and forty-six plays competing in the contest, her "Children of Earth" was adjudged best. By short-story rules it was faultless even though a drama. Evidently its fictional art outweighed its theatrical technique, for on the actual stage it was a failure.

Her later pen ran largely to novels, sometimes one or two with every year. Brilliant in passages, excellent here and there in characterization, they fall down almost all of them in structure. She fails in the architectonic, in sustained dramatic power. Some of her volumes like "The Black Drop" are dull from start to finish.

The fatal weakness of Alice Brown has ever been her

multiplicity, her ability to do many things well—she has even published a volume of poems, and with Miss Guiney made a critical study of Stevenson. Excellent, but nothing done uniquely well, nothing that has invited disciples, nothing that will force its way down, as will Miss Jewett's, into the years to come. A dependable literary workman, watchful of times and manners, alert, tireless, she has constantly through four decades been high in public favor, but her best, as compared with the best of Miss Jewett and Mary E. Wilkins, lacks depth and color and permanence.

III

The second decade of the period, the first decade of the new century, stands in short-story history as the age of O. Henry. Suddenly the short story became a startling thing, with tricks and quirks and unexpected explosions. It was the age, too, of Jack London, of the "Call of the Wild" tale, the "red-blooded" tale, the tale of the raw red areas where "men with the bark on" did their superman deeds, tales recorded if possible by one who himself had been an actor in the drama. The most distinctive short-story collections and single short stories issued as independent volumes during the opening years of the decade were:

1900. "The Son of the Wolf," Jack London.
1900. "Shadowings," Lafcadio Hearn.
1900. "Whilomville Stories," Stephen Crane.
1901. "Stratagems and Spoils, Stories of Love and Politics," William Allen White.
1901. "Crucial Instances," Edith Wharton.
1901. "Held for Orders," Frank H. Spearman.
1902. "The Kindred of the Wild," Charles G. D. Roberts.
1902. "Melomaniacs," James Gibbons Huneker [Sketches].
1902. "Out of Gloucester," James B. Connolly.
1902. "The Splendid Idle Forties," Gertrude Atherton.
1902. "Our Josephine," Opie Percival Read.
1903. "Philosophy Four," Owen Wister.
1903. "The Way of the Sea," Norman Duncan.

Throughout the decade the Jack London, "Blazed Trail" atmosphere. It was the era of the John Fox "Hell fer Sartain" tale and of the James B. Connolly "Out of Gloucester" yarn. With Connolly had come a new breath from the sea—the new actuality, realism, veritism, transferred to deep water. Its author was a physical superman of the Jack London type. He had won in 1896 "the first Olympic championship of modern times at Athens"; he had been a marine at the battle of Santiago; he had seen much of life in the navy and had participated in all phases of marine adventure, including submarine work. His tales, for a time frequent in the magazines, were redolent not of books but of the sea. They were untheatric, genuine, the work of one who wrote of what he knew, wrote of what he had been a part of.

Constantly the emphasis was changing; two elements were becoming dominant: sheer story-telling art, the story told only for story-telling's sake, for entertainment; and, secondly, vivid characterization of a central figure, with striking newness in manner and background.

But characterization belongs to the novel; the short story is, from its very nature, brief, a single situation, a culminating moment. There is no time for character development. But more and more, even to the end of the period, demand came imperiously for sharply etched leading characters. A new discovery had been made, however, perhaps through the Sherlock Holmes stories of Conan Doyle, the discovery of what Grant Overton has called "integrated short stories": if a character cannot be presented in all his angles in a single story, then scatter him through a series until finally he emerges in fullness of individualization. The "Chimmie Fadden" stories of the mid-nineties; "The Country of the Pointed Firs" stories by Miss Jewett; "Old Chester Tales" by Margaret Deland with their inimitable Dr. Lavender; the running series of short stories published as if it were a novel by Owen Wister with the title "The Virginian"; the "Get-Rich-Quick Wallingford" stories of George R. Chester; and the detective stories of Melville Davisson Post. With such later writers as Cohen and Kelland and Glass, this character featuring became a veritable *cliché,* like that of the Mutt and Jeff and the Andy Gump cartoons, which have long since strangled their creators.

Post made a variation of the Sherlock Holmes detective tale and set more bells to ringing than he realized. He was a lawyer, as Conan Doyle was not, and his criminals were not hunted down by means of clues impossible save to the superman detective. The criminals were caught red-handed and they were allowed to slip through intricate loop-holes in the law to undeserved freedom. Uncannily skilled was he in the use of "code" mysteries, most fecund in the invention of plot and crime, as witness such titles as "The Strange Schemes of Randolph Mason," "The Man of Last Resort," and "The Corrector of Destinies." Following him came Mary Roberts Rinehart, plot novelist, skilled in mystery-weaving. Her "The Circular Staircase," 1908, "The Man in Lower Ten," and "The Amazing Adventures of Letitia Carberry" bring back the days of Anna Katharine Green when in the full glory of her work. Suspense, mystery, sheer story-telling power that holds the reader to the end. If a novel exists for no other end than mere entertainment, the trembling excitement of a thrilling hour, she has been a novelist of note.

More and more as we shall note in chapter 25, the detective story became a dominating thing until it had produced a mass of material that in itself would fill a library alcove, and more.

IV

As the century grew into its 'teens the short-story flood widened and shallowed until it well-nigh enveloped all the literary field. Every living fictionist during the decade was pouring out short stories, and in addition to the old group with every season came new recruits. Sixteen "arrivals" I would cite, and these their first noteworthy volumes:

1911. Mary Roberts Rinehart, "The Amazing Adventures of Letitia Carberry."
1912. Arthur B. Reeve, "The Silent Bullet."
1912. Irvin S. Cobb, "Back Home."
1912. Montague Glass, "Object: Matrimony."
1913. Elsie Singmaster, "Gettysburg."
1913. Owen Johnson, "Murder in any Degree."
1913. Edna Ferber, "Roast Beef, Medium."
1914. Katharine Fullerton Gerould, "Vain Oblations."
1914. Gouverneur Morris, "The Incandescent Lily."
1915. Dorothy Canfield, "Hillsboro People."
1916. Fanny Hurst, "Every Soul Hath Its Song."
1918. Wilbur Daniel Steele, "Land's End."
1918. Theodore Dreiser, "Free, and Other Stories."
1918. Joseph Hergesheimer, "Gold and Iron."
1919. Sherwood Anderson, "Winesburg, Ohio."
1919. Octavus Roy Cohen, "Polished Ivory."

The outstanding short-story events of the decade were the death of O. Henry in 1910 and the publication of his collected writings in a popular set sensationally advertised and widely sold. For a time O. Henryism—everywhere O. Henry. Magazine fiction leaned heavily toward eccentricity of manner, up-to-dateness of vocabulary and setting, smartness and unusualness in characterization and in culminating paragraph.

In an age of standardization an elaborate attempt was made now to standardize even fiction. The short story was made more and more a matter of rules, of fixed requirements, of standard varieties and lengths like Ford machines. These requirements filled dozens of handbooks and became the subject matter even of correspondence courses. With all the standards and parts and patterns thoroughly understood even the unliterary could make short stories. It was a mere matter of six weeks in a correspondence course.

Noteworthy was the rise of Edna Ferber, born in Kalamazoo, Michigan, in 1887—second generation of the period. Again a blow at the old Anglo-Saxon régime. Her father was a Hungarian Jew, her mother an American, Milwaukee-born of Teutonic ancestry—one thinks of Bret Harte. Never personality more vivid and vital than the daughter of this marriage. Unlike most of her literary generation, she could not wait for college. Through with high school at seventeen, she became a newspaper reporter, at first on local journals and finally on the "Chicago Tribune." Six years in all. In her work everywhere the newspaper slant: timeliness, practicality, concentration upon middle-class readers who demand for the most part lavishness of color, sentiment, humor of the slapstick order, cleverness, and success—the O. Henry formula. The new realism, everywhere a contagion during the decade, disillusioned her not at all. She would write realism that touched life as bitingly as anything in Dreiser, and yet she would do it with optimism. Her story "Representing T. A. Buck," "American Magazine," March, 1911, is the opening note of her literary career. That it appeared in the "American" is in itself an illuminating fact: a business story, an American business type represented—how success was won by Emma McChesney, feminine commercial traveler. Before this vigorous personality was rounded out

in all the phases of her character, before she had poured
out all her business axioms and adages and up-to-date Poor
Richardisms, she had filled three volumes, "Roast Beef,
Medium," 1913, "Personality Plus," 1914, and "Emma
McChesney & Co.," 1915. A new type had been created:
the irresistible modern woman who has pushed her way
into the business areas formerly occupied exclusively by
men. Everywhere in all the series an overflow of vitality
and an enthusiasm in living that are contagious. Later in
her literary career she outgrew the short-story form and
wrote novels. Characterization from the first had been her
chief concern, and characterization is a matter of the novel,
unless one achieves it by piling short story upon short story
each centered upon a single individual. Her "So Big" and
her "Show Boat" novels, inordinately praised, pitched to
the key and the art demands of the average reader, and,
launched with all the machinery of modern advertising,
have been greatly successful. Clever, witty, vital with enthusiasm, she has been a good influence even though her
novels are destined to meet the fate which has come to all
work aimed at the mere market-place. Her Emma Mc-
Chesney studies, however, will endure long. Modeled at the
start upon O. Henry, they outgrew their model, improved
upon it, vitalized it with genuine content, and added a new
and picturesque character to the American gallery.

From the same decade and the same influence came another feminized O. Henry, Fannie Hurst, a native of
Missouri, a graduate of Washington University. School-
teaching had been her first venture, then literature. Before
she was twenty-one, with no resources but vigorous health
and determination, she went to New York to win recognition. She worked for years before she won a trace of it.
Life, which to her was what it had been to O. Henry, she
studied with intensity for the one purpose of securing literary material. She worked in shops and restaurants and
once crossed the Atlantic in the steerage. And her first
published collection had O. Henryism in the very title,

"Just Around the Corner," 1914. It was as up-to-date, vivacious, and vital as even her master's little old Bagdad sketchings or Edna Ferber's business adventurings. She has created characters, but no single character that dominates. With success won, she turned to the novel and became one of the best-seller candidates with every publishing season, strongest perhaps with her "Lummox," 1923, and "A President is Born," 1927. No writer of the period has been more successful. Her stories published weekly by a syndicate of newspapers are continually advertised as by the "highest-paid short-story writer in the world." An excellent type of the professional literary worker trained by hardest labor into New York standards, slavish follower of fashions soon to be outworn.

V

To list all the O. Henry "school" during the new century 'teens would be useless labor. Most of them perished with the decade, or else became biographers. The O. Henry contagion, it would seem, was more general in the outlying districts, notably in the Midwest. One case there was in Kentucky, Irvin Cobb, born in 1876 at Paducah. From early boyhood he has been a newspaper reporter and editor and writer. He was editor of a daily paper at nineteen, and before he was of age was in charge of a column—"Sour Mash"—in the Louisville "Evening Post." He has been the typical reporter of his generation, as Richard Harding Davis was of his. A list of his important assignments would fill a column. Literature has been with him a by-product, a part of the day's work—an abundant one, however. A mere list of his books fills a quarter of a Who's Who page. First of all he is a newspaper humorist, maker of the most volatile of all literary products. His short-story career began in 1910 with "The Escape of Mr. Trimm" published in the "Saturday Evening Post." Then had come "The Belled Buzzard," destined to remain his classic literary achievement, though several of his later Kentucky-life tales come near it in excellence. He has added one unique character, perhaps two, to the gallery of American fiction types; the Judge Priest of "Back Home" and "Old Judge Priest," and the Mr. Trimm of his earlier work. Leisure should have been his: he who could create "Fish Head" should have been given time to work out other Kentucky weirdnesses rather than to have to report Thaw and Goebel murder trials and make his mere "Stickfuls" and "A Laugh a Day" series. Like all other journalists, he has written in hot haste with newspaper ink that fades after its single day. In allusion, in vocabulary, in fictional fashions, in point of view, he is always as up to date as a college orchestra. He has greatly entertained his generation—no mean epitaph; but for the most part call his work not literature: call it farce, call it literary journalism. Perhaps in the future, and not long hence, all our literature will be on the flying leaves of journalism: stuff read with eagerness and thrown into the dust-box with the Sunday paper.

In still another way Cobb has been a new type: he was of the younger non-New England generation of literary workers which swarmed during the decade into New York from the West and the South. Note a random list of geographical varieties: Elsie Singmaster, Pennsylvania; Will Payne, Illinois; Mary Austin, Illinois; C. C. Dobie, California; Barry Benefield, Texas; W. D. Steele, North Carolina; Ring Lardner, Michigan; Octavus Roy Cohen, Alabama; Thomas Beer, Iowa; Ben Ames Williams, Mississippi. One might fill a page with such names and not once touch New England and the Middle States.

A single exception is Katharine Fullerton Gerould, born in Massachusetts and educated at Radcliffe College to the master's degree and for nearly ten years a member of the Bryn Mawr College faculty. Unlike the youngsters from the West and the South, she is no rebel: she stands with Henry James and Mrs. Wharton, and she has written the most caustic arraignment of O. Henry that has yet appeared, unless it be my own. Her sinister tale "Vain Oblations," 1914, placed her at a bound near the head of the new school of short-story writers. It is done with rare art: she has never since equaled it. One may class it with those few tales that burn themselves into one's memory like scorpion bites and will not be erased, that become abiding horrors, like Charlotte Perkins Stetson's "Yellow Wallpaper," 1892, and Frederick Stuart Greene's "The Cat of the Canebrake," 1916.

She has done excellent work as a critic. Her *causerie* in the "Yale Review" of July, 1924, dealing with the contemporary short story is distinctive. The art requirements in the early twenties she summed up in this paragraph:

> To be first-rate, a short story must first of all be well made. It must give us situation, suspense, and climax. The incident that informs and creates the story must be a significant one; either truly momentous for one person, or vividly typical of the lives of people, or—if you like—suggestively symbolic. It must carry more than its own weight. It cannot, that is, be simple anecdote, however trenchant. If it but chronicles an absurdity, the absurdity must carry implications concerning fate or human character. A short story that does not do this may be readable, and often is, but it is not a great short story.[2]

VI

The short story of the twenties more and more sought to throw off the O. Henry influence, the mold of form, the binding force of the crystallized handbook rules. As in the free-verse movement, the impelling motive was for freedom from the tyranny of convention, and—again as in the free-verse movement—freedom has gone often to absurd lengths. Realism and literary license have been pressed to extremes by such writers as Ernest Heming-

[2] For a complete survey of the requirements of editors in 1921 consult "The Stories Editors Buy and Why," Jean Wick, with letters from various editors of the time.

way who have deliberately violated every canon of the old handbooks and even the elementary rules of grammar. Literary scandal, like all other scandal, is tremendously arresting, but it is brief. The real artist does not flaunt himself, nor pose, nor perform bad-boy tricks for sensation in the presence of dignity, nor does he deliberately place strangeness and sex uncleanness and grotesque newness among his leading artistic canons.

The closing decade has been an era of prizes offered for short-story work, notably the "Harper's Magazine" prizes in surprisingly large figures. Then, too, there has been the five-hundred-dollar prize offered each year by the Society of Arts and Sciences in the so-called O. Henry Memorial Award for the most notable short story appearing in a magazine during the current year. The following have been winners of the prize:

> 1919. Margaret Prescott Montague
> 1920. Maxwell Struthers Burt
> 1921. Edison Marshall
> 1922. Irvin S. Cobb
> 1923. Edgar Valentine Smith
> 1924. Inez Haynes Irwin
> 1925. Julian Street
> 1926. Wilbur Daniel Steele
> 1927. Roark Bradford
> 1928. Walter Duranty
> 1929. Dorothy Parker

After reading the list one feels like Herbert S. Gorman, who reviewed the O. Henry collection in 1924:

One wonders a bit dejectedly what Sherwood Anderson, Edith Wharton, James Branch Cabell, Theodore Dreiser, Glenway Westcott, Alice Brown, Joseph Hergesheimer, Conrad Aiken, Katharine Fullerton Gerould, and a few others were doing all these years. Can it be possible that they wrote no short stories? And then it comes to mind that some of them wrote a number of their finest short stories in that time, any one of which—from an artistic standpoint—is worth the entire fifteen short stories in the O. Henry Memorial Award Prize Stories of 1924.

In conclusion allow me to repeat a single paragraph from an earlier criticism:

On the whole the short-story episode in American literary history has been not altogether a symptom of strength. "Short story writing is a young man's game," says H. G. Wells, and it may be added that it is also the natural device of the young nation just emerging from its adolescent period. To see life in true perspective, to know the truth in its breadth and depth, demands that we fix our attention not on fragments of life, on snatches of experience, on glimpses, swift impressions, but on wholes. America has not had the time to look steadily and long at any phase of the human play. All it has wanted has been momentary impressions artistically given, surfaces and sensations. It has been satisfied with cleverness rather than mastery, entertainment rather than instruction, with journalism rather than literature. What the coming period is to be it is not within the province of the historian to seek.[3]

BIBLIOGRAPHICAL REFERENCES

"The Advance of the American Short Story," Edward J. O'Brien, 1923.

"The Development of the American Short Story," F. L. Pattee, 1923.

"Our Short Story Writers," Blanche Colton Williams, 1920.

"The Writing of Fiction," Edith Wharton, 1925.

"Modern Short Stories," F. H. Law, 1918.

"Best Short Stories for 1915" and a volume for each year following, Edward J. O'Brien.

"O. Henry Memorial Award Prize Stories," edited by Blanche Colton Williams and published yearly. 1919 and every year following.

"Representative American Short Stories," Alexander Jessup, 1923.

"Stickfuls. Myself to Date," by Irvin S. Cobb, 1923.

[3] Introduction to "American Short Stories," Fred Lewis Pattee, 1925.

CHAPTER XX

REVOLT FROM THE FRONTIER

I

THE spirit of revolt which had started in the early nineties under such names as "veritism" and "naturalism" grew stronger with every decade. From the first it was a Midwestern affair, centering in the midland capital.

The muck-rake episode of the Roosevelt era, and a decade later the free verse revolt which had its inception in the heart of the midlands, were but phases of a greater movement, a more significant rebellion, one that voiced its major demands through the medium of prose fiction. To understand this revolt one must read chronologically twenty novels—forty would be better—scattered over two decades. Here is the preliminary list:

1900. "Sister Carrie," Theodore Dreiser.
1903. "The Pit," Frank Norris.
1904. "The Common Lot," Robert Herrick.
1905. "Memoirs of an American Citizen," Robert Herrick.
1906. "The Jungle," Upton Sinclair.
1908. "Together," Robert Herrick.
1909. "A Certain Rich Man," William Allen White.
1911. "Jennie Gerhardt," Theodore Dreiser.
1912. "The Financier," Theodore Dreiser.
1914. "The Titan," Theodore Dreiser.
1915. "The Spoon River Anthology" [Not, however, a novel], Edgar Lee Masters.
1915. "The Harbor," Ernest Poole.
1916. "Windy McPherson's Son," Sherwood Anderson.
1918. "An American Family," Henry Kitchell Webster.
1918. "On the Stairs," Henry B. Fuller.

1918. "My Ántonia," Willa Cather.
1919. "Winesburg, Ohio," Sherwood Anderson.
1920. "Main Street," Sinclair Lewis.
1921. "Brass," Charles G. Norris.
1921. "Erik Dorn," Ben Hecht.
1922. "Babbitt," Sinclair Lewis.
1922. "Children of the Market Place," Edgar Lee Masters.

Behind this list, in the eighties and the nineties, lay the novels and the critiques of William Dean Howells, himself a Westerner, and the helpless shoutings and gesturings and pleadings of the early Garland, and Frank Norris, and Fuller.

A study of these twenty novels reveals much: they are documents in the history of the Middle West. First of all, they reveal the passing of the New England influence. A flood of immigrants ever since the mid-century had been pouring into the prairie lands. For millions of people the period had been another colonial era, with all the hardships of the early American settlement days. Whole States had become in population prevailingly Scandinavian or Teutonic. European ideals and manners and religions had over large areas become dominant. No longer New England and Anglo-Saxondom: a generation had arisen, trained in the American schools, able to speak English with no trace of accent, that was beginning to ask with bitterness: Why should I sing—

"Land where my fathers died,
Land of the Pilgrims' pride"?

With the new American had come European ideals to oppose the New Englandism of the earlier day. Millions there were to whom Puritanism was only a vague synonym for sinister repressions. More and more were creeping in European pessimism, European Sabbath observance, European ideals concerning sex conventions, European doubt and atheism.

The tide of young Westerners, many of them from little prairie colleges, poured, as already we have noted, into Chicago, hungry for literary expression, and most of them found work in newspaper offices. Some of them did not last long, some of them survived the ordeal and flourished until Chicago seemed small to them. Then on to New York, where they either sank at once or else swam into literary fame. Grilled into efficiency by the newspaper were such vigorous Westerners as Ade, Phillips, Dreiser, Willa Cather, Anderson, Lewis, and Sandburg. Their literary energies quickly overflowed in the form of fiction—short stories, novels, romances.

But it was fiction with a new tang, a step in advance of even the ultimate dreamings of the *fin de siècle* realists, fiction not only redolent of Continental influences, but distorted into new forms under the pressure of the new American journalism. Bound by long hours to newspaper offices, pruned without mercy by city editors, blue-penciled and bludgeoned into news-making efficiency, the new school brought to their fiction journalistic technique: factuality, truth to observed details, a style forged for the ten millions of the daily press. Make sentences short, paragraphs short, a vocabulary tuned to the ordinary even as far as slang. Strip the story of plot and all other devices of the artificial age; make it simple with no slightest suspicion of literary overtones. And tell it in pictures—always pictures; make it visible, make it move; hit the high spots, the vivid *news* elements; shock your reader, thrill him, hold him, he is *blasé,* fed up on such stuff, but "get him." Sentences snappy, each paragraph a bunch of Chinese crackers. "A short-breathed sentence," says a recent handbook for journalists, "is like the crack of a whip. It arouses jaded intellects to attention." And especially make your man, your woman, alive. Characterization, always characterization! Thus the new realism, the new utter modernness.

Another newness: the young Lochinvar school had all of them been reared in small towns only lately the frontier.

To come into civilization opened their eyes to the barrenness of their early environment. It shocked and disillusioned them. It was not until he had lived two years in Boston that Garland was able to see the West as he later portrayed it in "Main-Travelled Roads." And now with Dreiser and Masters and Anderson and Lewis and the rest came a vivid picturing of the crudeness of the passing frontier. Satire, even cynicism, they poured upon their own home towns, with hideous picturings often, picturings with the implied suggestion that they were typical of all American towns. So at least it was gathered by Europeans. Fundamentally all of them were untrue to fact, or at least to facts. It was like dwelling upon the horrors of unsightly scaffolding and forgetting the growing cathedral beneath.

Dreiser and Masters we have already dwelt upon. Other modern instances are Sherwood Anderson and Sinclair Lewis.

II

Anderson was peculiarly a product of the "Spoon River Anthology" period, 1915–1919. While readers and critics were wrangling over the strange Caliban thing that had shambled out of the frontier wilds into the cultivated areas of poetry, Anderson "went the poet one better" with his homely album of "Winesburg, Ohio" daguerreotypes.

The man himself had originated in the social area he describes. He was born in Camden, Ohio, in 1876, his father an ex-soldier, a harness-maker, a man ruined by a plethora of imagination; his son has completely preserved him in "A Story-Teller's Story," in "Tar," and in "Windy Mc-Pherson's Son." The mother, a more practical soul, reared her little family alone and with incredible toil. On Hallowe'en nights when the neighborhood boys threw cabbages at her door, she railed at them in screaming fury, she the gentlest of all gentle souls, and so drew their fire again and again until she had secured cabbages enough for her winter's supply.

The little flock scattered early. The boy, forced into self-support, saw life in its coarsest areas. He was mechanic's apprentice, stable boy, factory hand and, at seventeen, adventurer without money or job on the streets of Chicago. His book "Tar" is a penetrating study of the primitivism, the Westernism, the virgin soil that produced him. It is an introspective autobiography, and it is more: it is a rural album of coarse daguerreotypes illustrating the psychology, the manners, the view of life, the institutions, the personalities of an area left behind by the retreating frontier.

In Chicago the boy found employment in rolling kegs of nails in a warehouse, assembling bicycles in a factory, and learning his first lessons in metropolitan civilization. He had no clear ideals, no formulated philosophy of life, no constructive plan. Eager, curious, formless, he drifted hobo-like and wondered. His early books are autobiographic. No writer more self-centered, more introspective: even now he can talk only about himself and about his wonder at the meaning of things.

When he was twenty-two there came the Spanish War, and he enlisted, for the mere adventure of it. For a few weeks he was a hero.

"When with the others of my company I marched away to the railroad station to entrain for war the entire town turned out and cheered. Girls ran out of houses to kiss us, and old veterans of the Civil War—they had known that of battles we would never know—stood with tears in their eyes."

Then suddenly had come the war collapse and again he was nobody, disillusioned, adrift—what was life after all but a series of disillusions? "Windy McPherson's Son" and "Marching Men," his earliest work, are stories of small-town youngsters filled with idealism and romance who seek their fortune in the city and are disillusioned to utter surrender of all ambition. So Anderson. "Having no God," he says of himself, "the gods have been taken from me by the life about me."

Back again in the Ohio of his birth, he found work as he could, was married, and in time was manager of a small paint factory. But the spirit of the frontier still bubbled in the little prairie town; his father's exuberant romanticism had been a part of his birthright. Like Babbitt in Lewis's novel he yearned to break away from it all, and one bright morning, unlike Babbitt he did break away; he cut loose from everything and went to Chicago where he found employment in an advertising agency.

And now a new butterfly fluttered across his romanticism. He would write, not "ads" but literature. Weeks and months of agonizing practice, then on an impulse New York City. In Chicago, in New York, in his voluminous reading he was with rebels. They shaped his thinking, and fed the wild tides within him. For months he worked as Jack London had worked as described in his " Martin Eden."

Out of the West an individualist, a frontiersman, in step with nobody, self-centered as a desperado and as confident. Life to him is a thing good or bad only as it reacts on *him*. When he writes he will write like nobody else, he will think like nobody else. Hear him as he reflects upon literary art.

There was a notion that ran through all story-telling in America that stories must be built about a plot, and that absurd Anglo-Saxon notion that they must point a moral, uplift the people, make better citizens, etc. The magazines were flooded with these plot stories. . . . The plot notions did seem to me to poison all story-telling."

And again:

Would the common words of our daily speech in shops and offices do the trick? Surely the Americans among whom one sat talking had felt everything that the Greeks had felt, everything that the English felt. Deaths came to them, the tricks of fate assailed their lives. I was certain none of them lived, felt or talked as the average American novel made them live, feel and talk; and as for the plot short stories of the magazines— those bastard children of de Maupassant, Poe, and O.

Henry—it was certain there were no plot stories ever lived in any life I had known anything about.

He would record the actualities of life as he knew them, he would hold up his mirror and reflect life unrevised, undiminished. If it was shocking, so much the worse for life. He knew how men talked, he had heard stories by the hour told by advertising agents in his office, by hired men on farms and in shops, by young soldier bucks in tents and latrines. That was actuality, that to him was Truth: it devolved upon him simply to record it.

When one told a tale to a group of advertising men sitting in a barroom in Chicago or to a group of laborers by a factory door in Indiana one instinctively disbanded the army of classic English words. There were moments then for what have always been called by our correct writers "unprintable words." One got now and then a certain effect by a bit of profanity. One dropped instinctively into the vocabulary of the men about, was compelled to do so to get the full effect sought for the tale. What had the words of such a tale to do with Thackeray or Fielding? . . . Had one ventured into the classic English models for tale-telling, at that moment there would have been a roar. "What the devil! Don't you go high-toning us!"

One is prepared now for what follows. "Windy McPherson's Son," like all he writes, is autobiographic, is a close-up, strongly scented with soil of the new-broken frontier: the primal stench is not out of it. Publishers were afraid of such a book; it brought him only rejection slips, until the miracle happened as it had happened to Frost: an English publisher took it, the British public hailed it as something racily American, and New York as always fell into line with a shout of welcome. "Marching Men" came next: another study in defeated romanticism, another golden frontier proved nothing but the old ordinary thing.

Then came the Freud period in the man's fiction. Sex-repression had been a peculiar phase of the frontier period.

The conquest of the American forest and the wild plains had been a masculine matter. It had made not only for the absurd over-chivalry one finds recorded in Bret Harte, but for monk-like dreamings, coarse story-telling, base sex orgies at times. The frontier attitude toward femininity, a growth from three centuries, accounts for the place of women in American society at the present time, a condition that has been criticized with harshness by such novelists as Robert Herrick and Sinclair Lewis. The full significance of the frontier attitude one may learn from the wise old Kansas philosopher Ed Howe, author of "The Story of a Country Town":

> As a boy and young man I absorbed from my surroundings tremendous respect for women. I was not taught it; men naturally felt that way; it was their religion. Women and girls didn't want to do the rough things men were engaged in; they were cleaner, gentler; better in every way. I was almost grown before I heard of a foolish or incapable mother, or of a rowdy girl. When I first heard of a woman appearing as a public speaker, it seemed sacrilege; I became interested in a children's magazine, and when I found it edited by a woman, lost interest. . . . I suppose that was the old savage way; certainly it was not at all like the present fashion, wherein men criticize women as freely as Democrats criticize Republicans.

With Freud's volume before him, Anderson found the answer to some of his questionings. Sexual inhibitions, concealed eroticism, sex aberrations—these were the hidden causes of conduct. His volumes "Poor White," "Winesburg, Ohio," and "Many Marriages" aroused criticism that had in its tones at times something like horror, and as a result the circulation of the volumes and the fame of the author grew rapidly.

"Many Marriages," like "The Triumph of the Egg" and other volumes that followed it, was a book made with honest intent. If there is coarseness in it, evidences of a heavy masculine hand that at times bears on too hard, one may defend it when one remembers the man's origin and training. Unquestionably he is a lover of beauty—this came from his mother, who was half-Italian; he was romantic of soul—this came from his temperamental father; he was a Westerner, who had dreamed as all Westerners do that perfection lay in the East, and had been disillusioned. H. S. Canby could call the book "a new Pilgrim's Progress in which the pilgrim goes crying for 'Life, Life,' in a very different sense from that intended by Bunyan."

On his later life, his Whitman-like chants, his various books, his second breaking-away period when he settled in a small Virginia town and edited a country newspaper in the spirit of "escape," we need not dwell. He has spread himself widely—too widely; hardly a literary form that he has not touched. He is best in his confessional moods, as in "Tar" and "A Story-Teller's Story." A hobo soul, he has settled nothing, he has settled down to nothing.

"I want in everywhere. To go in is my aim in life. I want into fashionable hotels and clubs, I want into banks, into people's houses, into labor meetings, into courthouses. I want to see all I can of how people live in their lives. That is my business in life—to find out what I can, to go in."

At every point he provokes paradox. H. L. Mencken could say of his novel "Dark Laughter," "It has all the cruel truthfulness of a snap-shot, and it is at the same time a moving and beautiful poem."

Anderson is a paradox in our hopeful America, a literary agnostic, an intellectual hobo, a grown man still adolescent, an agitator with no program, a poet soul with no foundations, a romanticist turned cynic, a man from the westward march deflected eastward, a frontier individualist who has lived into the age of industrialism and chain stores and combinations. Such men build no foundations. They stir the waters to muddiness but they do nothing permanent.

III

The successor to David Graham Phillips as fictional critic of the American social régime has been Sinclair Lewis, one of the earliest of the second generation of the new period—his birth-year was 1885. The change in literary tones and methods wrought by the twenty years which separate the two men is more radical than often is caused by the evolution of a century. To read one of Phillips's novels, say "The Cost," after "Main Street" and "Elmer Gantry" is like sitting for tea in a Victorian drawing-room after a matinée session with the "talkies." Lewis was reared not at all on Victorianism, and there was in him no childhood impress of Puritanism. From earliest boyhood literature to him was Kipling and Shaw and Wells, Crane and Norris, London and O. Henry, Phillips and Upton Sinclair and Mencken and Masters.

He was latest member of that Young Lochinvar school which during two decades rode in knight-errant procession into the East to reform it. His home was Sauk Centre, Minnesota; eighteen years he lived there; his father was the physician of the town. Concerning these primal years upon the prairie we need not question. Stuart Sherman has described them in a phrase: "a healthy athletic boy-hood in an American small town where a spark is dropped by a village radical who has read Robert Ingersoll, Karl Marx, and Napoleon." Lewis himself has summed up the years in this more condensed formula: "the eternal aching comedy of expectant youth."

The "spark," the "expectancy," working their will in the lad, sent him to New England, that dream of the prairie-born since the days of the Cary sisters. There was "culture" in New England, civilization, beauty—that was his dream; and he went to Yale, where in four years he added to the college curriculum several things, including two summer voyages to Europe on cattle-boats. No youth more headlong, more hungry for life. Following his graduation, "for eight years," he writes—

1907–1915—I was a literary jack-of-all-trades: newspaper reporter on the New Haven *Courier and Journal,* San Francisco *Bulletin,* and for the Associated Press; magazine editor —*Transatlantic Tales, Volta Review, Adventure, Publishers' Newspaper Syndicate;* manuscript reader for F. A. Stokes Co. and George Doran Co. I wandered down to Panama, going steerage, returning stowaway, and in between failing to get a job on the Panama railroad. A year and a half I spent in California, part of it reporting, part trying (vainly) to "free lance," sharing a bungalow at Carmel with William Rose Benét. And once Allan Updegraff and I shared miserable rooms on the East Side of New York.[1]

He might have added that he worked for his board for Upton Sinclair in his Helicon Hall experiment, that he vagabonded over Europe and over twenty-six of the United States and through Mexico. Journalism taught him to write, and headed him toward literary expression. His apprentice work—short stories, sketches—he published as best he could—in the wood-pulp magazines, in the "Saturday Evening Post." He roomed, he toured, he argued with the young literary rebels: he was completely in tune with the times that made him. Then in 1914 he issued his first novel, "Our Mr. Wren," and followed it with "The Trail of the Hawk" and "The Job."

Enormously important these first three novels if one would understand the man. Always does the first book lay bare the soul of its creator: himself he reveals first of all; there is no more intimate autobiography. Everywhere in these first three fictions we find illusions shattered by life; eager attempt at escape; golden dreams that end in hideous awakenings. In all of them attempts at escape— a clerk bound to his counter and dreaming of Europe, a Jack London superman bound to his squalid acres and dreaming of conquests of the upper air, a small-town girl visioning

[1] "The Men Who Make Our Novels," C. C. Baldwin, 1919.

the glories of "a job" in the great city. All of them accomplish escape and drink to the full of their desire, but at a price not at all in the early dream. Everywhere disillusionment to the extremes of tragedy: everywhere the pathos of life inharmonious, life unequally yoked. The young prairie dreamer has turned pessimist; the "spark" has flamed into rebellion and adolescent cynicism.

Not until "The Job" did he evolve his method fully. He had read "The Spoon River Anthology," he had read "Jennie Gerhardt" and discussed it, he had read in earlier days "The Damnation of Theron Ware"—and he had been steadily lifted by the rising tide of what was then called realism: actuality to the boundaries of visibility, characterization to the extreme of forcing from his delighted reader exclamations of "Gee! I know the very man. I've seen him a thousand times."

Never young novelist more fortunate: the time, the public, the publisher all were ready. And in 1920 came the novel "Main Street," amazingly advertised and amazingly worth advertising. In the whole history of American literature no other novel has been so lavishly, so scientifically advertised as this and the two or three novels which followed it. And the public was ready: no previous generation would have responded with such unanimity—could have responded. They had been reading Dreiser, and Jack London, and O. Henry and Masters and the book reviews of the Baltimore cynic, Mencken.

"Main Street" came to the world as a novelty. It was a *salmagundi* peculiarly mixed: at first it was repellant—one must learn to like it. The main ingredient was characterization—nothing new perhaps, but never before so emphasized. Back in the nineties an album was popular called "Mental Photographs." The victim must answer "What is your favorite color? quotation? novel? hour of the day?" and the like. To Lewis the foundation of a novel was an endless series of "mental photographs." In "The Job," for instance, he casually introduces Captain

Lew Gordon on the earliest page, never again to use him; yet he must make for us a complete photograph, one as minute as the description on a police circular advertising an escaped bandit:

He carried a quite visible mustache-comb and wore a collar, but no tie. On warm days he appeared on the street in his shirt-sleeves, and discussed the comparative temperature of the past thirty years with Doctor Smith and the Mansion House bus driver. He never used the word "beauty" except in reference to a setter dog—beauty of words or music, of faith or rebellion, did not exist for him. He rather fancied large, ambitous, banal, red-and-gold sunsets, but he merely glanced at them as he straggled home, and remarked that they were "nice." He believed that all Parisians, artists, millionaires, and socialists were immoral. His entire system of theology was comprised in the Bible, which he never read, and the Methodist Church which he rarely attended; and he desired no system of economics beyond the current platform of the Republican party. He was aimlessly industrious, crotchety but kind, and almost quixotically honest. He believed that Panama, Pennsylvania, was good enough for anybody.

Evidently the maker of this daguerreotype had read with approval Mencken and Nathan's "Pistols for Two," issued the same year. Strip the novels of these mental photographs and you attenuate them to startling thinness. "Babbitt" would be reduced to a pamphlet.

Other elements there are in the surprising mixture: a dominating flavor of vulgarity, a universal showing of the worse side of things, an emphasis upon the commonplace; a dash of humor of the O. Henry distillate, showing oftenest in felicity of phrase and unexpectedness of comparison; a copious ladleful of that *chile con carne* we know as Mencken: "Treat 'em rough; stir the animals up." "Elmer Gantry" is dedicated to Mencken. And finally, in "Main Street," and "Babbitt" perhaps—never in "Elmer Gantry"—an oil of serious purpose, a groping after a soul for the mixture, an aim not merely destructive.

No one since Dickens has mixed his ingredients with such zest, such gusto, such curiosity concerning the amazing comedy of human life. He has seen everything, he has heard everything: his books overflow with his experiences, his opinions, his photographs. His whole biography is in them, including Yale and the cattle-boats. And he has let himself go in utter naturalness in the American vernacular—slang, slovenliness, profanity: the language as it is actually quoted and growled and murdered by the men of the daily round. No "mere literature" here; no aiming at style, no flourishes for beauty. His audacity at times mounts to impudence; he "pussy-foots" at nothing. If it is life, it goes into the record. And seemingly he delights in the hideousness and vulgarity he uncovers at every probing. It is a "Spoon River Anthology" in prose. Whom in the whole brotherhood of border vulgarians has he missed?

That "Main Street" was created by its author in all sincerity cannot be doubted by one who re-reads the book, and that it is true to actual conditions must also be admitted, though with the reservation that it was written to demonstrate a thesis, that his findings are often exaggerated for effect, and that often he has overlooked the happier things that might have made impossible his final Q.E.D. He is exposing, like all the other muck-rakers, to the utter limits, ugliness and inefficiency in order that it may be seen and deplored and remedied. And he is aiming at no one single town. As he himself expressed it, "Main Street" was written to reveal "not only the heart of a place called Gopher Prairie, but ten thousand towns from Albany to San Diego." A dismal picture it is: American culture lamentably low when seen in its totality. And the picture ends in pessimism complete. Carol's attempts at beautification and reform, and Babbitt's dream of what he might have been had his environment not smothered the soul within him, give us glimpses of a suggested standard, but Carol and Babbitt alike surrender in the end and go out of the record debauched and defeated. It typifies futility: the gradual decadence of American culture. Europe takes notice and smiles, and knows not that one great element of hope has been totally overlooked in the novels. These ten thousand prairie towns have sprung up, with millions of acres of prosperous wheat and corn, from utter wilderness—roamed, within the memory of men still living, only by buffaloes and warring Indians and frontiersmen as wild. Culture and Victorian manners and estheticism do not come to the border in a single generation. And what land in all the world has less of poverty and suffering and oppression?

But Lewis has not lived up to the mark which he set for himself in "Main Street" and "Babbitt." Success has brought decadence in the man's art. There is lack of fine workmanship more and more in the later volumes. Even "Arrowsmith" is debauched with muck-raking protest, querulous at times. Pressed by the publisher and a clamorous public, he has worked not with gusto and painstaking as in "Main Street," but as a special reporter rushed to his job and given no time for revision. The distinction of phrase and the concentration into epigram marking "Main Street" are gone. Again and again he has simply applied the old formula until now it is worn thin. The infection of the Mencken philosophy has increased until at times it completely masters the man. The culmination came with "Elmer Gantry," exposure of the utter depravity of the Christian ministry, a concentration into one character of all the charges ever made against ministerial hypocrisy, with the unescapable implication that the picture presents a type. "Main Street" might cause protest, but its facts could not be combated. One might ask after reading it, "What of it?" but one could not criticize it on the side of its truthfulness. "Elmer Gantry," however, was too strong, it was too much, and art is "nothing too much."

Steadily since "Babbitt" there has been decline. The decay of Carol's dream for the uplifting of Gopher

Prairie is typical of the decay of the man's own art. Nothing he can write can matter much now. Sherman's summary nearly a decade ago has in it the inspiration of prophecy: After "Babbitt" he said:

> The artistic charm and vivacity of this novel, to say nothing of its social stimulation, would have been heightened by somewhat freer employment of those devices of dramatic contrast of which Mr. Lewis is a master—by the introduction of some character or group capable of reflecting upon the Babbitts oblique rays from a social and personal felicity, more genuine, more inward than any of the summoned witnesses possesses. Eventually, if Mr. Lewis does not wish to pass for a hardened pessimist, he will have to produce a hero qualified to register in some fashion the result of his own quest of the desirable; he will have to give us his Portrait of a Lady, his Pendennis, his Warrington and his Colonel Newcome.[2]

For a time his influence was considerable, but after "Elmer Gantry," a work done in heat and haste, on its face untrue in its implications, his day was over. In "Dodsworth" he worked hard to come back, and he partly succeeded, but the golden moment had passed. One of the youngest generation, a man in college when "Main Street" was published, wrote this not long ago: "We of our generation think that Sinclair Lewis rearranged Main Street into a pattern no less false than Gene Stratton Porter would have created," and he believes that the "generation devoted almost exclusively to debunking and cudgel reaction" is to pass quickly and give way to one able to see all sides of life and to be strictly impartial. "The era of protest, of desire to shock the unsophisticated, of wild experiment, must soon end."

T. K. Whipple's critique in "Spokesmen," by far the wisest treatment of Lewis's fiction thus far, has this caustic summary of the man:

[2] "The Significance of Sinclair Lewis," in "Points of View," S. P. Sherman, 1924.

The reviewer who said that in *Elmer Gantry* Lewis had sent the preachers a comic valentine hit off Lewis's style to perfection. Lewis seems to aim at much the same stage of mental development as the movies, which is said to be the average age of fourteen. His manner is founded on the best uses of salesmanship, publicity, and advertising. It is heavily playful and vivacious, highly and crudely colored, brisk and snappy. He avails himself of all the stock tricks of a reporter to give a fillip to jaded attention. His people do not run, they "gallop"; instead of speaking they "warble" or "gurgle" or "carol"; commonplace folk are "vanilla-flavored"; interior decorators are "daffodillic young men," "achingly well-dressed"; dancing becomes "the refined titillations of communal embracing." No wonder Lewis has sold satire to the nation—he has made it attractive with a coat of brilliant if expensive varnish.

He has added two words to the vocabulary of criticism, words useful and everywhere understood, "Main Street" and "Babbitt." Perhaps with the passing of years this may be reckoned his leading achievement.

IV

The increasing thrust of frontier life and spirit into fiction and poetry as the new century advanced had two effects: the Dreiser-Masters-Lewis-Anderson reaction—satire, exaggerated picturings, muck-raking protest, over-emphasis upon crudeness and frontier lack of "civilization"; and the escape reaction—an ostrich-like head-hiding from unpleasant realities. Chief among these refugees from reality one may name Joseph Hergesheimer, who, even when the world was afire about him and the whole of America was an excited camp with the totality of its youth for good or for bad enrolled for war, sat in his study and dreamed of old Salem, Massachusetts, in the 1840's, and the clipper ships that sailed the spice and tea routes to Cathay and Singapore, his final product the gorgeous dreaming "Java Head." And the second of the school was

James Branch Cabell who, out of step with the sorry here and now in his own America, even in his native Virginia, attempted escape even from the working laws of the planet which held him, and remolded the scheme of things entire in a world of his own building.

The coming of Hergesheimer into the "Spoon River-Winesburg, Ohio" decade was like the coming into the old Salem family of the Manchu princess Tao Yuen, new wife of the old sea captain, with her dainty Orientalness, her colors, her poppy dreamings, her pagan soul. Philadelphia produced the man, a fact never to be lost sight of. He was reared in a home of the old régime, with traditions, inherited usages, bells night and morning for prayers, furniture and furnishings from long lines of ancestry, onyx-topped tables, mahogany and rosewood and ebony, highboys from Windsor, marble mantels and tall mirrors, perhaps from Holland.

Despite copious autobiographical data the early period of his life does not stand out sharply. Everywhere he has romanticized his realism. It is like the photographic plate elaborately touched with color for the screen—the truth and yet not the truth. This at least we know: he was frail and sickly as a child and acquired early the convalescent reflex. It kept him from the public schools, it rendered him a dabbler at life, one who worked by impulse only along the lines of whim and fancy. Not at all a unique specimen: there was Washington Irving.

Self-educated by means of desultory reading, largely in fiction, without compulsions, a dawdler without job or profession or orderly education, he dabbled in art, attended an art school for two days in the week, an enthusiastic amateur. Then another night moth, escaped from the books he was reading, fluttered him—literature. Why not write? One must do something. It was fourteen years before he published anything. "The Lay Anthony," fantasy woven of classic myth stuff and picturesque modernity, was the first. Then came "The Three Black Pennys," 1917, which gave him his first fame. History was the basis of it with enough of thesis to hold it erect, the age-old *motif* of recurring inherited traits in later generations—three generations of furnace men in Pennsylvania tracing back to a single episode that damned them all. But as one reads it one is conscious, first of all, of the setting and the surfaces. As the English critic J. B. Priestley has phrased it, "When he gives us an eighteenth-century story, we do not see that century and enter into its life, but merely see Joseph Hergesheimer in wig and satin breeches, dreaming in an Adam room."

He is a man of the senses and his appeal is to the senses. He is perfectly in key with his age: he will make moving pictures—the eye first of all must be satisfied. Hence color like a Turner painting, hence costume in minutest detail— the outer inventory of his feminine characters is like that of the social column of a fashionable ladies' weekly. Everywhere lingerie and old lace. Open him at random.

Howat saw, in the yellow candlelight, a woman not, he decided, any better-looking than Caroline, in an extremely low-cut gown of scarlet, with a rigid girdle of saffron brocade, a fluted tulle ruff tied with a scarlet string about a long, slim neck, and a cap of sheer cambric with a knot of black ribbons.

Open again:

A young woman with a chalk-white face and oleaginous bandeaux of dead-black hair, in scarlet and green tartan over an extravagant crinoline, was seated on a sofa between two men, each with an arm around her waist and wine glasses elevated in their free hands. Essie was facing them from a circular floor hassock, in a blue satin informal robe over mussed cambric ruffles, heedless nonchalants, and her hair elaborately dressed with roses, white ribbons and a short ostrich feather. Her body, at once slim and full, was consciously seductive, and her face, slightly swollen and pasty in the shadows, bore the same heedless unrestraint. Her dark, widely-opened eyes, an insignificant nose and shortly curved, scarlet lips, held almost the fixed, painted impudence of a cynically debased doll.

Enough! Every noun has its color adjective, every verb its adverb, and when he touches a shawl he is the master of the bazaar: no one has surpassed him.

The world he remolded nearer to his heart's desire is a world of the five senses, only the five senses. Life is a dream of fair women, instinct not with life but with sensuous longing. His Manchu princess is not alive, she is a hand-made doll with Oriental accompaniments and a colorful wardrobe. Linda Condon, *roué* among saints, a saint among roués, is impossible, as untrue to actuality as Mr. Rochester in "Jane Eyre." "Cytherea" is the dream of a sophomore who has gone to sleep over his Freud, the dream made objective by a colorist. Truth is not the soul of it: it breathes of the make-up room, it is heavy with civet and patchouli, it is brocaded, it is silked in with artistry to be looked at only in the stage half-lights of romance. How narrow his range, how pitiful his conceptions of the human tragedy and comedy! Of the common lot, with its plethora of toil, its denials, its genuine religious aspirations, its sacrifices, he knows little. Beauty as an abstraction, embodied in the feminine, a dream, a narcotic, a Nirvana ecstasy acquired by imagination, this is his world. All that the race in its long living has acquired of hope, of vision, of purity, of ultimate satisfactions, he dismissed with irony and sneers—disillusion.

And his decade followed him, the younger generation of it, and placed him among the leaders. There was a period during and after the war, call it from 1918 to 1923, when humanity would forget, would escape from the jungle of horror that is war into a Garden of Allah, into a Maxwell Parrish dream, where nothing was real, where maidens like the Madeline of Keats's "Eve" floated in amorous perfectness, where banquets embraced in their menu—

". . . lucent syrops, tinct with cinnamon;
Manna and dates, in argosy transferr'd
From Fez."

Adolescence, dreams, escape. Then it was that Hergesheimer filled a need. But the mood did not last long. It was
hoped that at length the dreamer of empty nothingness
might awake to life and be of help to the new world of
the West so sadly in need of leaders and prophets and
strong directors of its civilization. In vain. Behold him in
his latest rôle as reporter for the ephemeral press of the
femininity of Hollywood and of the thrills that come from
the finding of a pewter plate.

To James Branch Cabell the man is an "anchorite,"
an "artist who labors primarily to divert himself," as if
life were a curse put upon humanity to be avoided by
drownings in drugs, by Nirvana dreamings, by the destruction of time by means of diverting imaginings.[3] He is
"no more concerned with moral values than is the Dec-
alogue," continues Cabell with fine irony, for "Beauty is
divine; a power superior and somewhat elfinly inimical to
all human moralities and rules of thumb, and a divinity
that must unflinchingly be served: that . . . is Mr. Hergesheimer's text." But beauty to the Hergesheimer clan
is a fleshly and feminine thing, a "worship of woman's
beauty as, upon the whole, Heaven's finest sample of artistic self-expression."

Deploring his minute detailing of weather and landscape and sartorial equipment and household furniture,
like "every other phase of 'realism' . . . untrue to life,"
Cabell finds "magic" in the style of the man, the magic of
the most exquisite art. With such magic in his own lines
does Cabell describe Hergesheimer's Linda Condon that I
was compelled to reread the novel for fear the magic
might have escaped my eye. In vain. The woman is an

[3] Part VII of "Straws and Prayer-Books," 1924; "Joseph Hergesheimer: an Essay in Interpretation," 1921.

abstraction, an "ornamental odalisque," not alive—with the life of this world at least. The magic is in Mr. Cabell's pen. His friendship has drugged his judgment. If one be a critic then one must exclude from his fireside all creators of books.

V

And this leads us to James Branch Cabell himself, more permanent stuff. He is only slightly a product of the war period, though the "Jurgen" episode, which enlarged his audience and gave him a fame that otherwise might not have been his, came in 1919 within the mad period when no one was wholly sane. Born only one year earlier than Hergesheimer—1879 it was—he had been publishing fiction for ten years before the Philadelphian's earliest work appeared. His novel "The Eagle's Shadow" came in 1904, and his "Jurgen" was suppressed for its alleged pornography three years before "Cytherea" was boosted into popularity by the same experience.

With Cabell we come to Virginia, a State (save for Thomas Nelson Page, Mary Johnston, and Ellen Glasgow) scantily supplied with literary creators. Richmond was his birthplace, as it was Miss Glasgow's, and to understand him one must understand first the Richmond "complex" just as to understand Hergesheimer one must know the Philadelphianess of the man. Note a single ironic sample of the Cabell aristocracy:

We Virginians cannot ever quite overcome our feeling that the Puritans are parvenus, deriving from families too recently arrived in this country to be yet completely Americanized. We have never, for that matter, learned to think of the Pilgrim Fathers and their descendants as belonging, exactly, to the gentry.

His biography has been as short and simple as that of a professor: a course in William and Mary, teacher of

Greek and French in that college, newspaper work in Richmond and New York City, coal-mining in West Virginia, genealogist and historian for various organizations, and then for years a seclusion that has produced something like thirty volumes.

The approach to the man as a literary artist is by way of certain of his own volumes, notably "Straws and Prayer-Books" and "Beyond Life," "The Judging of Jurgen," and "Taboo." Here he has meticulously explained himself and his attitude toward life, toward realism, toward romance. The literary artist, he explains, is a "minion of the moon":

That art is a criticism of life appears a favorite apothegm among those who know least about either. Yet the statement is true enough, in the sense that prison-breaking is a criticism of the penitentiary. Art is, in its last terms, an evasion of the distasteful. The artist simply does not like the earth he inhabits: for the laws of nature his admiration has always been remarkably temperate; and with the laws of society he has never had any patience whatever.

So the literary artist leaves the earth which he inhabits, daily and with no more to-do than daily is made over the same feat by professional aëronauts. And the literary artist diverts himself by constructing other worlds, whose orderings are different, and to his mind more approvable. All creative writers have thus, whether consciously or no, embarked in an undertaking compared with which the axiomatic attempt to weave ropes out of sand or to construct silk purses from even less adapt material is a quite sane and unassuming enterprise.

Literature he approached as a patrician and a scholar. He had taught Greek and French in his college; his reading was in esoteric areas: King Arthur legends, Spenser, the eighteenth and seventeenth century dreamers and intellectuals. Genealogy gave him strange flavors. When he would write fiction of his own he found himself bound by strangling inhibitions. First, he was a patrician shrinking from the democratic frontier: Main Street recordings; "realism," which at basis was but recorded mediocrity; best-seller cheapness; and, as he himself expressed it, "such Pollyannas among fiction writers as Mr. Theodore Dreiser and Mr. Sinclair Lewis, who can derive a species of obscure esthetic comfort from considering persons even less pleasantly situated than themselves—somewhat as a cabin passenger on a sinking ship might consider the poor devils in the steerage—and so turn rhyparographer, and write 'realism.' "

Furthermore, there was in the man a certain fastidiousness as to literary style and diction that was Johnsonian in its quality. The crude slovenliness and pleonasm of Dreiser, and the debonair up-to-dateness of Lewis and Anderson filled him with disgust. He could even assign George Moore to the limbo of the world's worst authors because in four chance openings of one of his volumes he found these four sentences:

"A word sufficed to set the whole gang recounting experiences and comparing notes."
"At the end of the act she received an ovation."
"As is generally the case, there was right upon both sides."
"It never rains but it pours."

Enough. "I close the book: for really nobody, no matter how widely he be acclaimed a master of vigorous and delightful prose, is privileged to talk to me in just that flat and meagre tone."

The episode tells much. To him literature must have distinction of style: first, a Johnsonian elevation of vocabulary. George Washington is not to be dismissed with the vigorous Saxon monosyllables "he could not tell a lie": he was the man "congenitally incapable of prevarication." But it is also a style that has rare poetic charm. Whole paragraphs become, by mere dislocation into short lines, "free verse." And the vocabulary is unique in these days of slipshodness and journalism, a vocabulary that sends one often to the dictionary, every word seemingly inevitable. No such stylist in modern times, at least in America. There is wizardry in it—magic. One who is tuned to it—and not at all is it for the unesoteric many—surrenders completely, no matter what may be the logic or what the wild conclusions.

Again, a fastidious repulsion from "Puritanism"—devil of the young intellectuals—which somehow he located in northern areas, central in New England, narrowed his horizon. For a time, at the start, he concentered upon Virginia romance. "The Rivet in Grandfather's Neck" was a novelty: one needs but to glance at the title to realize that. But Mary Johnston and even the New England Mary E. Wilkins had spread great banquets of Virginia romance, even to the vulgarizing of it into best-seller compounds. And he threw off all conventions and bonds, and in "The Cream of the Jest" made a book, to quote his own words, "different from any of his previous compositions." He had determined in this story lovingly to deal with an epoch and a society and even a geography whose comeliness had escaped the wear-and-tear of ever actually existing.

The result was his invention of the Empire of Poictesme, " 'a happy, harmless Fable-land' which is bounded by Avalon and Phæacia and Sea-coast Bohemia, and the contiguous forests of Arden and Broceliande, and on the west of course by the Hesperides, because he believed this country to be the one possible setting for a really successful novel." Here, abolishing space and time and natural laws, he created a world after his own definitions of beauty, striving only "to write perfectly of beautiful happenings." Book after book he added to his records of this enchanted mesa in fairyland. A detailed map he added, most marvelously complicated, and complete genealogies. And over it all he threw the wizardry of style, one, to quote him again, that had a "prodigality in the transforming magic which—heaven knows, in how few books!

—quite incommunicably lends romantic beauty to this or that not necessarily unusual or fertile theme, somewhat as sunset tinges the wooded and the barren mountain with equal glamour." And again let me quote the author in a sentence I would fain make my own: "I am by no means sure this curious *tour de force* was worth performing; but I am unshakably convinced that [he] 'brings it off' to a nicety."

He has made himself a Camelot and has peopled it with a King Arthur court of his own creation. He has worked out a unique mythology with personages as *sui generis* as if from the newly discovered record of a lost civilization. It is not easy to read his various dreamings in "Chivalry," in "Jurgen," in "The Cream of the Jest," in "Gallantry: Dizain de Fêtes Galantes," in "From the Hidden Way." If one is enamoured of plot and reads for the sheer story, one throws the books to the dust-heap after ten pages. Not for the many, this work, not even for the unsifted few. Only the adept can follow and understand. Not often is there perfect clearness, seldom is there logic. Instead, the reader is always confounded by a myriad of medieval cognomens and genealogical references. Leave-taking at every point from "realism," from religious convention- alities, from logic.

If one has the time to plough through this wilderness of eccentricities and idioms, this maze of innuendo and ironic criticism, one may find what undoubtedly is present, a "biography" of a living soul, a parable perhaps illustra- tive of human life. Doubts assail me at times whether this be after all fiction. This is philosophy, a philosophy of negation, thrown into narrative form.

As to the further progress of the amazing cycle only the future may know. Perchance it may be a germinal thing like the Arthur cycle, setting future poets and ro- mancers into creative moods; but this is hardly possible. In all the history of literature no great thing has come from the prophets of futility, from disillusion and ironic contemplation of human life.

BIBLIOGRAPHICAL REFERENCES

Anderson and Lewis are each given a chapter in "Spokesmen," "Modern Writers and American Life," T. K. Whipple, 1928.

Lewis and Hergesheimer are each given a chapter in "Contemporary American Authors," J. C. Squire and Associated Critics of the "London Mercury," 1928.

"Our America," Waldo Frank, 1919.

"Sherwood Anderson," C. B. Chase, 1927.

"The Phenomenon of Sherwood Anderson," N. B. Fagin, 1927.

"Sherwood Anderson and Other Famous Creoles," W. P. Spratling, 1926.

"Sinclair Lewis," O. Harrison, 1927.

"Sinclair Lewis," V. L. Parrington, 1927.

"The Significance of Sinclair Lewis" in "Points of View," 1924, Stuart P. Sherman.

"The Prairie and The Making of Middle America," Dorothy A. Dondore, p. 406.

"The Frontier in American Literature," Lucy L. Hazard, 1927, p. 281.

"The Presbyterian Child," Joseph Hergesheimer, 1923. Autobiographical.

"From an Old House," Joseph Hergesheimer, 1925. Autobiographical.

"Joseph Hergesheimer," W. Follett, 1922.

"Joseph Hergesheimer," J. B. Cabell, 1921.

"Joseph Hergesheimer," Llewellyn Jones, 1923.

"Bibliography of the Works of Joseph Hergesheimer," H. L. R. Swire, 1922.

"James Branch Cabell," H. L. Mencken, 1927.

"Cabellian Harmonics," W. A. McNeill, 1928.

"Round-Table in Poictesme: a Symposium," Don M. Bregenzer and S. Loveman, 1924.

"A Bibliography of the Writings of J. B. Cabell," Guy Holt,
    1924.
The Storisende Edition of James Branch Cabell, 18 Volumes,
    1930.

CHAPTER XXI

REVALUATIONS

I

THE era of disillusion following the World War saw the evolution of a strange myth, the Ambrose Bierce case, not yet settled. Born in 1842, a soldier who saw in his youth every phase of war realism and horror, Bierce came into the new period as a hold-over from an earlier post-war futility era. He had had a varied and colorful career, largely journalistic. In 1871 he had gone to London and for five or six years was a literary adventurer, boon companion of the young makers of ephemeral magazines— "Fun" and the "Lantern." His caustic hits and *bons mots* he gathered while there into a volume "Cobwebs from an Empty Skull." Then for twenty years he knocked about among the newspaper offices of San Francisco, a man with a cold pen tipped with poison. In 1881, William Randolph Hearst added him to the staff of his new journal the "Examiner" to do what would now be called a "column," and he had found congenial soil. Now it was that he vented the full volume of his bitterness; just how bitter we do not realize, for the original occasion for each jibe we cannot fully know, and moreover, it has never been entirely reprinted; but we can judge shrewdly from his "The Cynic's Word Book," republished with the title "The Devil's Dictionary." They called him "Bitter Bierce."

The first work of the man to attract general attention was his short-story collection, "Tales of Soldiers and Civilians," 1891, later issued with the title "In the Midst of Life." The preface is unique: "Denied existence by the chief publishing houses of the country, this book owes itself to Mr. E. L. G. Steele, merchant, of this city." "Too strong" had been the general verdict of the magazines. "The public will not endure such horrors." Ah, the timid eighties! Later came a second collection, "Can Such Things Be?"

Upon these two the literary standing of the man is chiefly based. They undoubtedly influenced the younger writers of the period. Stephen Crane was inspired after reading them to write his "Red Badge of Courage." But the collections as a whole have been greatly over-rated. They are metallic, they are coldly artistic, they are lacking in real pathos. In my "Development of the American Short Story" I said this of the tales:

The man was an artist, cold, cynical, conscious of his art. He was not bound by rules: he was heedless sometimes even of fundamentals. . . . Artificial as was the material in which he worked, and deliberate and ironic as were his motifs, nevertheless he was able to create situations hauntingly suggestive. Many of his stories begin for the reader where the last sentence ends. His ghost stories, totally unexplained, recorded with circumstances of actual history, nevertheless have within them suggestions of an abnormal psychological world, possible within each of us, and those more terrifying than even a supernatural apparition.

He published a dozen volumes, strange mixtures, "Black Beetles in Amber," "Shapes of Clay," "The Monk and the Hangman's Daughter," "The Shadow on the Dial," and the like, followed at last by a hodgepodge limited-edition set in twelve volumes; all these are certainly unique in our literature. Little read, soon forgotten save for a few tales that still haunt the anthologies, tales with an atmosphere of horror like the recollection of a visit to a morgue, he is not likely long to be held up as a leader even by the group of youngsters that is resurrecting him.

The post-war generation seeking futility and strong flavors found in the Civil War veteran what seemed to them a prophet. His sudden disappearance in the early days of the World War rendered his case dramatic. Gradually there was evolved a most elaborate series of Bierce myths: he had joined the insurgent Villa's forces (he an invalid seventy years old), and had been executed by a firing squad; he had gone down with Kitchener in the torpedoed British gunboat in the North Sea. Between these two extremes a dozen other mythical endings, the latest, perhaps, assigning him to a suicide's end in some obscure gulch in the Yosemite.

Much pother over a disillusioned old man and his literary remains. In a single year four biographies of him have appeared, the most noteworthy being "Bitter Bierce, a Mystery of American Letters," 1929, by C. Hartley Grattan, and "Ambrose Bierce; a Biography," by Carey McWilliams, 1929.

Ambrose Bierce, however, is poor material from which to shape a leader and a prophet—a picturesque myth but never a major influence.

II

The strangest reversal of values, however, the most amazing commandeering of leadership from the forgotten, has been the case of Herman Melville. A decade ago a tenth-magnitude luminary to be found only in such a forgotten literary ephemera as that of Duyckinck or of Allibone, he has suddenly blazed into first magnitude—has been as completely taken into the new period as if he had been born in it. It is like the case of the popular old alumnus who has been voted in as a member by the new freshman class.

That even until yesterday the man was held as a minor figure is known to all readers. John Nichol in 1882 dismissed him from his British survey of American letters with ten words—he was a mere traveler. Four years later, Richardson in his two-volume history, which devoted forty-seven pages to Longfellow and sixty to Hawthorne, accorded to him a scant half-page—Melville was a cheap panderer for popularity. At the opening of the new century, Barrett Wendell in his Harvardo-centric survey which accorded to Holmes eighteen pages summed Melville up in forty words and these chiefly to combat Stevenson's recent praise. Higginson did not mention the man; Abernethy referred to him simply as "another forgotten New York novelist." We might go on and on. A mild curiosity was created in the eighties by Stevenson and Clark Russell, but these two dwelt solely upon the man's realism, his ability to transport his reader into the actual forecastle of a ship at sea. Even these two neutral observers sensed not at all the real powers of the man. Then silence again for a generation.

In 1890, the western frontier, since colonial days the boundary line of American romance, had reached the Pacific. A decade later it was in Alaska, the new Eldorado; a decade later, discovered by youngsters of the new period, Jack London, and others, it was found to be in the South Sea Isles of the Pacific, the ultimate West. Then in 1919 had come Frederick O'Brien's "White Shadows in the South Seas," followed in 1921 by his "Mystic Isles of the South Seas." Never discovery exploited with more rapturous superlatives. At last the land where mere actuality was melodrama: enchanted islands languorous with tropic beauty, peopled by voluptuous nymphs, Ultima Thule of romance. O'Brien's first gorgeous book became a best seller—he had broken into enchanted lands beyond the sunset.

Then suddenly, almost by accident, it was found that the same thing had been done two generations before, and with a literary power that out-Londoned London and that surpassed even the glamorous O'Brien in gorgeous picturings and fleshly abandon and ability to cast over its readers the lotos-eating spell of the tropics. Then as they read, they awoke to the epic power of "Moby-Dick," the lyric charm of "Mardi," and the mad torrential cynicism of "Pierre." Over night Melville became a classic, rated by the young critics as the peer of Whitman and Mark Twain and the superior of Poe. His writings were for the first time gathered and published in editions, some of them magnificent; an adequate biography was prepared; richly illustrated single volumes began to appear on the book-stands, and, as with Whitman and Poe, every scrap of his composition, even the inanities, was sought out and issued, sometimes in *de luxe* editions. After seventy-five years Herman Melville had "arrived" and that in the teeth of his own prediction in "Mardi": "He who on all hands passes for a cypher to-day, if at all remembered hereafter, will be sure to pass for the same. For there is more likelihood of being over-rated while living than of being under-rated when dead."

Now it was that the full mystery of the man began to be felt. Why should a genius capable of creating "Moby-Dick" have lapsed all at once into silence and for a generation have lived sterile of vital literary product? Why the amazing inequalities in his work? Was the man not insane? Were his books, like Blake's, powerful because of their affinity with madness? No American author, not even Poe, offers the critic problems more fascinating— and more baffling.

III

The year 1819 was marked in America by the birth of three major literary forces, three men in revolt, breakers-away: Lowell, New England "Brahmin," undiluted Puritan, born under the shadow of Harvard College; Whitman, completely bourgeois, untouched by New England, born on a Long Island farm not far from New York; Melville, aristocrat and proletarian, mingled Knicker-bocker and Puritan and to be classified with neither element, born in New York City and yet schooled through all his childhood in the straitest sect of Calvinism by a Boston father. And of the three the one most completely thewed for leadership was Melville, a Titan in soul, in courage and daring surpassing Lowell, in imagination and intellect surpassing Whitman, in epic sweep and superman force surpassing both. Lowell, the first to rise, hailed while in his thirties as an iconoclast, literary leader of his generation, and a contemporary classic, is in eclipse today. He was hamstrung, we now see, by his New Englandism. To maintain the "quality of Boston" he surrendered his originality and the fire that was his birthright and became a parlor poet, a maker of puns and exquisite brilliances, of stylistic critiques, smart and cocksure, aimed often at the destruction of the unconventional as in the case of the Thoreau bombshell, writer of expositions of democracy—western democracy expounded in rhetoric with a gold pen from a Harvard chair. Whitman was of slower growth: full recognition came late, almost too late for him to realize personally its full limits. There was no New Englandism in his work, and New England spurned him. He was totally of New York: he was cosmopolitan, tolerant, unpolished, outspoken. A drop possibly of the Harvard cordial in his Bohemian beer might have helped him, might have given to his poetry a wider appeal. Probably not, for we see what the mixture did to Melville. Melville was of both regions, and of neither. He fell between the thorns of New York and the rocks of New England, and seemingly he perished. For two generations he lay dormant until, watered by the appreciation of a new era, he sprang to life and like the fabled beanstalk filled the whole sky.

To realize what happened to the man one must begin with his two grandfathers, Revolutionary War officers: on the paternal side Major Melville of Boston—Scotch; New England-born in the mid-eighteenth century; A.B., Princeton, A.M., Harvard; married early into the old

Boston family of Scollays; Puritanic; conservative to the degree of wearing in his old age the cocked hat and knee-breeches of his boyhood era. (See Holmes's "The Last Leaf.") No rebel here. No come-outer fires in this Beacon Street ancient with his patrician air and chiseled features, in this gentle scholar branded with the Harvard herd-mark. No Titan surely this elder dandy with the silver shoe-buckles and the courtly bow. But the maternal grand-father of Herman Melville had been of sterner stuff: General Peter Gansevoort of New York—Knickerbocker Dutch; gigantic in frame, six feet four, like Washington, and correspondingly broad; as blue-eyed as a Viking, and as impetuous. "During a fire in the old manorial mansion, with one dash of the foot, he had smitten down the oaken door, to admit the buckets of his negro slaves. . . . In a night scuffle in the wilderness before the Revolutionary War, he had annihilated two Indian savages by making reciprocal bludgeons of their heads." It was this old giant-killer, so Melville declares in "Pierre," that first fired his youthful imagination and furnished him with his first superman hero. Amidst the relics of this old Titan the youngster dreamed of glory.

The son of the Bostonian, Allen Melville, had broken early the New England fetter and had become a wander-ing trader, even to the crossing of the Atlantic in repeated voyages. Once he had spent a whole year in Paris where he had learned to speak the language like a native. Then in Albany on a trading venture he had found Maria Gansevoort, blue-eyed, full-bosomed, voluptuous; and the result was the forsaking of New England forever and the adoption of New York State henceforth as home. Of this extra-tribal union, which produced in time eleven children, Herman was the fourth child. In physique, in animal perfection, in impetuosity, in lawless imagination he was a Gansevoort, the child of his mother; in con-science, in sympathies, in patrician instincts, in pride, in intellectual power, he was a Melville. The cosmopolitanism of his father was a molding influence. He grew up in an atmosphere of romance: tales of ocean voyages, of giant waves that all but swamped the ship, of adventure in strange cities, of the fascinating influence of a strange language that sometimes he heard from his father's lips. So vivid became this romance that two of the boys of the family in time ran away to sea, one of them to become captain of deep-sea packets. But despite his seeming Bohemianism, the father was inflexibly a Puritan: he indoctrinated his children with Scotch thoroughness. Until late in Melville's adolescence he never once dreamed that his father's elaborate system was not as infallible as the circling sun and stars.

The father's sudden death when the boy was thirteen left the family in dire poverty. All the children who were old enough were obliged to seek employment. Further schooling was impossible: the boy, like Whitman and Mark Twain, grew up practically self-educated, self-directed in his reading and his thinking. At seventeen he made his first break with conventional life: he was off to sea, the summer voyage of four months recorded in "Redburn." Brief as it was, it was a turning point in his life. It was his fitting school, his preparatory course, just as his later voyages were his university career. He was off to realize on the dreams of his youth, to explore the wild regions that his boyish imagination had peopled with demigods and warriors in lands of gold.

One thinks inevitably here of Mark Twain: his tiny boyhood world, the main street of a squalid village where he knew intimately every soul, where he was taught that fundamentally men are good, that in the long run right conquers, that God is in his Heaven and the wicked infallibly suffer; his dreaming of the golden world beyond the horizon from which the steamboats came and into which they disappeared; his boyhood break from this world to find the rainbow's end; his schooling in the filth and abysmal wickedness of the Great River and the wild western mining-camps with their elemental men and their standards of value that rated a man only for what he actually could do; his return at last to the golden areas of civilization disillusioned but still dreaming; his marriage into the old conservative Eastern family and his residence on the Brahmin avenue of a New England city; then utter climax of disillusion; the heartsick world-wanderings, and the final utter pessimism and despair. It is a phenomenon peculiarly American.

Again at twenty-one Melville broke from the conventional. The Gansevoort blood within him lusted for life, for adventure, for fellowship with elemental men. He had heard the yell of the demoniac Jackson as he had been torn from the yard-arm in the storm, defying men and gods, and swallowed by the sea still blasphemous and unconquered; he had seen a brutal captain unsoftened by civilization driving men and working his imperious will, and he dreamed of Titans of the measure of his old grandfather, the Indian-killer. "Parlor men, dancing masters, graduates of the Albe Bellgrade who shrug their lace shoulders at boisterousness—faugh!" He was off on a New Bedford whaler for his college course, which was to last, as it proved, for three years and nine months, which was to throw him into four different ships, and give him for teachers and classmates the human sewage from the open cess-pools of the world. For fifteen months he was on the whaler *Acushnet,* and "with very few exceptions, our crew was composed of a parcel of dastardly and mean-spirited wretches." So brutal was this first breaking-in that while at an island of the Marquesas group where they had touched for supplies, he broke from the ship and plunged into the jungle, where, all declared, only death awaited a fugitive. For four months he lived in utter savagery with cannibals. Then, rescued by the whaler *Julia,* he continued his education, his classmates now a crew of "villains of all nations and dyes picked up in the lawless Spanish Main and among the savages of the islands." He was in a mutiny, he was thrust into the bilboes at Tahiti, for weeks and months he lived as a fugitive with beach-combers—the offscourings of humanity. Then life on another whaler, and finally a transfer to an American ship of war where for a year he lived in the school of the utterly worldly and the physical; "the pent-up wickedness of five hundred men nearly overcame all my previous theories." At twenty-five he was home again in New York, having completed a university course not recognized by Harvard, yet one that had been exhaustively thorough in the fundamentals of actual human life, a course that had controverted all of the early conventional teachings of his Puritan father, one that had admitted him into the red-blooded fellowship of Men, or, as he himself expressed it, "that stark stripped human relationship which is deeper than the depths of sex."

IV

Home from his amazing adventure, the boy of twenty-five settled to a career of authorship—one of his youthful dreams. There had been no apprenticeship: his four years in the forecastle had been anything but literary. Mark Twain had stood long at a printer's case, most exacting of universities; so had Whitman; but the young Melville, scarce out of his sailor's togs, without experience and without models, sat down to tell his story in his own words. Time and again he had told it before to forecastle groups skilled in nautical narrative, and to eager relatives. Certainly the tale had lost nothing in the frequent tellings. Varnished unquestionably it was, spiced freely with the marvelous, and worked always to surprising climaxes; but it squared at every point with forecastle knowledge and nautical technique: his early audiences had been imperious here.

The result was "Typee," a forecastle yarn, one of the

most original books of the mid-century, a book as completely without prototype as "Roughing It" and "Life on the Mississippi" were to be in years to come.

That the book was a product of New York just as the "Knickerbocker History" was a product, and Cooper's novels and "Leaves of Grass" were products, was no accident. None of them could have come from New England. The original creations of American literature, our *American* classics, with exceptions have been extra-New England in origin. For flouters of the old order, whether in religion or in literature, the Puritan had only damnation. The novel from the first he condemned, and as a result no great piece of fiction, Hawthorne's alone excepted, to the present day has come from New England. "Uncle Tom's Cabin" would never have been written but for its author's seventeen years in the Middle West. The "North American Review" never once in its whole New England career mentioned Whitman or Poe or Melville, the trio declared by our younger critics to be our major classics. Even Hawthorne had to fight twenty-five years for recognition, and he received it only because "The Scarlet Letter" seemed to be a Puritan document sermonic at heart.

But even cosmopolitan New York hesitated at "Typee." The English edition was pruned a bit before the Putnams dared issue it. Melville, son of his Gansevoort mother, educated in the forecastle of whalers at sea, deemed it no *faux pas* to tell the whole truth of Polynesian voluptuousness and of the actuality of the happenings when naked South Seas maidens swarmed the decks of whale-ships in tropic harbors, or to record his honest observations upon missionary efforts among the Polynesian heathen. The book was scarce off the press when both in England and America it was attacked with ferocity. It was lecherous, it was blasphemous, it was deliberately untrue. The man by his own confession was an outcast: of course he would have no sympathy with missions or with anything that stood for decency. Leading magazines, widely circulated, like the "Living Age," lashed him with superlatives:

With this tribe he remained about four months, during which he cohabited with a native girl, named Fayaway. We shall not pollute our pages by transferring to them the scenes in which this wretched profligate appears, self-confessed as the chief actor. . . . When they left jail no captain in the harbor would have anything to do with them on account of their desperate character. They even leagued with a reckless gang of seamen known in the Pacific as "Beachcombers."

Thus was Herman Melville first presented to the reading world.

FitzJames O'Brien, New York Bohemian, was the first to review the book adequately. It was its originality, he declared, that was damning it, its frank sensuousness in an age of mawkishness and religiosity. No later critic has surpassed some phases of his diagnosis. "The man," he declared,

"is essentially exotical in feeling. Matter is his god. His dreams are material. His philosophy is sensual. Beautiful women, shadowy lakes, nodding plumy trees, and succulent banquets make Melville's scenery, unless his theme utterly preclude all such. His language is rich and heavy with a plating of imagery. He has barbaric love of ornament and does not mind how much it is put on. Swept away by his sensual longing, he frequently writes at random. One can see that he uses certain words only because they roll off his pen lusciously and roundly.

In other words the author was adolescent, over-sexed, untrained, unschooled in literary art, and let his romantic soul go without restraint or thought of models. But even O'Brien missed the real secret of "Typee." The book is woven of three strands. One, as the later Frederick O'Brien was to discover in the teeming tropic islands, is realistic and sensuous backgrounds; everywhere first-hand observation: the manufacture of poee-poee, and tappa, the laws of the taboo, the personal habits and daily life of the natives. It is a handbook of South Seas information. Some have seen only this element in the work. But the book fundamently is a romance. Its affinity is with "Robinson Crusoe": the infernal whaleship, the exciting escape, the desert island with its strange flora and fauna, the cannibals, the Man Friday, the minutiæ of life and psychological reactions of a man cast away among savages, the final escape. Everything is heightened even to melodrama, everywhere the marvelous, everywhere the hero central. The landscape through which he flees is melodramatic—the mighty waterfalls in a series, three hundred feet high, the final break from captivity with the death of the villain Mow-Mow at the hero's hands. Obviously it is romance, so completely so that one may be inclined to suspect, as did its earliest readers, that the whole yarn is not a real experience at all, but a deliberately manufactured thing.

Consider the beauty of Fayaway. Three pages of description in superlatives he lavishes upon her: "I would have matched the charming Fayaway against any beauty in the world." "Her figure was the very perfection of feminine grace and beauty . . . her rosy mouth with teeth of dazzling whiteness . . . her hands soft and delicate as those of any countess." A Bertha M. Clay heroine could not be more perfect. But this is not enough: *all* the maidens of Typee are beautiful. "To compare them with the gallery of coronation beauties in Westminster Abbey: it would be the Venus de Medici placed beside a milliner's doll." Mere superlatives are too feeble to embody his dream. To see a Peruvian lady inhale a cigarro under orange trees, he declares, is ravishment, "but Fayaway, holding in her delicately formed olive hand the long yellow reed of her pipe, with its quaintly carved bowl, and every few moments languishingly giving forth light wreaths of vapor from her mouth and nostrils, looks still more engaging; . . . to the mild fumes of the tobacco her rosy breath added a fresh perfume." It is too much: we begin to be suspicious of the whole story. "I boldly pronounce the teeth of the Typees to be far more beautiful than ivory itself. . . . Nearly every individual of their number might have been taken for a sculptor's model." Everywhere superlatives. At the touch of a Typee cook even fat pork is glorified: "most docile and amiable pork, a morsel of which placed on the tongue melts like a soft smile from the lips of beauty." This is not a book of travels, a record of mere fact: it is romance, it is adolescent rhapsody, it is a Rasselas dream of an Eden in a happy valley far away from the sad realism of civilization.

Which leads us to the next strand, the heart of the book. Starting as a "Robinson Crusoe" it ends as a "Utopia." The Knickerbocker romancer is interrupted by the Puritan. The superlatives of the book are but a foil for the rottenness of civilization. The whole is a Carlyle sermon, a young man's Utopia. In the valley of the Typees only physical perfection, naked symmetry, radiant health; but "stripped of the cunning artifices of the tailor and standing forth in the garb of Eden, what a sorry set of round-shouldered, spindle-shanked, crane-necked varlets would civilized men appear! Stuffed calves, padded breasts, and scientifically cut pantaloons would then avail them nothing." Life was elementally simple among the happy Typees. "No mortgages, no protested notes, no bills payable, no debts of honor in Typee; no unreasonable tailors and shoemakers, perversely bent on being paid; no duns of any description; no assault and battery attorneys to foment discord, backing their clients up in a quarrel, and then knocking their heads together; no poor relations everlastingly occupying the spare bed-chamber, and diminishing the elbow room at the family table; no desti- tute widows with their children starving on the cold char- ities of the world; no beggars; no debtors' prisons; no proud and hard-hearted nabobs in Typee; or to sum up all in one word—no Money!" Without wealth there was no need of laws. "In darkest nights the natives slept securely, with all their worldly wealth around them, in homes the doors of which were never fastened. . . . They lived in great harmony with each other. . . . I never witnessed a single quarrel. . . . An unbounded liberty of conscience seemed to prevail."

Completely was the book in the key of the reforming forties—the era of the transcendental ferment. It should be placed on the same shelf as "Walden," as "The New England Reformers," as the Brook Farm story, as "The Blithedale Romance," and as Cooper's "The Crater," a book written in supreme contempt of all the New England gospels. Thoreau would lessen the denominator of civilization by the practice of New England parsimony and by the using of Nature as a cathartic and a balm; but the young Melville would go to the utter extreme: he would return to the savagery from which the race sprang, to primitive morals when mankind was naked and unashamed, and to primitive health of body and of soul. Turn the whole world into a happy Typee valley, was his thesis, where the laws created by Nature in the beginning have not been overruled and modified by the stupidity of man.

"Typee" was followed by "Omoo," second volume of the amazing Odyssey of his four years in the Pacific; then somewhat later, by "White Jacket," which is the third volume.

v

Thus chapter one of Melville's literary life. His first books were sensationally received on both sides of the water. The fierce criticism of the religious press helped rather than hindered the circulation of these earlier volumes. More cannibal stories were eagerly demanded: they were a new sensation. But Melville had developed during the two years since he had left the sea. "Typee" and

"Omoo" were but apprentice work. "To go down to posterity as a man who has lived among cannibals!" he sneered. Intolerable. "Until I was twenty-five I had no development at all. From my twenty-fifth year I date my life." He had begun to read—eagerly, impetuously; the wealth of literary allusion in his later volumes is remarkable. His New England ancestry was confronting him: he would write, if he wrote at all, in major key. He would write as a master, a literary superman. No more mere entertainment of the forecastle element, who could appreciate only the moving picture and the marvelous. He would write books of power. Cooper at the same stage had the same experience: merely to tell Indian stories seemed trivial, and he had written "The Bravo" and "The Heidenmauer" and the "Headsman."

Then came another break in the life of young Melville —a definite turning-point. This dreamer of supermen, this watcher for months and years of far ocean horizons from the whaler's main-top, this rover with elemental men in the vast lawlessness of the Pacific, behold him shorn of his Samson locks, married to the only daughter of the Chief Justice of Massachusetts, Elizabeth Shaw of the Boston aristocracy, dainty, conventional, ingrained to helplessness with the New England taboos. Behold him with a family about him, removed to a New England farm, fighting amid rocks and polypod for mere livelihood; and in vain—for he will nothing of the hoe, he will toil only with his pen, and he will write no more of cannibals. Failure, poverty among the New England rocks, support at length by the wife's father. A jungle lion chained by the leg, burning out his soul in rage, powerless save for his roar.

Books he would write commensurate with those of his new-found superman Hawthorne, but he could center upon nothing objective. Like Byron's, his genius was lyric: he could write only of himself. Unless he had personally felt, or actually experienced, his imagination refused to take fire. All that he ever wrote was auto-biographic, egocentric, and always with the egotism of rebellion, the saying of "No in thunder"—a Puritan dis-illusioned. The vividness of his early ideals was balanced by a corresponding intensity of bitterness.

All of Melville's major characters are Byronic, Titans in rebellion, supermen who flaunt their defiance even in the face of the Almighty. Like Jack London in later years, the man had looked into hell; he had seen ruthless power, sea-wolves in authority, and always triumphant. It revolutionized, after four years of it, his early philos-ophy. He was a Nietzsche before Nietzsche had written a word. Be hard, smite down, trample, be a superman, or else be yourself trampled, that was the law of Nature,—of God, if there be a God. "De god wat made shark," ruled Queequeg, "must be one dam Ingin." He felt the sea-wolf lust of domination in his own soul and would ex-press it. He himself was a superman. In all his characters we see only Melville. He is Taji, a god, in "Mardi." He is Jack Chase, "the masterpiece of all God's works," in "White Jacket." He is Jackson in "Redburn," rotted to a skeleton by consumption yet claiming to the last ounce of his strength his master place on the sail in the hurri-cane and hurled to death with yells of blasphemy. In "Israel Potter" he is Paul Jones, "the Coriolanus of the sea—a cross between the gentleman and the wolf . . . his wild lonely heart incapable of sympathizing with cuddled natures made humdrum by long exemption from pain"—Paul Jones who single-handed went forth in a bowl to fight the whole British empire. In "Moby-Dick" he is Captain Ahab, "the man who like Russia," as he explained to Hawthorne, "or the British empire, declares himself a sovereign nature (in himself) amid the powers of heaven, hell, and earth. He may perish; but so long as he exists he insists upon treating with all powers upon an equal basis." He was Ethan Allen: in him he saw his gigantic grandfather—himself. Captured by the English, Allen, as he explains, found that he had "fallen into the hands of Dyaks." He was turned brutally over to the Indians to be butchered, but "with desperate intrepidity, he availed himself of his enormous physical strength, by twitching a British officer to him, and using him for a living target, whirling him round and round against the murderous tomahawks of the savages." And again he was Allen—Allen taken to England to be hanged, and in London while on his way, as he believed, to the gallows, defying the whole British empire with curses and roars of contempt. And he was Israel Potter, living his young life in an ecstasy of mad adventure, capturing single-handed a British vessel and killing its crew, fighting shoulder to shoulder with Jones on the *Bonhomme Richard;* then a soldier of fortune, a fugitive, the sport of chance; then married to an English girl; then crushed by family cares, dogged by creditors; then forty years of squalor and exile; then death.

Into his third volume, "Mardi," Melville threw all his powers. Again, opening chapters of exciting adventure and closing chapters of didactics and cynical criticism: "Robinson Crusoe" shading into Ecclesiastes. No book has been more misunderstood. It is not an insane jumble, it is a book of power: no other American could have written it, and no Englishmen save perhaps Swift. It is Gulliver in a South Sea setting: an epic of disillusion, precisely in the key of the post-war nineteen-twenties. The central figure, Taji, self-elected god—Melville himself, hemmed in by the intolerable commonplace and dreaming of adventure and knight-errant chivalry beyond the blank horizon which bound him to littleness, breaks from the ship in mid-ocean, and in a cockle-shell boat begins an independent voyage, himself as captain—sheer madness. But glorious adventure rewards him: he becomes master of an abandoned wreck, rich in treasure. Still unsatisfied, he hurls himself again upon the deep, and he finds Yillah, a goddess, the maiden of a thousand dreams. A few days of perfect joy on the isle, and she is gone. And now he too has become a god moving with gods and island kings, but Yillah is gone and without her life is inconceivable. Companioned by gods and seers, he scours the islands of the world for the ideal, the illusion, he has lost. It is the blue flower of Novalis; it is the lost dreams of youth: "For, oh, Yillah! were you not the earthly semblance of that sweet vision that haunted my earliest thoughts?" One by one the Isles of the Blessed are found to be but habitations of the wretched; one by one all things deemed glorious by man: the glory of kings, the joys of love, the sacredness of the church, the dreams of liberty, the democracy of the New World, the ideals of faith, hope, charity—all that humanity has deemed valuable, he finds but vanity and a striving after the wind. On only two islands would he fain linger for a moment—the one where Bacchus rules as king, and the other where the teachings of Jesus are *actually* lived in all their literalness. But even here he finds not Yillah. It is Ecclesiastes with a South Sea setting: it is the drama of his own life. And it ends in sordidness and despair: he finds not Yillah, but Hautia—Circe, the maliciously carnal. "As my hand touched Hautia's, down dropped a dead bird from the clouds."

Some of Melville's most distinctive work is in "Mardi." An anthology of amorphous lyrics, as original and as compelling as Whitman's, might be culled from its paragraphs. "Mardi" appeared in 1851 when Whitman was at the crossroads of his poetic career, four years before "Leaves of Grass" was issued in its earliest phase. Was "Mardi" the source of Whitman's inspiration? Consider this random paragraph which I have ventured to throw into the Whitman line-length:

West, West! West, West!
Whitherward point Hope and prophet-fingers;
Whitherward, at sunset, kneel all worshippers of fire;

Whitherward in mid-ocean, the great whales turn to die;
Whitherward face all the Moslem dead in Persia;
Whitherward lie Heaven and Hell!

West, West!
Whitherward mankind and empires—flocks, caravans, armies,
    navies, worlds, suns, and stars all wend!

West, West!
Oh, boundless boundary! Eternal goal!
Whitherward rush, in thousand worlds, ten thousand keels!
Beacon, by which the universe is steered!—
Like the north-star, attracting all needles!
Unattainable forever; but for ever leading to great things this
    side thyself!
Hive of all sunsets!
Gabriel's pinions may not overtake thee!

Cymbals, drums, and psalteries!
The air beat like a pulse with music!
High land! high land, and moving lights, and painted lan-
    terns!
What grand shore is this?

Reverence we render thee, Old Orienda! . . .
Original of all empires and emperors!
A crowned king salutes thee!

A dozen more passages as Whitman-like: "A king on
his throne," chapter 60; "The Moose," chapter 184; "The
Lion," chapter 180. Everywhere poetry: tropic picturings
flaming with color; whole chapters languid as a tropic
noon. Nora-Bamma is Tennyson's Land of the Lotus-
eaters. Arranged in the Whitman line-length:

Its beetling crags, bent poppies, shadows, willowy shores, all
    nod;
Its streams are murmuring down the hills;
Its wavelets hush the shore.

Who dwells in Nora-Bamma?
Dreamers, hypochondriacs, somnambulists;
Who, from the cark and care of outer Mardi fleeing,
In the poppy's jaded odors,
Seek oblivion for the past, and ecstasies to come.

Open-eyed, they sleep and dream;
On their roof-trees, grapes unheeded drop.
In Nora-Bamma, whispers are as shouts;
And at a zephyr's breath, from the woodlands shake the
    leaves,
As of humming-birds, a flight.

Everywhere, after the escape of Yillah, poetry in rhap-
sodic prose. "As if Mardi were a poem, and every island
a canto, the shore now in sight was called Flozella-a-Nina,
or The-Last-Verse-of-the-Song." It is a book to live with,
to study long. It plunges one into thought; it bathes
one's soul with beauty.

VI

The masterpiece of Melville, the Caliban "Moby-Dick,"
was born in travail that all but destroyed its creator. It
was written by compulsion—headlong, convulsive. Part
I was on the press before Part II had been started. It
was written for money, for dear life, some of it in the
cool stillness of the Berkshires, some of it in the "Baby-
lonish brick-kiln" heat of a New York attic in August.
"Dollars damn me!" There was a mortgaged home, there
was a young family growing ever more expensive, there
were debts—and to fight them there was but his single
pen. "Mardi" had not sold well: it had been brutally
criticized. A new book must be written and at once: no
time for revision, no time for finish, no time even for
careful thought. "The calm, the coolness, the silent grass-
growing mood in which a man *ought* always to compose
—that can seldom be mine. . . . What I feel most moved
to write, that is damned—it will not pay. Yet, altogether

write the other way I cannot. So the product is a final hash, and all my books are botches."

Sad words, yet always must they serve as the first description of "Moby-Dick." The book is indeed a "hash": it is a headlong, lawless hodgepodge, the most chaotic book that ever rose to the dignity of a classic. What a volume! Encyclopedia of the whaling industry, biologic study of marine fauna, nautical anthology, history, gargoyle portraiture, sermons in whaleskin, prose, poetry, realism, romanticism, metaphysics—where in all English can you find a mix-up to equal it?

Not long do you read, however, before the strange tale compels you. You are one of the wild crew, you are pulling at an oar in mad pursuit; you are in the try-works at midnight toiling like a gnome; you are at the helm steering through blackness and storm; you are in the forecastle discussing monsters, religion, tropical metaphysics, exotic gastronomics, mad old Captain Ahab with the whalebone leg, and in the last climax you hear with tingling nerves his dying challenge to fate, a climax that renders the death of Long Tom Coffin in "The Pilot" mere commonplace. And you awake as from a nightmare, you are home from a four years' voyage. And then it bursts upon you that the book is not a hodgepodge at all but a unit; it is a voyage, and what is a voyage but a vast miscellany? Then again it bursts upon you that it is more than a mere voyage: it is an infernal "Pilgrim's Progress"; it is a study of the fundamentals of human life; it is a clinic; it is a mad attempt to thrust aside the veil that hides the supreme mystery of man; it is an "Invictus" hurled at "whatever gods may be."

The metaphysics of the thing, "the hell-fire in which the whole book is broiled," to use Melville's own phrase, is best explained in Captain Ahab's own words:

"All visible objects, man, are but as pasteboard masks. But in each event—in the living act, the undoubted deed—there,

some unknown but still reasoning thing puts forth the mould-
ings of its features from behind the unreasoning mask. If man
will strike, strike through the mask! How can the prisoner
reach outside except by thrusting through the wall? To me,
the white whale is that wall, shoved near to me. Sometimes I
think there's naught beyond. But 'tis enough. He tasks me;
he heaps me; I see in him outrageous strength, with an inscrutable malice sinewing it. That inscrutable thing is chiefly
what I hate; and be the white whale agent, or be the white
whale principal, I will wreak that hate upon him. Talk not
to me of blasphemy, man; I'd strike the sun if it insulted me."

And again:

The white whale swam before him as the monomaniac in-
carnation of all those malicious agencies which some deep men
feel eating in them, till they are left living on with half a
heart and half a lung. That intangible malignity which has
been from the beginning; to whose dominion even the modern
Christians ascribe one-half the worlds. . . .

Melville was anatomizing his own soul: his contempt
for the herd, his No-saying in thunder. The monomania
of Ahab was his own. There is no blasphemer like a
Puritan backslider, but such renegade blasphemy is always accompanied by brooding moroseness and secret
horror leading often to insanity. To Hawthorne the man
talked interminably of metaphysics: it had become a
cliché. Indoctrinate a boy until he is thirteen and the
marks are inerasable forever.

But apart from its colossal Ahab and its fierce light upon
Melville himself and the universal human soul, "Moby-
Dick" has literary values that place it among the few
great books of the mid-nineteenth century. Its graphic
narratives of elemental men fighting, in a cockle-shell
of a boat on a vast ocean, against the most powerful of
all God's created animals—"the mightiest elephant is but a
terrier to Leviathan, so, compared with Leviathan's tail,
his trunk is but the stalk of a lily"; its quivering

excitements; its stove boats; its insane moments when a Titan arm darts the harpoon to the mad yell "Starn all!"; its hissing line leaping from the tubs; its league-long tows at racing speed; its colossal death scenes—the dying monster heading at last toward the sun—all this stirs a reader like a powerful drug. This is Life: "as the swift monster drags you deeper and deeper into the frantic shoal, you bid adieu to circumspect life and only exist in a delirious throb."

Nothing else in all American literature is keyed in the pitch of some chapters of this mighty saga. The picture of the try-works at midnight casts a shadow that is infernal, "a redness, and madness, and ghastliness" of horror that is not the conscious and theatric art of Poe but the very soul of its creator. Take this Dantean climax:

As they narrated to each other their unholy adventures, their tales of terror told in words of mirth; as their uncivilized laughter forked upwards out of them, like the flames from the furnace; as to and fro, in their front, the harpooners wildly gesticulated with their huge pronged forks and dippers; as the wind howled on, and the sea leaped, and the ship groaned and dived, and yet steadfastly shot her red hell further and further into the blackness of the sea and the night, and scornfully champed the white bone in her mouth, and viciously spat round her on all sides; then the rushing Pequod, freighted with savages, and laden with fire, and burning a corpse, and plunging into that blackness of darkness, seemed the material counterpart of her monomaniac commander's soul.

VII

The book "Pierre" which quickly followed "Moby-Dick" is autobiography written in lunar caustic by a man who, as he expressed it himself, "began to feel that in him the thews of a Titan were forestallingly cut by the scissors of fate . . . who felt as a moose hamstrung." It is a mid-century "Education of Henry Adams" with tenfold more of cynicism and twenty-fold more of despair—and it is the product of a man of thirty-two. Disillusion and self-pity have become monomania, and monomania has become an unbalancing which is but another name for insanity. The book is a study in abnormality, it is auto-diagnosis, an intense chapter from an over-intense life. The section "Pierre and His Book," telling of the agony from which "Moby-Dick" emerged, illumines the man as with lightning flashes:

All things that think, or move, or lie still, seemed as created to mock and torment him. Still, the profound wilfulness in him would not give up. Against the breaking heart, and the bursting head; against all the dismal lassitude, and dreadful faintness and sleeplessness, and whirlingness, and craziness, still he bore up. His soul's ship foresaw the inevitable rocks, but resolved to sail on, and make a courageous wreck. In that lofty little garret of his, Pierre foretasted all that this world hath either of praise or dispraise; and thus foretasting both goblets, anticipatingly hurled them both in its teeth. All panegyric, all denunciation, all criticism of any sort, would come too late for Pierre.

Too late indeed! His generation was not ready for him and he cursed them and quit. He would not, could not yield to their demands. The feminine fifties with their "Wide Wide World," their "Lamplighter," their "Uncle Tom's Cabin," were in full career. Even Hawthorne was near despair: American Literature was in the hands of "a damned mob of scribbling women." Fate for Melville struck the final blow: the Harpers fire of 1852 destroyed all the plates and most of the sheets of his books, and he was not popular enough to be republished. He was ruined, he who already was ruined. Seven years of struggle there had been, seven years of "clamorous pennilessness," of caustic criticism—seven years and seven volumes; and then—save for "Israel Potter" four years later and a few magazine articles, a flaring-up of the embers—silence for forty years. It was 1891 when he died—just at the opening of the period that was to discover him and to crown his genius.

VIII

We can appraise the man to-day. The prejudices and the timidity that damned him in the nineteenth century have for the most part died by now. We can see to-day that for literary power and sweep of imagination and sheer originality no other in the range of our American literature can measure up to him, save only Whitman. There is a startling likeness between the two men: in their literary independence, their irreverence for the ordinary and the established, their sympathies that included all men of all conditions, their physical perfection before hardship and all had broken them down, their dominating egotism, their compelling masculinity and their frank acceptance of Nature, their originality of expression that voiced itself in self-created literary forms—they were radically beyond their own generation. Of the two Melville excelled in sheer literary power. It was in him to write in Whitman's own measure poetry commensurate in power with Whitman's. There are in his volumes turns of expression, Homeric similes, compelling bursts of narrative, adjective touches, poetic rhapsodies, paragraphs of impressionism, paintings in tropic color, unsurpassed in American literature. Note for instance his lurid picturings of London, his psychoanalysis of Benjamin Franklin, and his description of the fight of Jones in the *Bonhomme Richard,* his impressionistic characterizings of the islands of the Encantadas, his prose lyric flights in the later chapters of "Mardi." But such flights were seldom sustained. His genius was like that of Coleridge: lyric bursts rather than finished wholes, and then silence.

Whitman was without New England conscience or New England training; he fell into no harassing religious doubts, no brooding or melancholy; his philosophy was not grounded upon formal metaphysics. He had moreover infinite patience and the gift of totality. "Leaves of Grass," for all its accretions, is a unity. It grew. It was remorselessly pruned, revised, reconsidered. He was unhurried, unhampered by family, unvexed by financial necessities. And early he selected his poetical instrument and tuned it to his own touch, so that with full freedom and economy he could bring to bear the maximum of his powers.

Melville had none of this: his temperament undoubtedly was autocratic and mercurial. Had wealth been his, and perfect freedom of foot, doubtless it would have been the same story. Jack London, who at many points startlingly resembled him, surrendered to the reading public, gave it precisely what it demanded, and prospered; Melville despised the public, refused to yield at any point to its demand, hurled his contempt into its face with blasphemy, and wrote to satisfy his own imperious soul. Like Byron, he was over-intense, over-impetuous: the fire within him burned out his soul at thirty-two. He was a genius born into a perverse generation which stoned him and left him (as they supposed) for dead; a genius born two generations too soon. Furthermore, the audience for which he wrote has not appeared even yet.

BIBLIOGRAPHICAL REFERENCES

AMBROSE BIERCE, 1842–?

"Portrait of Ambrose Bierce," Adolphe de Castro, 1929.
"Bitter Bierce; A Mystery of American Letters," C. Hartley
    Grattan, 1929.
"Life of Ambrose Bierce," Walter Neale, 1929.
"Ambrose Bierce: A Biography," Carey McWilliams, 1929.
"Ambrose Bierce: A Bibliography," Vincent Starrett, 1929.

HERMAN MELVILLE, 1819–91

"Herman Melville, Mariner and Mystic," Raymond Weaver,
    1921. It has the distinction of being the first life of Mel-

ville and one of the first elements in the Melville revival of the twenties.

"Herman Melville" in "English Men of Letters series," John Freeman, 1926.

"Herman Melville," Lewis Mumford, 1929, containing much information undiscovered at the time of Weaver's volume, is at present the best biography. In a bibliographical note he says, "Among the critics whose studies of Melville have contributed to his revival and to a proper evaluation of his work I would mention especially Mr. Frank Jewett Mather, Jr., Miss Viola Meynell, Mr. Percy Boynton, Mr. J. W. N. Sullivan, Mr. E. L. Grant Watson, and, not least, Mr. Van Wyck Brooks."

Several editions of Melville are now on the market. The definitive edition is that published by Constable & Company (London), 1923–1924.

CHAPTER XXII

THE POETRY DÉBÂCLE

I

By 1917 the new poetry renaissance was at its height. Anthologies and books *about* the movement had already filled a five-foot shelf and were coming in increasing numbers. The seed volume, "Des Imagistes," had been followed in 1915, 1916, and 1917, by "Some Imagist Poets," a series that inspired a swarm of experimenters. In 1916, 1917, and 1918 Alfred Kreymborg issued his "Others," an anthology of new forms, and in 1915 Miss Zoë Akins ran for twenty-two weeks in "Reedy's Mirror" a minute topographic survey of the whole contemporary field, with specimens, entitling it "The Shadow of Parnassus, a Critical Anthology of American Verse." The younger generation was poetry-obsessed—everywhere new poetic contortions, experiments, lawlessness.

As early as 1908 Ezra Pound had issued in Venice, Italy, a collection of lyrics with the title "A Lume Spento," and then had followed it with "Exultations," "Canzoni," and in 1912, "Ripostes." Poetry, as he defined it, "is a kind of inspired mathematics"—mathematics so intricate at length that he could express its utter soarings with no term less infinite than "vorticism." T. S. Eliot, leading eccentric of the period, for a time was also a highly intoxicating element. Following his lead came an excited group of poetlings who scrambled poetry into contortions like this:

> in Just
> spring when the world is mud—

385

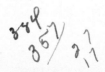

> luscious the little
> lame balloon man
>
> whistles far and wee
>
> and eddieandbill come
> running from marbles and
> piracies and it's
> spring
>
> when the world is puddle-wonderful

John Gould Fletcher, too, was a disturbing force. In 1915 came his "Irradiations," and a year later his "Goblins and Pagodas," each with an elaborate introduction explaining his complicated methods. Then had come the headstrong leadership of Amy Lowell—leadership from France at the first: her "Six French Poets" came in 1915, and her "Some Imagist Poets" in 1916. A year later her highly temperamental "Tendencies in Modern American Poetry" marshaled the scattered elements and creators into a movement. It was the first attempt at a serious evaluation of the new poetry, and its appearance is the high-tide mark of the so-termed poetical renaissance.

Poetry during the five years after 1912 came surging out from the vacant niches and end pages of magazines and the poets' corners of weekly papers where so long it had furtively lurked, into an unheard-of prominence. It was a subject now for newspaper front pages even, and popular weeklies. Everybody was reading it, or professing to read it, or intending to read it. It burst even into the Sunday "funnies" and the comic journals:

> There's a grand poetical "boom," they say.
>   (Climb on it, chime on it, brothers of mine!)
> 'Twixt the dawn and the dusk of each lyrical day
> There's another school started, and all of 'em pay.
>   (A dollar a line!
> Think of it, Ferdy, a dollar a line!)

In the year 1916, the year before Miss Lowell's "Tendencies in Modern American Poetry," more volumes of verse and drama were issued than of any other variety of literary product. Poetry had somehow laid hold of the younger generation. Three years before this, 1913 it was, William Stanley Braithwaite had issued an "Anthology of Magazine Verse and Year Book of American Poetry," a work to be repeated yearly to the present day—an amazing mass of mediocrity. Every one seemed to be writing verse and publishing it in elegant tiny volumes, for the most part at the author's expense.

To list even the names of those who issued poetry during this verse-mad decade would fill pages, and to attempt criticism of individual volumes would be like geodesizing a prairie village of molehills. Dozens of anthologies, glowing reviews, poetry magazines—a dozen of them, with large prizes awarded by committees (never so many prizes in the history of the world), coronation banquets to adolescent twitterers, glorification of high school Miltons, winners of poetry prizes, all have been powerless to save mediocrity from oblivion. Manly in his "Contemporary Literature" lists two hundred and fifteen poets who have written since 1900; Kreymborg in his index to "Our Singing Strength" adds several hundred more. Some have been enormously productive. Ezra Pound's poetry-book titles number nineteen, Louis Untermeyer's (counting his anthologies) swell to something like twenty, Witter Bynner's ten, Arthur Davison Ficke's twelve, John Gould Fletcher's fourteen, and Percy MacKaye's (including his dramatic work) forty. Hardly a prose writer who has not added at least a volume of poetry—even Mencken, Dreiser, Dos Passos, Edith Wharton, and Gamaliel Bradford.

In the words of Bruce Weirick, "The list soon became appalling. . . . It is incredible that they should all have written poetry. And not all have. Indeed it is well to take most of these lyrists quite sparingly, or one will soon begin to loathe the taste of sugar." And he lists among the uninspired versifiers Grace Hazard Conkling, Grace Fallow Norton, Margaret Widdemer, Elinor Wylie, Alice Corbin, Mary Carolyn Davies, Aline Kilmer, Edith Wyatt, Witter Bynner, William Rose Benét, Hermann Hagedorn, Charles Hanson Towne, and John Hall Wheelock.

II

The inherent weakness of this poetry-intoxicated school, the pitiful failure of what for a moment promised to be a new American voicing of life, was exposed most cruelly when an unforeseen demand was laid suddenly upon them. When the group was in fullest voice, pouring out with elaborate gesturings its amazing volume, suddenly there was a call for *poetry*. Never before such need for bards, for seers, for voices: the very fabric of civilization was on fire and seemingly doomed.

A war long continued needs interpreters: what is the soul of it? Why are men willing to die in it? What say the young men as they go to their sacrifice? What agony of lament from mothers, what outpourings from souls stirred to the very deeps?

Out of our Civil War, out of the tragic third year of it when the heart of the nation was wrung tight, came practically all of our national anthems, our martial lyrics, our expressions of the soul of America. To sing "Rally Round the Flag, Boys," "We're Coming, Father Abraham, Three Hundred Thousand More," "Maryland, My Maryland," "Dixie," "Tramp, Tramp, Tramp, the Boys are Marching," "My Eyes Have Seen the Glory of the Coming of the Lord," "Tenting Tonight on the Old Camp Ground," and a dozen others is to recreate the soul of the great conflict.

And out of it came a supreme bard, Walt Whitman: without the Civil War he would have been but a phase of transcendentalism, as forgotten now perhaps as even Alcott. The war it was that flooded his "Leaves of Grass" with light, that added to them what really is the vital spark. He interpreted the hour when America in her Gethsemane found her soul, and it was in the same hour that he found his own.

But with the World War crisis, when the demand came for *voices,* for dominating interpreters, for makers, for seers; when the whole young manhood of America was war-clad, and embarking on a crusade, it fondly believed, to the old battle-fields from which had emerged our civilization, when France and Germany and England and Italy, with their backs to the wall, were fighting at the last ditch for their very lives, what of these five hundred new poets of Kreymborg's "Our Singing Strength"? Let us examine the bibliography of the current poets: Ezra Pound was issuing "Quia Pauper Amavi" and "Umbra," translations from Guido Cavalcanti and others, and was explaining "vorticism"; John Gould Fletcher was issuing "Japanese Prints"; Arthur Davison Ficke, writing under the pseudonym Anne Knish, was issuing "Spectra" with Witter Bynner; and Amy Lowell was writing "Tendencies in Modern American Poetry," emphasizing little save form and technique—"Imagism," "polyphonic prose," "tone color," Chinese effects, Japanese irradiations. And this when the world was ablaze and the very foundations of civilization were threatened. Poetry is the voice of the highest living. The soul of it is its content and not its manner. Technique is incidental. The poet is a voice, a prophet, a seer, a leader in the days of crisis, interpreter after the days of storm.

III

One voice there was that was genuine, one cry from a human soul at life's zero-hour—the "I Have a Rendezvous with Death" of Alan Seeger. A Harvard man, class of 1910, a born poet, though doubtful and groping for expression, for his hour had not come, he went in 1913 to France as a graduate student. And hardly was he settled when suddenly the Germans plunged into Belgium, the Battle of the Marne was on, and the whole world was red with war. Impulsively he enlisted in the Foreign Legion and for two years was almost daily in battle. And as he could he wrote poems, not at all the conventional and imitative stuff he had dabbled with in his student years. Poetry was life now, a thing that came of itself and would not be controlled. In the spring of 1916, while within sound of the German guns, he wrote what is doubtless one of the finest lyrics called forth by the war.

> I have a rendezvous with Death
> At some disputed barricade,
> When Spring comes back with rustling shade
> And apple-blossoms fill the air—
> I have a rendezvous with Death
> When Spring brings back blue days and fair.
>
> It may be he shall take my hand
> And lead me into his dark land
> And close my eyes and quench my breath—
> It may be I shall pass him still.
> I have a rendezvous with Death
> On some scarred slope of battered hill,
> When Spring comes round again this year
> And the first meadow-flowers appear.
>
> God knows 'twere better to be deep
> Pillowed in silk and scented down,
> Where Love throbs out in blissful sleep,
> Pulse nigh to pulse and breath to breath,
> Where hushed awakenings are dear. . . .
> But I've a rendezvous with Death
> At midnight in some flaming town,
> When Spring trips north again this year,
> And I to my pledged word am true,
> I shall not fail that rendezvous.

He was wounded at the battle of Belloy-en-Santerre and died July 5, 1916. Only one other of his poems needs mention, his "Ode in Memory of American Volunteers Fallen for France," written to be read at a Memorial Day celebration in Paris. The twenty poems he wrote during the two years of his war service have been published in a volume with an introduction by William Archer.

Another American war lyric universally known was "In Flanders Fields" by the Canadian Colonel John McCrae:

> In Flanders fields the poppies blow
> Between the crosses, row on row,
> That mark our place; and in the sky
> The larks, still bravely singing, fly,
> Scarce heard amidst the guns below.
>
> We are the Dead. Short days ago
> We lived, felt dawn, saw sunset glow,
> Loved and were loved, and now we lie
> In Flanders fields.
>
> Take up our quarrel with the foe:
> To you from failing hands we throw
> The torch; be yours to hold it high.
> If ye break faith with us who die
> We shall not sleep, though poppies grow
> In Flanders fields.

Nor must we neglect another deep note, struck by Vachel Lindsay in his lyric "Abraham Lincoln Walks at Midnight (in Springfield, Illinois)":

> It is portentous, and a thing of state
> That here at midnight, in our little town,
> A mourning figure walks, and will not rest,
> Near the old court-house pacing up and down.
>
> .   .   .   .

It breaks his heart that kings must murder still,
That all his hours of travail here for men
Seem yet in vain. And who will bring white peace
That he may sleep upon his hill again?

The older poets, all of them pathetically minor singers, Henry van Dyke, Helen Gray Cone, Robert Underwood Johnson, Josephine Preston Peabody, and the rest, realizing the situation, tried the major key—in vain. George Edward Woodberry, for example, wrote beautifully finished sonnets—seven "Sonnets Written in the Fall of 1914." A man standing before his house on fire polishing sonnets!

The leading American victim of the war was Joyce Kilmer, killed in action in July, 1918. A journalist of promise, a nascent poet, much praised for his single lyric "Trees"—a poetic fragment greatly overpraised—he lives because of what he undoubtedly might have been had he been suffered to come back from his tremendous experience of life in the war zones of Europe. In a letter to Howard W. Cook, compiler of "Our Poets of Today," Kilmer declared that all he had written before the war was worthless:

I have very little chance to read contemporary poetry out here, but I hope it is reflecting the virtues which are blossoming on the blood-soaked soil of this land—courage and self-abnegation, and love, and faith—this last not faith in some abstract goodness, but faith in God and His Son and the Holy Ghost—I hope that our poets already see this tendency and rejoice in it—if they do not they are unworthy of their craft.

I would venture to surmise that the extravagances and decadence of the so-called "renascence of poetry" during the last five years—a renascence distinguished by the celebration of the queer and the nasty instead of the beautiful—have made the poet seem as silly a figure to the contemporary American as he seemed to the Englishman of the nineties, when the "æsthetic movement" was at its foolish height.

Kilmer was a native of New Brunswick, New Jersey, born December, 1886. After his course at Rutgers he became first a graduate student at Columbia, then an instructor of Latin, then editor of the "Churchman," and finally a member of the "New York Times" staff. His volume "Literature in the Making," 1917, containing interviews with twenty-three contemporary writers, among them Howells, Kathleen Norris, Booth Tarkington, Montague Glass, Rex Beach, Robert W. Chambers, James Lane Allen, Edward S. Martin, Robert Herrick, Arthur Guiterman, George Barr McCutcheon, John Erskine, Ellen Glasgow, Fannie Hurst, Amy Lowell, Edwin Arlington Robinson, Josephine Preston Peabody, and Percy MacKaye, is an admirable introduction to our period.

Out of this minor group from which so much was expected two or three have survived the deadly second decade of the movement and have been read even in the débâcle days of the nineteen twenties. The work of Stephen Vincent Benét has grown constantly in power and depth, culminating in his strong epic rendering of "John Brown's Body" in 1928. William Ellery Leonard, too, has sounded at least once the deeper notes of elegy in his "Two Lives," a quivering fragment cut from life itself—a latter-day classic. And Lew Sarett, woodsman, guide, student of Indian life, and college professor, in his "Many Many Moons" and "Slow Smoke" has caught a few times the most elusive atmosphere of wild life in the still untamed North Woods. Then, too, Cale Young Rice, enormously over-written, a vast flatness of sand, has here and there oases of tropic beauty. His "Night in Avignon" bursts upon one in the tropic beauty of a night-blooming cereus. An anthology from his poems, a thin volume, would possess surprisingly high merit.

To these one may add a few lyrics from the émigré philosopher and critic George Santayana, a genuine poet. It is futile to seek farther.

IV

One characteristic we must note in the entire new-century school as we leave it, one characteristic at least of the few major voices. It has not been a group of singers eager and excited like the Elizabethans, a group filled with hope and joy and belief in the glory of life and the greatness of the national hope; no, this characteristic has been an expression of glory missed, of dreams ending in disillusion, of beauty trampled down. On the old Fourth of July patriotism, hear Masters:

And these grand-children and great-grandchildren of the
    pioneers!
Truly did my camera record their faces too,
With so much of the old strength gone,
And the old faith gone
Which labors and loves and suffers and sings
Under the sun.

There is defeatism and futility in Robinson, and at times even in Frost. The period was an Indian summer so far as this outburst of poetry is concerned, strikingly colorful, yet unnatural, and quickly over. It was too self-conscious, it talked too much—it talked itself to death, it died of manners. Never before in the whole history of poetry was so much written *about* poetry. For the most part it expressed itself in lyric forms, seldom in the objective epic. The lyric is autobiographic, self-expressing, egotistic—and many of the poets of the decade have been egotistic to the verge of megalomania. After a brief Indian summer, with a few unseasonable yet spontaneous spring songs, now has come the ending of it all. May the new springtime bring a new outburst of glorious song!

The free-verse period—with its brief emphasis upon many little wrens exalted for a short time into nightingales—silenced or else obscured many real singers who

refused to retune their instruments. No one has expressed
the poetic dilemma of the period more clearly than Jessie
B. Rittenhouse (Mrs. Clinton Scollard): "At no period
in American literature," she writes, "has the poet who
holds his art as a consecration been so isolated as during
the last ten or twelve years, when the entire focus of
poetry has been upon form and when those who would not
turn to the startling or bizarre found themselves stig-
matized as conventional. The cynical strain which has
crept into modern poetry also, the ironical and satirical
vein, in line with the same vein in fiction and drama, still
further isolates the poet whose work belongs to the constructive rather than the destructive forces of life."

The result of the whole movement has been weakening
to poetry rather than strengthening. Its decline after the
death of Miss Lowell has been rapid, and the failure of
the movement has been accepted by many as a failure of
poetry itself rather than as the failure of a school. Surely
in the last half-decade poetry has become more and more
unmarketable and less and less discussed and read.

BIBLIOGRAPHICAL REFERENCES

"Our Singing Strength," Alfred Kreymborg, 1929.
"Troubadour," an autobiography, Alfred Kreymborg, 1926.
"Skepticisms, Notes on Contemporary Poetry," Conrad
      Aiken, 1919.
Anthologies of contemporary poetry, edited by Untermeyer,
      by Aiken, by French, Erskine, Stork, Wilkinson.
"Convention and Revolt in Poetry," John Livingstone Lowes,
      1919. A brilliant study.
"The Younger American Poets," Jessie B. Rittenhouse, 1904.
"From the Front," trench poetry, C. E. Andrews, 1918.
"A Treasury of War Poetry," edited with an introduction and
      notes by George H. Clarke, 1917.
"Our Poets of Today," Howard W. Cook, 1923. (See section
      including Alan Seeger, Charles Divine, Joyce Kilmer,
      John McClure, and other soldier poets.)

Works of Joyce Kilmer, edited by R. C. Holliday with a
    Memoir, 1918.
"Memories of My Son, Sergeant Joyce Kilmer," Annie E.
    Kilmer, 1920.
"From Whitman to Sandburg," Bruce Weirick, 1924.

CHAPTER XXIII

THE LATER CRITICISM

I

THE increasing stream of books and magazines and news-papers—by the close of the period a veritable inundation, flood-wide even if shallow—called forth at length an almost equal amount of printed comment and attempted assessment. Before 1900 criticism in America had been a sporadic thing, unoriginal and for the most part feeble, the feeblest of all our literary product. Lowell, whose leadership as critic had been unquestioned for a generation, died in 1891, the beginning of our new period. His voice had been a voice from the old quarterly review days, positive and dictatorial, stylistically artificial, even forced. Like Jeffrey and his editors, Lowell approached his subject by way of long detours; he was self-conscious in his witty turns and his circumlocutions; he salted his paragraphs everywhere with erudite allusions. His influence upon the younger critics, like Hamilton Wright Mabie, for instance, was demoralizing. Howells who came early under his influence escaped in time from Boston and after 1890 became more and more what Nature intended him to be, a voice from the West rather than from the East. His influence during the first twenty years of our period —an influence strengthened by his editorship of a "Harper's Magazine" department and by his series of autobiographical and critical volumes, like "Criticism and Fiction," 1891, "My Literary Passions," 1895, "Literary Friends and Acquaintance," 1900, "Literature and Life,"

1902—was undoubtedly one of the directing forces of the period.

The accepted professional critic, however, during the *fin de siècle* was Edmund Clarence Stedman of New York, a man, as we see him to-day, greatly in earnest, completely honest, but slenderly equipped for directive force in an age of transition. He was a gentle soul, an appreciator, an editor, an anthologist rather than a constructive critic, a timid appraiser with a taste for poetry of the Victorian order, a lecturer upon the theory and practice of poetry after classic formulæ, but no leader of forces in revolt. Timidly he accepted Whitman, but the new voices from the West were to him impossible. His "American Anthology," 1900, marks the line of finality between the old and the new in later American criticism.

For by 1900 new forces were transforming the literary field, forces vital, overpowering, universal—like the coming of springtime. Among them was the new organization and the sweeping advance of the American press. Book-reviewing now became a journalistic thing: soon it had become a minor profession. Before 1890 the author of a volume could look for adequate reviews in not more than four publications. First there was the "Atlantic Monthly," always authoritative. Then there was the New York "Nation," fearless, unbiased, often severe, but for a generation the most feared and respected of all the American reviews. Fiction it touched but gingerly and only its strongest productions. It was tremendously serious: fiction, even in the nineties, had not yet been admitted into the unquestioned areas of literature. For literary news and reviewings with lighter pen one looked to the New York "Critic," which under the editorship of the two Gilders, Jeannette and Joseph, was during the eighties and the nineties a pleasing journal of authority and influence. The establishment of the "Bookman" in 1895, the publication in 1900 of Stedman's "Anthology," and the death of Stedman in 1908 were events marking the close of an era. A new period was opening, one that the Chicago "Dial" was able to understand and direct in a distinctive career of some thirty years.

To the new journalism which came flooding into the new century, touching even the book-stands and the publishers' lists, book-reviewing was a reporter's job. Listen to the new voice from the sanctum:

A new book is primarily news, and the reviewer as a reporter has a journalistic job to perform. His ear must be attuned to the voice of the public, which says, "I wonder what this new book by Phineas Fog-Horn is all about, anyway."

Journalistic book-reviewing, then, was simply news-reporting. "Whatever else a review does it must make clear the value of the book reviewed, it must define and explain as well as criticize."

First came the book-review page in the Wednesday or the Saturday edition, then the Sunday-edition book supplement, one that grew into such magazine-like proportions as the "New York Times Book Review" and the "Herald-Tribune" section "Books." At first, much of this reviewing was non-critical, often the mere echoing of the publisher's sample review or of the superlatives on the book-jacket "blurb." Then came the signed review, and the superlatives lessened. Book-reviewing during the twenty years has steadily grown in compass and value. Most of the critical books of recent years, like S. P. Sherman's six volumes and Mencken's series of "Prejudices," appeared first as book-reviews.

Then came the professedly critical journals of the more scholarly type. In 1911 the old "Yale Review" changed its title from "A Journal for the Scientific Discussion of Economic, Political, and Social Questions" to "A Quarterly Magazine Devoted to Literature, Science, History, and Public Opinion." In 1914 came the "New Republic" and a little later the "Freeman," journals containing not only book-reviews but brilliant critical articles in the spirit of the new era. The negative in all questions intellectual and literary came with Henry Holt's "Unpopular Review," a vigorous interlude, and later with Mencken's "American Mercury." In 1924 appeared Henry Seidel Canby's "Saturday Review of Literature," a journal of increasing authority and influence.

In Mr. Canby's opinion, the newspapers during the decades since 1900 have been greatly helpful in the advancing of sound critical standards. They—

. . . have rendered one great service to criticism. In spite of their attempts to make even the most serious books newsy news, they, and they alone, have kept pace with the growing swarm of published books. . . . The literary supplement, which grew from the old book page, contained much reviewing which was in no bad sense journalistic. Without it the public would have had only the advertisements and the publishers' announcements to classify, analyze, and in some measure describe the regiment of books that marches in advance of our civilization.[1]

II

Since 1905 criticism, outside the book-reviewing-as-mere-news area, has flowed mainly in two channels, perhaps at times in three. First, there has been the conservative type, sometimes called the classical, sometimes the humanistic,—criticism opposed to romanticism when romanticism is defined in terms of revolt from the long-held conventional definitions. Secondly, there has been the liberal type, the voicings of the younger intellectuals, some of them of the "big bow-wow" quality. A still later type, the historical and the psychoanalytic, will require another chapter.

Of the leading older conservative critics of the period five only need be mentioned. These, and their earliest volumes of criticism, are as follows:

[1] Quoted in "Magazine Article Writing," Brennecke and Clark, 1930.

William C. Brownell (1851–1928)—"French Traits," 1889;
    "American Prose Masters," 1909.
George Edward Woodberry (1855–1930)—"Studies in Let-
    ters and Life," 1890; "America in Literature," 1903.
Paul Elmer More (1864–   )—"Shelburne Essays," first
    volume, 1904.
Irving Babbitt (1865–   )—"Literature and the American
    College," 1908; "The New Laokoön," 1910.
Stuart P. Sherman (1881–1927)—"On Contemporary Litera-
    ture," 1917.

All but one of the five—Brownell from Amherst—were
Harvard men; all but one of them—Brownell again—had
been college instructors; two of them—Brownell and
More—had been editors of the "Nation." It has been
against these men chiefly that Mencken and his followers
have hurled the taunt "campus critics," fruit perhaps of
an age-old conflict between the uncolleged and the colleged,
between town and gown. "The leaders of one party
sulk," said Stuart P. Sherman, "like Achilles, in the universities; the leaders of the other party rail, like Thersites,
in the newspapers. 'Academics!' cry the journalists. 'Barbarians!' cry the professors. The antagonism is acute, and
the consequences of this division are a tendency toward
sterility in the Party of Culture, and a tendency toward
ignorance and rawness in the Party of Nature." [2]
    Sherman himself was of the Harvard school, a disciple
of Irving Babbitt. Settled in the Midwest as professor of
English literature, he had savagely attacked the early work
of Theodore Dreiser, but had gradually become more sympathetic with the young rebels of his native West; and
later, in New York as editor of the "Herald-Tribune" review "Books," had grown decidedly liberal in his judgments of the new liberalism. His critical articles gathered
into some six or seven volumes, notably "On Contemporary Literature," 1917, "Americans," 1922, "The Genius
of America," 1923, and "Critical Woodcuts," 1926, rank

[2] "New York Evening Post Literary Review," December 31, 1921.

high among the literary products of the period. The death of Sherman in 1927 at the age of forty-six was a distinct loss to American criticism.[3] The transition critic between the mid-century criticism and the new humanism has been George E. Woodberry. "Mr. Woodberry, in 'The Heart of Man,' 'The Torch,' and 'Masters of Literature,' " says J. E. Spingarn in his essay "American Criticism Today," "is an inheritor of the Lowell tradition, in whom, despite many new influences, New England idealism carries on its appointed task of illuminating the meeting point of art and life. His biographies of Emerson and Hawthorne have few equals among the briefer histories of literary lives; and the best of his essays on the great writers have a unity and lift that make many of Lowell's seem those of a shrewd but old-fashioned amateur." More to the Lowell side he leaned, perhaps, than to the newer humanistic ideals, but to his death in 1930 he was a stabilizing influence in our criticism, a literary soul who preserved amid all the chaos of the new era something of the calm and beauty of the older days of art.

Between the philosophic Harvard group and the uncouth liberals and futilitarians, of late an increasing tribe, has stood stoutly all through the period the Amherst littérateur, journalist, and critic, William C. Brownell [4] on the staff of the "Nation" from 1879 to 1881, and for nearly forty years literary adviser of Charles Scribner's Sons. All in all, he has been the most consistent and helpful critic the period has produced. A thorough knowledge of French culture, voicing itself in two volumes, "French Traits," 1889, and "French Art," 1892, and a thorough grounding in the history and the content of critical theory in his volumes "Criticism," 1914, and "Standards," 1917, had placed him among the conservatives, defenders of the old

[3] See "Life and Letters of Stuart P. Sherman," by Jacob Zeitlin and Homer Woodbridge, 2 vols., 1929: a work throwing much light upon the period, especially in its critical areas.

[4] "American Prose Masters," W. C. Brownell, with an introduction by Stuart P. Sherman, 1923.

classical traditions. But he was more than a mere theorist, more than a mere conservative. He was sympathetic, as his colleagues were not, with the general trend of American culture. Insisting not at all upon the inflexible boundaries of the extremists, he was willing to accept the culture already acquired, to be thankful for it, and to be willing to build upon it gradually more perfect structures. His "Democratic Distinction in America," 1927, stands as one of the landmarks in later criticism.

Beginning with the thesis that "we differ from the world in general in being a democracy that has never been anything else," he studies the effects of this difference "upon our native character and its associated manners." "We had the best of all possible starts." We developed with no thought of social strata. It has made for idealism. Moreover, we laid our foundations upon morals. "Our philosophy has been preponderantly fraternal and equalitarian." We have been a kindly people and on the whole a polite people. "Our distinction, such as it is, at least is promising in being fundamentally a matter of the heart." The spirit of our society has been individualistic and so open to criticism, but we have been in a transitional stage, and "all transitional trails are uncomfortable." Social maturity is bound to come soon or late.

American humor and American sentiment he considered unique and distinctive. Our traditions he found woven of two strands, "the ancestral and the national, the remote and the recent." "Instead of being comparatively traditionless because so 'recent' we have a traditional advantage in being also 'remote.' In ethics we have a similarly dual tradition of corresponding strength—Puritanism and its alloys and modifications." The American attitude toward women he also classed among our distinctive traditions. But greatest of all the refining influences was, he believed, the American care for formal education. Nowhere else are there to be found so many agencies for popular culture. University extension, the rapidly increasing ranks of the professoriate with its growing extramural activities, the vast spread of libraries, newspapers, magazines, foundations, Chautauqua assemblies, lyceums, the gramophone and radios, and even the "movies" (though perforce they leave the cultivation of taste to other agencies)—all these obviously, he declared, are democratic achievements of no small significance.

"As a result our general culture is probably more general than elsewhere—general enough at all events to hold out the promise both of becoming more so and at the same time of rising to a higher level." Even in the esthetic field he finds encouragement. "In architecture, landscape gardening, music, there is already distinction, and in a lesser degree in the other arts. Slowly the herd is moving and it is steadily upwards."

For a generation he has stood inflexibly for better art, but never has he berated American uncouthness. He has been the mediator between the two critical factions, wholly approved of by neither, wholly rejected by neither, a constructive influence always for American betterment.

III

The leading critic of the conservative school has been Paul Elmer More, instructor in Sanskrit at Harvard and Bryn Mawr, literary editor of the "Independent" and the "New York Evening Post," editor of the "Nation," 1909–1914, author of the "Shelburne Essays," at present twelve volumes. The man, however, was a philosopher and a poet, rather than a professor and journalist. His book title of 1894, "A Dreamer in Gotham," is expressive. To him at the start literature was a matter of origins, of ghostly hands from the prehistoric India and all the Orient. Later he centered upon Hellenism, distilling the soul of it in five distinctive flagons—five volumes: "Platonism," "The Religion of Plato," "Hellenistic Philosophies," "The Christ of the New Testament," "Christ the Word." Ori-

entalism tranformed the man into a Gandhi-like recluse.
For two years he lived as a hermit and studied and medi-
tated and wrote.

In a secluded spot in the peaceful valley of the Androscog-
gin I took upon myself to live two years as a hermit, after a
mild Epicurean fashion of my own. As for the hermit . . .
having found it impossible to educe any meaning from the
tangled habits of mankind while he himself was whirled about
in the imbroglio, he had determined to try the efficiency of un-
disturbed meditation at a distance. So deficient had been
his education that he was actually better acquainted with the
aspirations and emotions of the old dwellers on the Ganges
than with those of the modern toilers by the Hudson or the
Potomac.

Poor method indeed for learning the meaning of the life
of one's day, this running away from it. It made him more
than ever a dweller in the past, a defender of ancient cultures, a man of the classics. Now began his critical papers.
Alone in his hermitage, he had discovered the secret of
Thoreau. One by one he investigated the great original
personalities, especially those who had stood solitary and
had lived from within: Pascal, Plato, Nietzsche, Hawthorne, Whitman. For such decadents and men of the mere
senses as Swinburne, he had only contempt. Year by year
came added volumes to the "Shelburne Essays," our
American *Causeries du Lundi,* until they have become one
of the most distinctive achievements of the new period.
In style they are distinctive. Brownell labored heavily
in his sentence structure. The course of his argument is
unmarked by the guide-boards of connectives and summaries. There is, indeed, a piling-up of abstract thought
until one is befogged and bewildered. But More's critical
prose rises to the levels of beautiful literature. Aside from
his critical message and the trend of his philosophy, he
belongs in our history of literature if but for his style
alone.

In his latest phase he has stood with Irving Babbitt as a protester against the modern literary currents. He preaches in his lay pulpit the ancient values in opposition to the new doctrines of futility. For him the "new humanism" must rest upon a religious basis, or as he himself has expressed it:

It does not follow . . . that the art and literature of a creative era must be exclusively or even predominantly religious in intention, or that every individual artist must be a believer. But I think it would not be difficult to prove from history that wherever great art has flourished, noble in theme as well as in technique, there religion such as I have described it, though the ingredients vary in tone, has been present in the background, coloring the thoughts and emotions of society and investing the natural world with the glamour of the supernatural. On the other hand it is equally true that religion, even when favorable in spirit, does not automatically produce a humanistic age, while in some of its manifestations it has been actually antagonistic to art and human letters; there is need also of a humanism, aroused to its own dignity and ardently concerned with the beautiful representation of life as well as with life itself.

Professor Irving Babbitt has been the heavy artillery of the new Humanism, a philosopher and dialectician rather than a littérateur. His position, and that of the whole group about him, is most elaborately presented in "Humanism and America," 1930, an anthology of defining articles edited by Professor Norman Foerster. The table of contents is instructive:

Norman Foerster: "Preface"
Louis Trenchard More: "The Pretensions of Science"
Irving Babbitt: "Humanism: an Essay at Definition"
Paul Elmer More: "The Humility of Common Sense"
G. R. Elliott: "The Pride of Modernity"
T. S. Eliot: "Religion without Humanism"
Frank Jewett Mather, Jr.: "The Plight of our Arts"
Alan Reynolds Thompson: "The Dilemma of Modern Tragedy"

Robert Shafer: "An American Tragedy"
Harry Hayden Clark: "Pandora's Box in American Fiction"
Stanley P. Chase: "Dionysus in Dismay"
Gorham B. Munson: "Our Critical Spokesmen"
Bernard Bandler, II: "Behaviour and Continuity"
Sherlock Bronson Gass: "The Well of Discipline"
Richard Lindley Brown: "Courage and Education"

A counter attack by the younger group opposed to the "negative philosophy" of More and Babbitt was issued immediately, a symposium entitled "The Critique of Humanism," edited by C. Hartley Grattan, but it settled nothing at all. On both sides nothing was accomplished; nothing new presented—a furious threshing of age-old straw.

IV

The group of liberals who have stood opposed—individualists, disillusioned dreamers, futility criers, younger generation revolters, intellectuals, sayers of No—has been a strange heterogeny, but one that has possessed growing power. The shadow of pessimism and doubt had been increasing with growing emphasis ever since the mid-century. In 1910, Samuel Clemens, leading humorist of America, died of disillusion, embittered against humanity as no one else had been since the creator of the "Yahoo." He was by all means the most distinctive and widely known personality of his period, and during the twenty years he lived in the period after 1890, the influence of his futility pose was tremendous. Says a critic of the period: "Mark Twain loved to be a figure in the public eye, shouted his doubts and forebodings from the house-tops, and dared his hearers to disprove. His white serge of later years, his ornate vocabulary of objurgation, and his violations of the drawing-room proprieties were all parts of his manner and his manners, which were calculated to display his contempt for the politer conventions of 'the damned human race.' " [5] And following his death came Paine's 1,600-page biography, collections of his letters, and a twenty-five-volume set of his works advertised with enormous display. The shadow of Mark Twain is dark upon the period. Five years after Twain's death "Bitter Bierce," devil's lexicographer, having gathered his bitterness into twelve volumes, cursed God and died, perhaps by his own hand in some wild gulch of the Sierras. In the eighteen nineties had rusted out in blackness and blasphemy after forty years of barrenness Herman Melville, creator of "Moby-Dick," that plesiosaurus of American fiction. Earlier, after a decade of sterility, had died Nathaniel Hawthorne of the disease diagnosed correctly only by Emerson: "the painful solitude of the man, which, I suppose, could not longer be endured, and he died of it."

A disease it was that blighted nearly all of our literary men. America in art and literature for a century after the establishment of the republic stood for mediocrity. Cooper, Poe, Melville, Thoreau—to mention but our unquestioned leaders—fought it, sought to alleviate it, perished of it even as Hawthorne. Others fled to Europe where civilization seemed old and matured and satisfying.

Then had grown another area of embittered criticism. From the days of Philip Freneau—who wrote,

> Can we never be said to have wisdom and grace
> Unless it is brought from that damnable place?

—to the present moment, our criticism has been caustic with denunciations of our subservience to English models. For a generation the Phi Beta Kappa orations of the colleges rang with demands for literary independence. One might fill a volume with these drastic flings at our grovelings before European critics and our slavery to British literary models, and only half-way through it would be Lowell's gibe in 1848:

[5] "Some Contemporary Americans," Percy H. Boynton, 1924.

"You steal Englishmen's books and think Englishmen's
    thought,
With their salt on her tail your wild eagle is caught."

But subservience has been forced upon us. One may not
expect a raw continent to be subdued and turned into refinement in a dozen decades. Behind the youth who, until
comparatively recent times, dreamed of a literary career,
there was nothing—could be nothing, of sustaining culture. The young Longfellow in 1825, just out of the backwoods college and attracted to literature as a profession
by his study of the European classics, was told by his practical father, a graduate of Harvard and a member of
Congress, that there was not wealth and refinement enough
in America to support a man of letters, that it would be a
century at least before the nation could ever dream of
native professional littérateurs. That was in 1825. Want
of a sustaining culture had compelled Freneau, a genuine
poet, to prostitute his muse and destroy almost completely
his native gift, and it had driven Charles Brockden Brown,
a romantic genius, into journalism and statistics. Irving,
lifeless in the tepid atmosphere of New York, had escaped
at last into the denser culture of Britain as a man escapes
from prison, and had lived abroad during all of the creative period of his literary life. Twenty-one years he spent
in Europe. Cooper, after his sixth book, also escaped to
the Continent where he resided for seven years. His verdicts written in the early thirties are illuminating:

Manners, tastes, knowledge, and tone are all too much dif-
fused in America to make head against the sturdy advances of
an overwhelming mediocrity.

Literature in America, he believed, was handicapped beyond all immediate remedy:

There are no annals for the historian; no follies (beyond
the most vulgar and commonplace) for the satirist; no manners for the dramatist; no obscure fictions for the writer of

romance; no gross and hardy offenders against decorum for the moralist; not any of the rich artificial auxiliaries of poetry.

Aside from Whittier and Thoreau and Whitman, every one of our major writers went abroad for long periods, escaping at the earliest possible moment. The roll-call of those who spent three years and more in Europe would include Ticknor, Everett, Hawthorne, Poe, Longfellow, Holmes, Willis, Taylor, Lowell, Howells, and Stephen Crane. Even one as redolent of America as Mark Twain was no exception. After his "arrival" with "The Innocents Abroad" in 1869, he spent one third of his remaining life in foreign lands. Many, as we have seen, shook off completely their American connections, notably Henry James, Bret Harte, Edgar Saltus, Harold Frederic, Henry Harland, T. S. Eliot. Others, like the mid-century feminine romancers and the contemporary Cabell, created alien provinces outside our actual domain and in imagination transferred their residence to domains of the air.

And from it all has come the inevitable result. Educated in Europe, our travelers have brought back from Europe worn-out ideals and conventions that have fitted not at all our vigorous new-world needs. They have tried, as did Longfellow, to bring cultures from feudal days into the wild backwoods freedom of our democracy, to graft upon the vigorous wild vine of our Western world the hot-house growths of an out-worn civilization. And right here has been the contended point of one school of the later liberal critics: the literature of a people, they say, is the voice of that people. It is not a mirror held up to another civilization or to mere models. Our literature is ourselves: "An ill-favoured thing," it may be, but our own. A negro spiritual that has been evolved from the actuality of a race in an unique environment is more valuable than a sequence of sonnets worked out from European models. Whoever writes the final history of American literature must define

"American" as Whitman defined it when he said, "All America is in my songs." It is the expression of what has been the evolution decade by decade of the American soul.

Disillusion and pessimism have been inevitable accompaniments of American criticism. They have become, in a way, an American disease, perhaps *the* American disease. One need not seek far for the reason—at least *a* reason. Never in the history of the race have dreams been more glorious than those which attended our earliest history—infinite picturings of wealth and happiness and freedom. Michael Drayton at the high noon of the Spacious Days sang of—

"Virginia, Earth's only Paradise."

To the New England Pilgrims it was a second Promised Land, a "New English Canaan." For centuries it was the world's sweet synonym for hope, for a second chance for the defeated, for glorious religious freedom to the bigot-ridden and the oppressed. Utopia it was in a world fresh from the hand of God. Millions of letters and clippings and documents and books scattered over three hundred years record the marvelousness of that dream which created the last great migration movement of the race.

Early American history is written in superlatives. Freneau, graduating from Princeton in 1771, depicted with true Commencement Day fervor "The Rising Glory of America," crying at the climax:

O I could weep
That I was born too soon,
Just at the dawning of that glorious day
When scenes are painting for eternity.

Reaction was inevitable. All through the nineteenth century it was a bitter growth increasing yearly, fed by the new spirit of industrialism and fabulous wealth in the hands of a few, by the revolutionizing advancing of science, and the establishment of cities. With departing adolescence came disillusion: America was "coming of age." The cultured few, the "intelligentsia," viewed with growing impatience the vulgar standards and the inertia of the mass. As the century passed toward its bitter end their criticism took at first the generalized name of "realism." More and more came the demand: We should see ourselves as we are; no more can we blind ourselves with childish legends, romanticism, everything working to happy endings. Truth is what we must have now, life depicted as it is, with no avoidance of disillusioning details.

American criticism had entered its second stage: it was calling for the Truth. Tradition no longer was to be trusted; dogma unsupported by evidence was to be discarded as rubbish; the resonant and the artificial in literature, mere rhetoric, were no longer to be endured. The new age, the age of science, demanded only Truth. The task of the artist it was to record the concrete in the artist's own experience, and inevitably this meant disillusion, for it is only when one is stripped of one's illusions, one's prejudices and pruderies, one's sentimentalism, that one is able to see actuality, to voice fundamentals in self and in externals. It was in view of such definitions as this that Whitman could voice his devastating verdict: "America has as yet morally and artistically originated nothing."

Hard indeed it is to explain when we view the epic nineteenth century of America with its vitality and its pushing vigor, its battles and its buildings, its conquering of a raw continent, its moral conquests and its wealth, its need for inspired utterance, for original ventures of the human spirit into fields undreamed of by Europe—it is truly hard to explain why its men of letters were content to be echoes and not voices.

V

Another element enters the problem to explain the bitterness of the young liberals especially in the culminating years of the old century—the loss of the American border. This element undoubtedly has been made far too much of during recent years since the discovery of it by Professor Turner, but it cannot be neglected as a dominating influence. For a century and more the western frontier was romance. The prairie lands—areas vast beyond all dreaming and rich with fertility and mineral storings totally untouched since the beginning of creation, for a time the golden dream of all the East, another "earth's only Paradise"—in a single generation lost their glory and became the chief area of dissatisfaction in the nation's geography. Optimism vanished in a night when the free land ended, when the frontier had reached the Pacific and was no more. That was in the early nineties, and from the nineties we may trace as a dominating force that creeping tide of disillusion, of revolt from the old standards, of futility and pessimism that has brought an amazing seaweed mass of criticism culminating in such symposiums as "Civilization in the United States: An Inquiry by Thirty Americans," edited by H. E. Stearns, 1922. And this in happy free America. The publication of this volume sets the high-tide mark of disillusion. Pessimism had produced its masterpiece.

BIBLIOGRAPHICAL REFERENCES

"Horizons: A Book of Criticism," Francis Hackett, 1918.
"Our Critics" in "Letters and Leadership," 1918. Van Wyck Brooks.
"America and the Young Intellectual," Harold E. Stearns, 1921.
"An Imaginary Conversation with Mr. P. E. More," in "Americans," 1922. Stuart P. Sherman.
"Criticism in America: Its Function and Status," essays by Irving Babbitt, Van Wyck Brooks, W. C. Brownell, Ernest Boyd, T. S. Eliot, H. L. Mencken, Stuart P. Sherman, J. E. Spingarn and George E. Woodberry, 1924.

"W. C. Brownell," in "Points of View," 1924. Stuart P. Sherman.

"The Newer Spirit: A Sociological Criticism of Literature," V. F. Calverton, 1925.

"American Criticism," W. A. Drake, 1926.

"Contemporary American Criticism," selected and arranged by James Cloyd Bowman, 1926.

"American Criticism: A Study in Literary Theory from Poe to the Present," Norman Foerster, 1928.

"Literary Renaissance in America," C. E. Bechhofer, 1923.

"Humanism and America," Norman Foerster, 1930. Essays by Irving Babbitt, Paul Elmer More, T. S. Eliot, Gorham B. Munson, and others.

"The New Humanism" number of the "Bookman," March 1930.

"The New Humanism," Leon Samson, 1930.

CHAPTER XXIV

MENCKEN

I

DURING the second and third decades of the new century the spirit of dissent, so long a smoldering fire, broke out, as we have seen, in such conflagrations as the "Civilization in the United States" symposium and in many volumes and articles similar in tone. Everywhere talk of a new and terrible "younger generation." For example, see Sherman's "Mr. Mencken, the Jeune Fille, and the New Spirit in Letters," in his volume "Americans." Though most of the members of it were forty years old or more, the "new generation" was discussed all at once as if it were a monster newly hatched, a Minotaur in his first adolescence raging to destroy all pure things. For a decade at least—the decade synchronous with the war epoch— newspapers and magazines overflowed with discussions of the unexplainable phenomenon: a new wild crop of youth disillusioned seemingly at birth, godless, incorrigible, at war with all things established (especially those ruled by law or discipline), in literature Fascisti overturning tables in all the temples and wrecking all the Victorian conventions.

And at the critical moment these Fascisti had found a leader, H. L. Mencken, compound of all things needed for such Fascism, a man with ten years of intensive training in journalism, uncolleged and therefore contemptuous of the academic, unchurched and therefore religiously skeptical. No ignoramus was he, however, no hobo type; a self-educated savant rather, with full courses in Bernard Shaw,

Nietzsche, and Ibsen, a well-to-do city man with all the urban complexes (a contempt for country "boobs," for instance), a dreamer of literary art in terms of the New York "Smart Set," in due time a newspaper soap-boxer and lay preacher with a syndicated column like Frank Crane and Arthur Brisbane. The evolution of this literary Mussolini is illuminating: to have evolved him in any other period would have been impossible.

The first approach to the man is by way of Baltimore. He was born there in 1880, he was educated in the schools there till he was sixteen, he has lived there ever since in the house in which he was born—most significant: the city complex as opposed to the country—one finds it everywhere in his writings; and the Baltimore complex, which is far more important. In him the quality of Baltimore. Let the man himself explain it:

Maryland . . . freed, by the providence of God, from the droughts and dervishes, the cyclones and circular insanities of the Middle West, and from the moldering doctrinairism and appalling bugaboos of the South, and from the biological decay of New England, and from the incurable corruption and menacing unrest of the other industrial States, it represents, in a sense, the ideal toward which the rest of the Republic is striving. . . . It has its own national hymn, and a flag older than the United States.

Was there ever more of provincialism even in Indiana? In Baltimore, as not even in Virginia, a patriarchal atmosphere, an old régime impenetrable by money or newness. The man is a Baltimore aristocrat in his conceptions, in fact in all his fundamentals: read his volume "Men versus Man." The underlying concept of American democracy he rejects with all the scorn of a Trotski. He is an individualist, an anti-socialist, an agnostic, an independent, a man refusing to keep step with any but himself and scarce with himself. Confronted with himself he will evade the issue with "I'm never twice alike. I'm no fundamentalist. I'm simply amusing myself." And yet with a Harvard education and a Ph.D. degree and a Harvard professorship, he would be an Irving Babbitt leading the forces of humanism against the vulgarity of the mob. Educated by city editors, by Shaw and Nietzsche and Ibsen, he has chosen un-Harvard-like weapons and methods and un-Babbitt-like shock troops as fellow-fighters, but still he is an aristocrat fighting "the moron majority," the American "mass," the triumphant "booboisie," all the forces arrayed against "humanism." Again the Baltimore complex.

Until 1916, thirty-six years of age, his literary life, for the most part journalistic, was wholly within the Baltimore area. He was as localized as Whittier, as completely provincial as Thoreau. Until well into his later youth, life had come to him largely through books. Fundamentally he was a romantic. Like most of his generation, he stormed the gate of literature first with poetry, voluptuous love lyrics. The little book should be reprinted—it will be. It is illuminating. The youthful lyrist had been touched by the earlier Kipling and had been outraged at Kipling's lapse into worldliness. Come back into the world that I love, he had cried:

> Unsung the East lies glimmering,
>   Unsung the palm-trees toss their frills,
> Unsung the seas their splendours fling
>   The while you prate of laws and tills.
>   Each man his destiny fulfills:
> Can it be yours to loose and stray,
>   In sophist garb to wash your quills?—
> Sing us again of Mandalay.
>
> Master, regard the plaint we bring
>   And hearken to the prayer we pray;
> Lay down your law and sermoning,
>   Sing us again of Mandalay.

This tiny volume, "Ventures into Verse," said I in an earlier review, is now extinct. "When it was issued it made no more impression upon the reading public than if it were a schoolgirl's yearnings published by Badger. The title was effeminate and timid; apologetic even. Had it been, say 'Hell after 8:15,' some poor devil of a newspaper reviewer might have glimpsed it in the heap, but 'Ventures into Verse'—it is rated in literary statistics as stillborn. Yet show me a more promising bit of poetic workmanship put to press that year by an American." Early was it impressed upon the young Baltimorean that if he was to make literary headway at all he must acquire sharper weapons.

The next test in our preliminary clinic concerns his education—self-administered, individualistic. His reading, as described by his biographer Goldberg, covered a surprising area: the leading nineteenth-century authors of England and America. Put in charge of the dramatic reviewing of his newspaper he lived for two years in the atmosphere of the current drama of the day—Shaw, Ibsen, Pinero. Resultant from reportings of the new Irish play-boy came a study of Shaw after Shaw's own pattern in "The Quintessence of Ibsenism,"—"George Bernard Shaw: His Plays," 1905, logical result, observes Ernest Boyd, of "an attack of Shavianitis at the appropriate age." Other rampant individualists, little known then in America, attracted the young enthusiast—first Nietzsche, to whose works he gave enormous toil. His "Philosophy of Frederick Nietzsche," 1908, a *tour de force,* represents diligence rather than scholarship. Through the mad chaos of Nietzsche he laid out no highways. Not at all did he attempt interpretation of the rounded philosophy of the man: like a special reporter at an interview he picked news values, phases of individualism that keyed with his own aristocratic ideals and ignored those that ran counter. A readable book he made, but the work is important not for light thrown upon Nietzsche, but for light thrown upon Mencken and the forces that molded him. His dramatic work led him next to Ibsen, then a newness in the Western world, a disturbing force. Seven volumes of translated work bear his name as editor with prefaces or introductions carefully wrought. All this is important: a youth in his early twenties throwing his leisure hours won from the most arduous of professions into a study of the archrebels of his day, editing them, interpreting them, making them accessible to the nascent "intelligentsia." His own little volume "Ventures into Verse" now began to appal him. He destroyed all the copies he could find. I know of only two that escaped his later adolescent rage.

Test three in our clinic: to his Baltimore provincialism, his anti-socialism, his anti-democracy, his Shavianism, Nietzscheism, Ibsenism, add, most important of all, journalism. Following the closing of his schoolboy text-books had come three years in his father's cigar factory, but at nineteen the death of his father had left him free to work his will. At once he began as reporter on a city daily. It is noteworthy that during the same month both Jack London and O. Henry made their first significant publications.

The apprenticeship of the youth was thorough and it was inclusive. During the next fifteen years he filled every position on the Baltimore journals from reporter and columnist and editorial writer and dramatic critic up to managing editor. During the last five years of this period he had charge of the "Free Lance" column—most significant. Note his own explanation of this column as quoted by his best biographer, Boyd:

General aim: to combat, chiefly by ridicule, American piety, stupidity, tin-pot morality, cheap Chauvinism in all their forms. Attacked moralists, progressives, boomers, patriots, reformers, and finally Methodists, etc., by name.

Invented many new words and terms, e.g., chemical purity, osseocaput, baltimoralist, smut-hound, honorary pall-bearer, snoutery, Boy Scout snoutism, snouteuse, booze-hound, malignant morality,—some of which got into circulation.

That was in 1915 in his valedictory when he left the Baltimore "Sun" for his new work as co-editor with

George Jean Nathan of the New York "Smart Set." That the man is not a mere destructive force, a typhoon in the jungle of growing America, lawless and aimless as often he calls himself, note here by way of parenthesis that at the ending of each period of his work he has summed up his aims and his accomplishments. Note, for instance, the résumé of his fifteen years of work on the "Smart Set"— from 1908 to 1914 as literary critic, and from 1914 to 1923 as associate editor. In it he contends that he made himself a constructive force in the literary history of the period. His ferocious "Sahara of the Bozart" he believes started a new literary period in the South.

It was early in his journalistic period at Baltimore that he discovered the secret of criticism that transformed Henry Louis Mencken into the H. L. Mencken that the world now knows. His early books, his Shaw, his Nietzsche, his Ibsen, his "Ventures into Verse," brilliant work for a youngster not far into his twenties, had made no impression: they were after the manner of their times. But the young journalist was eager: he had read Thackeray's "Book of Snobs," Ambrose Bierce, and the later Mark Twain; and he too felt wicked. And at this critical moment came the bit of advice that was to transform him. In a moment of confession he has told us how his purring little "Ventures into Verse" came to be followed by a book with the amazing title "Damn! A Book of Calumny":

Aspiring, toward the end of my nonage, to the black robes of a dramatic critic, I took counsel of an ancient whose service went back to the days of *Our American Cousin,* asking him what qualities were chiefly demanded by the craft.

And the Ancient had told him above all else to be interesting:

"All else is dross. Unless you can make people *read* your criticisms, you may as well shut up your shop. And the only way to make them read you is to give them something exciting."

"You suggest, then," I ventured, "a certain ferocity?"

"I do," replied my venerable friend. "Read George Henry Lewes, and see how *he* did it—sometimes with a bladder on a string, usually with a meat-ax. Knock somebody in the head every day—if not an actor, then the author, and if not the author, then the manager. And if the play and the performance are perfect, then excoriate someone who doesn't think so—a fellow-critic, a rival manager, the unappreciative public. But make it hearty; make it hot! The public would rather be the butt itself than to have no butt in the ring. That is rule No. 1 of American psychology—and of English, too, but more especially of American. You must give a good show to get a crowd, and a good show means one with slaughter in it." . . . The advice of my ancient counselor kept turning over and over in my memory, and as chance offered I began to act upon it, and whenever I acted upon it I found that it worked.

II

The literary advent of Mencken dates from 1908, the year he began to contribute regularly to "The Smart Set." For the first time now he had an adequate audience, one wider than Baltimore. His book-reviews, modeled after the pattern described by the Ancient who had taught him dramatic criticism, now began to bite and cauterize. Authors got now a decidedly new sensation. They began to talk of the "Smart Set" reviews. Who was this man Mencken who lashed about him so furiously, who in vocabulary and literary gymnastics seemed to "out-O. Henry" O. Henry himself in the O. Henry decade? By 1914, when he took the editorship of the "Smart Set" with George Jean Nathan, he had become the synonym for brutal reviewing.

Soon, however, with his articles in his magazine, his reviews, and his syndicated column in a series of newspapers, he struck the universal national consciousness. Never such seeming joy in denunciation, including even the scheme of Things Entire, such irreverence, such shameless confessions of futility,—a literary Malay running amuck. Especially did he seem to be infuriated by Methodists and Baptists and churches generally, by college professors, by 100% Americans, by "Comstockery," by Billy Sundayism and all reformers. The decade from 1914 to 1924 was his—the Mencken decade, the age of superlatives, of denunciation matched by counter-superlatives of approval by his growing circle of disciples, as radical as he but without his uncanny skill. In every syndicated column weekly he excoriated, often by name, every one, everything, in the American republic from the President to the rural man of God. And the come-back was bitter beyond belief and abundant beyond measure. No other writer in the history of literature has been so lambasted with adjectives, so Billy-Sundayed, so dangled over the pit of hell by all the ministers of America. And seemingly the man enjoyed it. He gathered with miserly care all the clippings, and—serene as a house-fly—pasted them into a manuscript, and, when enough Billingsgate had been hurled to be gathered into a volume, issued it as his regular book of the year with the astounding title "Menckeniana, A Schimpflexicon." And he sold the entire edition. In the rich diction of the college campus, "can you beat it?" It reminds one of Sherwood Anderson's mother and her method of obtaining cabbages.

Beginning with his "A Little Book in C Major," 1916, a book of epigrams selected from his earlier articles, his "Book of Burlesques," 1916, and his volume of the following year, "A Book of Prefaces," he now began on what we may call his second literary period, the period of his first independent literary criticism, articles issued first in his magazine and then in frequent volumes. Some twelve or thirteen volumes he issued between 1914 and 1924, the most important of them bearing the running title "Prejudices." Here lies the main body of work upon which his reputation as a critic must be based.

That consternation followed many of the articles is not to be wondered at. Even in America, the land of the wholly free press, one does not find extremes like this:

In the presence of the Methodist clergy, it is difficult to avoid giving way to the weakness of indignation. What one observes is a horde of uneducated and inflammatory dunder-heads, eager for power, intolerant of opposition, and full of a childish vanity—a mob of holy clerks but little raised, in intelligence and dignity, above the forlorn half-wits whose souls they chronically rack. In the whole United States there is scarcely one among them who stands forth as a man of sense and information. Illiterate in all save the elementals, untouched by the larger currents of thought, drunk with their power over dolts, crazed by their immunity to challenge by their betters, they carry over into the professional class of the country the spirit of the most stupid peasantry, and degrade religion to the estate of an idiotic phobia. There is not a village in America in which some preposterous jackass is not in irruption.

Or this of Virginia, mother of the Southern States, in his "Sahara of the Bozart":

Her education has sunk to the Baptist seminary level; not a single contribution to human knowledge has come out of her colleges in twenty-five years; she spends less than half upon her common schools, *per capita,* than any northern state spends. In brief, an intellectual Gobi or Lapland. Urbanity, *politesse,* chivalry? Go to! It was in Virginia that they invented the device of searching for contraband whisky in women's under-wear.

Or this *lèse majesté* of Roosevelt written in the period of laudation just following his death:

A glorified longshoreman engaged eternally in cleaning out bar-rooms—and not too proud to gouge when the inspiration came to him, or to bite in the clinches, or to oppose the relatively fragile brass knuckles of the code with chair-legs, bung-starters, cuspidors, demijohns, and ice-picks.

Or this of Miss Lowell of Boston, leader of the free-verse movement:

> Miss Lowell is the schoolmarm of the movement, and vastly more the pedagogue than the artist. She has written perhaps half a dozen excellent pieces in imitation of Richard Aldington and John Gould Fletcher, and a great deal of high-falutin bathos. Her "Dome of Many-Colored Glass" is full of infantile poppycock. . . . Her celebrity, I fancy, is largely extra-poetical. . . . Miss Lowell has been helped very much by her excellent social position. The majority, perhaps fully nine-tenths, of the revolutionary poets are of no social position at all—newspaper reporters, Jews, foreigners of vague nationality, school teachers, lawyers, advertisement writers, itinerant lecturers, Greenwich Village posturers, and so on. I have a suspicion that it has subtly flattered such denizens of the *demi-monde* to find the sister of a president of Harvard in their midst, and that their delight has materially corrupted their faculties. Miss Lowell's book of exposition, "Tendencies in Modern Poetry," is commonplace to the last degree.

> Poets fared hard with the Mencken of this middle period: Frost is "Whittier without whiskers." Ezra Pound . . . "the American in headlong flight from America. . . . A professor turned fantee, Abélard in grand opera." "Such cheap jacks as Alfred Kreymborg, out of Greenwich Village." "Vachel Lindsay with his nebulous vaporings and Chautauqua posturings." "As for Edgar Lee Masters, for a short season the undisputed Homer of the movement, I believe that he is already extinct. . . . The *Spoon River Anthology* fell upon the country at the height of the last sex wave—a wave eternally ebbing and flowing, now high, now low. It was read, not as a work of art, but as a document; its large circulation was undoubtedly mainly among persons to whom poetry *qua* poetry was as sour a dose as symphonic music."

It would be possible to gather from all the writings of the man materials for a Counter-Schimpflexicon with materials as startling as those he has quoted from the missiles hurled at himself. It would be a needless task to compile such a monstrosity. Mencken has been the play-boy of the period, feared, hated, despised; but on the other hand he has been the courageous voice, the self-appointed Amos, the able leader of the minority. His smashing attacks have angered us all, but it has been good for us to be angry. It has kept us young. For a decade—even his bitterest enemies cannot deny it—he was the leading American critic. Despite his waning influence, perhaps he is the most arresting voice even now.

III

The fundamental weakness of the man as a critic, literary or social, has been the journalism complex, an ingrained part of him now like the length of his stride and the lines of his autograph. Life he has seen from the standpoint of the city newspaper; he is always looking for news values; he is always obsessed with contemporaneousness. No repose here, no contemplation, no perspective, no basis of patient research. Everywhere impressions, everywhere snapshots, one-day classics, everywhere improvisations made with the infernal press-hour close at hand. It is flashily brilliant, with here and there an oasis of critical insight that is genius, flashes that make one wonder what might have been had journalism not infected the very marrow in his bones. For journalism, as I have said in an earlier study, is a deadly disease, a city disease engendered by the lack of moral and intellectual sanitation in journalistic centers and by the steady diet of one thing never varied. It is a disease that lays hold inevitably upon the newspaper worker who remains for any length of time in the miasma of this most deadly of all extra-hazardous trades. The phosphorus of it eats into the bones and turns the very sky into mucus. The blight that is upon our literature to-day comes from the fact that the greater number of its practitioners have at one time or another been gassed in this arsenical area and rendered unbalanced, unable thereafter to see life steadily or indeed to see it at all with sane eyes. The man has read few books, though he has skimmed many thousands for review; in his book reviews he has looked first of all for news values, like a reporter interviewing a celebrity and then printing only the one indiscreet statement made in half an hour's talking, decorating it with red headlines and "screamers." They are unbalanced, impressionistic. They are "prejudices," not open-minded criticism—good reporting.

Again to quote from my earlier estimate:

The curse of the journalist is that he has lost his horizon. His work he pitches ever to the almighty Now. He must be heard instantly: he must bring methods and materials startlingly new or see his work drop dead from the press. When he speaks he must speak in falsetto; when he means three he must say nine.

Hence O. Henry and O. Henryism, stuff spiced for jaded palates, hence Jack London and Upton Sinclair and Theodore Dreiser. Stronger and stronger must be the dose if the blasé reader, his senses dull to near deadness by repeated sensation, is to "sit up and take notice." Note such sweeping generalizations as these:

In the whole canon of O. Henry's work you will not find a single recognizable human character; his people are unanimously marionettes. . . .

The business of poetry, remember, is to set up a sweet denial of the harsh facts that confront each of us—to soothe us in our agonies with emollient words—in brief, to lie sonorously and reassuringly. . . .

Then a leap to the Victorians, the crape-clad pundits, the bombastic word-mongers of the campus school—H. W. Boynton, W. C. Brownell, Paul Elmer More, William Lyon Phelps, Frederick Taber Cooper, et al. Here, undoubtedly, we have learning of a sort. More, it appears, once taught Sanscrit to the adolescent suffragettes of Bryn Mawr—an enterprise as stimulating (and as intelligible) as that of setting off fire-works in a blind asylum. Boynton is a Master of Arts in Eng-glish literature, whatever that may mean. Brownell is both L.H.D. and Litt.D., thus surpassing Samuel Johnson by one point, and Hazlitt, Coleridge and Malone by two. The learn-ing of these august *umbilicarii,* for all its pretensions, is pre-cisely the sterile, foppish sort one looks for in second-rate college professors. The appearance is there but not the sub-stance.

Enough. The man has Ambrose Bierce's "Devil's Dic-tionary" at his elbow, a set of O. Henry for vocabulary use, and one of Mark Twain for cynicism.

To Newton Arvin he is a humorist, "a humorist of a very high order." I also so classified him a decade ago. Not now. He is a wit of the Ambrose Bierce order, a worker in burlesque most delightful at times, a phrase-maker extraordinary, a capturer of similes and metaphors of vaudeville quality; but humor is a thing of the heart, it is apart from slapstick and vaudeville, it is a glow from the regions of sentiment, not a slap on the back and a roar of laughter. Pathos is one of its ingredients, and to pathos our Baltimore cynic is aseptic completely. He turns from it with sneering contempt to contemplate with approval the gawky coarseness and primitive revelings of Jim Tully. The Greek and Latin classics with their piti-able Antigones and Jocastas are to him "geysers of pish-posh." Everywhere sneers at the strugglers for "culture" in "jerk-water colleges," "jitney geniuses," "fugitives from the six-day sock and saleratus *kultur* of the cow and hog states." As a newspaper man he wants news values, gusto, bounce, "punch," success, up-to-dateness, venture-someness, slang, newness, wit. His epigrams are all from the head, a "Devil's Dictionary" thicker than Bierce's.

IV

Mencken's is undoubtedly the most raucous and the most arresting voice that has been raised thus far in protest against the age of "Triumphant Democracy." In his literary criticisms he has stood for the autochthonous, the genuine, the unconventional, the uncensored. For poetry that is mere "pish-posh," to use his own diction, for sentiment that is mere sentimentality, for money-mindedness, for soulless jazz, he has unlimited contempt. And, therefore, on the whole he has been a constructive force constantly on the saner side of literary art.

One statement in Goldberg's colossal glorification, "The Man Mencken," I myself can approve: the comparison of Mencken's critical methods with those of Poe. Let me quote:

Coming to pure poetry, I find a curious resemblance between Poe and Mencken. Poe, you will recall, ruled out of the province of poetry all passion, which he defined as "intoxication of the heart." . . . Mencken's attitude toward poetry is similarly characterized by the suspicion of passionate abandon. . . . He enjoys poetry after he has told himself that it is *an illusion consciously entered into*. His surrender is conditional. There is, in Poe, something—nay, very much—of this desire consciously to control the creative impulse. At bottom, such a desire is Utopian. It assumes the impossible,— the ability to discover the unconscious origins of art, to trace its genesis from intuitive chaos to reasoned fulfillment. . . . In Poe the imagination conquered, though everywhere the reason throws its glaring light. In Mencken, the reason conquered, though almost everywhere the imagination sheds its grateful glow.

Then he quotes Lowell's lines:

Three fifths of him genius and two fifths sheer fudge,

.   .   .   .

Who has written some things quite the best of their kind,
But the heart somehow seems all squeezed out by the mind.

Now there are fudge and genius in Mencken. And in Mencken, too, "the heart somehow seems all squeezed out by the mind."

Excellent. The basis of Mencken's criticism most assuredly is Utopian. To condemn so large a proportion of things established implies a standard of measurement, a bench-mark from which to begin surveys of the political and social and literary area surveyed. Like Poe, he is an aristocrat with a contempt for the herd. Like Poe, he is an individualist, standing always on his own feet, demanding originality. Like Poe, he abhors feminism, reformers, and conventionality, and like Poe he will rush to the help of persecuted friends and laud them though their work—as does Dreiser's—violates all his standards of excellence. And, finally, like Poe, he is fundamentally intellectual with a flair for scholarship.

Scholar he is not, though his knowledge covers a most surprising area; no American critic has known more, or known stuff more varied. Diligence he has had to the last degree, but no great depth. When scholarship is mentioned his defenders point to his "The American Language," 1919, surely a remarkable book, but one not to be considered in connection with exact scholarship. Entertaining it is, unique, but hardly authoritative, the work of a reporter with a vast knowledge of the contemporary, but weak in the fundamentals of linguistic history and full of error.

For a decade his influence was enormous. He struck at American complacency, at narrow provincialism, at superstitious veneration for the outworn and for ignorance, and at the reduction of life's values to a material basis. An aristocrat in our American democracy, he has stood as a Greek patrician in the days of Pericles might have stood deploring the contaminating influences of barbarism. The things he has damned are for the most part things that needed damning. His exaggeration of current evils: the feebleness of the American clergy, the lack of stamina in the college professoriate, the inanity and illiteracy of the average American, the hollowness of 100% Americanism, and the like—was needful if anything was to be accomplished. A single Mencken, not a group nor a school of Menckenites, was needed in the war decade in our America, and he came. One may compare him to what in the oil regions is called a "go-devil," a bomb of dynamite exploded in a "petering" well. Sometimes the blast converts the lifeless thing into a gusher.

One must not overlook the courage of the man. He has stood against established orders, he has committed *lèse majesté* until, had he lived in the Germany of William the Little, in the days before the World War, he would have collected prison sentences aggregating a thousand years. He has always been the leading defender of an author when the charge of pruriency has been brought against him. He was one of the first to proclaim Dreiser and Cabell, and he has championed for the most part the more violent of the Western rebels. Nor does he scrap all writers save the contemporary. Of the gods of the old Valhalla he champions Emerson, Cooper, Melville, Poe, Mark Twain, and to a degree even Whittier and Thoreau.

A twentieth-century Amos, debauched by journalism: the temptation is irresistible to dwell most on the side of the debauchery. From a hundred angles has he laid himself open to attack. One is nettled most, however, by the superlatives of his admirers. To the least inspired and most voluminous of his biographers and critics he is "the man who debunked American literature," he is "the Baltimore anti-Christ," he is the man who "sits in judgment over judging America, shaping a new generation," he is "the Lucifer of the American Paradise, leading the revolt of the angels." There is need of Mencken items monthly under the head of *Maryland* in the "Americana" department of the "American Mercury," and there is need of a new prayer in the prayer-books for delivery from the superlatives of one's friends.

V

That his influence is on the wane does not need to be said. He rose on the wave of cynicism following the war, and he was powerless to adapt himself to returning normalcy. The change of base from the "Smart Set" magazine to the "American Mercury" in 1924 was the beginning of the end. The big horn ceases to startle if it is blown too often. The "Americana" department, once mildly amusing, is pathetic now. To the new generation in whose hands lies the future it is a weariness. Shouts of "boob" and "moron" and their synonyms are for schoolhouse play grounds. No people or class are ever reformed by invective or by muck-rake exposure long continued. One shout of "Wolf! Wolf!" is helpful, but not a thousand. To raise the taste and the standards of a nation one needs but to continue work of the standard required. To make your neighbor improve his grounds, improve your own. The shouting and the tumult dies; the loud cymbal solo quickly bores; the feet of the young men are at the door.

Those influenced by Mencken, the Menckenii, the "young intellectuals" deplored by Sherman, are for the most part to be found among the contributors to the volumes "Civilization in the United States," 1922, edited by Harold E. Stearns, and "These United States" (two volumes) edited by Ernest Gruening, 1923. Their methods have been for the most part like those of their leader Mencken—destruction with no attempt at reconstruction. But surely the older critics have given them cause for rebellion. According to Norman Foerster, self-appointed leader of the younger "new humanists," the period has been one "cursed with the obscurantism of mere facts, of historical data unvitalized by the higher activities of reason and imagination. Our literary scholars have fallen victims to the mechanistic tendencies of the age; and in their pseudo-scientific wanderings into the fields of literary history, general history, and psychology, have lost nearly all perspective and ability to evaluate the writings either of their own age or of the past." [1]

[1] "The American Scholar: A Study in Litterae Inhumaniones," 1929.

The more brilliant of the newer critics are Van Wyck Brooks, of Harvard, whose "Ordeal of Mark Twain," 1920, and "The Pilgrimage of Henry James," 1925, fluttered for a time the critical dove cotes; Joseph Wood Krutch, professor at Vassar since 1924, Carl Van Doren, professor at Columbia, Henry S. Canby, professor at Yale, and Lewis Mumford, authority on civic architecture.

BIBLIOGRAPHICAL REFERENCES

"Pistols for Two," Owen Hatteras, 1916. Hatteras is a pseudonym for Nathan and Mencken. The work is autobiographical and valuable, a storehouse of fundamental facts for future biographers. To be used, however, with caution.

"H. L. Mencken: Brief Appreciations and a Bibliography," Burton Rascoe and others, 1920.

"A Prophet in C Major" in "Sidelights on American Literature," F. L. Pattee, 1922.

"Americans," Stuart P. Sherman, 1922.

"Portraits Real and Imaginary," E. Boyd, 1924.

"Bibliography of the Writings of H. L. Mencken," C. Frey, 1924.

"The Man Mencken: A Biographical and Critical Survey," Isaac Goldberg, 1925.

"H. L. Mencken," Ernest Boyd, 1925.

"A Short View of Menckenism in Menckenese," J. B. Harrison, 1927.

"Menckeniana: a Schimpflexicon," 1928.

"The Critic and American Life," Irving Babbitt. "Forum," February, 1928.

"The Modern Currents in American Literature," Paul Elmer More, republished from the *Forum*, 1928, as "The Demon of the Absolute," New Shelburne Essays, volume I, 1929.

CHAPTER XXV

THE LATER ESSAY

I

THE old literary form variously defined under the general head Essay was ephemeralized during the period, contorted into new forms, and well-nigh lost. The so-called familiar essay, the personal essay, the "essay proper," gradually faded out. The period as a whole was not keyed to the contemplative and the unhurried. More and more it demanded the swift, the informative, the dramatically pitched: the condiments, the *hors d'œuvres,* the spiced evanescence of the one-day classics. The gentle, chatty monologue of the Elia essay could not endure the fierce sun of the journalistic age.

An aristocratic thing this personal, this familiar essay, "always written for a little clan." Democracy has been against it. The all-leveling daily and weekly press cares not at all for aristocratic traditions. The effect, says Odell Shepard, "has been two-fold. On the one hand we have a complete abandonment of every mark of distinction—the learning of Lowell, for example, the serene elevation of Emerson, the frosty individualism of Thoreau—and a frank catering to the multitude. On the other hand we have the innumerable writers of 'articles,' who struggle month by month and even day by day to satisfy America's enormous appetite for information upon things in general. In neither of these camps is anything done for the true essay." Editorials, "articles," book-reviews, "how to do it" papers, interviews, biographical sketches, critical articles, narratives of things seen and done, have come in a flood, but most of them have been mere ephemeræ, stuff made to perish with the pulp-paper news-sheet in which they appeared.

That survivals still persist—hold-overs from the more leisurely years, and that there still survives "a little clan" that demands the Elia salads with their evanescent flavors, the gentle, the unhurried, the stylistically turned, witness the twelve volumes of Agnes Repplier strewn in gentle fragments through the magazines of forty years, and the equally gentle essayings of Crothers, and Dallas Lore Sharp, and David Grayson with his adventures in contentment, and Louise Imogen Guiney, and Charles S. Brooks. Few indeed of all our better writers during the forty years past who have not at some time stolen into the quiet area and written their Elia musings, even Mencken among them, and Sinclair Lewis.

II

During all of the forty years of the period the Dean of our familiar essayists has been Agnes Repplier of Philadelphia. Spurning the more glittering rewards of the novel, the dominating art form of her time, she has clung to her one ancient instrument and has mastered it. The last she is, and the most worthy, of the vanishing tribe of the Elias.

So fully was she in major tune even in the eighties that I considered her at length in my earlier study, "American Literature since 1870." She first came into notice, I said, in 1886 when one of her essays came to Aldrich, who was delighted with it and who made haste to introduce her to the "Atlantic" circle. Two years later came her first volume, "Books and Men," and since that time, her essays, goodly in number and scattered through many magazines, have become a well-known feature of the times. Themes she takes to suit her fancy, apparently at random, though more often phases of her beloved "happy half-century".:

"A Short Defense of Villains," "Benefits of Superstition," "The Deathless Diary," "The Accursed Annual," "Marriage in Fiction," and all other topics pertinent to Dr. Johnson's little world.

There is French blood in her veins, therefore wit, vivacity, measure, style. Irony often is in her pen, and gentlest satire. The basis always is critical, yet never is she guilty of violence and Menckenese. One may open at random: this of a popular modernness:

There are American newspapers which print every day a sheet or a half-sheet of comic pictures, and there are American newspapers which print every Sunday a colored comic supplement. These sincere attempts to divert the public are well received. Their vulgarity does not offend. "What," asks the wise Santayana, "can we relish if we recoil at vulgarity?" Their dullness is condoned. Life, for all its antics, is confessedly dull. Our absurdities may amuse the angels (Walpole had a cheerful vision of their laughter); but we cannot be relied on to amuse our fellow men. Nevertheless, the colored supplement passes from hand to hand—from parents to children, from children to servants. Even the smudgy blacks and whites of the daily press are soberly and conscientiously scrutinized. A man, reading his paper on the train, seldom skips that page. He examines every little smudge with attention, not seemingly entertained, or seeking entertainment, but without visible depression at its incompetence.

Could anything be more gentle, anything more caustic?

Twelve volumes has she written, with something like one hundred and fifty of these Repplier "conversations," each the length of an Elia, and each as chattily brilliant as a Holland House dinner table with a Sydney Smith. Read "The Gaiety of Life" in "Compromises," or "A Kitten" in "In the Dozy Hours," or "Guides: A Protest" in "Varia." What Holmes did with his "Autocrat" she has done for our period, and with more of depth and sincerity.

Philadelphia, conservative, reverent toward the past, enamoured of ancestry, has preserved most completely the eighteenth-century atmospheres. Boston during our period has done little for the essay proper save to publish it in the "Atlantic" when supplied from extra-Bostonian pens. Her leading essayists after Holmes, Howells, and Crothers, she imported from the West. In New York the shadow of the sky-scrapers has cast a upas-tree blight upon everything not journalistic. Hear the latest young Philadelphian essayist, Christopher Morley, born in 1890, Rhodes Scholar at Oxford, columnist after 1920 in New York City:

In that frenzy of haste and friendliness, where the traveller must even struggle against his well-loved comrades for the endangered command of his own soul; where silly half-truths are so fashionable and so well rewarded that even the desire to write honorable candor easily grows dim; where sometimes one almost attains the ultimate and most fearful disillusion —that God Himself is in a hurry; in that jungle·be wary and be calm, my soul. The whole jungle conspires and rustles with menace; it is thick with beauty and terror; how swiftly the creepers wind you in if you try to pause for reason and peace. . . . Magnificent, terrible jungle of New York! Like Mowgli, you must learn to run with the wolves, and learn to love them, for they are lovable and brave. But be wary, O soul. There will come a time when you must return to live with men.

III

The most versatile literary figure—essayist, critic, Bohemian, scholar—that Philadelphia produced, however, during the period, the most remarkable indeed that the period produced anywhere, was James Gibbons Huneker, 1860–1921.

From the·first Huneker was for the few, the Bohemian few, who know thoroughly the *revolté* areas of modern European literature and art. To the commonalty he was first known, as far as he *was* known, in 1917 through Mencken's essay, later published in his "Book of Prefaces." No introduction more startling:

Huneker comes out of Philadelphia, that depressing intellectual slum, and his first writing was for the Philadelphia *Evening Bulletin*. He is purely Irish in blood, and is of very respectable ancestry, his maternal grandfather and godfather having been James Gibbons, the Irish poet and patriot, and president of the Fenian Brotherhood in America. . . . Philadelphia humanely disgorged Huneker in 1878. His father designed him for the law . . . but like Schumann, he was spoiled for briefs by the stronger pull of music. . . . In the year mentioned he set out for Paris to see Liszt; his aim was to make himself a piano virtuoso. . . . He stayed in Paris until the middle 80's, and then settled in New York.

For the rest of his life he was a journalist, a critic of music for various New York journals, becoming in time the leading critic in this especial province of art that America has produced. His first book, "Mezzotints in Modern Music," appeared in 1899, then a series of volumes dealing with music, among them "Chopin" and "Liszt." For ten years he was associated with Rafael Joseffy, as teacher of piano at the National Conservatory, New York.

But music, though his major interest, soon became only a part of his journalistic activities. In the prime of his powers he undoubtedly was, in all that concerned certain areas of contemporary European art and literature, the most erudite critic that America has yet produced. His knowledge of Bohemian Paris and all that emanated from it, including gossip and statistics of bibulous capacities, was most amazing. He knew personally and intimately a surprisingly vast circle of creative souls—all, perhaps, of any note in his own day, more especially, however, those of the Bohemian world. To our literary criticism he was what Whistler was to our art.

No other essayist and critic of the period, not even Mencken, has been more fearless in his advocacy of anti-Puritanism, or more outspoken concerning his Europeanized ideals. In style he was a Mencken before Mencken had begun to write. Painstakingly he had learned composition and vocabulary over his Poe and his Carlyle and his French decadents. Stumbling upon a paragraph like this unsigned, to whom would you attribute it?

Whether he [G. B. Shaw] will ever vouchsafe the world a masterpiece, who can say? Why demand so much? Is not he in himself a masterpiece? It depends on his relinquishment of a too puritanical attitude toward art, life, and roast beef. He is too pious. Never mind his second-hand Nietzsche, his Diabolonian ethics, and his modern version of Carlylean Baphometic Baptisms. They are all in his eye—that absolutely normal eye with the suppressed Celtic twinkle. He doesn't mean a word he utters. (Who does when writing of Shaw?) I firmly believe he says his prayers every night with the family before he goes to his Jaeger-flannel couch.

His versatility and his powers of swift composition—5,000 words a day for weeks—were almost unbelievable. In 1912 this was his outline of a month's work:

I've interviewed Lloyd George (*New York World*), Joseph Conrad (*Times*), Matisse (*Times*), the Futurists (*Metropolitan Magazine*), Richard Strauss (the same), also for the *Times;* and I must write specials on Vienna (*Century Magazine*), and Prague for *Scribner's;* not to mention articles on "Modern German Art" (which I abominate) and one on Vermeer.

Bohemianism was his undoing. With all his knowledge, he added little to our knowledge of things we would know. He has seen and conversed with all the demigods of his day, and he does nothing but tattle endlessly about their feet of clay. His "Steeplejack"—with his knowledge of music and of literature, what might it not have been? Instead, recorded Bohemian wassailings with the great. Mencken in his introduction to the Selected Essays of Huneker describes with high glee the increasing flow of scandal, bibulous adventure, and hitherto untold secrets concerning the great that came belching from the man with each added glass of beer, as if the thing were a deed to record for future years. "Variations" and "Ivory, Apes and Peacocks" have much in them worth while, but Bohemianism always is a squandering of powers. By temperament the man was headlong, impatient, a grasper at half-truths, a maker of epigrams at the expense of truth. His sarcasm was withering. His greatest pleasure was making "imbeciles realize their imbecility," and by imbeciles he meant all not in step with his own little company.

Imperatively is he for the few, the esoteric few, the adepts who can enter the penetralia of classic music or who can read with knowledge his adventures with Max Stirner, Villiers de l'Isle Adam, Paul Cézanne, "O. W.," and the like. Completely does he take for granted on the part of his reader his own omniscience; everywhere allusions which only the virtuoso may endure without gasping, for he is writing not for all, he is writing not at all for imbeciles.

And yet everywhere in his volumes there are illuminating flashes, even illuminating articles, that are for all. For example, I know of no other such penetrating estimate of Walt Whitman as he has given in a single brief essay. He searches every nerve and gland of the old poet—"hankering, gross, mystical, nude"—like a surgeon at a clinic, and despite your convictions as you open his report you leave it perforce with his.

Without suggesting effeminacy, he gave me the impression of a feminine soul in a masculine envelope. When President Lincoln first saw him he said: "Well, he *looks* like a man!" . . . The truth is, Walt was not the healthy hero he celebrates in his book. That he never dissipated we know; but his husky masculinity, his posing as the Great God Priapus in the garb of a Bowery boy, is discounted by facts. . . . With all his genius in mentioning certain unmentionable matters, I don't believe in the virility of these pieces, scintillating with sexual images. They leave one cold despite their erotic vehemence; the abuse of the vocative is not persuasive, their raptures are largely rhetorical. . . . But in the underhumming harmonics of "Calamus," where Walt really loafs and invites his soul, we get the real man, not the inflated humbuggery of These States, Camerados, or My Message, which fills the Leaves with their patriotic frounces. . . . He has at times the primal gift of the poet—ecstasy; but to attain it he often wades through shallow, ill-smelling sewers, scales arid hills, traverses drab levels where the slag covers rich ore, or plunges into subterrene pools of nocturnal abominations— veritable regions of "the mother of dead dogs." Probably the sexlessness of Emerson's, Poe's, and Hawthorne's writings sent Whitman to an orgiastic extreme, and the morbid nasty-nice Puritanism that then tainted English and American letters received its first challenge to come out into the open and face natural facts.

And so on to the end of the clinic.

A strange duality, this man of two worlds, two dominating natures at war, this Herman Melville back from epic adventure in Europe among demigods of Nature and of naturalism, and working out, ever in fevered haste, Moby-Dicks, chaotic, mostly trash, yet here and there glimpses of a serene on the highest levels of literary inspiration. Mencken has done his best, and I think wisely, to rescue the man from the fate of Herman Melville, but other generations alone can do the work. Perhaps, even as with the creator of "Omoo," a century from now he may be rated as first magnitude in the new American ephemeris. At present, however, he seems headed, despite his undoubted powers, for oblivion.

IV

For two decades one found often in the "Atlantic" and elsewhere contemplative little essays by Samuel McChord Crothers, a Westerner, born in 1857 in Illinois and educated for the ministry at Princeton and Union Seminary and Harvard. From 1894 to his death in 1928 he was pastor of the First Church of Cambridge and preacher to Harvard

University. Then his essays began to appear in the "Atlantic Monthly": soon they became one of the "features" of the magazine, sermons out of the pulpit many of them, books and men as seen by a Boston divine in his study and along the streets. Plentiful in humor, often gently satirical, always readable, they were a pleasant feature of the entire period. "A Social Survey of the Literary Slums" is a sample of his titles, and his volumes, some sixteen of them, bear such pleasant names as "The Gentle Reader," 1903, "The Pardoner's Wallet," 1905, "The Pleasures of an Absentee Landlord," and "Among Friends."

More widely known, however, to "Atlantic" readers, has been Bliss Perry, born in Williamstown, Massachusetts, in 1860, educated at Williams College, professor successively at Williams, Princeton, and Harvard, and for ten years after 1899 editor of the "Atlantic." As was naturally demanded of a successor to Lowell in the editorial chair, the slant of his essay work has been for the most part critical. Professorial, most of it, expository, often illuminating. Provincialism, however, has sat upon him like a birth-mark. Ten years in a University of Kansas chair would have helped him amazingly. The "quality of the 'Atlantic'" has been the bugbear that has shadowed him. His most distinctive work has been his editings and his little volume of familiar essays "Pools and Ripples," 1927.

The tribe of the essayists, one finds after all, has been large even in the un-Elia-like days of our jazzed-up period. With more space one might expand upon the critical work of John Jay Chapman, whose summation of Whitman in "He patiently lived on cold pie and tramped the earth with triumph" still clings to me; of Gerald Stanley Lee, who located philosophy reduced to epigrams on Mount Tom; Charles S. Brooks, whose "Chimney-Pot Papers," 1919, bring back for a moment the golden days of the old essay-forms; of Ludwig Lewisohn, Walter Pritchard Eaton, William Lyon Phelps, and George Jean Nathan.

V

One variety of the essay, the editorial, has been made every day like paving brick in enormous quantities through the entire period. And yet the day of the editorial had passed long before the new century opened. In the days of Horace Greeley the editorial was a power not only political, but social and even literary. But with the coming into journalism of three or four compelling personalities —Bennett, Dana, Pulitzer, Hearst—the emphasis was shifted to the news columns. The editorial became a mere tradition, made always in old-time quantities, but seldom read and usually lacking in "punch" and general effectiveness. Always, even in its most vigorous days, was it a thing of the moment. Says William Allen White:

> Probably no literary form is as evanescent as the editorial; perhaps it may not have sufficient distinction even to be called a literary form. Probably the editorial is a mere literary impulse, and a book of editorials, all gathered up and bound in book paper and in book type, is a book of vagrant fancies, passing wishes, hopes that died a-borning. It is like the record of a subconscious mind—curious, heterogeneous, helter-skelter, mad.[1]

White has the distinction of having written the one editorial of the period that achieved national and international attention and that has survived even to the present as a kind of classic. His "What is the Matter with Kansas?" published in the "Emporia (Kansas) Gazette," August 15, 1896, was undoubtedly an influence upon our national journalism. The spirit of the new West was in it; it was original and alive. Let us quote a sample paragraph:

> What's the matter with Kansas? Nothing under the shining sun. . . . What's the matter with Kansas? We all know;

[1] "The Editor and His People"—Editorials by William Allen White selected from the "Emporia Gazette," by Helen Ogden Mahim, 1924.

yet here we are at it again. We have an old mossback Jack-
sonian who snorts and howls because there is a bath-tub in the
State House; we are running that old jay for governor. We
have another shabby, wild-eyed, rattle-brained fanatic who
has said openly in a dozen speeches that "the rights of the
user are paramount to the rights of the owner"; we are running him for Chief Justice, so that capital will come tumbling
over itself to get into the State. We have raked the old ash-
heap of failure in the state and found an old human hoop-
skirt who has failed as a business man, who has failed as an
editor, who has failed as a preacher, and we are going to run
him for Congressman-at-large. He will help the looks of the
Kansas delegation at Washington.

White has achieved literary distinction in areas outside
of his newspaper work. His "The Court of Boyville,"
1899, became within its limited field a juvenile to compare
with "Tom Sawyer" and "Huckleberry Finn," his "Stratagems and Spoils," 1901, and "A Certain Rich Man,"
1909, were strong novels of the muck-rake period, and his
later volumes combining Kansas wisdom and humor have
been entertaining episodes.

VI

One of the most discussed of our *littérateurs* for three
decades of the period, and one of the most problematical,
was Elbert Hubbard, who aspired to be the American
William Morris and who achieved a unique following.
His Roycroft shop, his book-making experiments, his "Fra
Elbertus" clientele, his "Philistine," the last and most
permanent of the "Yellow Book" imitations, had at one
time an enormous vogue. As a lecturer he vied with Hamilton Wright Mabie and William Lyon Phelps in popularity, and his "Little Journeys" booklets circulated like
souvenirs from the Holy Land.

The man was a Westerner, Illinois-born in 1856. After
a varied career as a general worker, he became partner in
a soap-manufacturing concern and after accumulating

$75,000 resigned and went to Harvard, where the monotony quickly disgusted him. Then came a tour of England where he met G. B. Shaw and then William Morris, who inspired him with the fires of warfare against the conventional and the shoddy. The result was the Roycroft shop and the accumulation at length of the Fra Elbertus congregation—mostly feminine. His tragic death in the sinking of the *Lusitania* put a sudden end to his influence though not entirely to his Roycroft work.

A biography of the man, "Elbert Hubbard of East Aurora," by Felix Shay, has an introduction by Henry Ford. Ford, who was attracted by the shop-management ideas of his subject, wrote of him as a pioneer:

Elbert Hubbard demonstrated the power of an idea when conceived by an independent mind and supported by intelligent industry. His shop became a place of pilgrimage to men and women who were interested in the handicrafts and who dreamed of a greater idealization of common life. Whether Mr. Hubbard made a permanent contribution toward that end, the event will declare, but certainly he served to keep the thought alive in his time.

But Hubbard aspired to literary leadership and by many was hailed as a major writer, among them Edwin Markham the poet, to whom he was one of the leading literary forces of his day. His summing-up of Hubbard gives us the widely popular conception of the man during at least two decades:

The Roycroft work, of course, was only one phase of Hubbard's activities. He was known for his wide-spread lectures, his syndicated newspaper columns, his own magazines, and booklets. *The Philistine,* a magazine of protest, edited by Hubbard, was a national institution, and its smack and tang has not been repeated. His "Little Journeys to the Homes of the Good and the Great," a series of brief and vivid biographies, was an inspiration. The far-flung "Message to Garcia," casually issued in the March *Philistine* at the opening of the twentieth century, was another turning point in Hubbard's career. This parable on Initiative and Thoroughness was a message to American Youth. It caught the eye and ear of Big Business. "It has," says Shay, "been printed and reprinted more times than any other piece of literature in the world—the Bible excepted. It has been translated into forty or fifty languages and dialects. The New York Central issued a first edition of 100,-000 copies, then 400,000 more, then an edition of a half a million. For more than twenty-five years it has been printed and distributed in millions of copies each year."

Time has been less kind in its verdicts. More and more is it seen that the man was a showman, that his literary work was without originality and without wearing qualities. A picturesque figure he was, one much advertised, one perpetually in the public eye, but one with no more qualities for permanence than a morning newspaper.

BIBLIOGRAPHICAL REFERENCES

"Essays of Our Time," Sharon Brown, 1928.
"The Bookman Anthology of Essays," John Farrar, 1923.
"Contemporary Essays," W. T. Hastings.
"A Book of Modern Essays," B. W. McCullough and E. B. Burgum, 1926.
"Essays and Essay-Writing," W. M. Tanner, 1917.
"Modern Essays, Two Series," Christopher Morley, 1921, 1924.
"Contemporary Essays," edited by Odell Shepard, 1929.
"Modern Essays," edited by John M. Berdan, John R. Schultz, Hewette E. Joyce, 1915.

JAMES G. HUNEKER, 1860–1921

"James Huneker" in "A Book of Prefaces," H. L. Mencken, 1917.
"Steeplejack," 1920 [Autobiography].
"Letters," edited by Josephine Huneker, 1922.
"Intimate Letters," edited by Josephine Huneker, 1924.
"Bostonia and Bohemia" in "Some Contemporary Americans," Percy H. Boynton, 1924.

"Essays by James Huneker," selected, with an introduction by
    H. L. Mencken, 1929.
"James Huneker" in "A Book of Prefaces," 1917; and
    "Huneker, a Memory," in "Prejudices," Third Series,
    1922, H. L. Mencken.

CHAPTER XXVI

THE NEW BIOGRAPHY

I

FROM the days of Cotton Mather, with his "lives of sixty famous divines" and of the governors "that have been shields unto the churches of New England," down to the present day the making of biographies has been in America a diversion and a profession. The lives of Washington alone fill an alcove. All our "statesmen" from the days of the Revolution and all our writers, even those of minor note, have been made subjects for at least a volume. Every generation must rewrite the biographies—all of them. With every year the recording tribe grows larger. In a single twelve months of late have appeared seven lives of Lincoln, six of Woodrow Wilson, and eight of Napoleon.

To Washington Irving an adequate biography was chiefly setting and "times." Through the four volumes of his carefully wrought book George Washington moves as a majestic, shadowy super-presence riding like a god the clouds of war and directing the storm. With the passing of the New England school of writers came the era of authorized biographers, official lives done by designated literary executors, biographies made in the presence of all the letters and papers held by the family. The result always was the creation of mythical personages often saintlike in their uniform perfectness. The treatment of Longfellow by his brother Samuel, of Hawthorne and Emerson by their children, are examples. The printing of letters carefully selected and edited as in the case of Lowell's by

Charles Eliot Norton, or Mark Twain's by Albert Bigelow Paine, came as a later fashion.

With the beginnings of the new realism in the eighties and nineties came the advent of the "True" variety of biography. Paul Leicester Ford for instance in 1896 wrote "The True George Washington," and three years later did the same thing for Franklin. A historian's attempt it was to strip off the mythical furbishings and present only historical evidence.

After the opening of the new century, biographical methods changed rapidly. Realism had advanced into "Zolaism" and "Naturalism." A generation had arrived disillusioned, it would seem, in its very cradle, and it found the old biographies stuffed with "bunk," mere mythologies, repositories of carefully selected goody-goody letters. The time for "debunking" had come. The whole biographical alcove had to be reorganized to the fundamentals. Biography henceforth was to read like a novel by Dreiser. Especially was sentimentalizing to be wiped out, and the squeamish avoidance of all baser phases of the subject must be rectified. The man must be painted like Cromwell, warts and all.

Moreover, the *dramatis personæ* of biography soon suffered a revolutionary change. No longer "statesmen" alone, nobles, kings, distinctive men of letters, posed as subjects. No one too humble for biography; picturesqueness alone was needful. On the book-stands now were more and more to be found biographies of sensational minor figures: Anthony Comstock, John L. Sullivan, Lord Timothy Dexter, Kit Carson, Jim Fiske, and Jesse James.

A phase it was of the scientific trend of the period, the increasing worship of "the god of things as they are"—a phrase on all lips in the late nineties. "Truth!" everywhere, the demand for Truth,—the *whole* truth. S. S. McClure felt it in 1893. Of the first number of "McClure's" Albert Shaw wrote in the "Review of Reviews," "It throbs with actuality from beginning to end." Biography it gave in

what it called "Human Documents," "Interviews of
Famous People" by other famous people—everywhere
actuality. Bok's aim was precisely the same. It was time to
strip from the biographies the embroidery of romance and
get to grips with the facts. Even the new Nature writers
caught the spirit of the times, as witness Seton's psychoanalysis of "Old Silverspot" the crow in "Wild Animals
I Have Known," 1898, and "The Biography of a Grizzly,"
1900.

II

The modern psychographic treatment of biography as a
distinct art has as its most prominent American representative Gamaliel Bradford, who has done the major part of
his work in essay lengths. A Massachusetts man, born in
Boston in 1863, he essayed Harvard but was compelled to
relinquish his course early by ill health. Ill health also kept
him from the strenuousness of professional life and set his
thoughts upon authorship as a life-work. His first published book came in 1895, a book of essays with the title
"Types of American Character," a groping toward the
biographical form which later he was to make his own.
Not till 1912 with his study of "Lee the American" did he
gain full control of the method by which he is now known.
Then followed in 1914, "Confederate Portraits," in 1916
"Union Portraits," the same year "Portraits of Women,"
in 1923 "Damaged Souls." Other similar volumes have
come at frequent intervals. Already he has done what apparently he set out to do, made a national gallery of typical
Americans, both men and women.

To make his type of mental and physical portrait, the
biographer must be philosopher, research specialist, painter,
literary master. To quote George Alexander Johnston,
"The new biography . . . is essentially detached and dis-
passionate. The biographer of the new school is neither a
hero-worshipper nor a detractor. His standpoint is that of
the spectator, the impartial observer. It would not be pos-

sible for the biographer to interpret with perfect understanding the lives of diverse characters if he did not maintain a standpoint of detachment." And again:

However detached the new biography may be, it always insists on the enduring humanity of its characters. Its personages are not dead specimens to be examined through the microscope of time. "Human beings," says Strachey, in his preface to "Eminent Victorians," "are too important to be treated as mere symptoms of the past. They have a value which is independent of any temporal processes—which is eternal, and must be felt for its own sake."

For such portraits endless research is necessary, a notebook filled with special instances. Then from ten thousand jotted-down details the biographer must select the vital few that illuminate. Patiently, touch by touch, he builds up his character, creates the summation of an individuality by an accumulation of revealing moments, till the portrait is a speaking likeness. To Bradford, even as it was to Sainte-Beuve in his critical studies, nothing is unimportant, nothing too trivial to place in his balance or add to his analysis. From tiny straws may be charted the main currents of a life. More detached is he than his English rival Strachey, more unprejudiced, less artificial. The Englishman, to give a rounded impression of Queen Victoria's reign, reproduces the panoramic procession of men and events that must have reviewed themselves in her memory as she lay dying at Windsor. It is an artificiality, it is not the truth: who knows what passed through the mind of the dying queen? Bradford too has not escaped the "personal equation" error; who can free himself from it? His very title "Damaged Souls," for example, implies a thesis. Why select the seven he does: Benedict Arnold, Thomas Paine, Aaron Burr, John Randolph, John Brown, P. T. Barnum, and Ben Butler? All human souls are damaged. A thesis is a thing to defend, and to defend it one must select carefully his facts and ignore all counter facts.

Johnston in his review of the three European biographers, Maurois, Strachey, Ludwig, mentions Bradford not at all. A few dates are illuminating: Strachey's "Eminent Victorians" appeared in 1918, his "Queen Victoria" in 1921; Ludwig's "Goethe" came in 1919; and Maurois's "Ariel," based on the life of Shelley, came in 1923. By 1918, the date of Strachey's first volume in the new manner, Bradford had already issued his "Lee the American," "Confederate Portraits," "Union Portraits," "Portraits of Women," and "A Naturalist of Souls." Being an American, Bradford naturally has not attracted the attention of European or Europeanized critics.

In addition to all the rest, there is a literary quality to the man's work rare in biography. The work of the older school was all too often sub-literary, mere factual recordings for reference rather than for continued reading. To Bradford, biographical portraiture has but a single excuse for being: it is to be read, and read with pleasure to the reader, it must be interesting, it must be compelling in its interest. And early he evolved a style as well as a historical method, one combining clearness, dramatic movement, wit, humor, charm.

III

What the Europeans have introduced new in biographical method has been the novelized biography of the variety presented by Maurois and Ludwig. After the publication of "Ariel" the form swept over America like a contagion. It came at a critical moment. Realism in its extreme forms, realism as exemplified in such novels as those of the young Hemingway, of Dos Passos with his "Manhattan Transfer" novel, of the English Lawrence and Huxley, had alienated many readers. To go back to the sentimentalism of E. P. Roe or Harold Bell Wright romance was manifestly impossible: science and the new age had brought skepticism and disillusion. But now came a form with all the thrill and dramatic movement of the romance, yet based upon the actual happenings of an actual person. The springs of romance, supposedly stopped forever by the new science, were bursting out again through this hitherto solemn and prosaic stratum. The characters were not fictitious; they were real people, historical personages. One could be entertained and yet be learning the history of his country. Hence the amazing sweep of the movieized biography, the story biography, the reproduction of a picturesque life in terms of its most exciting episodes. Brigham Young, P. T. Barnum, John L. Sullivan, Aaron Burr— American history told in terms of the uniqueness of such lives became a thing that even lovers of Harold Bell Wright fiction could enjoy. Following the Shelley biographical talkie "Ariel," came such biographical-novelizations as "The Magnificent Idler," a story of Walt Whitman, by Cameron Rogers, and "The Dreamer," by Mary Newton Stanard, a movieizing of Poe. In such work, declares Clifford Smyth, "the weakness rather than the strength of the romance-biography is apparent. Flesh and blood never had part in these heroes of melodrama; they are distortions, impossible idealizations that bring into grateful relief the old-fashioned biographies, with their ample notes and fine array of 'authorities.' "

The result has been, during the decade of the twenties, an orgy of biographizing that has gone to extremes. Biography in the hands of many of the younger workers has meant a bringing forth of materials which have mercifully been covered by time and a making of them central. In the opinion of Albert Bushnell Hart there has come "the Historical School for Scandal," a debauching influence. "The public get all the 'kick' of fiction with the soothing sense that they are dealing with something 'real' and 'scientific.' " And he continues most wisely with this:

Democracy and universal education have combined to bring into existence a vast reading public, without cultural standards, which is anxious to consider itself as good as any other class in any other age. Was there in the past a statesman who was really great and incorruptible? Was there a poet or painter who believed in the greatness of his art? Were there scholars who cared nothing for the world? Were there men who, human enough and failing often for that reason, yet kept a sense of the intrinsic worth of human nature? Then away with them! Or show us that they not only sinned but were hypocrites, little men, smaller even than ourselves! Let us bolster up our self-esteem not by slowly working out for ourselves again a new philosophy of life but by pulling down all men of all times to our level. Set up the bebunking school of biography and be quick about it. The school has had an enormous vogue because its public is large.[1]

Dismissing such lives as those of Billy the Kid, and Jesse James, of Wild Bill Hickok, and John L. Sullivan—studies of America in terms of its lesser and its more sinister personalities (and these personalities presented only in terms of their most dramatic moments)—despite this element of melodrama, many remarkable biographies scholarly, critical, interesting, modern, have appeared during the past decade. Lives of Poe, notably "A Study in Genius," by Joseph Wood Krutch; of Longfellow—"A Victorian American," by Herbert S. Gorman; of Hawthorne—"The Rebellious Puritan," by Lloyd Morris; of Poe again— "Israfel," by Hervey Allen; of Franklin—"The First Civilized American," by Phillips Russell; of Lincoln— "The Prairie Years," by Sandburg—all these show the direction of the present times, the recataloguing and revaluation of the American Valhalla by the new generation. Nothing more natural: time alters all things. Trees that to one in the heart of the jungle hide the very sun in their seeming dominance, become mere shrubbery when viewed at length from the hill-top.

IV

The real soul of the later period one finds best perhaps in autobiography, a literary form that increased in viru-

[1] "Current History Magazine," November, 1929, and February, 1930.

lence, like an epidemic. The writers of no period have viewed themselves with more of consternation. A symptom again is it of realism, of wonder expiring in the presence of science, of a growing sense of futility. Failing to understand life, they could at least describe the phenomena of their own experiences with it. Hence such outpourings as Dreiser's "A Book About Myself," and Anderson's "A Story-Teller's Story."

Two varieties of autobiography there have been: first, the Howells variety—"how to be a Howells," Gerald Stanley Lee once expressed it. The realist turned his microscopes upon himself and told how to be a boy in a log cabin, told of the courses of reading it had taken to mold him, of the shaping influences of his literary friends and acquaintances. Then there was Garland, who spent the last years of his life telling of Garland and the Garlands—five volumes at present romanticizing the Middle Border and its central figure Hamlin Garland:

"A Son of the Middle Border," 1917
"A Daughter of the Middle Border," 1921
"Trailmakers of the Middle Border," 1926
"Back Trailers from the Middle Border," 1928
"Roadside Meetings of a Literary Nomad," 1930

But more influential, if less entertaining, have been the voices of futility, the most dominating being that of Henry Adams whose "The Education of Henry Adams," finally issued during the war period, 1918, drowned for a time even the war-voices and surpassed in sales even the British or Spanish novel which was leading all the best-selling fiction.

Chronologically Henry Adams, 1838–1918, belongs in the period before 1890. His influence, however, came in the *fin de siècle* and the two decades that followed. A man of remarkable endowments and remarkable opportunities— he was a son of Charles Francis Adams of the old Massachusetts dynasty, private secretary to his father in England, editor of the "North American Review," 1869–1876, professor in Harvard University, 1870–1877—he was admirably fitted for the work that after 1877 he proposed for himself, a rewriting of American history. Six works, some of them biographical, he produced, culminating in his distinctive "History of the United States During the Administrations of Jefferson and Madison," 1889–1891, nine volumes. With the ninth volume he laid aside his history disillusioned. Why write history? The foolishness of it!

The year 1891 was to him an intellectual and moral climacteric. The growing dominance of science and realism and commercialism and adventure with the materialistic forces—who could work in such a tide? And he retired in his studies to a monk-like contemplation of the Middle Ages. Modern life more and more he viewed as futility, an attempt to reap the wind. A decade before, he had thrown out a cynical novel "Democracy," withholding his name, however, from the title-page. For a decade he lived in spirit in the realms glorified by Scott, and in 1913 be emerged with a volume "Mont Saint-Michel and Chartres," in every way an American classic. In his introduction to the volume, Ralph Adams Cram, the architect, acclaimed it as "one of the most distinguished contributions to literature and one of the most valuable adjuncts to the study of mediævalism America has produced. . . . Seven centuries dissolve and vanish away, being as they were not, and the thirteenth century lives less for us than we live in it and are a part of its gaiety and light-heartedness, its youthful ardor, its childlike simplicity and frankness, its normal and healthy and all-embracing devotion."

But even as Henry Adams was bathing himself in his medievalism he was creating his masterpiece of negation, his autobiography of an American Hamlet; he who might have led his age, was "sicklied o'er by the pale cast of thought," content to sulk and cynicize, and quit. America

was in need of an intellectual leader, a Moses to conduct
her to the land of promise that was her right, and timidly
he could do nothing but publish fictional cynicism anonymously, and even, for very fear, withhold his "Education of
Henry Adams" for twelve years after it was finished. The
arraignment of Stuart Sherman was not too severe:

He and his kind, bred on the classics, and versed in law
and European diplomacy, were anachronisms, survivors out
of the classical eighteenth century, belated revelers in the
Capitol. A multitude of unknown or ignored forces had
developed in his absence, and had combined to antiquate him,
to extrude him from the current of national life, and to in-
capacitate him for a place in the public councils. This singular
new nation was no respecter of grandfathers. It took its superior men wherever it found them. It picked its chief statesman out of a log cabin in Illinois, its chief military hero out
of an Ohio tannery, its most eminent poet from a carpenter's
shop, and its leading man of letters from a pilot-house on the
Mississippi. Such standards! Henry spent a lifetime elaborating his grand principle of the degradation of energy, to
explain to himself why the three grandsons of two Presidents
of the United States all ended miserably: one as President of
the Kansas City stock-yards; one as a member of the Massachusetts bar; while one had sunk to the level of a professor
of history at Harvard.

A voice from the virile new West. But the brilliancy of
the book, the character-sketching, the international perspective at every point, made it at once one of the vital
creations of the period, a masterpiece of literature, a stone
in the road that—whatever be one's moral or intellectual
or national reactions—one cannot avoid. Its influence upon
the younger men has been pronounced. As a single example
consider such a paragraph as this from the young Harvard
Ph.D., Van Wyck Brooks:

Of the innumerable talents that are always emerging about
us there are few that come to any sort of fruition. The rest
wither early; they are transformed into those neuroses that

flourish in our soil as orchids flourish in the green jungle. The sense of this failure is written all over our literature. Do we not know what depths of disappointment underlay the cynicism of Mark Twain and Henry Adams and Ambrose Bierce? Have we failed to recognize, in the surly contempt in which the author of "The Story of a Country Town" habitually speaks of writers and writing, the unconscious cry of sour grapes of a man whose creative life was arrested in youth? Are we unaware of the bitterness with which, in certain letters of his later years, Jack London regretted the miscarriage of his gift? There is no denying that for half a century the American writer as a type has gone down to defeat.

To verdicts like this the older generation may object with all emphasis, but there is no court of appeal. The future of all of us is in the hands of the generation coming on. We may deplore, but it is well for us to listen to their voices and cease from egotism.

BIBLIOGRAPHICAL REFERENCES

"Aspects of Biography," André Maurois. Translated from the French by Sydney Castle Roberts. Based upon a series of lectures delivered at Cambridge, England.

"This Hard-Boiled Era," Katharine Fullerton Gerould, "Harper's Magazine," CLVIII–247.

"Modern Biography," edited by Marietta A. Hyde, 1926.

"Henry Adams" in "Shelburne Essays," Eleventh Series, Paul Elmer More, 1921.

"The Adams Family" in "Americans," Stuart P. Sherman, 1922.

"Literary Life in America" from "Emerson and Others," Van Wyck Brooks, 1927.

"Psychography" in "A Naturalist of Souls," Gamaliel Bradford, 1926.

A LIST OF FIFTY NOTEWORTHY BIOGRAPHIES AND AUTOBIOGRAPHIES OF THE PERIOD

Adams, Henry: "The Education of Henry Adams."

Addams, Jane: "Twenty Years at Hull-House."

Aldrich, Mrs. Thomas Bailey: "Crowding Memories."
Antin, Mary: "The Promised Land."
Atherton, Gertrude: "The Conqueror."
Barrus, Clara: "John Burroughs—Boy and Man."
Beer, Thomas: "Stephen Crane."
Beveridge, Albert J.: "The Life of John Marshall."
Bok, Edward: "The Americanization of Edward Bok."
Boyd, Ernest: "Guy de Maupassant."
Bradford, Gamaliel: "Damaged Souls."
Bruce, William Cabell: "Benjamin Franklin, Self Revealed."
Carnegie, Andrew: "Autobiography."
Chapman, John Jay: "William Lloyd Garrison."
Clemens, Samuel L.: "Autobiography."
Damrosch, Walter: "My Musical Life."
Davis, Charles Belmont: "Adventures and Letters of Richard Harding Davis."
Epler, Percy: "Life of Clara Barton."
Garland, Hamlin: "A Son of the Middle Border."
Gompers, Samuel: "Seventy Years of Life and Labor."
Hendrick, Burton J.: "Life and Letters of Walter Hines Page."
Howe, M. A. DeWolfe: "Barrett Wendell and His Letters."
Howells, William Dean: "My Mark Twain."
James, William: "Letters of William James."
Jefferson, Joseph: "Autobiography."
Keller, Helen: "The Story of My Life."
Kennan, George: "E. H. Harriman."
Lowell, Amy: "John Keats."
McClure, S. S.: "Autobiography."
McElroy, Robert: "Grover Cleveland."
Mitchell, E. P.: "Memoirs of an Editor."
Muir, John: "The Story of My Boyhood and Youth."
Paine, Albert B.: "Mark Twain, a Biography."
Palmer, G. H.: "The Life of Alice Freeman Palmer."
Perry, Bliss: "Walt Whitman."
Riis, Jacob A.: "The Making of an American."
Sandburg, Carl: "Abraham Lincoln: the Prairie Years."
Seitz, Don C.: "The Life and Letters of Joseph Pulitzer."
Steiner, Edward A.: "From Alien to Citizen."
Tarbell, Ida M.: "In the Footsteps of the Lincolns."
Thayer, William Roscoe: "Life and Letters of John Hay."

Thomas, Augustus: "The Print of My Remembrance."
Trudeau, Edward Livingston: "Autobiography."
Washington, Booker T.: "Up from Slavery."
Weaver, Raymond M.: "Herman Melville, Mariner and Mystic."
Werner, M. R.: "Brigham Young."
White, William Allen: "Woodrow Wilson."
Whitlock, Brand: "Forty Years of It."
Wiggin, Kate Douglas: "My Garden of Memory."
Woodberry, George Edward: "Edgar Allan Poe."

CHAPTER XXVII

THE LATER FLOOD OF FICTION

I

DURING the decade of the twenties prose fiction dominated all other literary forms. In the book-lists of a publishing season the fiction section has at times been longer than all the other literary sections combined. To go back over these lists for a decade is to discover that fiction-making is not a thing governed by inflexible laws. Fiction is a fashion that changes often and without apparent reason. Most of the best sellers of even a decade ago seem as out of date when we read them to-day as do the hats of the same period.

To chart the voluminous product of the period, to try to discover a passage through it and evaluate its thousand islands, is a task all but impossible. At the same time realism and romanticism—Dreiser and Cabell; at the same time the old and the new—Howells and Hemingway; at the same time Ben Hecht and Harold Bell Wright, Sinclair Lewis and Zane Grey, Mrs. Wharton and "Mrs. Wiggs of the Cabbage Patch," Henry Fuller and Ring Lardner.

The decade was shadowed heavily by the war-smoke that hung for years over the world after the guns had become silent. The generation that had furnished the shock-troops for the war had marched back into civil life disillusioned and bitter. They had been heroes, men sent out as on a crusade to save civilization, "to make the world safe for Democracy," and they were now reading the Versailles treaty. At home they found themselves no longer heroes but men out of a job, while the profiteers who remained at home flourished. The war and all war experiences were for a time taboo as themes for literature. Readers were supposed to be "fed up" on all war stuff. But the war nevertheless dominated the literary output. It had blunted the moral sensitiveness of the whole world. The license of war-time, trench coarseness and materialism, the sex-life of great masses of young males held long without feminine companionships of the better kind, the atheism and pessimism bred in the camps—had made for license, for a return to jungle ethics and ideals. A generation debauched by war was expressing itself in fiction. And there had come novels overloaded with sex, with coarseness, with the logic of futility.

Among the leaders of new after-the-war school of novelists we may name Ben Hecht, John Dos Passos, Scott Fitzgerald, Ernest Hemingway, Glenway Wescott, Elizabeth Madox Roberts, E. E. Cummings, Kenneth Burke, and Evelyn Scott, and with them such modern instances as Jim Tully. Honest doubters unquestionably, presenters of "God's Truth" it may be. One of their number has ventured to say that already this school has done work that it is safe to add to the undisputed classics: "The Enormous Room," by E. E. Cummings, "My Heart and My Flesh," by Elizabeth Madox Roberts, the introductory essay to "Goodbye, Wisconsin" by Glenway Wescott, "Orient Express" by John Dos Passos, certain short stories by Kenneth Burke, and "The Sun Also Rises" by Ernest Hemingway. He may be right.

II

Though I deal but little with the work of any writer whose first book was issued after 1920, let me for a moment dwell upon this modern school. Let me at sheer random select a typical volume: it is "Strange Fugitive," a first novel, written by young Morley Callaghan in 1928.

First of all, the story is placeless. The opening exposition has in it not a hint of locality. Manifestly, however, it is American—it touches the Canadian border where "boot-legging" is a big business, and for the most part the action takes place in a city. There is no plot, no working of all the lines of action to a culminating climax. It is a characterization novel of the Sinclair Lewis type. It is as exclusively concerned with the doings of Harry Trotter, brutal boss, wife-beater and wife-murderer, fugitive from justice, bootlegger, adventurer with women, as was Lewis's novel with the single figure of George Follansbee Babbitt. Everywhere Harry Trotter. The spot-light is always upon Harry Trotter. The sections of the story might be given such titles as "How Harry Trotter Bossed His Gang," "How He Thought He Had Murdered His Wife," "How He Played Checkers," "How He Behaved in a Road-house with a Mistress," "How He Killed in Cold Blood a Rival Boot-legger," and "How He Was Exterminated by Rival Gun-men."" Everywhere the influence of Lewis: his methods of making his central character alive by recording everything he does, even his habitual reflexes. Compare Trotter's bathing technique with that of Lewis's character in section three of "Babbitt." In both novels realistic detail with nothing omitted. It is "movie stuff," often ludicrous, but it renders the man alive. At least, he *seems* alive; he is a gargoyle like a Dickens character, yet he carries conviction to the reader.

Everything objective. Never does the author assume the omniscient attitude in presenting his characters: he shows them photographically with no synthesizing general statements to make us understand them better than they understood themselves. Soon we awake to the fact that we are not studying primarily an individual. The man is a type. In becoming acquainted with him we have been introduced to an area of masculinity. Here is the masterful, animal-istic, selfish, physically dominant male so abundant in our free America—the cave-man type, the sheik type. Women are fascinated with Trotter, they "fall for him," they pursue him. And the man gets to be fastidious in his choosing of mistresses. He has ideals of his own as to beauty. The old romancers described their heroines in terms of their hair, their complexions, their grace, their winsomeness, their feminine helplessness, their sylph-like forms. To Trotter a woman was beautiful only when she had perfect legs. Every female in the book is described first of all in terms of her legs.

The novel is short: it contains less than 80,000 words. Mrs. Wharton's "Ethan Frome," always reckoned as a short story, has 40,000; Henry James's short stories often were longer. "Henry Esmond" has 209,000 words; "Jane Eyre," 200,000; "Middlemarch," 163,000.

The leading characteristic everywhere is actuality, bare actuality. Why admit such vulgarians into the realms of serious literature and report as if they were important their sordid, often blasphemous, and even obscene picturings and conversations? "Why not?" answers Sinclair Lewis. "Folks are folks. The hobo, the itinerant tailor, and the hick, just as much as the college professor, the business man, and the society woman." And Henry K. Webster for the younger writers lays down this as the law:

The critical fashion of the day proscribes the exceptional. Unless the novelist wishes to rest under the imputation of romanticizing, let him write about commonplace people, dull, inarticulate and earthbound as the majority of mankind admittedly are.

There are other reasons than the war to account for such work. In an era when every one can write and every one is reading, one must do something out of the ordinary to be heard. Pessimism has more news value than optimism, illicit sex adventure more front-page importance than normal, virtuous living; divorce after a married week more "kick" for the reader than the records of silver weddings.

The chief indictment of the older critics, however, concerns quite another matter. These youngsters are illiterate:

they do not know the English language. Let George Santayana, scholar, philosopher, poet, critic, present the leading indictment against this most modern of literary generations:

They have had too much freedom, too much empty space,
too much practice in being spontaneous when there was nothing in them to bubble out. Their style is a sign of this: it is
not merely that they have no mastery of the English language as hitherto spoken, no clear sense of the value of words,
and no simplicity; they are without the vocabulary of the
idiom of cultivated people. That might all be healthy evolution, even if a little disconcerting to us old fogies, who can't
keep up with the progress of slang. America has a right to a
language of its own, and to the largest share in forming that
pigeon-English which is to be the "world-language" of the
future. But it is not comparatively only that the style of the
young radicals is bad, nor in view of traditional standards: it
is bad intrinsically; it is muddy, abstract, cumbrous, contorted, joyless, obscure. If their thoughts were clear, if the
images in their minds were definite and fondly cherished, if
their principles and allegiances were firm, we should soon
learn to read their languages and feel it to be pure and limpid,
however novel its forms.[1]

Writers of this younger school have not voiced themselves in the older and more conservative magazines, not
even those as modern as the "Saturday Evening Post."
The magazine editor lives in close touch with his subscribers and must not violate the ideals and the prejudices
of his readers and his advertisers. If a young writer is to
get a "Strange Fugitive" novel published he must issue it
as a book.

III

And this brings us to a second group of contemporary
novelists: the standard magazine group. There is no better

[1] "Young Radicals in America" ("Forum Papers," First Series),
edited by Benjamin A. Heydrick, 1924.

way to approach this school of fictionists, their work most often in the best-seller lists when freed from magazine serializing, than to consider the prize-contest conditions governing such work.

Preëminently has the past decade been sensational with prize contests for novels and short stories, in some cases the prizes offered running into five figures. The aim in every case has been purely commercial. Viewed without sentiment, they have been simply methods of securing a manufactured product that can be marketed with profit to the promoters. To succeed, this product must appeal strongly to the class that buys and reads magazines and afterwards books. The findings, therefore, of these boards of judges may be taken as voices of the period: their standards are the higher standards of the times.

Considering such novels as those winning the distinctive prizes offered by the Harpers, "The Able McLaughlins," Margaret Wilson, 1923; "The Perennial Bachelor," Anne Parrish, 1925–6; "The Grandmothers," Glenway Westcott, 1927–8; "The Dark Journey," Julian Green, 1929–30; "Wild Geese," Martha Ostenso, which won the "Pictorial Review" prize in 1925, and "Jalna," Mazo de la Roche, which won the $10,000 "Atlantic Monthly" prize in 1927 "from twelve hundred manuscripts entered from all parts of the world"—considering these, one is able to say that the elements conducive to winning are six in number.

The first quality demanded is originality: something having an atmosphere, a "feeling" that is different, modern, alive. Second, the treatment must be realistic. Everywhere the thrill of actuality: life as really lived by men and women, unidealized, untinted. Third, there must be no plot, no artificial ordering of episodes to a culmination at the end. In the formal romance of the past there was a hero and a heroine and a villain, and two casts of subsidiary characters, the good and the bad. The struggle for possession of the heroine against the machinations of the villain culminated usually in a victory for righteousness and the happy uniting of the persecuted couple. Such artificiality clashes with all the demands of actuality. Instead of plot, a series of episodes illustrative of the current of living in the area under observation.

The fourth demand concerns characterization, a major canon of late. The prize novelist must specialize carefully in character development. Each character, so far as the novelist is able to accomplish it, must live before the reader vividly, completely, and so compellingly that there shall always be the feeling of actuality. As to background, it must always be merely background, the drop-curtain before which the action moves. The tendency at present is to handle it impressionistically, by mere hints and implications rather than by photographic listing of details. An "atmosphere" is to be caught, implied in a phrase or a sentence, made subservient always to characterization and action.

Again, there must be good workmanship, or—as the workers themselves prefer to term it—artistry. Readers now are impatient of verbosity. They want quick results, movement, interest, sharply defined pictures, brilliant epithet, frequent "wise-cracking" epigram. And finally there must be humor. For a best seller a dash of humor is all but imperative.

The demands for the short story are fundamentally the same. In 1926 after the three contests conducted by "Harper's Magazine," contests that called forth ten thousand manuscripts, I made this observation upon the volume containing the winning stories:

A study of these prize-winners makes clear the canons for fiction held by this board of judges. First, it would seem that the short story of the present moment must avoid the conventional; it must be startlingly fresh and original in background and characters and atmosphere and situation, as compellingly fresh, indeed, as is the title of what to me is the best tale in the collection, W. D. Steele's "When Hell Froze." Again, a story must not end with its final sentence: it must end suggestively, tantalizingly, hauntingly. Then too, it must be human, built upon the bed-rock fundamentals of humanity as it actually is, a glimpse of naked souls. And last of all, the tale must be well-told with vigor of style, lightness of movement, flashes of epithet, and distinction of dialogue.

And right here a suggestive note. More and more the novel, in every area of it, has felt the pressure of the short-story technique. Almost all of our present-day writers of fiction served their apprenticeship as short-story writers, escaping to the novel as soon as they had won for themselves a market value, and they have not wholly outgrown the habits of their apprentice years. The older novel was long and complicated. Until well into the nineteenth century it was a three-volume affair. By the mid-century it had shrunk to two volumes: nearly all of Cooper's romances were "two-deckers," as were those of Paulding and Simms. By the end of the century the two-volume novel, save for the one paleozoic survival Dreiser, had become extinct. Then gradually the novel became thinner and thinner—I mean in physical proportions—more like the short story in its make-up.

The short story has taught the modern author the value of compression. The old romancer rambled at will. He might interrupt anywhere the flood of his narrative to preach a sermon or elucidate a matter or describe the circle of the horizon. Charles Egbert Craddock used to pause at an exciting moment and write a page descriptive of the shadows that were running along the sides of the mountains in her background. Everywhere to-day the demand for compression. Perhaps the "movies" too have exerted an influence: always the story must progress or the reader will "skip" to where it does progress.

Moreover the short-story technique as to dialogue has touched the novel. The endless "said he," "said she," "answered he," "tittered she," and all such "conversational tags" have been largely dropped. The dialogue runs now without tags, cracklingly, swiftly, often epigrammatically.

Finally, the modern novel is more and more concentrating upon brief intervals of life, even as the short story is. The older novel prided itself upon the fact that it had room in which to trace the growth of its characters. After living with a hero through three volumes which sometimes carried him from childhood perhaps to middle life, one understood the man. One has seen the evolution of his strengths and his weaknesses even as they are seen in actual life. In the short story, with its inexorable demands for brevity, this manifestly is impossible. The short story deals with a climactic moment. There is not time for development of character. More and more the novel is obeying the same law; more and more is it becoming a lengthened short story.

In this school of the more serious novelists are the five major women writers I have already treated, a half dozen of the leading short-story writers, notably Alice Brown and Zona Gale, and in addition Mary Austin, Dorothy Canfield Fisher, Elsie Singmaster, Elinor Wylie, and Kathleen Norris.

IV

In the next order come the professional best sellers who aim at hundreds of thousands in multiplied editions, of late largely feminine. Typical individuals of this amazing group are Gene Stratton Porter, Edna Ferber, Mary Roberts Rinehart, and Fannie Hurst. According to Mencken this variety of fiction constitutes the "middle layer" of contemporary American literature:

By the middle layer I mean the literature that fills the magazines and burdens the book-counters in the department-stores—the literature adorned by such artists as Richard Harding Davis, Rex Beach, Emerson Hough, O. Henry, James Whitcomb Riley, Augustus Thomas, Robert W. Cham-

bers, Henry Sydnor Harrison, Owen Johnson, Cyrus Townsend Brady, Irvin Cobb and Mary Roberts Rinehart.[2]

Mrs. Porter's day of fame began with her "Freckles,"
1904, a volume which in ten years sold 670,733 copies. "A
Girl of the Limberlost," 1909, and "The Harvester," 1911,
were almost equally successful. "At the time of her death,
December 6, 1924, more than ten million copies of her
books had been sold." "Altogether," says Overton, "it
seems reasonable to estimate her earnings at $2,000,000
in a productive period of twenty years and about twenty
books." Literature with her and her class had become "big
business." Mary Roberts Rinehart presents this picture of
the successful modern novelist:

My business with its various ramifications had been growing; an enormous correspondence, involving business details,
foreign rights, copyrights, moving picture rights, translation
rights, second serial rights, and dramatizations, had made
from the small beginnings of that book of poems a large and
complicated business. I had added political and editorial writing to my other work, and also records of travel. . . . Filing
cases entered into my life, card-index systems. To glance into
my study after working hours was dismaying.

The elements entering into "Freckles" and "The Harvester" are not greatly different from those composing E.
P. Roe's "Nature's Serial Story," a best seller of 1884: a
moral basis, a romantic and sentimentalized love interest,
and a liberal salting with specialized Nature study. It was
the formula for the Harold Bell Wright novels of later
years, as we shall see.

Other elements came into the recipe with every new
season. In 1913 came Eleanor H. Porter's "Pollyanna,"
a novel built upon the theme of the war lyric soon to come,
"Smile, Smile, Smile." For a year or more Polyannaism

[2] "Prejudices": Second Series—"The National Letters," H. L.
Mencken, 1920.

swept the nation; it added a new word to the American vocabulary, and incited "the intellectuals" to wrath.

Edna Ferber in 1915 added the modern business woman complex and became, according to her publishers, "the highest paid story-writer in the world."

In the fourth grouping is that vast area of fiction represented in the seventies and the eighties by E. P. Roe, an area lying in the lower reaches of Mencken's "middle layer," sub-literary yet enormously read. The American people do not *read* Mrs. Wharton and Margaret Deland, they pass by the standard magazines, they cannot read Cabell, they balk at Lewis and Dreiser, and Hemingway and Hecht and Wilder they never heard of. They want, vast numbers of them, action and sentiment and romance, with liberal spicery of morals: literature movie-minded, yet "safe."

Most typical is the case of Harold Bell Wright, whose books during the twenty years after 1903 ran second only to the Bible in number of sales. Expressed in modern newspaper "English," "the man has had more genuine reader-fans during the period than any other American novelist." The word is expressive. His publishers advertise that they can produce vouchers that they have sold, in America alone, 737,443 copies of each of twelve novels issued before "Exit," or 9,849,316 in all, and that two of them, "The Shepherd of the Hills" and "The Winning of Barbara Worth," sold each a million and a half copies. Though they were a full generation apart, one born in 1838 and the other in 1872, the parallel between Roe and Wright is close. Both were born in New York State in humble homes where toil came early and where schooling was perforce limited; both eventually entered the ministry, Roe as a Presbyterian, Wright as a Disciple; both were forced to retire from active pastoral work because of ill health, Roe to a farm in New York where he cultivated small fruits, and Wright, after eleven years in various churches in the rural West, to wanderings that finally ended at Tucson, Arizona, where he succeeded in winning a small farm from the desert. Both, denied a pulpit, sought to continue their religious work by means of fiction, and both, unliterary, untrained, largely unread save in religious classics, approached the novel from their own standpoints without models or masters. The result was the same in both cases: moral teachings first of all, sermons candied for "the general," novels readable even by Campbellites because written by a minister. Both talked to the multitude in language the multitude understood, and both touched only the major chords inherent in all life: mother, home, sentimental love, virtue rewarded, villainy triumphant for a time and then punished, and finally happiness for all the good.

Thus far the problem of Harold Bell Wright is simple. But there is a difficulty: not yet has it been explained how he found a man or men with faith enough in his fiction to organize a new publishing house that was to handle only his books. And it was to be no ordinary publishing house. Money for advertising was to be poured out without stint, the American News Company was to be ignored, distribution was to be pushed even into the smallest towns of even the sage-brush areas, and advertising was to be along the lines used by the manufacturers of soap, or collars, or breakfast foods. In the words of Grant Overton, this was the method:

Six months before a new Wright story is to be published, thousands of tradespeople all over the United States know that the story is to be published, and when, and with what enormous advertising placed in forty specified periodicals and several dozen newspapers it will be "pushed"; and then begins the steady succession of personal letters and even telegrams, circulars and placards and posters. Honest-minded persons in remote settlements discuss with enthusiasm and awe the prodigious sum of money to be expended on "just this one book, a *book,*" librarians grow anxious and advertising men eager, preachers prepare sermons, in thousands upon thousands of homes the Christmas gift to Mother is pre-determined,—until at last, in the wide-rolling wave of excitement, a vast surge of the people of simple faith and worthy ideals, the day comes when the book is born.

After they had issued some ten volumes the unique publishing firm was taken over by one of the old New York houses. These are Wright's books:

> "That Printer of Udell's," 1903
> "The Shepherd of the Hills," 1907
> "The Calling of Dan Matthews," 1909
> "The Uncrowned King," 1910
> "The Winning of Barbara Worth," 1911
> "Their Yesterdays," 1912
> "The Eyes of the World," 1914
> "When a Man's a Man," 1916
> "The Re-creation of Brian Kent," 1919
> "Helen of the Old House," 1921
> "The Mine With the Iron Door," 1923
> "A Son of His Father," 1925
> "God and the Groceryman," 1927
> "Exit," 1930.

Fundamentally the man is a preacher. "When I start to write a novel," he explains, "the first thing I do is to figure out why I am going to write it. Not what is the story, but why?" In other words, he selects a moral issue and announces a text.

I mull over this for a while, and when it is pretty straight in my mind, I write out an argument. No suggestion of plot, you see. No incidents, scenes, location, nothing done at first except the argument, but it is the heart and soul of the novel. The novel is merely this argument presented through the medium of characters, plots, incidents, and the other properties of the story. Next come the characters, each standing for some element or factor in the argument. Up to the last copying of *The Eyes of the World,* not a character had been named. They were called in the copy, Greed, Ambition, Youth, or whatever they represented to me in the writing of the story.

The moral basis determined upon, he could then work out an appealing setting—the Ozarks or the desert wilds "where a man's a man" and where Barbara Worths could be won. And he did it always with accuracy, calling in experts to check his statements at every point. One reads him with confidence. Earnest he is, honest, spontaneous, tremendously convinced of his own literary position, able as few others have been to speak the language of all the people and win them to the reading of books. Unliterary his work is, undoubtedly, as graded by absolute standards, but it has played its part in the literary education of the great American mass. No history of *American* literature can avoid him.

V

Since the war there has been an enormous demand for what Mencken would designate the third and bottom-layer variety of fiction. In the tragic epoch following the war every one sought escape. The demand was insistent: "Tell us stories that will take us out of ourselves; transport us to other scenes where life has no sadness; make us forget." In a late visit to Hollywood, California, Hamlin Garland found the town full of middle-aged winter tourists from his "Middle Border." They appeared to be "living on limited incomes, taking it easy after a life of hard work on the level lands of the blizzard belt"—people, in other words, of the vast American average. And this their intellectual life: "These farmers fill the moving-picture theaters and their taste is not high. . . . They also read books . . . but the books are not mine. They prefer, quite properly, Zane Grey and Edgar Burroughs; they are tireless consumers of detective stories."

The case is symptomatic: Harold Bell Wright no longer satisfies. The movies have come, and the "talkies." Completely in line is it, however, with all the American past. Only a short time ago we could have celebrated the centenary of Mrs. E. D. E. N. Southworth. Listen to Jay E. House, the columnist:

Mrs. Southworth's was the gentle hand which wrote seventy novels and encompassed the death of more than 200 arch-villains. For reasons now inconceivable, she persecuted approximately 500 heroes and heroines through interminable pages. It is likely that Mrs. Southworth held the all-time mortuary record. . . . If Mrs. Southworth was the queen of the killers, Mary J. Holmes was the princess of the lachrymal glands.

Then with the Civil War period came Robert Bonner's "Public Ledger," with Sylvanus Cobb, Jr.'s "The Gunmaker of Moscow," advertised as sensationally as the Wright novels a generation later. Thrilling, this early "Dumas of America," but moral. After pages of curdling melodrama he could end his novel with:

"And," added the pastor, while a tear of pride stood in his eye, as he looked for an instant into the face of his now happy wife, "all things above our proper sphere we will leave with God."

And there were Beadle's dime novels, and the Cap Collier detective stories, and "The Leavenworth Case" of Anna Katharine Green, early substitutes for movies and radio.

Every decade has its own brand: the nineteen twenties ran to Zane Grey, with his border tales of headlong adventure, cowboy movies in board covers, to Edgar Rice Burroughs with his amazing "Tarzan of the Apes" series, to Carolyn Wells, who in addition to a long list of detective tales, issued a volume entitled "Technique of the Mystery Story," presumably as a text-book for schools.

Completely has the decade surrendered to detective

stories. "The Circular Staircase" of Mary Roberts Rinehart, and later her dramatized thriller "The Bat," became for a time national events. The work of Willard Huntington Wright, who successfully concealed himself for a year behind the pseudonym S. S. Van Dine, has at times vied in sales even with the feminine best sellers. And there have been Melville Davisson Post, George Gibbs, Samuel Merwin, and names rapidly swelling into the dozens. The O. Henry audience they have inherited entire, and they have drawn recruits from even the "upper layer" of fictionists —Doyle and Chesterton in England, and Alice Brown in America.

So amazingly many these modern crime mystery tales that they are reviewed now in dozen lots several times, each publishing season. On a single page of a weekly journal, one finds reviews of eight such novels with these suggestive titles:

"Wild Justice," George A. Birmingham
"The Body in the Road," Moray Dalton
"The House of the Vanishing Goblets," The Edingtons
"The Black Door," Virgil Markham
"Who Killed Charmian Karslake?" Anne Hayes
"Mammon," Percival C. Wren
"Murder on the Marsh," John Ferguson
"The Gloyne Murder," Carl Clausen

And on the following page six more. The making of such tales has become an industry. Detective story magazines now, detective anthologies—among them "The Mammoth Mystery Book," "one thousand pages of excitement"; and, to crown all, The Crime Club, Inc., furnishing the best detective story of every month—"the newest thrillers." Note a few titles in their current advertising:

The Poisoned Chocolates Case, The Silent Murders, The Seven Stabs, Signed in Yellow, The Crooked Eye, The Body on the Floor, The Crimson Circle.

Surely the Deadwood Dick thrillers and the Nick Carters of the mid-nineteenth century "had nothing on" these lurid creations.

It is an inevitable accompaniment of a newspaper and "movie" age. Movement, action, plot, love interest primitive in its unconcealments, mystery prolonged until the last moment, and above all a masterful hero with whom the reader identifies himself. Narcotics, harmless perhaps as tobacco, but surely not literature as literature has been defined in the more spacious periods.

VI

Concerning the future of fiction in the new period that is soon to open, if it is not already with us, it is easy to be pessimistic. But hopeful signs are not wanting. James Branch Cabell, so many years with the minority, so many years a lonely soul refusing to surrender to cheapness and sensation, rendering only his best, has lately exulted in what he calls a "Dizain of the Doomed" (April, 1930, number of "Books") in finding himself with the new literary shock troops. "I had never hoped to include among my more enthusiastic followers such notabilities as Messrs. Norman Foerster, Harry Hayden Clark, Frank Jewett Mather, Gorham B. Munson, Granville Hicks, and Paul Elmer More." The "doomed" in his list are those who have taken from humanity the foundations they already had and have substituted nothing in return. For good or bad their work is done. "The manner of each of them is formed, is perfected and is known." They can add now nothing that is new. The period they represented is over. And what have they left us? Including himself in the list of the doomed, he contends that they are doomed because they worked without foundations, they took away hope, they merely destroyed.

Really that lack of a panacea is quite fatal to all literary pretensions. Man, breathing so precariously in the close shadow of death, and noting always the approach of the un-knowable, needs vitally some strong belief in one or another cure-all, very much as a child fretting in the night needs pare-goric. And almost any panacea will do—even our new human-ism will do, we fondly think, at a pinch—so long as the more happily obtuse of men can be hoodwinked into believing that tomorrow this talked-about panacea will begin to work, and everything will be put in apple-pie order everywhere. For it is the belief which matters: it is the belief which drugs. But these writers of the 'twenties have offered us nothing in espe-cial to believe in—and that, too, when almost any sort of polite lie would have served our despairing need.

Exquisite irony perhaps, the quintessence of pessimism in a way, yet based on truths fundamental.

CHAPTER XXVIII

NEWSPAPER BY-PRODUCTS

I

SINCE 1890 a new literary form has been evolved in America, the newspaper column, a phase of American humor, perhaps the latest development. Our humor, during the long evolution of it, has had three outlets: first, the spontaneous oral overflow wherever men may gather, especially at banquets and convivial assemblings, unrecorded, forgotten with its day; second, the humor of the professional entertainer—the Lyceum humor of such lecturers of the nineteenth century as Artemus Ward, Josh Billings, Robert J. Burdette, Mark Twain, James Whitcomb Riley, and Bill Nye; and third, the humor contributed to newspapers and comic journals.

During the eighties and the nineties this third class of humor entered the newspapers in small portions—"paragraphs"—to be inserted at random "in the run of the paper," wherever there might be space vacant. Some of it might be published under the head of "Jokes," "Small Shot," "Pebbles," and the like. O. Henry in 1887 was contributing to the Burlington "Free Press" what its editor called a "string of jokes"—"Your string for November just in." At the same time he was contributing to the New York "Truth," which classified its contributions as "Jokes, Ideas, Verses, Squibs, Poems, Sketches, Stories, and Pictures." It classified O. Henry's humorous contributions as "Sketches." "Paragraphs," however, was the inclusive name of all such newspaper ephemeræ. Says Jay E. House, veteran now among the columnists:

From along in the seventies until the late nineties a large class of paragraphers made mock and flourished. Many of them served small-town papers; all were anonymous and unknown outside the immediate neighborhood of their own narrow activities. . . . The old-timers were sung but unhonored. Their stuff permeated a nation. It was copied from Belfast to San Diego and from Bellingham to Tallahassee. But credit, when credit was given, accrued to the newspaper on which the paragrapher was employed. Thus *The Somerville Journal, The Germantown Telegraph, The Yonkers Statesman, The Danbury News, The Norristown Herald* and a number of other small-town newspapers impinged upon a national consciousness and became famous.[1]

This was the period of the "Danbury News" man— James Montgomery Bailey, 1841–1894; of the "Burlington (Iowa) Hawkeye" man—Robert Jones Burdette, 1844–1914; of Charles B. Lewis—"M. Quad," 1842–1924; of George W. Peck, who became notorious with his recordings of the doings of "Peck's Bad Boy"; and of dozens of others known equally well in their little day.

Between this group and the later columnists stand the transition figures of Eugene Field and George Ade, both of them employed on the same Chicago paper, Field to furnish one column daily and Ade two.

Despite the fact that others had furnished what might in a loose way be called "columns" long before his famous "Sharps and Flats" in the Chicago "News," Field is generally regarded as the father of the newspaper column. Certainly up to 1900 he was the only one who had ever made a column that was widely recognized. His Chicago work began in 1883 and continued until his death in 1896. Nearly everything of value to-day in his published works appeared first in this column. And yet it must be said that the greater bulk of all he wrote day after day for the woodpulp leaves of his newspaper is to-day veriest trash and

[1] "The Odyssey of a Columnist," Jay E. House, "Saturday Evening Post," September 5, 1925.

deservedly forgotten. Says Jay House in his revealing article:

> The work of the columnist is the most fleeting and ephemeral of all writing. I have so much of "Sharps and Flats" as was considered worthy of preservation between covers on the bookshelf at home. There is scarcely a gleam in it. Some years ago I had the impulse to reprint a column of Field's stuff. I was compelled to ravage the book from cover to cover to eke from it a thousand words which seemed to me to be worth the printing. Maybe I am no judge of that which is worthy of reproduction, but I doubt that Field wrote a column which would stand up in competition with a score of those turned out to-day.

II

In the opinion of House the modern column is a product of the new century: "the number of columnists in an active state of eruption in 1901 might have been counted on the fingers of one hand." "By 1900, the great club-swinging editors who lent to the always anonymous editorial page the color of individuality and the splendor of their names had passed, or were passing. . . . A pall of anonymity was settling over American newspapers. Then came the columnist marching singly and by twos and threes. In fewer than a dozen years, he was an army." No longer was he impersonal: the "ego" column had come. "Nothing so quickly palls upon the newspaper reader as a dead level of anonymity. For various reasons, he wants to know who 'wrote that piece.' He wants something to lay hold on or something to boot around. He likes to be in intimate touch with somebody on his favorite newspaper and he wants the individual identified. An 'I' or 'we' writer, properly identified, supplies the necessary individual touch and ties the reader to the newspaper with a silken bond. . . . Those who seek my *Capra hircus* may be broadly divided into two classes: one tries to humiliate me by direct expression of his loathing and disgust. The other goes to my employer in an effort to have me fired. The object of his concern is the newspaper itself."

III

Not all of this later army of columnists is by any means to be considered in a history of American *literature*. Only a few, by widest stretch of definition, may be reckoned as literary, and these only for infinitesimal bits from their daily outpourings. Looking at the "school" from the standpoint of good verse, Kreymborg for his "Our Singing Strength" selected eleven names, listing them alphabetically:

> Franklin P. Adams, 1881—
> Leonard Bacon, 1887—
> Gelett Burgess, 1866—
> Dana Burnett, 1888—
> Thomas A. Daly, 1871—
> Arthur Guiterman, 1871—
> Donald Robert Perry Marquis, 1878—
> Christopher Morley, 1890—
> Keith Preston, 1884–1927
> Edwin Meade Robinson, 1878—
> Bert Leston Taylor, 1866–1921

Not all of these are columnists, however, though all are skilful with the light guitar. Three of them stand preeminent as columnists, and they are leaders thus far in this most difficult of literary forms: Bert Leston Taylor, Franklin P. Adams, and Don Marquis. All of them were Westerners either by birth or by adoption. The column, indeed, has itself been Western by birth and evolution, from the vast midlands sprawling about Chicago, their center; then finally it was taken over by New York City which originates nothing. To quote Stuart P. Sherman, "Don Marquis is a typical New Yorker—that is to say, he was born in Walnut, Bureau County, Ill.—some sixty miles to the west of F. P. A., and three years earlier." [2]

Taylor was a New Englander, born in Goshen, Mass., but educated in the College of the City of New York. Entering journalism in 1895, by way of Chicago, he was able to establish in the "Daily Tribune" there a column, "A Line o' Type or Two," that soon attracted wide attention. Says Henry B. Fuller: "His broad column—broad by measurement, broad in scope, and a bit broad, now and again, in its tone—cheered hundreds of thousands at the breakfast-tables of the Middle West, and on its trains and trolleys." [3] With common sense and wit and exquisite verse and homely personalities and whimsies and critical comment on everything in the daily run of life, he became a veritable literary dictator, molding the thinking of thousands. And his death in 1921—he died of pneumonia—brought a peculiar sense of loss to a whole people.

Most of his flimsy-winged stuff perished with its day, but Taylor was a poet, a maker of *vers de société* of exquisite texture—light, faultless in technique, unstrained, tipped skilfully with irony but with irony never forced or harsh, and always at the end a climactic burst or an unexpected rhyme that brought a glow or often a laugh. Quoting from the well-known Preface to "Pride and Prejudice" the sentence: "This novel was written between October 1796 and August 1797, and offered to Mr. Cadell, who declined to see the manuscript," he could add such caustic comment as this:

> Deathless Cadell! Though long since turned to clay,
>   Your name lives on with the immortal Jane's.
> She sought you one rememberable day,
>   Humbly and had her labor for her pains.

[2] "Don Marquis, Poet"—"Critical Woodcuts," 1926.
[3] Preface to "The So-Called Human Race," Bert Leston Taylor, 1922.

To you the chance was offered to inscribe
 Upon her title-page your lustrous name,
But, true to the traditions of your tribe,
 You turned her down, and—gained a lasting fame!

At the heading of his column there were often such kindred lyrics as "The Dinosaur," the ballad "Bread Puddynge," "The Passionate Professor," and "Canopus":

When quacks with pills political would dope us,
 When politics absorbs the livelong day,
I like to think about that star Canopus,
 So far, so far away.

Greatest of visioned suns, they say who list 'em;
 To weigh it, science almost must despair.
Its shell would hold our whole dinged solar system,
 Nor even know 'twas there.

When temporary chairmen utter speeches,
 And frenzied henchmen howl their battle hymns,
My thoughts float out across the cosmic reaches
 To where Canopus swims.

When men are calling names and making faces,
 And all the world's ajangle and ajar,
I meditate on interstellar spaces
 And smoke a mild seegar.

For after one has had about a week of
 The argument of friends as well as foes,
A star that has no parallax to speak of
 Conduces to repose.

Often came Nature lyrics, bursts of lyricism uncynical and unhumorous in intent: poems distinctive, neglected as yet by anthologists. Like his prototype of an earlier decade, H. C. Bunner, he himself selected from his enormous mass of daily doings only the most carefully finished of his many lyrics for publication in book form. Two volumes only he permitted: "A Line-o'-Verse or Two," 1911, and "Motley Measures," 1913. Other collections have been made since his death but all his published work is now out of print, a thing that should not be.

The estimate of Franklin P. Adams, himself a master-columnist, is significant:

Though, to my mind, he was easily the best paragrapher that ever achieved the art of putting the front page, or the leading editorial, or a whole political, literary, or artistic situation into twenty-five words, his verses were even better than his paragraphs. . . . His output for twenty years was greater and its quality higher than those of anybody else in the same high profession of writing light, satirical verse. I hate the ranking system applied to artistic endeavor; but I place B. L. T. always on a plane with Calverley, and frequently far above him.

Taylor never wrote when he had nothing to say, and when he wrote he said what he had to say so much better than anybody else could say it that he must have been the despair of every columnist in the country. Nowhere in literature have results been achieved with greater or surer simplicity. The Taylor verse is sure; in each line is the utmost effort; he used to say that if you could write a 99% line in three minutes and a 100% line in nine hours, or nine days, there should be no problem of conduct; that though maybe nobody would know the difference, you were writing for yourself and nothing short of your uttermost was thinkable.[4]

Adams and Marquis are later, indeed latest, expressions, both working in the New York area, the former with a column entitled "The Conning Tower," the latter in one bearing the heading "The Lantern." Both are poets—first of all poets; both are of the "ego" group of self-recorders, intimately personal, chatty, gossipy, admitting the public seemingly into their very skeleton closets and inmost lives.

[4] Preface to "A Penny Whistle," Bert Leston Taylor, 1921.

Of the two Adams is the wit, Don Marquis the light guitarist.

Adams, born in Chicago, educated for a year in the University of Michigan, entered journalism in 1903 in his native city under the influence of B. L. T. A year later he was in New York working for the "Evening Mail." Like Field, he was enamoured of Horace, the columnist of old Roman days, and paraphrased him often in purposely outrageous diction. Surely the very human old lyrist, patronized so generously by the wealthy Mæcenas, must have been reincarnated in Franklin P. Adams. Here is Horace in twentieth-century Americanese:

TO HIS LYRE

Ad Lyram

Horace: Book I, Ode 32

"Poscimur. Si quid vacui sub umbra—"

If ever, as I struck thy strings,
    I've sounded one enduring note,
Let me, O Lyre, think up some things
    That folks will simply have to quote.

A Lesbian lyrist owned thee once;
    He used to sing a lot, he did,
Of dames and demijohns and stunts
    Like that. He was the Tuneful Kid.

Help me, mine ancient ukulele,
    Sing songs of sorrow and of joy,
Such as composed and printed daily,
    Will make the public yell, "Oh, *boy!*"

No lyrist to-day surpasses him in lightness of touch, in witty turns of expression, in all that goes to make up that exquisite lyric *tour de force* in sheer desperation called by the French phrase *vers de société.*

From his column have come six collections of lyrics: "Tobogganing on Parnassus," 1909; "In Other Words," 1912; "By and Large," 1914; "Weights and Measures," 1917; "Something Else Again," 1920; "So There," 1923. Not up to B. L. T.'s delicious mockery, but near it.

Don Marquis, working for the most part in higher spirits than Adams, letting himself go in what at times comes dangerously near to slapstick comic-strip stuff, as in his "Old Soak" characterizations, nevertheless is capable of deeper notes than Adams or any of the other day workers of the time. His column in the New York "Sun" long was famous. He is an entertainer, but he is more: he is a poet, at his best hauntingly suggestive, thrillingly beautiful. Even in his lyrics of lighter vein, he is original and often compelling, as in this random selection from his riches:

THE TOM CAT

At midnight in the alley,
  A tom-cat comes to wail,
And he chants the hate of a million years
  As he swings his snaky tail.

Malevolent, bony, brindled,
  Tiger and devil and bard,
His eyes are coals from the middle of Hell
  And his heart is black and hard.

He twists and crouches and capers
  And bares his curved sharp claws,
And he sings to the stars of the jungle nights
  Ere cities were, or laws.

Beast from a world primeval,
  He and his leaping clan,
When the blotched red moon leers over the roofs,
  Give voice to their scorn of man.

He will lie on a rug tomorrow
    And lick his silky fur,
And veil the brute in his yellow eyes
    And play he's tame, and purr.

But at midnight in the alley
    He will crouch again and wail,
And beat the time for his demon's song
    With the swing of his demon's tail.

Like Adams, he has collected from his column several volumes of miscellany: "Hermione," 1916; "Prefaces," 1919; "Dreams and Dust," 1915; "Poems and Portraits," 1922. "The Old Soak," too, he has republished, and others in the same movie-pitched key.

IV

But the lyrist of powers among the columnists is decidedly a rare bird, and not often among the hundreds of the regular variety is one to be found whose product is worthy of republication. Carl Van Doren characteristically makes New York the center of this peculiar industry.

In New York, to which so many things are drawn by its sheer magnitude, the column has at present its greatest prestige and influence. There the successful members of the guild enjoy reputations which are unequalled by those of any other contemporary authors. They have, of course, advantages. Not perhaps monthly, like story-writers, nor perhaps annually, like novelists or dramatists, but daily they appear before their publics; and their publics daily number hundreds of thousands of readers in New York, with possible millions elsewhere for those of the columnists who are taken up by newspaper syndicates. Appearing thus punctually, these wits can pounce first upon the news and make, or publish, the earliest *mots* on topics that invite them. Appearing thus regularly, these same wits, having beat up their game, can chase it with comic persistence as long as need or interest lasts.

For the most part, like Heywood Broun in his column, "It Seems to Me," the appeal to readers is wholly personal. The columnist exhibits constantly himself, his whim-whams, his prejudices, his convictions, his comic adventures, even his bill of fare. He gradually builds himself up into a mythical personage like a character in a novel. He interprets the news for his reader, putting it often into delightful shaded light with wise philosophizings. Literary criticism, even, he can bring into the hearts and homes of those who read but books of their own kind. This for instance from the New York "World" of 1924:

So Laura Jean Libbey is dead. What recollections her name calls up! School-days, strawride days, days when the bees bumbled outside and the smell of flowers floated in; days when boys, as though by psychic agreement, stoutly refused to work and hid "Nick Carter" and "Dick Merriwell' behind their geometries. And those terrifying, mysterious, alluring crea-tures across the aisle, those perverse creatures with ribbons on their hair and ringlets to their waists—what were they hiding behind their geometries? Laura Jean Libbey. Laura the incomparable, the delightful; Laura who could evoke pink-and-lavender glamour right from page 1; Laura who never failed to deliver the loving couple into each other's arms, while bells banged the nuptials and friends wept into their kerchiefs. She is said to be the author of eighty-two novels and forty plays. She once said she never had any trouble writing; no halting or doubt, no tramping the floor at midnight to capture an elusive concept, no temperamental fits, starts, or sulks, no waiting for inspiration. She always knew where she was go-ing; right always conquered might, wrong, or what-not, and right was always perfectly easy to perceive. Well, all honor to her. Her works may not be great literature, but they were in key with youth. If she was not profound, girls found her readable; and who shall say that her influence was not as good as the movie, which has usurped her place?

Whether the column is but the modern survival of the old *genre* invented by Steele and Addison in the Queen

Anne days of the "Spectator" and later of the "Tatler" and (later still in America) of Washington Irving's high-spirited echo of it in "Salmagundi," who can say? It has in a way always been a magazine "feature," as witness the "Easy Chair" of "Harper's," and the present "As I Like It," of William Lyon Phelps in "Scribner's." Personally, however, I believe it to be an evolution from American journalism and I am convinced that its birthplace was the Middle West.

V

Closely akin to the column is the syndicated daily sketch or poem, notably those creations furnished the press by Walt Mason and Eddie Guest—one fundamentally humorous the other fundamentally serious. For the most part newspaper humor is sub-literary, especially in its poetry. But Walt Mason in his daily stunt verses, each of them looking like a solid paragraph of prose, has a unique atmosphere and point of view. Only America and America's western areas could have produced Walt Mason. He is as "different" as the looks of his verses are different. He has collected some of his "stuff" into volumes. Open him at random:

I have read your latest book, Oppenheim; it involves a swarthy crook, Oppenheim; and a maid with languid eyes, and a diplomat who lies, and a dowager who sighs, Oppenheim, Oppenheim, and your glory never dies, Oppenheim. Oh, your formula is great, Oppenheim! Write your novels by the crate, Oppenheim! When we buy your latest book we are sure to find the crook, and the diplomat and dook, Oppenheim, Oppenheim, and the countess and the cook, Oppenheim! You are surely baling hay, Oppenheim, for you write a book a day, Oppenheim; from your fertile brain the rot comes a-pouring, smoking hot, and you use the same old plot, Oppenheim, Oppenheim, but it seems to hit the spot, Oppenheim! You're in all the magazines, Oppenheim; same old figures, same old scenes, Oppenheim; same old counts and diplomats, dime musée aristocrats, same old cozy-corner chats, Oppenheim,

Oppenheim, and we cry the same old "Rats!" Oppenheim. If you'd only rest a day, Oppenheim! If you'd throw your pen away, Oppenheim! If there'd only come a time when we'd see no yarn or rhyme 'neath the name of Oppenheim, Oppenheim, Oppenheim, it would surely be sublime, Oppenheim!

William Allen White, in an introduction to the *Uncle Walt* edition of the poet in 1910, called him "The Poet Laureate of the American Democracy." He is the voice of the people. His "prose rhymes are read daily by approximately ten million readers. A newspaper service sells these rhymes to two hundred newspapers," and he adds this:

It will interest the ten million readers of Walt Mason's rhymes to know that they were written in Emporia, Kansas, in the office of the *Emporia Gazette* after Mr. Mason had done a day's work as editorial writer and telegraph editor of an afternoon paper. . . . His philosophy is the philosophy of America. Briefly it is this: The fiddler must be paid; if you don't care to pay, don't dance. In the meantime—grin and bear it, because you've got to bear it, and you might as well grin. But don't try to lie out of it. The Lord hates a cheerful liar.

Out of the same section comes another syndicated product, the Kansas philosophy of E. W. Howe, the modern Poor Richard. His sayings vie in number now with those of Solomon, whose proverbs were three thousand. There is no escaping his wisdom:

When a man tries himself, the verdict is usually in his favor.
Every one hates a martyr; it's no wonder martyrs were burned at the stake.
The man who can call women angels in a new way succeeds best in love and literature.
A man of considerable sense may engage in prayer, to show off before the women and children, but if a man should be chased by a bear, and drop on his knees to pray, instead of running, I should doubt his sanity.
The people are forever asking too much: failing to get it, they often go to war, and destroy what they have.

I have heard the question asked thousands of times: "Is life
worth living?" It doesn't make any difference whether it
is or not; we have it, and must make the best of it. And so
long as we do not blow our brains out, we have decided
life is worth living.

In private life, a fool finds his proper level, but in public affairs he is encouraged by those who would rob him.

From north of Kansas another daily versifier, syndicated
by hundreds of newspapers and read daily by millions, is
Edgar A. Guest, born in 1881 and since 1895 an employee
of the "Detroit Free Press." His column "Chaff" ex-
panded in time to "Breakfast Table Chaff" and the daily
poem it contained became at length a national affair. As a
poet "Eddie Guest," as all America knows him, is the
legatee of Will Carleton and Field and Riley of the older
group, and of Sam Walter Foss of later years, trafficker
in sentiment, moralizer and lay preacher, thumbing always
the major chords of home and mother and children and
happy married living. Sub-literary, most of his poetry;
and yet, as Bill Nye said of Wagner's music, it is to casual
readers really better than it sounds. Criticism troubles
him not at all: his motto, let me write the heart and home
songs of my people, let him who will write to please the
professional critics. He is for the millions, not the few. To
sneer at him is to sneer at America itself, for the great
average reader loves him and reads him and quotes him.

That vast areas of his work are commonplace is not to
be wondered at. Pegasus cannot be harnessed and hired
out by the day, nor can he be scheduled for daily soarings at
so much the month or year. He makes few lofty flights in
these headlong newspaper days. But to rule Guest from
all the anthologies is bad judgment. Despite his daily handicap he is a poet. His hymn notes are often distinctive:

> God grant me these; the strength to do
>   Some needed service here;
> The wisdom to be brave and true;

The gift of vision clear,
That in each task that comes to me
Some purpose I may plainly see.

  .   .   .   .   .

God grant me faith to stand on guard,
  Uncheered, unspoke, alone,
And see behind such duty hard,
  My service to the throne.
Whate'er my task, be this may creed:
  I am on earth to fill a need.

In a pessimistic age he is always optimistic:

I've feared a thousand failures an' a thousand deaths I've died;
I've had this world in ruins by the gloom I've prophesied.
But the sun shines out this mornin' an' the skies above are blue,
An' with all my griefs an' trouble, I have somehow lived 'em
    through.
There may be cares before me, much like those that I have met;
Death will come some day an' take me, but I
              Ain't
                  Dead
                      Yet!

Always his philosophy is built on common sense and practicality. Creeds that are adhered to simply because they are
old he excoriates with anger. He preaches, but always his
texts concern the sacredness of home, the duty that comes
with children, the joys of humble life lived in the areas of
love and honesty and sensible toil.

VI

Of the makers of what may be called "light verse" there
have been many of late. At no other time in the history of
poetry have there been so many who could do the exquisite
work required of pens that would run without awkwardness in the lines of old Herrick, or Locker Lampson, or
Calverley, or T. B. Aldrich, or H. C. Bunner. To follow "The Wit's Weekly" department of the "Saturday

Review of Literature" is to wonder at the widespread lightness of poetic touch in these latter days. For a single example, this prize-poem of the week of April 12, the winner Helen Gray. The prize was to be for the best poem in the manner of Herrick, to be entitled "To Julia (1930) Not to bob her hair":

> My Julia, reap not, I entreat,
> That rippling gold like ripen'd wheat;
> Why should sad autumn's stubble show
> On that bright head, presaging snow?
>
> Time flies, and Fashion faster flies;
> To watch her whims methinks 'twere wise.
> Sylvia and choice Corinna now
> Wear lengthen'd locks, and why not thou?
>
> Wouldst in thy liquid mirror see
> Boy Hylas, though more fair than he?
> Rather let Cyprian Venus there
> Spread in soft waves her floating hair.

Most exquisitely has the light guitar been handled by Arthur Guiterman, born in 1871, reared in New York, and educated in the College of the City of New York. Journalism has been his job, but as with Poe, poetry became his passion and at length his profession. In his own words:

For the last nine years I have been the principal contributor of verse to *Life*, and I suppose that I am popularly known as the originator of "Rhymed Reviews" and other humorous metrical stunts in that paper. But don't try to pigeon-hole me in any compartment, or I'll fool you; because I have always written, and shall continue to write, on any theme that interests me or fills me with enthusiasm, and in whatever style happens.

No other poet of recent times so completely the master of technique in all its phases. Especially is he expert with rhyme. No word so impossible that he cannot rhyme it again and again with seeming effortless inevitableness. When Tutankhamen's tomb •was furnishing headlines to all the papers of the world, this lyric he threw off with the title "Egyptomania":

> At present we're throwing conniptions
> About the Egyptians,
> And lifting our Western sombreros
> To all the old Pharaohs,
> Though he who must bear the gravamen
> Is Prince Tutankamen
> Whose sepulcher, bared to the gapers,
> Gives news to the papers.
> Now Mr. and Mrs. Schapiro
> Are headed for Cairo,
> While Timothy Jenkins *et uxor*
> Have tickets to Luxor;
> And soon shall our wandering teachers
> Descant on the features
> Of cities and temples of Nilus
> With eloquent stylus
> And each shall return with his booty,
> A petrified cootie—
> A warranted-genuine scarab
> Purveyed by an Arab.

In the same pleasant choir Gelett Burgess of early "Purple Cow" and later "Goops" fame; his self-written epitaph is as murderous as Shakespeare's:

> Ah, yes, I wrote the "Purple Cow"—
>   I'm sorry, now, I wrote it!
> But I can tell you, anyhow,
>   I'll kill you if you quote it!

On this ferocious note we close our review of the light guitarists of the latter day with a partial roll-call of the choir, lyrists whose work in time will be drawn upon for the most distinctive collection of lighter verse to be found anywhere in English.[5] Here at least our poetry is distinctive: James J. Montague, Berton Braley, T. A. Daly, Burges Johnson, Edwin Meade Robinson, Christopher Morley, Wallace Irwin, Jessie Rittenhouse Scollard, Carolyn Wells, and many another the omission of whose name will doubtless be mentioned by my reviewers.

BIBLIOGRAPHICAL REFERENCES

"Day In and Day Out: Manhattan Wits" in "Many Minds," Carl Van Doren, 1924, gives a view of several of the columnists.

"Anthology of American Humor in Verse," 1917.

"A Little Book of American Humorous Verse," T. A. Daly, 1926.

"The Bowling Green; an Anthology of Verse," Christopher Morley, 1924.

"The Little Book of Modern Verse," three series, Jessie B. Rittenhouse, 1913–1927.

[5] See "Our Poets of Today," Howard Willard Cook, 3d edition, 1922.

INDEX

Numbers in bold type refer to pages where authors are treated at length.